An English Library

SIXTH EDITION

An English Library

SIXTH EDITION

Edited by

NIGEL FARROW

BRIAN LAST

VERNON PRATT

PUBLISHED IN ASSOCIATION
WITH BOOK TRUST
Gower

Published by
Gower Publishing Company Limited
Gower House
Croft Road
Aldershot
Hants   GU11 3HR
England

Gower Publishing Company
Old Post Road
Brookfield
Vermont   05036
USA

ISBN 0 566 05818 9

Printed in Great Britain by
Billing & Sons Ltd, Worcester

CONTENTS

INTRODUCTION

An English Library is for everyone who likes reading books. It has been compiled with one objective: to identify the books from the classical and modern heritage that will extend your enjoyment of reading. Over 2500 titles have been selected by a group of some 20 men and women who write, teach or publish books for a living but read them for enjoyment. If a book is listed in these pages it is because it has given an experienced reader real pleasure, not because it fits a particular critical theory of literary excellence.

An English Library should be used in the same spirit. If reading a recommended work is not proving to be a rewarding experience, do not persist with it. Perhaps its selection or its assessment was ill-judged, or perhaps you have a 'blind spot' for this type of book. Reading is not a competition: challenge yourself but do not waste valuable time reading without enjoyment. On the other hand, no book which is generally accepted as a great work should be written off by a disappointed reader for all time. One of the joys of literature is that personal taste changes both under the influence of reading and through the experience of life itself. It is one of the purposes of *An English Library* to be ready with a word of explanation or encouragement about a book which has been abandoned in the past and to which the reader now feels like returning.

HISTORY

The origin of *An English Library* lies in two contrasting effects of the Second World War. The bombing of London destroyed publishers' stocks of books and paper just when the demand for books increased. As the public had little idea what was available, the National Book Council invited F Seymour Smith in 1941 to compile a forty-page booklet entitled *The English Classics*. Its success prompted the first edition of *An English Library* in 1943, a greatly expanded work, aimed at librarians, booksellers, students and book buyers. Up to 1963, five editions of *An English Library* were compiled by F Seymour Smith and published in association with the National Book League, the successor to the National Book Council. This edition is published in association with the National Book League's successor, the Book Trust.

NEW FEATURES IN THIS EDITION

An English Library is built around its representation of the English classics. Previous editions excluded writers who were alive at the time of publication and only included nineteenth century classics from the literature of the United States of America. Children's literature was included but only if the books were classics which continued to be read throughout adult life.

This new, sixth edition appears more than 25 years after the last one. It remains true to the spirit of the original work but a number of changes in the scope and treatment of the entries have been made in order to serve the needs of a reader in the last decade of the twentieth century. As in previous editions, the coverage is based on the humanities subjects. It is these creative disciplines that most readers turn to in their hours of leisure.

Certain sections are entirely new: *Children's Literature*, *World Literature in English*, *The Bible* and *Fine Arts*. *Children's Literature* has been included in order to acknowledge both the volume and quality of literature for children that is now available. In this section specific editions of the texts are recommended where appropriate, so as to guide readers — or parents of readers — to the version which may be most suitable for a young reader. The presence and excellence of illustrations has particularly influenced the choice of edition. Another completely new section appears under the heading *World Literature in English* and includes some of the writing from beyond the UK and the USA which has clearly developed our understanding of the capabilities of the English language as well as widening our cultural heritage.

American Fiction is presented as a separate and substantial unit within the *Fiction* section. The previous edition accepted nineteenth century Americans that were 'part of the main traditional streams of English writing'. The same criterion now clearly admits such 'universal' twentieth century American writers as Scott Fitzgerald, Hemmingway, Faulkner, Salinger, Bellow and Heller. A section on *The Bible* has been added. To read much of classical English Literature and history without a knowledge of the content and language of the Bible in English is to read through a glass darkly.

The ban in previous editions on living authors has been lifted. Writers, like the rest of the population, are living longer and today many great names live to see their works become classics. However, two specific pieces of information provided in previous editions have been omitted: price and edition. Stable prices are as much a thing of the past as the three-decker novel, although the growth of paperback publishing in the last 25 years has made much good literature available at a reasonable cost. Indeed the 'paperback revolution' is one reason why specific editions are no longer cited. There are too many editions available of the major classics, such as Dickens and Shakespeare, to list all of them and choosing the 'right' edition is a personal choice that depends on your taste, budget, and reason for reading the particular work.

In certain sections, notably *History* and *Biography*, the texts cited may be out of print. These are included because of the perennial nature of their content and authority and because they will be available from a good library. Alternatively, a second-hand copy can be purchased both as a joy and often as a good investment.

ARRANGEMENT OF ENTRIES
Each section has a short introduction which discusses the range of literature that is included in the list and the principles used in the selection of

individual titles. The entries are arranged alphabetically by author. The author's selected titles are then given with their date of first publication, so that the reader can place the texts in their historical context. In the *Reference* section, the title of the text only is given since such works are often collective efforts.

Every entry is annotated with a brief comment which is designed to indicate why the book is well regarded. Where appropriate to the content of the book, the comment highlights those aspects of the work which may attract new readers.

The arrangement by author is for convenience of use: the objective of the selection and annotation is to focus attention on individual books rather than their authors. There are several good reference books which give details of author's lives and works (see the *Reference* section). For those searching for a particular book there is a title index which lists all the books in *An English Library* alphabetically by their title. There is also an author index which is of particular use when checking whether there are books by the same author listed in other sections.

ACKNOWLEDGEMENTS

The books which appear in this edition of *An English Library* have been selected by a process of consultation within the group of contributors and editors, as well as individual suggestions from a larger number of people. The introductions and annotations were largely written by the sections' compilers, with additions and amendments made by the editors in order to achieve a general consistency in the treatment of the works described. This edition of *An English Library* is therefore very much a collective work.

All the contributors are named in the list which follows this introduction and I thank them for their patient work which was done largely for the love of their particular subjects. The editorial work was divided between three of us: Vernon Pratt assembled and organised the contributors to many of the sections, and Brian Last undertook much of the text editing as well as making a substantial contribution to the annotations. I enjoyed selecting and annotating many of the entries, especially in the *Fiction* and related sections, and taking overall editorial responsibility for this edition.

In the early planning stage of this edition we benefited from advice from a number of distinguished writers and commentators who are closely associated with the work of the Book Trust. Martyn Goff, Margaret Drabble, Michael Holroyd, Richard Hoggart, Martin Seymour Smith and Peter Stockham were among those who made helpful comments on the structure of the edition and the criteria for selection of entries.

Andrea Spurling undertook much of the research work in the early stages of preparing this edition. I am also grateful to Lesley Brown who entered the text into a computerised database so the editors could make repeated revisions and updates.

The final acknowledgement must go to F Seymour Smith who developed the original concept of *An English Library* and compiled the first five editions. In his introduction to the first edition Edward Blunden hailed it as 'a masterly list of standard reading'. Today we are less certain about the existence of absolute standards in literature or in life. But the editors and contributors to this edition have tried to carry on F Seymour Smith's commitment to persuading people to read and to read well.

Nigel Farrow

CONTRIBUTORS

Candice Arthur David Baron

Patrick Colton Richard Dutton

Robert Godber Nigel Farrow

William Fuge Ian House

Gordon Inkster Beryl Jones

Brian Last Margaret Marshall

Sue McNaughton Andrea Spurling

David Spurling Anne Stubbins

Alan Windsor

FICTION

This section is concerned with fiction in the form of the novel or the short story. Other sections of *An English Library* embrace works which contain large elements of fiction: drama, poetry, essays and even (or especially) autobiography. Conversely, the story or characters in a novel do not have to be pure invention in order to qualify as fiction. The entertaining guide *The Originals: Who's Really Who in Fiction* illustrates the extent to which novelists draw from life, or are drawn into their own fiction, as in the 'faction' novels of Norman Mailer and Truman Capote.

The short stories included in this list are mostly in the form of recommended collections by individual writers. The titles of some specific stories are given where these are generally recognized as outstanding examples of the author's work. There is a view that in classic short story writing English fiction cannot compete with French or Russian fiction. However, the modern English team has probably had the better of the match in the twentieth century when the emigrés (James and Conrad) and the Americans (Hemingway, Scott Fitzgerald, Malamud and Updike) are included.

English fiction means fiction in English. As the novel was born after the Act of Union and before Irish Home Rule it grew up within one political boundary as well as one linguistic tradition, and the works of writers from all four countries of the British Isles have been included in this section. The special relationship between English and American fiction is recognized by providing a listing in a sub-section entitled 'Some American Fiction'. It is not a comprehensive survey of American works but a selection of those which are studied and enjoyed by readers in Britain and elsewhere as frequently as home-grown fiction.

A rapidly growing body of fiction in English is written by those who are neither British nor American. Their works are presented in a separate section, *World Literature in English*. In this section can be found the works of such major authors as Patrick White and Chinua Achebe.

Another issue of selection has been the publication date for works which are eligible for inclusion. There needs to be some distance between the immediate reputation of works by new authors and their acceptance as part of an established body of English fiction. A clear line would be to exclude the works of living authors, but in an age when, happily, novelists like the rest of the population are living longer such a rule would exclude a large number of modern classics. Another clear cut approach would be to set a specific date, say 1960 or 1970, by when a work had to be published in order to be eligible. This would severely limit the usefulness of the list for those whose enjoyment of fiction is based on exploring the works of particular authors. A cut off at a specific date of publication would preclude the listing of recent and possibly superior works by authors who were well established as modern masters before that date. For instance, a line drawn at 1960 would remove the last volume of Evelyn Waugh's *Sword of Honour* trilogy. Iris Murdoch, Angus Wilson and Anthony Burgess would only be represented by their earliest works.

For these reasons the selection has been made from the works of authors who had achieved their first publication by 1980; this allows the list to include relatively recent novels by established authors and thereby reflect their mature achievements. Inevitably a wobbly boundary line is drawn through the work of contemporary fiction, with a few authors excluded even though their works are as meritorious as those of contemporaries who achieved their first publication a year or two earlier.

The great majority of fiction of the past and the present takes the form of popular novels written in a particular genre: the murder mystery, the thriller or spy-novel, the historical romance, science fiction, or the mass-market bodice-rippers and pulp westerns. There is much craft and enjoyment to be found in genre fiction, although much of it is written with the sole aim of amusing the reader for as long as it takes to turn the pages. Such works have only been included in this list if, as well as belonging to a particular genre, they have gained a literary status. However, a few writers and their works are listed as sign posts towards the large, popular genres which lie outside the boundaries of this list: Agatha Christie points to the many skilled authors of who-dunnits and Elmore Leonard is a distinguished representative of the hard-boiled crime novel, while John Cleland's *Fanny Hill* is the sole example of a specialist form of imaginative writing. Reference books, such as *Now Read On* and the *Bloomsbury Good Reading Guide* (see the *Reference* section) will provide a path to and through the works of some of the best writers of contemporary popular genre fiction.

The largest single genre today is children's fiction. More and more children's books have been published over the last thirty years as it has become possible to issue both classics and new works in well designed and colourfully illustrated editions at popular prices. This literature is considered separately in the *Children's Literature* section. A few of these works appear in this section because they are also read as adult fiction: the best example being the enjoyable but disturbing adventures of Alice.

Some genres and sources of fiction may not be as well represented in this list as their supporters might wish, for limitations of choice rather than reasons of literary merit. The predominant experience of life reflected in the English novel of the last two hundred and fifty years is that of the middle class male. Although some of the greatest fiction in this list was written by women more than a hundred years before the 1980 cut-off date, it has taken the intervening century for a consciously feminist fiction to be established. Some of this work has been published too recently to be eligible for consideration, but the reprinting by publishers such as Virago of earlier twentieth century novels has ensured that writers like Rebecca West, F Tennyson Jesse or Jean Rhys are not overlooked.

The apparent class bias in the source and subject of fictional writing is more difficult to correct: the genuine working class novel is a rare item. The themes of

1950s novels like Alan Sillitoe's *Saturday Night and Sunday Morning* or Keith Waterhouse's *Billy Liar* have more recently been developed in drama, especially for television, or in the lyrics of John Lennon than in contemporary novels. The following generation of potential working class heroes went to university and wrote the campus novel and the novel about the novel.

It is only possible to select from what is available and only right to choose those works that are considered to have lasting merit. What distinguishes the authors of such works from the writers of popular genre fiction is not the treatment of socially significant subjects or the making of fine moral judgements, but the intensity and richness of their imagination. In the best works this imagination is communicated through a high degree of literary skill to a general, continuing readership.

Brian ALDISS (1925–)

Non-Stop 1958
Aldiss has done more than most to make science-fiction respectable – although he is also a good 'straight' novelist, as in *Hand Reared Boy* or the later *Life in the West*. In this early novel, a space-ship inhabited by the degenerate descendants of its crew, and choked by flourishing vegetation, is the setting for a 'quest' novel.

Hothouse 1962
In the world of the far future, the land is covered by one giant tree, and a variety of fierce, vegetable life-forms rule. A kind of odyssey, full of humour, and containing some remarkable visions.

The Dark Light Years 1964
A sharp satire on the well-worn theme of the meeting between man and alien. What if the aliens are repulsive?

Eric AMBLER (1909–)

The Mask of Dimitrios 1939
An early work by a masterly writer of thrillers whose stories are comic–sinister sub-plots to the world of international politics and business. Latimer, a detective story writer, encounters mystery and adventure as he uncovers the strange life of Dimitrios, whose body he believes he has seen in a Turkish morgue.

Dirty Story 1967
The shady exploits of the dubious Arthur Simpson are described with humour and a powerful economy of words.

Kingsley AMIS (1922–)

Lucky Jim 1954
A pioneering work in the campus novel genre, and still the funniest. Jim Dixon, sufferer from every kind of complex, fights for respectability and love through a world peopled by ghastly academic bourgeoisie.

Take a Girl Like You 1960
The virginal Jenny Bunn comes down from the North to teach in an infant school. This is the story of her efforts to hold out in the face of a variety of seduction ploys – nicely ridiculed by a sense of the crudeness and sham of sexual confrontations.

Jake's Thing 1978
An example of later Amis. Back to the campus, but youthful frustration has been succeeded by middle-aged impotence and what was previously ridiculed as the comic pretentions of modern science and manners are now feared as the enemies of civilization.

Martin AMIS (1949–)

Money – A Suicide Note 1984
New York, the film world and the sexy Selina Street are good subjects for the younger Amis's flashing phrases and well developed sense of disgust. So far, moments and attitudes in Amis's novels are stronger than the works as a whole.

Daisy ASHFORD (1881–1972)

The Young Visiters 1919
A remarkable, misspelled, precocious piece of writing completed at the turn of the century by Daisy Ashford, aged nine. It has all the ingredients of a traditional novel distilled by its author's innocence into a refreshing clarity of perception.

Jane AUSTEN (1775–1817)

Sense and Sensibility 1811
The title refers to each of two sisters, Elinor and Marianne, and their respective reactions to the dastardliness of their lovers, as they set about the necessary search for, and final attainment of, husbands.

Pride and Prejudice 1813
Although *Pride and Prejudice* is 'lighter' than Jane Austen's later works, her irony is here at its best. For this reason, and for the delightful portrayal of the Bennet family, *Pride and Prejudice* is probably the most read and quoted of Jane Austen's novels.

Mansfield Park 1814
Fanny Price is the stoic heroine who is rewarded with the conventional happy marriage by the end of this delicate and detailed study of the affairs, intrigues and betrayals of a group of young people gathered in a country house.

Emma 1816
Emma Woodhouse is one of the great character portraits in English fiction: simultaneously fascinating and appalling. Her self-satisfied attempts at match-making and social manipulation go wildly astray. All is well in the end – by the standards of the times – thanks to the virtuous Mr Knightley, but some modern readers may prefer the unreconstructed Emma.

Northanger Abbey 1818
The dark and draughty mansion at the centre of this satire on both readers and writers of fashionable Gothic fiction is the catalyst for the active imagination of Catherine Morland, in love, of course, with its owner.

Persuasion 1818
Less sharp in its satire and ironic wit than previous works, Jane Austen's last completed novel deals sensitively, almost romantically, with the intricate love affairs of Anne Elliot and her sisters.

Beryl BAINBRIDGE (1934–)

Another Part of the Wood 1968
Joseph and his girlfriend, Dotty, take his son Roland to the remote Welsh countryside along with several other friends, one of whom, the strange boy Kidney, provokes different reactions from the various characters.

Harriet Said ... 1972
Harriet and the narrator become obsessed with the 'Tsar', a middle-aged man whom they wish to study at a distance but towards whom they gradually begin to approach more and more closely. Centred on Beryl Bainbridge's common themes of responsibility, respect and selfishness disguised as altruism.

The Bottle Factory Outing 1974
A black comedy of ordinary people caught up in extraordinary circumstances.

J G BALLARD (1930–)

Short Stories 1976
Starting as a leading writer of science-fiction in the fifties and sixties, he has more recently emerged as a novelist producing the vivid, autobiographical story of the Second World War in China, *The Empire of the Sun*. His short stories are full of powerful and distressful episodes as in the collections *The Terminal Beast* and *The Disaster Area*.

H E BATES (1905–74)

My Uncle Silas 1939
'Uncle Silas' features in a series of short stories in which this rural reprobate recounts his adventures, which vary from his being the all-conquering hero in the Crimean War to the seducer of many beautiful women.

Fair Stood the Wind for France 1944
An adventure set in occupied France, following story-lines used before and after. An airman escapes from the wreckage of his plane and seeks shelter and sexual comfort from a native girl.

The Darling Buds of May 1958
A comedy featuring the crazy Larkin family, made up of caricatures with predictable idiosyncrasies.

Samuel BECKETT (1906–)

More Pricks than Kicks 1934
A series of ten stories centering on Belacqua Shuah, an outsider in Dublin. His life largely consists of his various adventures with women, until death on an operating table, followed by burial and simultaneous disappearance from the minds of all.

Watt 1953
What does not happen to Watt in Mr Knott's house is the basis of this punning, funny novel that philosophizes on the non-events of everyday life through the mind of an inmate of a lunatic asylum.
See also: *Trilogy* – published separately as *Molloy, Malone Dies* and *The Unnameable*.

William BECKFORD (1759–1844)

Vathek 1786
An extraordinary little book which alone has given Beckford a name in literary history. A Voltairean tale of oriental adventure, suffused with gloomy and terrible perception.

Sybille BEDFORD (1911–)

A Legacy 1957
A first novel which is interesting for its social and historical setting. It deals with the dubious marriages between two families in Germany, followed by the introduction of the saving spirit of an English woman.

A Favourite of the Gods 1963
A Compass Error 1968
Set in Italy and France, these two novels follow the fortunes of three generations of women – Anna, her daughter Constanza, and her daughter Flavia – all of whom, as sexual and intellectual rebels, must face the problems of living in a rigid society.

Sir Max BEERBOHM (1872–1956)

Zuleika Dobson 1911
Mildly amusing story of the effect of the arrival of a beautiful woman on the young in Oxford. As Zuleika says, for people who like this kind of thing, this is the kind of thing they like.

Aphra BEHN (1640–89)

Oroonoko, or the History of the Royal Slave 1688
Although often forgotten, this is the first English philosophical novel. Significantly, it is written by a woman, and is remarkable for showing sympathy for oppressed Negro slaves in the colonized West Indies.

Arnold BENNETT (1867–1931)

Anna of the Five Towns 1902
One of the first of Bennett's novels to use the five pottery towns as dismal background to detailed representations of life. Anna, who refuses to conform in a Methodist society, is portrayed with care and sympathy, whilst the dispassionate style of writing represents the Methodists without passing explicit judgement.

The Old Wives' Tale 1908
A brilliant portrait of the lower middle classes. Set partly in the Potteries and partly in Paris, this is a story of Constance and Sophia Baines who begin life in a draper's shop.

The Clayhanger Trilogy – Clayhanger 1910, *Hilda Lessways* 1911, *These Twain* 1916
The most celebrated of Bennett's works, following the life of Edwin Clayhanger, his undulating relationship with Hilda Lessways, and his strange friendship with Hilda's son, George.

R D BLACKMORE (1825–1900)

Lorna Doone 1869
The times of Charles II and James II and the valleys of Exmoor are the settings for this much-loved story of the conflicts of passion and family loyalty in the romance between Lorna Doone and John Ridd.

George BORROW (1803–81)

Lavengro 1851
Romany Brye 1857
Adventures of gypsies and vagrants, tinkers and thieves, as the central character wanders from place to place in this inextricable mixture of fiction and autobiography.

Elizabeth BOWEN (1899–1973)

The Death of the Heart 1938
A subtle story of innocence and sophistication.

The Heat of the Day 1949
Set in Second World War London, Stella Rodway is in love with a traitor to his country and her values.

William BOYD (1952–)

A Good Man in Africa 1980
The setting is West Africa (where Boyd was born) and tells of Morgan Leafy's attempts to come to terms with the environment.

An Ice-Cream War 1982
No-one told the English and German armies in East Africa that World War I had ended, so they carried on fighting for three weeks after the armistice. The novel is told through the eyes of various characters such as Temple Smith, a boisterous American, and two contrasting brothers, Felix and Gabriel Cobb. Amusing and compassionate.

Malcolm BRADBURY (1932–)

Stepping Westward 1965
Like Malcolm Bradbury's first novels *Eating People is Wrong*, a satire on academic life, this time set in America. With its convoluted story-line and caricatures of people, it is less funny than Amis's *Lucky Jim*, but more savage in its humour.

The History Man 1975
An exact record of the era of hopes and betrayals that is epitomized in life at a new university in the sixties and seventies. Funny, sad, and serious, with a style which apparently removes authorial judgement, but not the moral of the story.

Ray BRADBURY (1920–)

Fahrenheit 451 1953
'The temperature at which book-paper catches fire and burns.' A science-fiction story in which imagination is threatened by the destruction of books, until a resistance group is formed and creativity is finally allowed to triumph.

Dandelion Wine 1951
This work bears out Ray Bradbury's reputation as a short story writer. Lawnmowers, trolleys and cars become objects of horror in these fantastic tales, each of which represents a flask of dandelion wine stored away for winter use in the summer of 1928.

John BRAINE (1922–)

Room at the Top 1957
Angry young man, Joe Lampton, plans to use the system whilst maintaining his hatred of it. But his working-class rebellion loses its power and we are left to wonder if there can be room at the top for any but the unprincipled.

Charlotte BRONTE (1816–55)

Jane Eyre 1847
A great, romantic novel: the first to present a woman as a passionate and independent being. Orphan Jane survives the hardships of the cruel Lowood school to become governess to the illegitimate daughter of the dark, byronic Mr Rochester and ultimately, his redeemer or his emasculator, if D H Lawrence's view of the relationship is preferred.

Shirley 1849
Less of a consuming read than *Jane Eyre* but again remarkable for its strong and wilful characters. Set in Yorkshire at the time of the Luddite riots, a mill-owner marries Shirley for her wealth, but both their loves lie elsewhere.

Villette 1853
A reworking of the plainly autobiographical work *The Professor*, this story is set in Brussels and concerns the heroine's passion for a professor, who is transformed from despot into angel.

Emily BRONTE (1818–48)

Wuthering Heights 1847
An intensely powerful novel of passion and violence, love and cruelty between Heathcliffe and Catherine, two kindred spirits who can unite only in death. It marries a poetic imagination with a complex structure to produce a work which is at once a Gothic romance and a harsh story in a real place.

George Mackay BROWN (1921–)

A Calendar of Love and Other Stories 1967
A volume of short stories set in the Orkneys. A sense of the cyclical quality of life, the toil of man on land or at sea having a continuity with life in Viking times, told in simple but poetic language.

John BUCHAN (1875–1940)

The Thirty-Nine Steps 1915
John Buchan's best-known thriller. Though dated, the tale of Scudder's notebook, and the skulduggery in London and on the moors of Scotland to which it leads, has seldom been bettered.

John Macnab 1925
Three important men, bored with their jobs, compete in a poaching wager. The taking of stags and salmon in an atmosphere of gentle aristocratic naughtiness is gripping enough to enthrall all but the most fervent egalitarian.

Edward BULWER-LYTTON (1803–73)

The Last Days of Pompeii 1834
A sombre historical picture of Roman life shortly before the destruction of Pompeii in AD 79. Historical romance was just one of several fictional genres successfully practiced by this writer – politician. A huge contemporary reputation now nearly disappeared.

John BUNYAN (1628–88)

The Pilgrim's Progress 1678
The famous allegorical journey of Christian from the City of Destruction to the Celestial City through such well-known obstacles and temptations as the Slough of Despond, the Valley of the Shadow of Death, Vanity Fair and Doubting Castle. Written in the beautiful, simple prose style of the English version of The Bible.

Anthony BURGESS (1917–)

A Clockwork Orange 1962
Burgess's best-known and possibly best novel is set in an uncomfortably near future, and told in the vernacular by the young delinquent Alex, who has chosen violence as a statement of his identity. After treatment to curtail his criminality the reader is left asking which is the lesser evil: violence or authoritarian mind-bending.

Malayan Trilogy – Time for a Tiger 1956, *The Enemy in the Blanket* 1958, *Beds in the East* 1974
Victor Grabbe is the tragic-comic hero in Malaya during the last years of British rule. A highly episodic, blackly comic story line with a distinct sense of sadness at the decline of England.

Earthly Powers 1980
A memorable novel which strikes the reader from the very first sentence; it spans six decades and follows the fortunes of Toomey, a novelist and intellectual, as he grapples with his homosexuality and his feelings towards the outstanding events of the twentieth century. Full of Burgess cleverness – witty puns, linguistic jokes – but involved in a serious debate at the same time.

Fanny BURNEY (1752–1840)

Evelina 1778
The first English novel to concentrate on the home life of a young middle class girl. Evelina's adventures on being sent out into the world are related by means of letters, containing inventive descriptions of comic characters and events.

Samuel BUTLER (1835–1902)

Erewhon 1872
The title is an anagram of 'nowhere' and is a satire in the Utopian mode, ridiculing the religion and morality of mid-Victorian society.

The Way of All Flesh 1903
A clearly autobiographical study of the troubled relationships between parents and children through a number of generations of the Pontifex family. Butler's wit relieves the general gloom and rancour.

John LE CARRÉ (1931–)

The Spy Who Came in from the Cold 1963
It is tempting to think that Le Carré uses his experience in the Foreign Office as background for the elaborate plots of his spy novels, many of which are constructed around the character of George Smiley, the quiet but obsessed secret agent. This early novel is set in Berlin and deals with many of the issues raised by the cold war, while

later novels such as *Tinker, Tailor, Soldier, Spy* (1974) concern Smiley's attempts to track down the 'mole' in the British Secret Service.

Lewis CARROLL (Charles Lutwidge DODGSON) (1832–98)

Alice's Adventures in Wonderland 1865
The White Rabbit, the Mad Hatter and company continue to provide joyous entertainment and a series of surreal images of adult life – which is why *Alice* continues to be read at all levels from the nursery to the university seminar.

Alice Through the Looking Glass 1872
Alice climbs through a mirror and finds herself in a chess problem. Carroll's love of logic, numbers and semantics provides frustration, puzzlement and delight. *The Annotated Alice* (ed. Gardner) is a useful companion for those coming back to Alice as adults.

Angela CARTER (1940–)

The Magic Toyshop 1966
Nights at the Circus 1984
Angela Carter writes disturbing novels which combine familiar mythical or fairy-tale stories with contemporary events. The language is rich and sensuous, the plots are bizarre and visionary. *Nights at the Circus* takes the reader back into the nineteenth century as the heroine, Fewers, struggles in what seems to be a dreamworld containing the nightmare of a wrecked society. There are collections of short stories: *Bloody Chamber* (1979) and *Black Venus* (1985).

Joyce CARY (1888–1957)

Mister Johnson 1939
This is an early novel based on Cary's experience as a magistrate in Nigeria. Humour is drawn from an account of an African who, caught between two cultures, manages to retain an innocence and charm even as he is made ridiculous and finally pathetic.

The Horse's Mouth 1944
The modern, Joycean techniques of Cary's later novels appear incongruous with their rather outdated, moralist ideas. Thus the 'anarchist' artist, Gulley Jimson, is presented, in a trilogy of which this is the last part, against an unchallenged background of institutional order.

G K CHESTERTON (1874–1936)

Father Brown: Selected Stories 1911–35
A Roman Catholic detective priest solves mysteries by virtue of the amazing powers of observation and profound insight into human nature which underlie his battered exterior.

Erskine CHILDERS (1870–1922)

The Riddle of the Sands 1903
An uncannily timely warning of a German invasion of England, this is a technically informative story about yachting and at the same time a tale of espionage. The author's own life ended in front of a firing squad.

Agatha CHRISTIE (1891–1976)

Her skill and ingenuity in constructing plots to obscure the murderer's identity have given Agatha Christie her reputation as the queen of the whodunnit. Her two favourite detectives, the Belgian Hercule Poirot, and the very British Miss Marple, have become institutions in crime fiction, repeatedly saving society from threats of murderous disruption.

Amongst the best of her numerous works are *The Murder of Roger Ackroyd*, 1926, *Murder on the Orient Express*, 1934, *Death on the Nile*, 1937, and *4.50 from Paddington*, 1956.

John CLELAND (1709–89)

Fanny Hill: Memoirs of a Woman of Pleasure 1749
The most famous 'dirty book' in English fiction is just that.

Wilkie COLLINS (1824–89)

The Woman in White 1860
A great mystery thriller which spellbinds its readers with an intricate and suspenseful plot and clever characterization, notably that of the Napoleonic villain, Count Fosco.

The Moonstone 1868
This early detective novel depicts the search for a huge diamond and the contest of wits between the villainous Godfrey Ablewhite, three Indians suspected of stealing the stone, and one of the first fictional detectives, Sergeant Cuff.

Ivy COMPTON BURNETT (1892–1969)

From *Pastors and Masters* (1925) to *The Mighty and their Fall* (1961) the most terrible family crimes and abuses are obliquely recorded in 18 novels, almost all of them set in Edwardian upper class households – Greek tragedies told through drawing room conversation. Among the most admired novels are *Brothers and Sisters* (1929), *A House and its Head* (1935), *Elders and Betters* (1944) and *Manservant and Maidservant* (1947).

Joseph CONRAD (1857–1924)

The Nigger of the 'Narcissus' 1898
Probably the finest tale of life at sea, subtly and sinisterly symbolic, in which James Wait, a massive Negro, undermines the unity of the whole crew of a ship by falling ill and seeming to be on the verge of death. Other sea stories cover a wide range of settings and subjects, although many concern the reaction of men under stress and their codes of behaviour. Among the best stories are *The End of the Tether, Typhoon, The Shadow-Line* and *The Secret Sharer*.

Lord Jim 1900
The guilt-stricken, idealist Jim becomes benevolent despot of a south-east Asian community, until nemesis in the shape of Gentleman Brown catches up with him.

Heart of Darkness 1902
A terrifying journey into the soul. Marlow, Conrad's narrator, plunges into the heart of the Dark Continent in an atmosphere of purposelessness and horror. One of the most powerful short novels in the English language.

Nostromo 1904
Set in an imaginary South American country and revolving around the quest for silver, this is Conrad's longest and most carefully constructed novel. It lacks the immediacy of the novels based on his own experience, and the characters are mostly two-dimensional representations of types. But the symbolic structure is a triumph; the character and suicide of Decoud is disturbingly real; and the black humour of the political scenes pre-figures the events of the twentieth century.

The Secret Agent 1907
A melodramatic story that recalls Dickens in its use of London locations and a cast of comic-sinister characters. Particularly memorable is the figure of the Professor, the perfect anarchist, in the face of whom the moral vacilliations of the miserable *agent provocateur* Verloc and his hapless wife are chillingly irrelevant.

Under Western Eyes 1911
Young Razumov becomes involved against his will with revolutionary politics. The novel reflects Conrad's view that terrorists are no better than the autocracy they attempt to overthrow. Set in Tsarist Russia and Geneva, the portrayal of the expatriate revolutionaries is simultaneously funny and frightening.

William COOPER (1910–)

Scenes from Provincial Life 1950
A precursor of the 'Angry Young Men' books and plays of the 1950s, this is the first and most successful of a sequence of novels which carries Joe Lynn from provincial schoolmastering and mild rebellion to a fairly conventional accommodation with English middle-class life.

A E COPPARD (1878–1957)

Collected Tales 1948
A self-educated master craftsman of the short story, Coppard's tales are often about outsiders in a country setting. Recommended stories are 'The Higgler' and 'Dusty Ruth'.

Daniel DEFOE (1661–1731)

Robinson Crusoe 1719
The unabridged *Robinson Crusoe* is less concerned with the day-to-day life of a castaway than with the trials of faith faced by a religious man in circumstances of isolation and adversity. But it is the imaginative picture of the marooned voyager rather than the religious element which fascinates most readers today.

Moll Flanders 1722
This novel – perhaps the first genuine novel in the language – purports to be the autobiographical confession of Moll Flanders, whore and thief. In fact it is a satire on acquisitive society, trenchantly and unconsciously exposed by Moll herself – whose personality is the most attractive feature of the book.

A Journal of the Plague Year 1722
A brilliantly detailed and convincing account of London in 1664–5, describing the spread of disease and its effects, supposedly from the pen of a resident of the city.

Len DEIGHTON (1929–)

The Ipcress File 1962
This established Deighton as a superior spy-story writer. His early novels all centre around the same eccentric character who finds himself involved in situations which, though often absurd, are frighteningly realistic.

Walter DE LA MARE (1873–1956)

Memoirs of a Midget 1921
De La Mare's skill at writing dream-like tales full of ghostly mystery, fantasy and gentle humour has made him a children's favourite. His interest in psychological and social issues is apparent in this novel which takes the form of an autobiographical record by a woman seen as a freak.

Nigel DENNIS (1912–)

Cards of Identity 1955
In the post-war period of ration books and identity cards, the Identity Club meets at an English country house to listen to case histories of identity problems. A skilfully contrived satire on the tradition of English life.

Charles DICKENS (1812–70)

The Posthumous Papers of the Pickwick Club 1836–7
The rambling and fantastical adventures of the eccentric members of the Pickwick Club. Mr Pickwick's prosecution for breach of promise (Bardell v. Pickwick) is one of the comic highlights.

The Adventures of Oliver Twist 1837–9
Helped by successful screen and stage adaptations, Oliver, Fagin, the Artful Dodger, Mr Bumble and Bill Sykes are among the best known characters in English fiction. Not Dicken's most powerful plea for social justice, but one of his most enduring.

The Life and Adventures of Nicholas Nickleby 1838–9
A picaresque novel of adventure set in the Georgian world of stage coaches and decadent aristocrats. Good, penniless Nicholas flees from Wackford Squeers and his awful orphanage with half-witted Smike. Life is then made miserable by Sir Mulberry Hawk and warmed by the Cheerybles. Wonderfully comic and affectionate scenes with Vincent Crummles' travelling theatre company.

The Old Curiosity Shop 1841
Little Nell and her grandfather are forced out of their gloomy shop when the evil dwarf Quilp discovers that his money has been gambled away. The death of Nell, closely followed by the old man, made a nation weep as the monthly episodes were devoured.

Barnaby Rudge 1841
Unsuccessful on publication and little read since, this historical novel about the Gordon Riots of 1780 has some strong characterizations and vivid scenes of the riots and subsequent executions.

A Christmas Carol 1843
The famous story of Scrooge, transformed from miser to a benevolent old fellow by the appearance on Christmas Eve of Marley's ghost and subsequent vision of the happy family life of his clerk, Bob Cratchit.
    This novel was followed in successive years by other Christmas books, *The Chimes, The Cricket on the Hearth, The Battle of Life* and *The Haunted Man*, each intended to propagate goodwill and the right of everyone to joy at Christmas-time.

The Life and Adventures of Martin Chuzzlewit 1843–4
An interesting, entertaining novel that is distorted (amusingly) by the introduction of the American scenes which were designed to boost sales of the serialized instalments. The serious targets of selfishness and fraud (The Anglo-Bengalese Disinterested Loan and Life Assurance Company) are almost obscured by the dazzling comedy in the scenes of Mr Pecksmith, the hypocritical architect, and Mrs Sairey Gamp, the tippling midwife.

Dombey and Son 1848
Heralding the themes of the later novels, this is a story of family life corrupted by money and pride. The descriptions of the construction of the London and Birmingham Railway document contemporary social change and also provide powerful symbolism.

The Personal History of David Copperfield 1849–50
Dickens' favourite novel and for long regarded as his greatest work, today it justly retains its popularity as an unrivalled child's view of life. The grown-up David's world is less convincing, although many of the famous characters – Mr Micawber, Uriah Heep, Traddles, the Peggotys – last throughout the story.

Bleak House 1852–3
An enormous panorama of English society, marred for some by the narrative being partly in the first person of the self-consciously saintly heroine, Esther Summerson. The legal world of Chancery is the corrupted and corrupting core around which all sorts of persons and professions revolve. The novel's power lies in the representation of its characters' moral life through environments and actions which are both symbolic and real: the fog in the City, the flight of Lady Dedlock.

Hard Times 1854
The shortest, most tightly-plotted novel is a counterblast to the mechanistic philosophy of the utilitarians and the political economists. Set against the industrial background of a Northern mill town, it also exposes the rigidity of Victorian divorce law. A forceful book, it is often admired by people who find Dickens' longer works too loose and over-emphatic.

Little Dorritt 1855–7
Do not be put off by the title; this sombre, complex novel is now widely regarded as one of the great works of English literature. The Marshalsea debtors' prison – remembered from Dickens' own youth – provides both a location for the central characters and a symbol of their imprisonment in their own personalities and delusions. English society is morally bankrupt, preferring stagnation and speculation to creativity and invention. The characterization is largely subservient to the themes but still achieves a painful reality (William Dorritt, Henry Gowan, Mr Merdle) and one comic-serious masterpiece (Flora Finching). A novel for our time.

A Tale of Two Cities 1859
Long popular through stage and screen versions, this story of the French Revolution is less lively than many of Dickens's others. Christian themes of renunciation and personal love are mingled in a forced and affecting ending; artistically, Dickens achieved, far, far better things.

Great Expectations 1860–61
A beautifully woven tale of intrigue, excitement, and love, in which the themes of late Dickens – fake gentility, the corruption of money, manipulation by anti-life forces

and the redemption of simple goodness – are well balanced. The characterization unites a new naturalism in the central figures, Pip and Estella, with the comic-poetic range of early Dickens: Joe Gargery, Miss Haversham, Wemmick and Trabb's Boy.

Our Mutual Friend 1864–5
Painful for the ailing Dickens to write and sometimes difficult to follow, his last complete novel contains powerful scenes, images and characters. Like the River Thames, the struggle for money flows through the novel. The love interest is carried by a group of strongly realized, young characters: the wilful Bella Wilfer, the indolent Eugene Wrayburn and the murderous Bradley Headstone.

Benjamin DISRAELI (1804–81)

Sybil, or The Two Nations 1845
This is a sequel to *Coningsby, or The New Generation*, which described the history of party politics. *Sybil* concentrates on the effect of these parties on the people they govern, studying the conditions of the working classes and analysing the events that led up to the Chartist riots. The two nations of the sub-title are the rich and the poor, ever divided.

J P DONLEAVY (1926–)

The Ginger Man 1955
The first and best-known of Donleavy's novels in his clipped, disjointed, comic style, which represents the perceptions of the anti-hero attempting to find fulfilment in an unwelcoming world.

The Onion Eaters 1971
Less exuberant than the earlier novels, but with an outrageous plot centering on Clayton Clay Cleaver Clementine and his claim to Charnal Castle through the distinction of his having three testicles.

George DOUGLAS (1809–1902)

The House with the Green Shutters 1901
Notable for its powerful characterization and evocation of the atmosphere of a small Scottish town. The once successful inhabitants of this particular house are finally ruined by debt after the son kills his father in rage at the purposelessness of his own existence.

Norman DOUGLAS (1868–1952)

South Wind 1917
Much admired in its time, this novel of chatter and expatriate hedonism is probably less read than Douglas's travel books.

Arthur Conan DOYLE (1859–1930)

The Complete Sherlock Holmes
The characterization and pairing of the brilliant but humanly eccentric Great Detective and his earnest but slightly slow witted assistant, Dr Watson, have given the Holmes stories an eternal appeal as well as a cult following. Today the plots' appeal lies at least as much in the detailed evocation of the life and values of Edwardian England as in the mysterious goings-on. Among the novels, *The White Company* is a good read and *The Exploits of Brigadier Gerard* are very enjoyable short stories for young adults.

Margaret DRABBLE (1939–)

The Millstone 1965
Rosamund is quite happy going about her simple routine existence: but then she meets George and she promptly becomes pregnant, unleashing hitherto unanticipated problems. A tale told with the sensitivity one expects from this novelist who has a great depth of insight into feminine psychology and the problems of intense human relationships. Drabble's more recent novel *The Radiant Way*, widens the social range of her characterization.

Daphne DU MAURIER (1907–89)

Rebecca 1938
A famous story of mystery and romance, a suspense-filled plot with elements of the strange and supernatural, of intrigue and irony. See also *The Flight of the Falcon*, another well-loved tale, and short stories in *The Rendezvous and Other Stories*.

George DU MAURIER (1834–96)

Trilby 1894
The sinister supernatural character Svengali, and Trilby, the golden-hearted whore, are two of the inhabitants of Du Maurier's world of student life in Paris, based on the artist-writer's own Bohemian experiences.

Lawrence DURRELL (1912–)

The Alexandria Quartet – Justine 1957, *Balthazar* 1958, *Mount Olive* 1959, *Clea* 1960
From an impressionistic writer of experimental novels, this work has as its theme the theory of novel-writing, with most of the characters being writers. Each of the four books describe an overlapping sequence of events from various shifting viewpoints.

Maria EDGEWORTH (1767–1849)

Castle Rackrent 1801
A forerunner in the family saga novel, this is a chronicle of reckless Irish life told by Thady Quirk, old steward to the Rackrent family. Immensely influential in its time – and still very readable.

George ELIOT (1819–80)

Adam Bede 1859
A rather cold novel for those not inspired by Methodism. Its tells of the love affair between Hetty Sorrel and Arthur Dennithorne, and of its tragic ending. George Eliot's scrupulous linking of consequence to actions is the best thing about it.

The Mill on the Floss 1860
The figure of Maggie Tulliver – independent, high-spirited, and emotionally stifled by the rural society in which she lives – dominates the book. A good introduction to George Eliot.

Silas Marner 1861
A slim but technically accomplished book, with an unusually simple theme. Driven to misery, alleviated only by the hoarding of money, the life and character of Silas are under scrutiny after a baby is abandoned on his doorstep.

Felix Holt, the Radical 1866
A less convincing novel, a political work rather too much given to melodrama. There is a choice to be made by the heroine Esther between the honest poverty offered by Felix and the wealthy lifestyle she has been used to.

Middlemarch 1871
One of the great peaks of the 19th century English novel: the daunting prospect of its ascent – nearly 1000 pages devoted to English provincial life – should never deter a reader who takes pleasure in masterful characterization, moral insights and a sense of place. Above all, it is a timeless human story of relationships based on the mistaken attraction of opposites: the idealistic Dorothea Brooke with the sham scholar Casaubon; the reforming doctor Lydgate with the flirt Rosamund Vincey.

Daniel Deronda 1876
A long, uneven novel, combining excellent characterization of English types with a plea for Zionism. The portrait of Gwendoline Harleth is one of the landmarks in the evolution of women in fiction, pointing forward to the heroines of Henry James, Hardy and D H Lawrence.

J G FARRELL (1935–79)

The Singapore Grip 1978
In the earlier and excellent *Siege of Krishnapur*, Farrell almost too carefully mixed historical research with a modern viewpoint of the men and women of a failing Empire. In this novel he found an ideal subject – the expatriate English society in Singapore that surrendered to the Japanese in the Second World War – in which the irony is mixed with compassion.

Henry FIELDING (1707–54)

Joseph Andrews 1742
Originally begun as a continuation of his 'Shamela', a satire on Richardson's *Pamela*, this first novel became much more than a parody. The hero and his naive father-figure Parson Adams follow a picaresque journey of comic adventures and draw various moral conclusions.

Jonathan Wild, the Great 1743
In a world which worships and rewards success, the 'greatness' of Wild lies in his perfection of the art of being a criminal. His career is traced from childhood to the gallows.

Tom Jones 1749
A milestone in the development of the English novel, this mock-heroic prose epic remains entertaining despite its age and great length. Tom Jones is a humanly flawed, likeable young man, who must learn something of the world and its immorality before being allowed to win the hand of the virtuous Sophia. It would be nearly another 150 years before a major novel could deal as frankly with the sexuality of its central character.

Ronald FIRBANK (1886–1926)

Valmouth 1919
Firbank's satirical novels are, for some, an eccentric, dreamlike version of reality, and for others, decadent camp. This one is set in an English resort for centenarians, where the niece of a black masseuse gets married to the son of an English woman.

Ford Madox FORD (1873–1939)

The Good Soldier 1915
An attempt to formulate a 'new form' in fiction, this novel displays distorted chronology, a mass of cross-references and allusions, and the story is told by a protagonist who is too emotionally involved to be a dispassionate narrator.

Parade's End: a tetralogy – *Some Do Not ...* 1924, *No More Parades* 1925,
Man Could Stand Up 1926, *Last Post* 1928
These four books analyse the effects of the First World War on English society by
charting the career of Christopher Tietjens, from the horrors of life at the front
through his marriage to a ruthless and malicious wife. The author later wished to
discount *Last Post*, an over-sentimental happy ending, and leave the series as a
trilogy. A work of social as much as literary significance.

E M FORSTER (1879–1970)

Where Angels Fear to Tread 1905
In this first novel, the marriage of an impetuous English woman to an irresponsible
Italian is described with characteristic mixture of wry humour and passionate interest
in human relationships.

The Longest Journey 1907
We follow the progress of the sensitive Rickie from free-thinking Cambridge to the
strictures of a public school and a convenient marriage. The conflict of public and
personal values lead to the downfall of a man unable to be selfish in a selfish society.

A Room with a View 1908
Against an Italian background, two factions of the British middle class are set to fight
out the issues of humanism.

Howards End 1910
The Schlegel sisters, Helen and Margaret, are concerned with art, literature and
music, whilst the Wilcox family deals in the practical business world of 'telegrams
and anger'. The opposing interests of the two families create the theme of one of
Forster's most brilliant novels, of people trying to 'only connect' across barriers of
class, race and character.

A Passage to India 1924
Forster's finest novel depicts the complex relationships between Hindus, Moslems
and the English in India. The dramatic results of the elaborate trip made by Adela
Quested, Dr Aziz and Mrs Moore to the mysteriously ominous Marabar Caves act as
catalyst to the intense feelings harboured on all sides, and are symbolic of far more
than the events themselves. Indian opinion is divided over the depiction of the Indian
characters but generally supports the novel's moral and artistic integrity.

John FOWLES (1926–)

The Collector 1960
A psychological probe into the minds of a young man and the middle class art student
he sets out to capture and imprison like one of his mounted butterflies. Isolated, they
find their class differences impossible to overcome, and the conflict between the
values of art and money is elemental in the final tragedy.

The Magus 1964
A complex, highly allusive work of magic and mystery, this novel has achieved a cult following. Conchis is the magician who blurs the lines between reality and fantasy for Nicholas, a young English teacher arrived on a Greek island, and raises the question of how responsible we are for our experiences.

The French Lieutenant's Woman 1969
Ostensibly writing a Victorian romance, Fowles, by repeatedly reminding us of his authorial presence in the text, along with his inclusion of three different endings, leads us to question all aspects of novel-writing as well as the values of Victorian society.

Michael FRAYN (1933–)

Towards the End of the Morning 1967
Although Frayn has turned to drama with greater success, this is a delightfully funny book about Fleet Street and suburban Sixties London.

John GALSWORTHY (1867–1933)

The Forsyte Saga 1922
A long series of books which takes the upper middle class Forsyte family from late Victorian times to the flapper twenties. The central theme of possession, as epitomized by Soames Forsyte, contrasted with beauty and love is clearly and effectively realized in the first and best novel, *Man of Property* (1906), but degenerates into sentiment towards the end of the sequence. The *Saga* itself contains three novels, with two interludes, but there is a second Forsyte novel sequence and several other stories.

David GARNETT (1892–1981)

Lady into Fox 1922
The fantastic tale of the transformation of a young woman into a vixen, and its subsequent effects on the relationship with her husband, told in lucid, ironic prose.

Elizabeth GASKELL (1810–65)

North and South 1854–5
A study of conflicts between the two halves of England, embodied by Margaret Hale brought from comfortable London to a dismal Northern town, and John Thornton, an unscrupulous employer whom she meets and finally falls in love with.

Cranford 1853
A gently humorous account of genteel life in a Cheshire village, describing characters and events with intimacy and compassion. Less of a 'social and political' novel than its predecessors, it remains the favourite for its delicacy and originality.

Mary Barton – A Tale of Manchester Life 1848
A grim and powerful story set in the 'hungry forties' – one of the first 'social' novels. John Barton, an upright trade unionist, finds himself the murderer of his employer for the cause of the working classes. His daughter Mary then has the difficult task of protecting her father and defending her lover who is suspected of the crime.

Stella GIBBONS (1902–)

Cold Comfort Farm 1932
A lively burlesque on the philosophy of D H Lawrence, the pessimism of Thomas Hardy, and the absurdity of popular romantic, pastoral fiction. The brisk wit is balanced by a strong sense of moral values.

Beside the Pearly Water 1954
A set of short stories from this prolific writer, dealing with love and marriage, money and power. A sense of fun lightens the serious undertones.

George GISSING (1857–1903)

New Grub Street 1891
A grim depiction of the hack literary world of poverty and intrigue, in which self-advertisement has a better chance of bringing success than artistic endeavour.

The Odd Women 1893
A refreshingly sympathetic portrayal of the beginnings of the feminist movement.

William GODWIN (1756–1836)

Caleb Williams 1794
In this early propagandist novel, the humble Caleb is persecuted by his evil master and thus exposes the injustices of the class system and the law. The interest lies mainly in its statement of Godwin's political philosophy.

William GOLDING (1911–)

The Lord of the Flies 1954
A group of schoolboys stranded on an island are left to form their own society. Golding's pessimism about human nature makes the result a horrific tale of superstition and terror. It has rightly earned the status of a modern 'classic'.

Pincher Martin 1956
The drowning seconds of a self-centred and nasty man are described in immense detail to create one of Golding's best novels.

The Inheritors 1955
Another struggle for survival, this time of Neanderthal Man before their fall and the advent of the race of man who carry evil in their souls.

Freefall 1959
Sammy Mountjoy is an artist reviewing his life to discover how he lost his soul in the transition from innocent childhood to guilt-ridden adulthood.

Rites of Passage 1980
The first novel in a recently completed triology, this Booker Prize winner is perhaps more impressive for its vivid recreation of life aboard an eighteenth century passenger ship than for its portrayals of class barriers and human failings. The story continues in *Close Quarters* and *Fire Down Below*.

Oliver GOLDSMITH (1728–74)

The Vicar of Wakefield 1766
Goldsmith's only novel, narrated by the vicar, Dr Primrose. An uninspiring story-line develops a certain charm, and the characters – a happy family upset by bankruptcy and marital misadventures – provide a warm, gentle comedy and a happy ending.

Robert GRAVES (1895–1986)

I Claudius 1934
Claudius the God 1934
A lively narrative of events, both public and private, in first century imperial Rome. Claudius, emperor from AD 41 to AD 54 tells the tales of his predecessors, and in the second novel, of his own affairs.

Henry GREEN (1905–73)

Living 1929
A vivid picture of English factory life, this novel deals (unpolitically) with the living and working conditions of foundry workers in Birmingham.

Party Going 1939
A group of rich, idle, young people are catching a boat-train to a party in France, until the descent of fog puts them into a hotel. In the few hours covered, trivia is made vastly important and the sexual inclinations of the party, like their expedition, are immersed in confusion. A poetic, resonant novel.

Loving 1945
The complicated events proceeding from a housemaid's discovery of the mistress of an Irish castle in bed with her lover are described with Green's objective, unconventional and experimental style, thick with symbolism, yet bright and funny.

Graham GREENE (1904–)

Brighton Rock 1938
The deprived youth seeking kicks out of life is now a stereotype, but this terrifying portrait of heartless Pinkie – as well as the counterbalancing concern of the book's heroine – is as good as anything ever written on the subject.

The Power and the Glory 1940
Along with *The Heart of the Matter*, this is a contender as Greene's best novel. A
whisky priest is pursued across a state in Mexico in which the church is outlawed, by a
police lieutenant of incorruptible and inflexible morals.

The Heart of the Matter 1948
The compassion of Major Scobie, Deputy Commissioner of Police in a West African
port during the Second World War, leads to his downfall as he struggles with the
conflicts between his Catholicism and his love for two women.

The End of the Affair 1951
An adulterous affair is brought to an end when he is knocked down in an air-raid and
she makes a bargain with God to save him if she agrees to give him up for ever.

A Burnt Out Case 1961
The title refers to Querry, a famous architect who has lost all motivation for love and
work. He now finds contentment working in a leper hospital, where the patients'
physical mutilation matches his spiritual degeneration.

The novels listed above are those generally accepted as major landmarks in
'Greeneland', but the variety and quality of Greene's work in novels and short stories
is probably unrivalled in contemporary fiction, including thrillers (*Gun for Sale, The
Human Factor*); humour (*Our Man in Havana, Travels with my Aunt*); and
contemporary politics (*The Quiet American, The Comedians*).

Walter GREENWOOD (1903–74)

Love on the Dole 1933
An outcry against the poverty of the '30s, this is a novel of abortive rebellion against
the pettiness of bureaucracy. Love is a possibility, but can it survive?

George and Weedon GROSSMITH (1847–1912 and 1852–1919)

The Diary of a Nobody 1892
First published in parts in *Punch*, Mr Pooter's struggle for respectability in the face of
untrustworthy tradesmen, unemployed offspring (young Lupin), the subversive
Murray Posh and the less than wholehearted support of friends and colleagues is one
of the funniest books in English about the English.

Neil GUNN (1891–1973)

The Silver Darlings 1941
A poetic imagination and a fervent belief in humanity pervade this story of a
settlement of crofters, evicted from their homestead, who are forced to struggle
against the forces of sea and plague to make a livelihood from herring fishing in the
early nineteenth century.

Henry Rider HAGGARD (1856–1925)

King Solomon's Mines 1886
One of the best adventure stories. Unfashionable imperialistic overtones there may
be, but the excitement of the journey into the unknown, and the horror of the grisly
climax are unbeatable.

Thomas HARDY (1840–1928)

Under the Greenwood Tree 1872
An idyllic romance between the improbably named Dick Dewey and Fancy Day runs
almost smoothly against a background of rustic characters struggling to retain
traditional country codes – the church choir versus the harmonium.

Far From the Madding Crowd 1874
Hardy's first major novel and for some the best because it is not overweighted with
cosmic significance. A beautifully balanced central quartet: Bathsheba Everdene, a
beautiful heiress, entangled with different suitors; the selfless shepherd, Gabriel Oak;
the 'macho', Sergeant Troy; and the obsessed Farmer Boldwood.

The Return of the Native 1878
Egdon Heath, one of the most powerful of the Wessex locations, is a brooding witness
to the dramatic goings-on of Hardy's passionate characters, set against the mild
comedy of his rural bumpkins.

The Trumpet Major 1880
An untypically simple and happy tale in which the good are allowed to triumph. Set in
the time of the Napoleonic Wars, it covers the affairs of Anne Garland and her
prospective husbands.

Two on a Tower 1882
This romantic and less well-known novel concerns the amorous fortunes of Lady
Constantine and her numerous marriages, resulting in various tragedies.

The Mayor of Casterbridge 1886
The famous wife-selling opening scene introduces a tragic hero of Shakespearean
proportions. Michael Henchard's character predicates both his rise and fall, but fate –
in the Hardy manner – contributes some strong nudges.

The Woodlanders 1887
A Sophoclean tragedy at Little Hintock, which Hardy liked 'as a story' best of all his
works. General opinion is less favourable.

Wessex Tales 1888
A series of 'dreams, and not records', which draw on the history, folklore and
atmosphere of Hardy's Wessex, and are full of characters both real and fantastic.

Tess of the D'Urbervilles 1891
'I have felt that the doll of English fiction must be demolished'. But Tess herself is more than a reaction, she is a moving creation of animal force and instinct. She is relentlessly punished for the sins of others in a world of corrupt laws. Although contrived, the tragedy of the story and its natural and emotional landscape will stir readers for as long as the English novel is read.

Jude the Obscure 1896
Jude Fawley aspires to great intellectual heights, but circumstances, drawn with Hardy's characteristic pessimism, are against him. This is the last and most desperate of the novels. Its hostile reception led Hardy to stop novel writing and concentrate on poetry.

L P HARTLEY (1895–1972)

The Go-Between 1953
The wonderfully touching story of Leo Colston, who looks back to a childhood summer in 1900 and remembers his unwitting discovery of the complexities of adult life and love in upper class England.

Eustace and Hilda Trilogy -- The Shrimp and the Anemone 1944, *The Sixth Heaven* 1946, *Eustace and Hilda* 1947
Young, sensitive Eustace is dominated by his wilful and passionate sister Hilda and persecuted by his dependence on her as he reaches adulthood. The second of the novels is less effective than the others, but the trilogy displays Hartley's masterful evocation of time and place, and powerful psychological insights into the dangerous strength of the brother–sister relationship.

Patricia HIGHSMITH (1921–)

The Talented Mr Ripley 1956
The first of Patricia Highsmith's crime novels about the Iago-figure, Mr Ripley. A fine writer of this genre of fiction.

Susan HILL (1942–)

Strange Meeting 1971
An accomplished novel about the horrors and waste of the First World War, and the contrasting friendship it could produce.

The Bird of Night 1972
A moving novel which examines the nature of friendship and madness through the two characters of Harvey and Francis.

Russell HOBAN (1925–)

Riddley Walker 1980
Broken fragments of language, culture and technology have survived a nuclear holocaust and are being crudely re-assembled in a harsh tribal existence. An intensely imagined, dark, disturbing book.

James HOGG (1770–1835)

The Private Memoirs and Confessions of a Justified Sinner 1824
The 'Ettrick Shepherd's' only novel is a powerful criticism of Calvinism, a doctrine detested by both him and his idol Burns. The 'justified sinner' is a product of the belief that Christians are freed from the obligations of moral law by virtue of their faith.

Richard HUGHES (1900–1976)

A High Wind in Jamaica 1929
A compelling story of a group of children being mistakenly captured by pirates on the way from Jamaica to school in England. This is a study of the conflicts which arise when children are present but unwanted in a grown-up world.

The Human Predicament – The Fox in the Attic 1961, *The Wooden Shepherdess* 1972
Two novels of a planned but unrealized sequence spanning the rise of Hitler from 1923 to 1934, and covering a wide social, political and geographical canvas, including England, Germany, America and North Africa.

R C HUTCHINSON (1897–1975)

Testament 1938
The depictions of human suffering in this and his later, prizewinning novel, *A Child Possessed* 1964, illustrate the acuteness of perception which has made Hutchinson an important recorder of recent times. His fundamentally Christian belief in the essential goodness and dignity within people underlies his work.

Aldous HUXLEY (1894–1963)

Chrome Yellow 1921
De rigeur for the young intellectual when it first appeared. A collection of witty people, including caricatures of contemporaries such as Bertrand Russell and Lady Ottoline Morrell, gather for a house party.

Point Counter Point 1928
Eyeless in Gaza 1936
Post-war London is the setting for the first novel, a satire on the absurdities of human behaviour – cynical and scathing, witty and sharp in its description of types in a

society obsessed by self-indulgence and self-analysis. The autobiographical *Eyeless in Gaza* takes the reader on to the author's discovery of mysticism and pacifism and contains the famous death of a dog.

Brave New World 1932
A futuristic fable of life scientifically pre-destined right from birth in a bottle, and graded to keep a hierarchy of ability and power. Creativity and romance are squashed. Mass entertainment is provided through controlled media. Still one of the best guesses about the worst aspects of a technological world.

There are also the excellent short stories in the *Collected Short Stories* and for those who like the novel of ideas, the later works such as *Apes and Essence* and the Utopian *The Island* one of the first books about the world after nuclear war.

Christopher ISHERWOOD (1904–)

Mr Norris Changes Trains 1935
Like *Goodbye to Berlin*, which includes as an episode the short story *Sally Bowles*, this is based on the author's experience of teaching in Berlin. Both of these works are series of episodes rather than complex novels, and are told with the 'I am a camera' technique, which abstains from judgement but nevertheless movingly depicts the upheaval and misery which came in the rise of the Nazis.

M R JAMES (1862–1936)

Collected Ghost Stories 1931
Knowledgeable reference to witchcraft, legends, historical documents and facts gives a pseudo-scholarly authenticity to these unsolved mysteries with their underlying sense of evil and ancient devilry.

Richard JEFFERIES (1845–87)

After London 1884
Along with *Amaryllis at the Fair*, this is regarded as the best of Jefferies' imaginative work, written with loving attention to nature and rural life and his own brands of poetry and philosophy.

Bevis: The Story of a Boy 1882
A forerunner of the kind of children's adventure stories later made popular by the likes of Arthur Ransome, this was republished in 1904 as a book for young people.

Jerome K JEROME (1859–1927)

Three Men in a Boat 1889
A famous, humorous work, ever-popular for its depiction of three friends (and a dog) on a farcical rowing expedition up the Thames.

B S JOHNSON (1933–73)

The Unfortunates 1969
Close to the last stop on the branch line of the experimental novel. Memories of a dead friend mix with a particular afternoon's activities and are presented in a box of 27 unbound sections of differing lengths – a tangible metaphor for the randomness of life and the disease of cancer.

Samuel JOHNSON (1709–84)

The History of Rasselas, Prince of Abyssinia 1759
A short, philosophical tale of an escape from the comforts of the Happy Valley, and a journey through the misery and dissatisfaction of the world outside. In Johnson's only prose fiction, his deep humanity and style are ever-present, while the moral is lightened more by the slanting, ironic humour than by the Christian message of renunciation of the world's vanities.

James JOYCE (1882–1941)

Dubliners 1914
A collection of stories each centering on characters who somehow fail to achieve true recognition of themselves and their destinies. The 'Dead', the last and best of these chapters in the life of Dublin and its inhabitants, skilfully brings together the previous protagonists and ends the book on a note of lyricism.

A Portrait of the Artist as a Young Man 1916
The arresting style of the very first page immediately insists that this book be read. Stephen Daedalus characterizes the artistic temperament which must break through the oppressions of family, society and religion (in Ireland) to achieve the spiritual and aesthetic freedom sought by Joyce himself.

Ulysses 1922
One day (16th June 1914) in the Dublin life of advertisement salesman Leopold Bloom embraces events simultaneously insignificant and universal and is recorded in a variety of manners – straight narrative, stylistic parodies, and the so-called 'stream of consciousness'. Individual episodes can be read with great enjoyment, especially with the help of a sympathetic but not too literary commentary such as Nabokov's notes in *Lectures on Literature*. Through the word-play and the allusions, shine the humanity of Joyce's treatment of everyman Bloom, and his contrasted companions, his vulgar, earth-bound wife Molly, and the would-be intellectual, high flyer Stephen Daedalus. A twentieth century epic.

Finnegan's Wake 1939
New Joyce readers do not begin here! *Finnegan's Wake* is so experimental in its use of language that it is largely incomprehensible. This long and difficult novel covers a night in Dublin through the dreams and imaginings of its central character, H C

Earwhicker. Burgess's commentary *Here Comes Everybody* is a useful starting-point for anyone who wishes to untangle Joyce's complexities.

Charles KINGSLEY (1819–75)

Alton Locke, Tailor and Poet 1850
A political pamphlet in the guise of a novel, stating the case of the working classes but disapproving of the directness of the Chartist movement. His theory that improvement lies in Christianity and individual endeavour sits at odds with his socialist ideals.

The Water Babies 1863
Kingsley has lately been the subject of posthumous psycho-analysis. Queen Victoria was not aware of the author's obsessions when she read this story to her children, who probably enjoyed the imaginative location of under-water life and profited from the moral of Mrs Doasyouwouldbedoneby.

Rudyard KIPLING (1865–1936)

The Jungle Books 1894, 1895
These stories intended for children focus on Mowgli, a boy brought up by a mother wolf, and his gradual acceptance by the animals of the jungle who teach him the lore of their kingdom.

Kim 1901
The best of his novels, none of which is as successful as his short stories. Kim is an Irish orphan who wanders across India with a Buddhist priest, playing the Great. Game (espionage) for the British Raj and mixing with the crowds, colour and chatter of Indian life. It is a British experience of India – which, however one-sided, still haunts the collective imagination.

Just So Stories 1902
Stories for young children, memories of which remain throughout life. How the elephant got its trunk and the giraffe its neck are 'explained' with ingenuity and humour.

Short Stories
Kipling is a master of the short story although in their large range they display, in sentiment and subject both the most and least attractive aspects of his writing and sympathies. Childhood and youth is both realized and sentimentalized ('Baa Ba Black Sheep', 'The Brushwood Boy'); Indian life – in the barracks ('Love-O-Women') and in the bazaar ('Without Benefit of Clergy') or among the dedicated administrators ('The Bridge Builders') and the fortune hunters ('The Man Who Would Be King'). Some of the best stories are achieved by the combination of Kipling's skill as a reporter and his love of the mystical and fantastic: 'The Finest Story In The World', 'Wireless' and 'The Gardner'.

Arthur KOESTLER (1905–83)

Darkness at Noon 1940
Rubashov is an old Bolshevik awaiting death in a GPU prison, forced to admit to 'crimes' that he has never committed. Although written out of the disgust of a former communist for the persecutions and trials of Stalin's purges of the 1930s, it has survived its immediate context both as a condemnation of totalitarian methods and for its portrait of Rubashov.

D H LAWRENCE (1885–1930)

Sons and Lovers 1913
A vivid, strongly autobiographical novel centering on young Paul Morel brought up in a Midlands mining family. The intimate bond between Paul and his mother, firmly excluding his father, taints his efforts at any fulfilling relationship while she lives.

The Rainbow 1915
Women in Love 1920
A novel concentrating on three generations of the Brangwen family in Nottinghamshire, and particularly on their male–female relationships. Ursula is seeking the wholeness of the rainbow, having transcended the prevailing mentality of mechanization. *Women in Love* follows the two sisters, Ursula and Gudrun Brangwen, in their search for perfect union with their respective lovers. At times the ideological dialogue mingles incongruously with tempestuous scenes of passion. *The Rainbow* and *Women in Love* are the central expression in novel form of Lawrence's anti-intellectual, anti-material, pro-animal, pro-sexual view of life. Those who are sympathetic to the view but not to his style as a novelist should try the energetic argument in his essays and letters or – better still – in his poetry.

Kangaroo 1923
Never very popular, this work is a somewhat self-indulgent account of the harassment experienced by Lawrence and his wife, but the Australian landscape brings out the true artist.

The Plumed Serpent 1926
An exploration against a Mexican background of the dark sexual consciousness lying beneath the rational mind of civilized man. Lawrence's enthusiastic indulgence in the violence of the book is rather disconcerting, as is his explicit belief that women must submit to the authority of men.

Lady Chatterley's Lover 1928
Controversial for its use of four-letter words and explicit sex scenes – between the lady and her gamekeeper – this last novel has neither the fluidity nor power of earlier works.

Short Stories
Lawrence's skills grew in the shorter story as they decreased in the novel. Among the best are the novella 'The Man Who Died', a moving reworking of the Christian resurrection; 'St. Mawr', about a woman giving up her husband for a horse; and 'The Woman Who Rode Away', dealing with ancient powers possessed by Indians.

Joseph Sheridan LE FANU (1814–73)

In a Glass Darkly 1872
A collection of chilling stories dealing with mysteries of the occult and the uncanny. The most notable amongst these are *The Watcher* and *Uncle Silas*.

Rosamund LEHMANN (1901–)

The Echoing Grove 1953
This is the most lastingly valuable of her books – the earlier *Invitation to the Waltz* followed by *The Weather in the Streets*, have dated somewhat. *The Echoing Grove*, whilst dealing with the same themes of a girl's awakening to social and political life, is maturer and more stylistically accomplished.

Doris LESSING (1919–)

The Grass is Singing 1950
Mary Turner, a white woman in Africa, is gradually overtaken by schizophrenia until she is violently killed by her houseboy. The representatives of a corrupt society in which blacks and women are oppressed make only a superficial inquiry into the complex background to the murder, in the first and possibly the best of Lessing's works of fiction.

The Golden Notebook 1962
An important work attempting to describe what it is to be a woman in a society of dehumanized males who see women as brainless objects. Anna Wulf keeps four notebooks in order to prevent chaos and madness. Together they can form something new, but like her anguished life, they can never be complete.

Children of Violence a sequence of five novels – *Martha Quest* 1952, *A Proper Marriage* 1954, *The Ripple from the Storm* 1958, *Landlocked* 1965, *The Four Gated City* 1969
The themes of identity and survival introduced in *The Grass is Singing* are pursued extensively in these five volumes. The aptly named Martha Quest, searching for her female self, rejects the prejudices of her society and adopts the Marxism of the author. Finally, in *The Four Gated City*, the prospect of a cataclysmic future destroys all hope for any kind of humanism.

Matthew Gregory LEWIS (1775–1818)

The Monk 1796
Lewis became known as 'The Monk Lewis' after writing this Gothic tale of Ambrosio who, despite his monkish exterior, seeks to gratify his senses. It is a tale of lust and debauchery as the reader follows Ambrosio from his first escapade to his inevitable end. The book uses many of the techniques of Gothic fiction, taken to their extremes.

Percy Wyndham LEWIS (1884–1957)

The Human Age a trilogy – *The Childermass* 1928, *Monstre Gai* 1955, *Malign Fiesta* 1955.
In a wasteland outside heaven a grotesque Bailiff examines the potential inhabitants with an alarming absence of scruple. The Joycean style of the first book gives way to Lewis's own in the later two, evoking a nightmarish atmosphere suffused with symbolism. As a painter, novelist, poet, critic and polemicist, Lewis's life and work reflects the most turbulent years of art and politics in modern history. See also the satirical novels *Tarr* and *The Apes of God*.

David LODGE (1935–)

How Far Can You Go? 1978
A very funny novel about a group of Roman Catholics, struggling with their all-too-obvious Catholicism and the clashes it produces when forced against the fast world of the twentieth-century.

Small World 1984
Morris Zapp, an American professor of literature, and Philip Swallow, an English professor, jet across the Atlantic to attend interminable conferences and to read long papers to other academics, all of whom seem to be playing a game with no fixed rules. In many ways the book is a literary joke, but it has a satiric purpose. Re-introduces several characters from the earlier *Changing Places*.

Clarence Malcolm LOWRY (1909–57)

Under the Volcano 1947
A partly autobiographical masterpiece set in Mexico. Geoffrey Firmin is a Faustian figure whose gradual death from drink and drugs is agonizingly documented in complex, allusive prose and a tangled network of plots and themes.

Hear Us O Lord from Heaven Thy Dwelling Place 1962
A series of interlocking stories discovered after Lowry's death, and dealing with his preoccupations with sexuality and identity, suffering and freedom.

Rose MACAULAY (1881–1958)

The Towers of Trebizond 1956
Her last novel is a highly comic travel adventure in which the narrator, Laurie, goes to Turkey with an aunt and an Anglican canon and an expression of the author's anxieties about Christianity.

Colin MacINNES (1914–76)

City of Spades 1957
Renowned for his sympathetic and honest portrayal of adolescents, West Indians and the underworld in London in the 1950s, this is an original novel about Johny Fortune, the black underdog in the big city.

Compton MACKENZIE (1883–1972)

Sinister Street 1913–14
Written before his huge outpouring of light novels, this is an autobiographical study of problems arising from being educated at public school and university.

Whisky Galore 1947
The best of the later lighter novels, ingeniously funny although the characters are stereotypes, about a boat-load of whisky stranded off a Hebridean island.

Sir Thomas MALORY (? –1471)

Le Morte D'Arthur 1485
Malory blended information from various sources to create the first major prose narrative in English fiction. A rather disjointed series of stories about King Arthur's Round Table and the quest of the Holy Grail is unified by the growing mistrust and betrayal among the principals.

Olivia MANNING (1908–80)

The Balkan Trilogy – The Great Fortune 1960, *The Spoilt City* 1962, *Friends and Heroes* 1965
A detailed observation of a husband and wife relationship against a background of the Second World War, she discovering new facets of his character in their life of travel in Eastern Europe and the Middle East. A remarkable piece of post-war fiction, combining historical fact with sensitive human analysis.

Katherine MANSFIELD (1888–1923)

Collected Stories 1945
Katherine Mansfield helped to give the short story a new footing as a form of fiction separate from the novel. These stories are a poetic evocation of the author's native

New Zealand in times present and past. *Prelude, Sun and Moon* and *The Fly* are specially recommended.

William Somerset MAUGHAN (1874–1965)

Of Human Bondage 1915
A directly autobiographical novel about the intense loneliness of a boy tortured throughout his life by the disfigurement of a club foot.

The Moon and Sixpence 1919
Based on the life of Gaugin, this is the story of a man who opts out of society to pursue a consuming urge to paint.

Cakes and Ale 1930
Probably his best novel in which his cynicism is at its sharpest. The narrator looks down his nose at the games played in literary circles in the early twentieth century, two members of which have been presumed to be caricatures of Thomas Hardy and Hugh Walpole.

The Complete Short Stories 1951
Three volumes of stories, among the best of which are 'Rain', 'The Letter', 'The Alien Corn', 'Red' and 'Episode'. All prove his ability as a strong narrator and perceptive observer – often of colonial life in the Far East – and display sardonic and somewhat supercilious opinions of human behaviour.

George MEREDITH (1828–1909)

The Ordeal of Richard Feverel 1859
An author less read than known, Meredith specializes in offputting flourishes of language. This is the tale of young Richard's strict upbringing and his thwarted attempts to attach himself to the woman he loves.

The Egoist 1879
A 'comedy in narrative', different from the rest of Meredith's novels for its originality of technique. Sir Willoughby Patterne is the narcissistic central figure, whose various female conquests succeed in humiliating, although not in transforming him.

Nancy MITFORD (1904–73)

The Pursuit of Love 1945
A jolly British comedy about the English ruling class. Her monstrously conceited characters speak with the tongues of upper class fools and flit about the social scene with an intentness only the wealthy can afford.

Brian MOORE (1921–)

Catholics 1972
Father Kinsella arrives at Muck Abbey, Ireland, in order to bring the traditional practices of the monks into line with the modern teachings of Rome. He finds an unusual ally in the figure of the old Abbot, but few of the others welcome his modernism. A novel about faith, compromise and choice.

The Doctor's Wife 1976
Sheila Reddon is married to a successful Irish doctor; for the first time in many years she finds herself outside Ireland, alone and with a chance to alleviate her boredom. In the romantic setting of Nice, can she do anything else but fall in love? A tender novel, concerning fidelity, self-discovery and self-fulfilment.

The Temptation of Eileen Hughes 1981
Eileen Hughes is an ordinary shop worker, or so she thinks, until the McAuleys invite her to spend more and more time with them. Why should she receive special treatment, gifts, status? As the novel unfolds it reveals human weaknesses: the greed for power, the need for control and how these aims may be achieved.

George MOORE (1852–1933)

Esther Waters 1894
Pure, young Esther is sent into the service of the Barfields, a household which revolves around gambling. She is seduced and deserted by another of the servants who finally marries her; she suffers all the while in poverty and humiliation. Influenced by the French realists, Moore's novels scandalized the late Victorian reading public.

Sir Thomas MORE (c.1477–1535)

Utopia 1516
See *Philosophy* section.

Iris MURDOCH (1919–)

Under the Net 1954
The first novel by this prolific and popular philosopher-novelist. Reading too much like a paper on existentialist philosophy at times, but also very funny, as the feckless hero wanders through a series of scrapes in the underground art world.

The Bell 1958
The symbolism is insistent but the narrative is compelling and this is often considered her finest work. A Benedictine lay community is the retreat for characters who must learn to come to terms with failure, in life and in love.

A Severed Head 1961
A farcical quest for freedom and identity through the various sexual games engaged in by the larger-than-life characters. A fantasy novel but one of her most convincing.

An Unofficial Rose 1962
Roses symbolize the well-worn conflicts between wild passion and cultivated discipline. Characters representing each type find they must take Sartrian responsibility for their actions.

The Sea, The Sea 1978
An aging theatre director attempts to escape from his past by moving to a quiet village, but his life catches up with him in the form of two women and a surprisingly adult young boy. A story of growth, maturity, understanding and baptism.

V S NAIPAUL (1932–)

Naipaul's work is placed here in English fiction: he was born in Trinidad of Indian descent and settled in England in his twenties. Like Conrad, whom he resembles in philosophic and psychological outlook, the widely different locales of his novels increases rather than decreases the universality of their themes.

The Mystic Masseur 1957
The first of three early comic novels set in Trinidad, although not well received by Caribbean writers and critics. A masseur exploits popular mysticism to become a celebrity and politician.

The House for Mr Biswas 1961
Spanning the period from the beginning of the century to the end of the Second World War, this major novel charts the efforts of Mr Biswas to 'escape' from his environment through the purchase of his own house. Mr Biswas is one of the most successful realizations of that common literary hero: the small man with a large imagination.

A Bend in the River 1979
The location in the heart of modern Africa's darkness – a violent, impoverished dictatorship – the large cast of characters differently obsessed and the pessimistic view of human nature and its attempts to progress by political means inevitably recall Conrad. The novel is both worthy of such a comparison and a work with its own voice.

Thomas NASHE (1567–1601)

The Unfortunate Traveller 1594
An early example of the 'picaresque' form of fiction in which the hero (Jacke Wilton in this case) wanders from adventure to adventure and learns to survive by using his wits. An entertaining book.

Flann O'BRIEN (1911–66)

At Swim-Two-Birds 1939
A surrealist, hilarious book, praised by James Joyce, of complex plots narrated by lots of different people telling lots of different tales.

The Dalkey Archive 1964
Less accessible and less amusing than *The Third Policeman* although similar in some of the devices that it employs. James Joyce comes back to life after a faked death and the mad scientist, who becomes De Selby in *The Third Policeman*, makes his entrance.

The Third Policeman 1967
The finest and funniest of these weird and wonderful novels. O'Brien explores the after-life with great invention and wit – a fantasy world of mystery and murder, love and bicycles.

Sean O'FAOLAIN (1900–)

The Collected Stories 1980–82 (3 vols)
O'Faolain's novels have never been as well-received as his short stories which, collected together here, exemplify his wide-ranging skills in the form. He writes of Irish life – of its characters and political tensions – with a mind able to both romanticize and satirize.

George ORWELL (Eric Arthur Blair) (1903–50)

Burmese Days 1934
Based on his police experience in Burma, this novel has as its central character the jaded Flory who, in common with most of Orwell's heroes, is handicapped by half-heartedness of intent and shabbiness of character.

Keep the Aspidistra Flying 1936
Gordon Comstook represents the average man, here endowed with a literary sensitivity and no money. His poverty infects his will and spirit, to such an extent that he can finally only submit to convention.

Animal Farm 1945
A famous parable on the dangers of totalitarianism. The animals revolt against their human masters to form their own society with the pigs as leaders. The memorable slogan to emerge from this is 'All animals are equal but some animals are more equal than others'.

Nineteen Eighty Four 1949
Now the real year has passed, it is safe to assume that most people have read, or heard about, this frightening anti-utopia. It did not arrive – but it still might. The anguish provoked by the rat episode will remain in readers minds indefinitely.

Thomas Love PEACOCK (1785–1866)

Nightmare Abbey 1818
A satire on the literature of doom and gloom presented mostly in dialogue between characters who nearly resemble the literary leaders of the day: Coleridge, Byron, Shelley etc.

Crotchet Castle 1831
A further short satirical novel on the ideas and personalities of the times with a dash of romantic interest.

Mervyn PEAKE (1911–68)

Gormenghast Trilogy – Titus Groan 1946, *Gormenghast* 1950, *Titus Alone* 1959
Peake creates a sinister fantasy world which is a version of the awful reality that he observed as a war artist. The hierarchical bureaucratic absurdity of Gormenghast Castle is inhabited by grotesque characters, the principals of whom, Steerpike and Titus, seek to escape.

Anthony POWELL (1905–)

A Dance to the Music of Time 1951–1975
A sequence of twelve novels which appeared at two yearly intervals. They cover the period from the 1920s to the 1970s and embrace schooldays, university, literary work, the Second World War, business, politics and the London life of fashion, foolery, money and power. Onwards and downwards or simply around in circles, dances the twentieth century: like music, small moments are given significance or beauty through the grace of Powell's writing or positioning in the overall movement. And if the narrator, Jenkins, and his class seem too enervated, in Kenneth Widmerpool the sequence develops from schoolboy buffoon to cabinet *eminence grise*, one of modern fiction's great characters – a comic creation that says something serious about life.

John Cowper POWYS (1872–1963)

Glastonbury Romance 1932
The best of Powys' novels, despite his great gift of story-telling, is labouriously long. A tale which revises and completes the Arthurian legend.

T F POWYS (1875–1953)

Mr Weston's Good Wine 1927
God sells the wines of Love and Death from a van in a Dorset village. The satire in this allegory is greater than the deliberately horrifying stories in *Mr Tasher's Gods*.

J B PRIESTLY (1894–1984)

The Good Companions 1929
An attempt to return to the long and diverse novel form of the eighteenth century, concentrating on the adventures of three characters whose various talents come together to form *The Good Companions* concert party. Humour of differing degrees of subtlety is present throughout.

Angel Pavement 1930
Against a background of post-war unemployment another firm collapses under the commercial exploitation of an unscrupulous Mr Golspie. It conveys the effects of pending poverty on the employees and their families through minute, 'realist' descriptions.

Bright Day 1946
Autobiographical content is high in this reminiscence of Bruddersford (Bradford) before the war and the subsequent destruction both of the place itself and of the general morale of the people.

V S PRITCHETT (1900–)

Dead Man Leading 1937
Explorer Harry Johnson follows too closely in his father's footsteps as he investigates his disappearance as a missionary in the Brazilian jungle.

Collected Stories 1982
The author's own selection from seven volumes of short stories spanning fifty years of his career and recording the changing social scene during that time. Pritchett is at his best in the short story, distilling a potential novel into a shorter form – he is, in his own words, 'something of an architect'.

Mrs Ann RADCLIFFE (1764–1823)

The Mysteries of Udolpho 1794
A famous gothic romance full of dark castles and hints of supernatural sorcery, which unfortunately are given clear and clinical explanations at the end. The fearful character Montoni foreshadows the Byronic hero.

Jean RHYS (1890–1979)

Quartet (originally *Postures*) 1929
Like *Voyage in the Dark* and *Good Morning, Midnight*, this short, compact novel draws on the author's roving life in bohemian Paris and London. The main character is a woman struggling against poverty and neglect, caught up in a sexual tangle in which she is emotionally and financially defenceless.

Wide Sargasso Sea 1966
Jean Rhys's finest novel concerns the mad wife in *Jane Eyre*. Bertha Mason (her real name is Antoinette) and Mr Rochester both present their own versions of the story; she is a Creole in the West Indies who believes her husband has married her for her dowry and attempts to retrieve his love through 'beah' or magic. Her loneliness and dependence force her into the insanity originally attributed to her by gossip.

Tigers are Better-Looking 1968
A volume of stories exemplifying Jean Rhys's gift for presenting the case of women victimized by men unable to understand them.

Dorothy RICHARDSON (1873–1957)

Pilgrimage 1938
Originally thirteen novels written over thirty years, here gathered into four volumes. *Pilgrimage* is critically important, primarily for its use of the interior monologue, antedating both Virginia Woolf and James Joyce. The length and unselectiveness of the work brings some tedium but it presents the world from a female perspective rather than the concrete masculine 'realism' of traditional novels.

Samuel RICHARDSON (1689–1761)

Pamela, or Virtue Rewarded 1740
A landmark in the development of the novel, it takes some dedication to read the whole book in its epistolary form. The virtuous heroine scribbles away in the most unlikely situations in order to record every moment of her attempts to escape the amorous clutches of her master. Even now our emotions can be engaged.

Clarissa Harlowe, or *The History of a Young Lady* 1748
A tragic version of *Pamela*, where virtue is not rewarded by cash, but with violation by an unscrupulous man which results in the heroine's death. Possibly the longest novel in English at over a million words, it even tried the patience of eighteenth century readers: 'if you were to read Richardson for the story your patience would be so much fretted that you would hang yourself' – Dr Johnson. However the epistolary form is suited to Clarissa's slowly dawning realization of Loveless' evil intent and there is great psychological depth to the characterizations and the universal story of the destruction of innocence.

Sir Charles Grandison 1753–4
Hardly read today because of its moralistic bearing, but containing some convincing characterization. In response to contemporary public demand, it is about a good man, as opposed to his previous good women.

Frederick William ROLFE (1860–1913)

Hadrian the Seventh 1904
An autobiographical novel based on the disappointment of Rolfe's personal aspirations to the priesthood. His extraordinary lifestory is recorded in A J A Simons' biography, *The Quest of Corvo*.

Salman RUSHDIE (1947–)

Midnight's Children 1981
The hero is born on the stroke of midnight, at exactly the same time as India becomes independent; the novel then traces the story of the development of both 'characters' in a combination of tragedy, comedy and farce.

Shame 1983
A more focussed work than the brilliant Booker Prize winning *Midnight's Children*. The fantastic and fabulous elements give a universality to this satire on the politics of modern Pakistan.

Victoria (Vita) SACKVILLE-WEST (1892–1962)

All Passion Spent 1931
An elegant study of an eighty-eight-year-old widow who has relinquished her artistic passion in wealthy marriage. When an elderly admirer leaves her millions, she gives it away to hospitals, much to the pleasure of her granddaughter who can pursue her own artistic ambitions free from the constraints imposed by possession of a fortune.

SAKI (Hector Hugh MUNRO) (1870–1916)

The Complete Short Stories 1930
Saki's stories are economical and written in witty and often satirical style. His Toryism manifests itself in much of his work, particularly some of his war pieces, but his best work shows a clever malice controlled and fashioned into an unique story-telling technique.

William SANSOM (1926–76)

The Loving Eye 1956
Sansom's writing seems less suited to the novel than to the short story. This is about a girl the main character, Matthew, sees through a window and the same but different girl he sees working at a night club.

The Stories of William Sansom 1963
Thirty-three stories selected from previous volumes and introduced by Elizabeth Bowen. The style is drily ironic, the descriptive detail is immaculate, and the dialogue and characterization convincing. A more recent volume of short stories is *The Marmalade Bird*.

Siegfried SASSOON (1886–1967)

The Complete Memoirs of George Sheraton Sassoon's fictional autobiography in three volumes – *Memoirs of a Fox Hunting Man* 1928, *Memoirs of an Infantry Officer* 1930, *Sheraton's Progress* 1936

A classic personal account of the events of the First World War period, from George's hunting and fishing upbringing, to his drift into the army, the horrors of battle and his subsequent formal protest, to a voluntary return to the front.

Dorothy L SAYERS (1893–1957)

The success of Dorothy Sayers' detective novels is largely due to the invention of the sophisticated aristocratic amateur sleuth, Lord Peter Wimsey, who solves mysteries and murders with charm and clever quotation, aided by his faithful servant, Bunter, and the basic Parker, from Scotland Yard. Among the most popular stories are *Murder Must Advertise* (1933), *The Nine Tailors* (1934) and *Busman's Honeymoon* (1937).

Paul SCOTT (1920–78)

The Jewel in the Crown 1966
The first volume of the Raj Quartet, Scott's best achievement, which deals with the momentous events of the last years of British rule in India. *The Jewel in the Crown* recalls, perhaps too closely, Forster's *A Passage to India* in its use of an assault on an earnest young English woman to bring to a climax the conflicting racial and social undercurrents, but in narrative technique and unprejudiced characterization, the work is a fine achievement in its own right.

The Day of the Scorpion 1968
The second of the quartet, extending the scope of the series to cover all aspects of this period of history, here showing the disruptive effects of war on an individual family and on the whole balance of Anglo-Indian life. The two later novels in the quartet are *The Towers of Silence* and *A Division of the Spoils*.

Staying On 1977
A touching portrayal of a retired ex-army couple staying on in independent India. Suffering from conditioned prejudice and conditioned British stiffness and stroppiness, their eccentric behaviour is viewed humorously and with affection.

Walter SCOTT (1771–1832)

Guy Mannering 1815
The Antiquary 1816
These novels followed the huge success of Scott's first novel *Waverley*, but unlike their predecessor they portray contemporary, rather than historical life. They

demonstrate Scott's power and massive influence as a writer of fiction and his weakness as a novelist, which has lead to a decline in his readership in the twentieth century. On one hand there are the vivid characterizations of villains, gypsies, smugglers, vagrants and country gentlemen set in the living tradition of Scots history and culture, on the other; there are the contrived plots, which are often carelessly worked out.

Old Mortality 1816
A return to the historical novel, here going back to 1679 and the rising of the Scottish Covenanters. Scott pictures the absurdities to which the Convenanters carried their religious fervour.

The Heart of Midlothian 1818
A domestic tragedy of Effie Deans, a girl imprisoned for child murder, whose sister Jeannie must face her conflicting inner emotions of love for her sister and honesty to herself and to God. Often seen as Scott's best work for the characterization of Jeannie Deans, the sympathetic treatment of everyday tragedy and the narrative account of the storming of the Tolbooth.

Rob Roy 1818
Business and personal worlds are contrasted in this novel of brilliant characters and annoying dialect. Rob Roy is the romantic adventurer rebelling against the laws of the greedy world.

Ivanhoe 1820
A historical romance – the first of Scott's to be set in England. Placed in the time of Richard I, the story deals with the supposed hostility between Norman and Saxon, and includes a huge cast of characters, including Robin Hood and Friar Tuck. Kenilworth is another still popular historical novel about the murder of Amy Robsart and the life of the Elizabethan Court.

The Fortunes of Nigel 1822
Contains a celebrated portait of James I, demonstrating Scott's ability to fuse personal interest and historical reconstruction.

Redgauntlet 1824
Portraying Prince Charles Edward (Bonnie Prince Charles) and his grotesquely unsuccessful attempt to regain his fortunes in England, this novel contains some of Scott's finest writing, particularly in the episode 'Wandering Willie's Tale'.

Short Stories
'The Two Drovers' and 'The Highland Widow' are tragic stories which appeared in the first Chronicle of Connegate (1827) and are recognized as pioneering classics of the short story form.

Mary Wollstonecraft SHELLEY (1797–1851)

Frankenstein, or the Modern Prometheus 1818
The original horror story. A monster created from inanimate matter becomes uncontrollable and wreaks revenge on the scientist responsible for its lonely and miserable existence.

Neville SHUTE (1899–1960)

No Highway 1948
As an aeronautical engineer who settled in Australia, Shute wrote his many novels from an exceptionally non-literary standpoint. He achieved popular success with works like *A Town Like Alice* (about the Second World War in the Pacific) and *On The Beach* (concerning the end of the world by nuclear fall out). *No Highway* remains a rare, fictional portrait of an engineer/scientist in the world of technology.

Sir Philip SIDNEY (1554–86)

Arcadia 1590
A prose romance written for and revised by Sidney's sister, the Countess of Pembroke. It is a long and extravagant pastoral fiction, deliberately picturesque and interspersed with verse. Of little interest to the twentieth century reader, but important in the history of literature for being an early example of a prose fiction approaching the recognized form of the novel.

Alan SILLITOE (1928–)

Saturday Night and Sunday Morning 1958
Arthur Seaton is one of the few genuine working class heroes in English fiction. The Nottingham factory worker who spends his leisure time getting drunk and chasing girls seeks to establish his identity in the face of the financial necessity of a life of boredom and subservience.

The Loneliness of the Long-Distance Runner 1959
A long short story about a Borstal boy, whose personal integrity demands that he lose a race he is expected to win. In the course of the action it is the governor of the prison who is shown to have his own corrupt interests at heart.

Tobias SMOLLETT (1721–71)

The Adventures of Roderick Random 1748
A rambling, episodic novel of rascaldom and vitality in which Roderick studies medicine, goes to sea (several times), falls among thieves, becomes a footman, fails to marry Miss Melinda Goosetrap but gains a father, wealth and a suitable wife.

The Expedition of Humphrey Clinker 1771
The last novel, with a more coherent plot than previous attempts, using the epistolary technique to tell another tale of episodic adventures about a family travelling around Britain. Like all his novels, it takes time to relate Smollett's views on a wide variety of current issues and personal prejudices.

C P SNOW (1905–)

Strangers and Brothers 1940–70
A series of eleven novels that chronicle life in England from the beginning of the First World War until 1968, all narrated by Lewis Elliot, who rises from the provincial, lower middle class to the 'corridors of power'. Elliot struggles with personal relationship and increasingly with the issues created by the applications of science and politics in modern society. For some, the work of a mid-twentieth century Trollope and, for others, a flat mixture of autobiography and power-snobbery. Of the sequence, *The Masters* is best known and is a good, suspenseful read.

E O SOMERVILLE (1858–1949) and Martin ROSS (1862–1915)

Some Experiences of an Irish R.M. 1890
A partnership between two female cousins produced these humorous tales of upper class rural Irish life, circulating around the R.M. (Resident Magistrate), Major Sinclair Yeates and his formidable wife. Within a comic format, a real world of horsebreeding/riding/stealing, hard drinking and rural poverty is vividly recorded. Follow-ups were *Further Experiences of an Irish R.M.* and *In Mr Knox's Country*.

MURIEL SPARK (1918–)

The Ballad of Peckham Rye 1960
The devil visits a South London factory, and both spoils and enhances the lives of the inmates.

The Prime of Miss Jean Brodie 1962
Jean Brodie has been stamped on popular consciousness by the play and screen versions of this novel. The original novel is both less substantial and more subtle in its treatment of the corruption or stimulation of adolescent intellect and sexuality by a charismatic school mistress.

The Girls of Slender Means 1963
Perhaps the best of her works, this funny, poignant, short novel gives a detailed picture of London life in 1945, the period between war and peace. An ignored, unexploded bomb ticks away in the garden of the May of Teck Club, as the young girls and their lovers pursue life in their individual ways.

LAURENCE STERNE (1713–68)

The Life and Opinions of Tristram Shandy 1759–67
A nine volume narrative of deliberate digression, brilliant parody, and seaside-postcard double entendre is interrupted by dashes, asterisks, blank chapters, and a black page. But *Tristram Shandy* is also a work of enduring humour and eccentric characterizations: Uncle Toby, Widow Wadman, Corporal Trim, Dr. Slop etc. It confused the newly-formed expectations of novel-readers and offended the moral sensibilities of Dr Johnson, but from the opening page, where the narrator is present at his own conception, the book still has the power to amuse and provoke.

A Sentimental Journey 1768
Parson Yorick narrates his journey through France; as the title states, it is often a 'sentimental' book, written as Sterne said 'to teach us to love the world and our fellow creatures'. Sympathetic observation, ironic insights and down-to-earth humour.

R L STEVENSON (1850–94)

The Strange Case of Dr Jekyll and Mr Hyde 1886
A short book, which has entered the popular imagination. The dual personality discovered by Dr Jekyll through dalliance with drugs had huge implications for society at the turn of the century.

The Wrong Box 1889
The Ebb-Tide 1894
Two novellas written with his son-in-law, Lloyd Osbourne. The first is full of black humour and the second a discomforting account of colonialism in the South Seas. Stevenson is a more 'modern' writer than is suggested by his popular reputation as the author of historical romances, which are listed in the Children's Fiction section.

Weir of Hermiston 1896
A work left unfinished at Stevenson's death, but which promised to be greater than any earlier achievement. There is little more than a scene set (in Stevenson's native Scotland) and characters outlined, but it is written with a maturity and restraint absent from previous writing.

Bram STOKER (1847–1912)

Dracula 1897
The vampire story set in the mountains of Transylvania and told in the form of dramatic diary entries. Van Helsing is the professor whose science is called upon to defend the necks of two beautiful women.

David STOREY (1933–)

This Sporting Life 1960
The rough, corrupt world of Rugby League football is an expression of the futile violence of twentieth century society, presented directly through the warrior-like mind of the hero.

Radcliffe 1963
An intense story of passion between two men, springing obliquely from the isolation of the hero who searches for the soul of his inflexible lover. Unable to compromise, the consequences for them must be tragic.

Saville 1976
The longest of Storey's novels is autobiographical in its painstaking depiction of the hero Colin's life in a Yorkshire mining village and his efforts to break away from its comfortable bonds.

R S SURTEES (1805–64)

Jorrocks' Jaunts and Jollities 1838
First published in *The New Sporting Magazine*, hunting and broad humour predominates in these stories of Jorrocks, the sporting grocer. A later novel, *Mr Sponge's Sporting Tour* introduces two more vivid characters, Mr Sponge and Mr Facey Romford.

Jonathan SWIFT (1667–1745)

Gulliver's Travels 1726
The enduring travels of gullible Gulliver from 'little' Lilliput to the land of the Houyhnhnms and Yahoos constitute a fantasy adventure story for children (after some necessary abridgement) and a savage political satire for adults. Should also be enjoyed for the prose style of the master of irony.

William Makepeace THACKERAY (1811–63)

Vanity Fair 1847–8
As Thackery's masterpiece this novel has outlasted the great majority of his work – and yet it is probably less read than many later, lesser novels by 19th century authors. In spirit, style and setting – the Napoleonic wars – it belongs to the Regency rather than Victorian age, although the realism of its plotting and narrative bring it closer to our own times. The story revolves around the contrasting personalities and fates of the 'good' Amelia Sedley and the 'bad' Becky Sharp. The Waterloo scenes are among the best narrative passages in an English novel. Of her type, Becky has never been bettered, and the author's famed irony still amuses and stings.

The History of Henry Esmond 1852
A historical drama set in Queen Anne's time, told in appropriate eighteenth century style, with portraits of literary personages including Swift, Addison and Steele. The hero is an unassuming chap who tells his own life-story which is influenced by the false supposition that he is illegitimate.

The History of Pendennis 1848–50
The empirical education of a young man is the central theme of this, one of the best of the lesser novels. The social satire is along the same lines as in *Vanity Fair*.

The Rose and the Ring 1855
A delightful fairy-tale produced for his eager readers at Christmas time.

Dylan THOMAS (1914–53)

A Portrait of the Artist as a Young Dog 1940
A collection of autobiographical stories of Thomas's childhood and early adulthood, told in his characteristically rich and sub-Joycean prose.

J R R TOLKIEN (1892–1973)

The Lord of the Rings 1954–5
A trilogy of novels produced as an epic sequel to the earlier fairy tale *The Hobbit*, expanding enormously the cast of fabulous characters and fantastical setting. *The Lord of the Rings* and its internal mythology became a cult for the hippy generation of the 1960s, which may or may not be proof that Tolkien's fantasy is, as he intended, more appropriate to adults than to children.

Robert TRESSELL (1870–1922)

The Ragged-Trousered Philanthropists 1914
A novel more likely to convert its readers to socialism than the characters in the story who are not disposed to accept the socialist doctrines proposed by their fellow workman, Owen. An important record of the poverty-stricken conditions and complacent attitudes of the working class in Edwardian England.

William TREVOR (1928–)

The Old Boys 1964
A class reunion is the device for bringing together Trevor's elderly male characters in the first of his novels to be recognized. It shows skilful characterization and contains cryptic, Beckett-like dialogue.

The Boarding House 1965
Similar vein to *The Old Boys*, this novel concentrates on an odd collection of elderly eccentrics in a boarding house. The dry humour and irony expose the fatuity of his unenlightened characters' lives.

Short Stories
Trevor is one of the best contemporary writers of short stories. Disappointment, ageing and the problems of his native Ireland are recurring themes in collections such as *Angel at the Ritz* and *Beyond the Pale*.

Anthony TROLLOPE (1815–82)

The Warden 1855
Visiting Salisbury on Post Office business, Trollope wandered into the Cathedral Close: Barsetshire was born. Politics – in the sense of people's everlasting attempts to manipulate others in the pursuit of power – is the mainspring of most of Trollope's novels. In Barsetshire the setting is provincial and ecclesiastical. *The Warden* has more warmth and economy of effect than many of its successors and a cheering particle of goodness in Rev. Septimas Harding.

Barchester Towers 1857
Perhaps the most generally popular of the novels for the comic machinations of Mrs Proudie and Reverend Slope, respectively the Bishop's wife and chaplain. The character of the ambitious Archdeacon Grantly has much realism.

The Last Chronicle of Barset 1867
Trollope thought this conclusion of the sequence to be his best and, as a portrait of a failure, the Rev. Josiah Crawley (who is accused of embezzlement), has depth beyond the author's normal range. The Barsetshire sequence is: *The Warden, Barchester Towers, Dr. Thorne, Framley Parsonage, The Small House at Allington, The Last Chronicle of Barset*.

Can You Forgive Her? 1864
The first in the Palliser sequence of novels which are the result of an unusual marriage of the imagination of a near-great novelist and the real world experience of a high ranking civil servant. Plantagenet Palliser and his wife, Lady Glencora, just avoid personal and professional catastrophe and their marriage and relationship are the continuing thread in the rest of the sequence.

Phineas Finn 1869
Phineas gets a seat in Parliament and is torn between the needs of love, friendship, money and political influence. The women are given strong personalities with more independence of thought and action than is usual in the fiction of the time. Kennedy, the manic Scottish millionaire, is a powerful study of obsession.

The Eustace Diamonds 1873
In the third Palliser novel, the greedy and unscrupulous Lady Eustace is portrayed with sustained skill as she devises numerous ways of keeping her ill-gotten diamonds. The Palliser sequence is: *Can You Forgive Her?, Phineas Finn, The Eustace Diamonds, Phineas Redux, The Prime Minister, The Duke's Children*.

He Knew He Was Right 1869
Remarkable for its portrayal of the mental breakdown of the leading character.

The Way We Live Now 1875
If Trollope had written only this novel – and not 46 others – its merits might be better appreciated. It presents the power and money world of finance, society, journalism and politics with precision and prescience. The story revolves around Melmotte, a crooked financier who achieves social and political prominence in a society that almost wants to be deluded and defrauded, and Lady Carbury, who promotes her family by writing bad books as deliberately as Melmotte issues dud stock.

John WAIN (1925–)

Hurry on Down 1954
Charles Lumley, like John Braine's Joe Lampton and Amis's Jim Dixon, is a protesting young man of the Fifties. Attempting to escape from the bonds of society he takes a series of socially unacceptable jobs until he finds a niche of neutrality.

Edgar WALLACE (1875–1932)

The Four Just Men 1905
The first of a phenomenal outpouring of popular books, this is a mystery story of great dexterity. Edgar Wallace became the best, well-known thriller writer of the early twentieth century, with titles including *Crimson Circle* and *Green Archer*. (Margaret Lane's *Edgar Wallace: The Biography of a Phenomenon* is a fascinating revelation of his strange life.)

Horace WALPOLE (1717–97)

The Castle of Otranto 1764
Valuable mainly for being the first of its 'gothic' kind, this is a romance of medieval extravagance with the supernatural manifesting itself in ghostly apparitions, walking portraits and lumps of metal falling out of the sky.

Hugh WALPOLE (1884–1941)

The Cathedral 1922
A contrived but readable story centering on the Archdeacon of Polchester, and recording his downfall, both public and private.

Rogue Herries 1930
The first of The Herries Chronicle which also comprises *Judith Paris* and *The Fortress*. This is a popular historical series, covering one hundred years in the life of the Herries family.

Keith WATERHOUSE (1929–)

Billy Liar 1959
A comic novel about Billy Fisher and the tangle of lies he manufactures in order to resolve the conflict between his real, dull, provincial world and the imagined world of his compulsive daydreams.

Evelyn WAUGH (1903–66)

Decline and Fall 1928
Waugh's first novel which established him as a writer of comic genius with such memorable caricatures as Paul Pennyfather and Captain Grimes. A satirical poke at upper-class corruption and institutionalized schooling.

Vile Bodies 1930
A second novel about the bright young things of the 1920s and their parties, full of vile bodies. Adam Fenwick-Symes needs money to marry Nina and in order to become part of the 'set'.

A Handful of Dust 1934
With a title taken from T S Eliot's *The Waste Land* ('I will show you fear in a handful of dust'), this novel anticipates the more serious tone of Waugh's later work. Death and the deserting of his wife combine to trigger the collapse of Tony Last's world, and he sets off on a fantastic voyage into the jungle.

Scoop 1938
By mistake, William Boot, writer of nature notes on the *Daily Beast* is sent to cover a Middle Eastern war. Funniest book about journalism – at least until Michael Frayn's *Towards the End of the Morning*.

Brideshead Revisited 1945
Waugh's romantic story of nostalgia for aristocratic culture, although the central reality is the Roman Catholic version of God, whom all the characters are enticed or driven to recognize. The snobbery no longer seems to trouble readers and the certainty has a great appeal.

Sword of Honour a trilogy – Men at Arms 1952, *Officers and Gentlemen* 1955, *Unconditional Surrender* 1961.
An unplanned trilogy of novels mixing the author's Second World War experience with his social and religious views. Near middle-aged, aristocratic, Catholic Guy Crouchback embraces the war as an escape from his own defeats only to be repelled in due course by the ethics of the 'people's war' and the farcical horror of battle. The downbeat character of Crouchback is offset by the vigorous and pointed comedy of Apthorpe, Brigadier Richie Hook, the awful 'new man', Trimmer, and the simple, religious conviction of Guy's old father. Possibly the best English novel to come out of the Second World War.

The Ordeal of Gilbert Pinfold 1957
A strikingly frank autobiographical account of a middle-aged writer who suffers a nervous breakdown which brings fantastic and humiliating hallucinations.

Mary WEBB (1881–1927)

Precious Bane 1924
Public praise from Prime Minister, Stanley Baldwin, led to the success of this rural novel. It is set in the author's home county of Shropshire which is brought to life by the use of local dialect, customs and superstitions.

Fay WELDON (1933–)

Down Among the Women 1971
Praxis 1978
Puffball 1980
Fay Weldon may be described as a 'feminist novelist' in that she explores women's relationships with each other and with the men and children in their lives. She writes sympathetically about women, but she is never sentimental and has a satirical sense of humour and an eye for realism.

H G WELLS (1866–1946)

The Time Machine 1895
The pioneering novel in the science fiction genre may lose its impact in comparison with the elaborate inventions of today, but the historical importance of *The Time Machine* cannot be denied. The Time Traveller is transported to a future in which human beings are divided into the beautiful, idle Eloi and their subterranean servants, the Morlocks.

The War of the Worlds 1898
Wells' scientific training gave him an almost uncanny ability to prophesy events and technological developments, so that although his fiction is fantastic invention it did have an air of plausibility at the time. See also *When the Sleeper Wakes* and the *The Invisible Man*.

Kipps 1905
One of Wells's social novels, in which the acquisition of wealth by an ingenuous draper's assistant leads to a humorous, though ultimately failed, attempt to become a 'gentleman'. The arbitrary distribution of money and its irrelevance to happiness are clearly-made points.

Tuno-Bungay 1909
The title refers to a bogus medicine sold at great profit by Uncle Ponderevo. A comic novel containing, like many of Wells's works, elements of autobiography and social satire.

Ann Veronica 1909
A novel, shocking for its time, about a student who rebels against her social and sexual experience as a woman and who, after involvement with the Fabians and the suffragettes, runs off to be the happy mistress of her biology tutor.

The History of Mr Polly 1910
A lively, humorous tale of a down-trodden shopkeeper who opts out of numbing drudgery by burning down his shop and becoming a handyman at a country pub.

Rebecca WEST (1892–1983)

The Fountain Overflows 1957
Possibly the best of Rebecca West's rather sprawling novels, containing strong autobiographical elements in its depiction of the Aubrey family and their dependence upon one another necessitated by the father's hopelessness with money. Earlier novels like *Return of the Soldier, Harriet Hume* and *The Thinking Reed* have been reprinted as the interest has increased in women writers of the recent past.

T H WHITE (1906–64)

The Once and Future King 1958 a tetralogy – *The Sword in the Stone* 1939, *The Witch in the Wood* 1940, *The Ill-made Knight* 1941, *The Candle in the Wind* 1958
There is room for doubt as to the success with which the later novels of this Arthurian sequence mix fable, entertainment and their serious message on the nature of man and war, but few would deny the romance and humanity of *The Sword in the Stone*. A children's classic, the magic and morality of Merlyn's education of the young Arthur in the timeless shires of England will repay adult reading. An epilogue to the four books was published posthumously, *The Book of Merlyn*.

Oscar WILDE (1854–1900)

The Picture of Dorian Gray 1891
The hidden portrait of beautiful Dorian is ravaged by time and evil-doings in the place of Dorian himself who retains his outer youth. A work which expounds the aesthetic theories of Wilde.

The Happy Prince and Other Stories 1888
A delightful set of fairy-tales, probably written initially for Wilde's two young sons.

Henry WILLIAMSON (1895–1977)

Tarka the Otter 1927
Williamson's strength lies in his short animal tales which do not raise the political and moral problems of his other fiction. *Tarka the Otter* and *Salar the Salmon* display the keen observation of a naturalist, and an unsentimental but touching method of approaching his delicate subjects.

A Patriot's Progress 1930
This tale concerns a lowly clerk at the Somme: a short, powerful indictment of war on the front line.

A Chronicle of Ancient Sunlight 1951–69
A few fervent admirers and some critics insist on the merits of this sequence of fifteen novels which take Philip Maddison through the author's own experience of the First World War. The hero's response to nature and animals add to Williamson's previous achievements in these areas, just as the passages justifying his fascist philosophy detract from his reputation as a writer and thinker.

Angus WILSON (1913–)

The Wrong Set 1949
Such Darling Dodos 1950
Two collections of dextrous, satirical, short stories which expose the apparent inability of the middle class to understand themselves.

Anglo-Saxon Attitudes 1956
A long, deliberately Dickensian satire containing a large social range of characters portrayed with psychological insight, but lacking overall intensity and cohesion.

The Old Men at the Zoo 1961
Regents Park Zoo, in a near future which will soon be at war, is the setting for a satirical political fable. The relationship between human beings and nature is explored through the spiritual journey of discovery undergone by bureaucratic zoologist, Simon Carter and a switch in style from realism into horrific fantasy. A fine novel.

Late Call 1964
A subtle and humorous novel that analyses the effects of class and age on human beings – and the spiritual inadequacies of social engineering. Retired hotel manageress, Sylvia Calvert, attempts to adapt to living with her son's family in a 'classless' New Town.

P G WODEHOUSE (1881–1975)

My Man Jeeves 1919
The first of a whole series of famous comic stories and novels continuing right up to *Much Obliged, Jeeves* in 1971. His artificial, but completely articulated, world is that of the upper classes where people speak in dated slang and have nothing more to do than to go to the Drones Club and get into awful (but harmless) fixes. The characters – Bertie Wooster, Jeeves the butler, Psmith, Lord Emsworth (and his pig) and Aunt Agatha – have become some of the best known and well-loved figures in English fiction. See in particular *Right Ho, Jeeves, Carry on Jeeves, Aunts aren't Gentlemen, Leave it to Psmith* and *The World of Psmith*.

Virginia WOOLF (1882–1941)

Mrs Dalloway 1922
In her third book, Virginia Woolf departed from the realist conventions to produce this pioneering, 'stream-of-consciousness' novel. This is a portrait of a society hostess and her various potential guests drawn from their feelings and memories on the London day she is to give a party. A short, accessible work.

To the Lighthouse 1927
Probably the most popular of her novels, this is the nearest she comes to combining life and art in a story. The wonderfully characterized Ramsay family and their guests gather to spend the summer on a Hebridean island in the shadow of the lighthouse. Each consciousness tells a different story, and for each the impact of war is different. A great feminine novel in its treatment of relationships and bereavements.

Orlando 1928
A fanciful biography of Orlando who starts off as a young boy in the Elizabethan age and then lives through four centuries, having changed sex in the time of Charles II.

The Waves 1931
The climax of her endeavour to imagine the workings of the subconscious, this is Virginia Woolf's most poetically beautiful novel, narrated from inside the minds of its six characters through childhood to old age.

Between the Acts 1941
Virginia Woolf's last and most experimental novel. The characters are amateur theatricals who are to take part in a staging of *Orlando*.

John WYNDHAM (1903–69)

The Kraken Wakes 1953
The Day of the Triffids made Wyndham's reputation as a science fiction writer (see *Children's Literature*). Subsequent novels including *The Kraken Wakes, The Chrysalids* and *The Midwich Cuckoos* also pursue the potential threat to human life and order from the unfathomed forces of nature.

Charlotte YONGE (1823–1901)

The Heir of Redclyffe 1853
The only one of her 150 books – mostly historical romances – still read today. The 'Oxford Movement' Anglo-Catholicism of the nineteenth century greatly influenced the production of these novels, which embody moral and religious ideals. The tragic young heir sacrifices himself for the sake of a disreputable uncle.

SOME AMERICAN FICTION

Sherwood ANDERSON (1876–1941)

Winesburg, Ohio 1919
When Anderson walked out of his middle-America paint business in 1912 he created
a formative legend and symbol of the struggle for the soul of America: art and nature
versus machinery and materialism. The short stories and sketches in *Winesburg*
reflect the struggle through the representation of ordinary small town life. The oral
narrative style is a mixture of native American and a conscious development of
Gertrude Stein's work.

Djuna BARNES (1892–1982)

Nightwood 1936
Famously praised by T S Eliot for its 'horror and doom', this surreal story of a group
of sexually obsessed people is more influential as an act of style than as a work of
readable fiction.

John BARTH (1930–)

Giles Goat-Boy 1967
Both this novel about the education of a goat-boy prophet on the computerized
campus of the modern university and the earlier history of 18th century Maryland,
The Sot Weed Factor, are very long and very clever books. Opinion is divided – often
across the gap of the Atlantic – between those who find the brilliant linguistics,
literary parodies and philosophical debate as just cleverness and those who see the
books as a detailed critique of the modern world.

Saul BELLOW (1915–)

Henderson the Rain King 1959
Millionaire Henderson has a revelation in Africa that fulfilment can come only
through love of man and a oneness with nature. Bellow's optimism shines through his
unconventionally told stories and gives hope for man's living salvation.

Herzog 1964
Moses Herzog is a Jewish intellectual, a victim in modern America, who refuses to
accept the fate that seems ordained. By the end of this comic novel, the disastrous,
compulsive letter-writer achieves some kind of salvation.

Humboldt's Gift 1976
Citrine – like his creator – is a successful Chicago-born writer. He is harassed by his
ex-wife, mistress, gangster chum and the gangster's wife. He is haunted and enriched
by his dead mentor, the poet Humboldt Fleischer. In Bellow's very real, yet absurd,
world the tragedy and the comedy are united with wit and sympathy. For Bellow's
short stories see *Mosby's Memoirs* and *He With His Foot in His Mouth*.

Erskine CALDWELL (1903–)

Tobacco Road 1932
Caldwell's novels record social history in the Southern region of America with directness and grim humour. They have made him one of the all-time, world-wide bestsellers. This well-known work celebrates the staying-power of the locals in the face of redundancy.

God's Little Acre 1933
Originally famed for its supposed violence and obscenity, this is a novel about sterility, with clear and clever portraits of Georgian characters and the conflicts between them. See also the short stories in *Men and Women* and *We are the Living*.

Truman CAPOTE (1924–84)

Other Voices, Other Rooms 1948
An early fantasy novel about the monstrous adventures which befall young Joel Knox on the loss of his boyhood innocence, described in original, poetic language.

Breakfast at Tiffany's: A Short Novel and Three Stories 1958
The exploits of Holly Golightly, who, as her name suggests, is flighty, but fervently honest and full of spirit. Set mainly in New York we are given a sociological picture of American life at the time.

In Cold Blood: A True Account of a Multiple Murder and its Consequences 1966
This grim, powerful book heralds the birth of the 'non-fiction novel'. Every detail is carefully based on the facts of the brutal murder of a Kansas family and yet the final account reads like fiction. It raises questions about the workings of justice, the place of the human being in American society, and the relationship of the author to the protagonists in a piece of 'faction'.

Raymond CHANDLER (1888–1959)

The Big Sleep 1939
The first Philip Marlowe story. There is a tendency to overclaim Chandler's literary status, but there is imaginative life in the seedy Californian world of this modern knight in tarnished armour. Of later books, *The Long Goodbye* is as strong on atmosphere and character as it is hazy on plot.

Walter CLARK (1909–71)

The Ox-Bow Incident 1940
One of the few authors of 'Westerns' to make it to literary respectability. A lynching provides a classic Western study of mob violence and universal types.

James Fenimore COOPER (1789–1851)

The Last of the Mohicans 1826
Cooper's best known novel is in fact the second of the 'Leatherstocking Tales' about Natty Bumppo. The novels trace the development of Natty from childhood to youth to maturity as he discovers the beauty and harshness of both man and nature. All the stories are concerned with the 'frontier' – both of the physical landscape and of the new American soul. The other titles are (in order of Natty's age) *The Deerslayer, The Pathfinder, The Pioneers* and *The Prairie*.

Stephen CRANE (1871–1900)

The Red Badge of Courage 1895
Henry Fleming, a young immature soldier in the American Civil War dreams of glory but becomes aware of his fear of battle. As we follow his struggles, the dehumanizing effect of war strikes home through the use of imagery and a straightforward narrative.

Theodore DREISER (1871–1945)

Sister Carrie 1900
Dreiser, in awkward but direct prose, chronicles the rise to stardom of Caroline Meeber, an eighteen year old whose casual sexual adventures shocked contemporary readers. Seedy life in New York and Chicago is skilfully portrayed.

An American Tragedy 1925
Based on an actual murder case, it is the story of a poor, provincial boy trying to climb out of his class. Dreiser's unsentimental representation of facts makes for powerful reading-matter; still clumsy in style but ultimately one of the important works of American fiction.

Ralph ELLISON (1914–)

Invisible Man 1952
Perhaps the first black American novel to reach a national and then international readership. The unnamed hero moves from an Uncle Tom world in his native South to Harlem and black activitism, but people around him 'see only my surroundings, themselves or figments of their imagination indeed everybody and anything except me'.

William FAULKNER (1897–1962)

Sartoris 1929
The first of the series of novels about Mississippi, for which Faulkner created the mystical and morally degenerate Yoknapatawpha County with its old families in decline (the Compson and Sartoris families), white trash (the Snopes) and descendants of black slaves. Young Bayard returning from the war sees violence as something positive in a hollow life, but such an attitude conflicts with the stability of his native South.

The Sound and the Fury 1929
One of the best known of Faulkner's novels, this is a complex and difficult work told in four parts through the interior monologues of three different characters, the first being an idiot, Benjy. Each tells the story of the Compson family and its degeneration and disintegration.

As I Lay Dying 1930
A short novel which combines grotesque humour and horror in a technically complex but brilliant exposition of the stream of consciousness. The Bundrens are a poor white family who set off on a pilgrimage to fulfil the only wish of their mother they have ever heeded – to be buried in Jefferson.

Light in August 1932
A complicated plot telling two stories simultaneously – of racial conflict and of a girl searching for the father of her unborn child.

Absalom, Absalom! 1936
Faulkner's masterpiece, but also his most difficult work, with Quentin Compson (from *The Sound and the Fury*) and his room-mate reviewing the fragmentary information available on the doomed life of Thomas Sutpen, whose failure to found an enduring plantation and dynasty is symbolic of the fate of the South.

Go Down Moses and Other Stories 1942
This volume contains the most celebrated of the short stories, 'The Bear', exposing man's needs to possess and violate both other human beings and the land. Also significant in this collection is 'The Fire and the Hearth', and altogether they document the history of the South through the fortunes of the McCaslin family.

Novels not concerned with Yoknapatawpha include *Pylon* and *A Fable*, a long allegorical novel set in the 1917 French army mutinies.

F Scott FITZGERALD (1896–1940)

This Side of Paradise 1920
Semi-autobiographical novel about a young man's first attempt to fit into American society. It now seems a slight book but it made Fitzgerald famous in the roaring twenties.

The Great Gatsby 1925
If not *the* great American novel, the novel which achieves greatness with most economy. The figure of Jay Gatsby – arch-romantic, criminal, idealist and corrupted man – is an ironic comment on American morality and sentiment. And yet there is sympathy for his loneliness and loss of love. Other aspects of the already fading American dream are also presented in a style which fuses poetry, irony and comedy.

Tender is the Night 1934
The marriage between the schizophrenic Nicole and a young psychiatrist, Dick Diver, is symbolic of the moral and spiritual disease underlying the decadence of post-First World War Europe. Set in the Riviera and Paris, the novel documents the unattractive milieu of wealth and indolence; critics have argued that the novel's structural problems mar a moving record of a relationship.

The Last Tycoon 1941
A return to his best form, but unfinished at Fitzgerald's death. The central character is based on the wonderboy of Hollywood, Irving Thalberg. A genuine love affair is doomed in a false world.

Fitzgerald's short stories are mostly 'jazz-age' tales written for contemporary magazines and include fine pieces such as 'The Rich Boy', and 'Absolution', and the fairy story 'A Diamond as Big as the Ritz'.

Dashiell HAMMETT (1894–1961)

The Maltese Falcon 1930
Enter Sam Spade and 'hard-boiled' crime writing. Hammett used his real life experience in the Pinkerton agency to create the modern, street-wise detective who is as violent as his quarry.

Joel Chandler HARRIS (1848–1908)

The Essential Uncle Remus
Modern sensitivities have rendered Negro dialect stories suspect, but these delightful stories of Negro myth and folklore were collected in the nineteenth century by a journalist and re-phrased for the telling of Uncle Remus to a small boy. Who would want to lose Brer Rabbit and the briar patch?

John HAWKES (1925–)

Lunar Landscapes 1969
This collection of often blackly humorous and surrealistic short stories and novellas is recommended as an introduction to one of the few writers to continue the experimental novel of Djuna Barnes. The novels include *The Lime Twig* and *The Blood Oranges*.

Nathaniel HAWTHORNE (1804–64)

The Scarlet Letter 1850
A disturbing story of the narrowness of Puritanism in seventeenth century New England. The scarlet letter is a capital 'A' (for adultory) which young Hester Prynne is forced to wear.

Complete Short Stories
Included here is *Endicott and the Red Cross*, which was the germ for the *Scarlet Letter*. Most of the stories deal with Puritan life and the suppression of human feeling which inevitably results in guilt.

Joseph HELLER (1923–)

Catch 22 1961
The title is now part of our language, and the farcical treatment of the least funny of human activities has influenced many literary and dramatic works since its publication. It is a bitterly satirical story of the Second World War, revealing the lethal absurdities of army bureaucracy and the ghastly attitudes of power-crazed officers.

Good as Gold 1975
A later novel in the same satirical, surreal vein as *Catch 22* only this time the context is family life and Washington politics. The Jewish family scenes are hilarious and sad and the politics are believable – thanks to Watergate.

Ernest HEMINGWAY (1899–1961)

Short Stories
Hemingway started as a short story writer and perhaps his best work is in this form. *In Our Time* (1925) contains fifteen short stories, which display his characteristic sparse, unemotional style. They are largely concerned with the life of Nick Adams, in the Great Lakes regions of his boyhood, and later at war. *Men without Women* (1927) contains three of his finest stories: 'The Killers' and 'The Undefeated' return to Hemingway's preoccupation with death and danger as a kind of affirmation of existence, and 'Fifty Grand' is a cynical tale of a man betting on his own defeat.

The Sun Also Rises (published under the title *Fiesta* in British editions) 1926
From his experience of expatriate Parisian literary life came this tersely written story of desperate souls trying to fill their emptiness with bullfighting and drinking. It made Hemingway's reputation as a spokesman for the 'lost generation' of post-First World War liberation and disillusionment.

A Farewell to Arms 1929
A powerful and moving love-story between an English nurse and the American lieutenant she helps back to health during the First World War. A novel celebrated for its brilliant account of the retreat of the Italian Army, and for its conviction of the dignity of man in the face of death.

For Whom The Bell Tolls 1940
Set against the background of the Spanish Civil War, and hence an atmosphere of violence and tragedy, this is the longest and most ambitious of the novels. The set piece narratives are more memorable than the characters.

The Old Man and the Sea 1952
A novella which reaffirmed Hemingway's reputation after the production of some lesser works. This is a fable about an old fisherman's stoical fight against nature and human defeat as he struggles to bring home a great marlin.

William Dean HOWELLS (1837–1920)

The Rise of Silas Lapham 1885
Howells insisted that fiction should 'cease to lie about life' and that it should portray people as they were. Silas Lapham of the title is a self-made businessman who attempts to break into Boston's wealthy traditional society, but who risks his fortune and his family's happiness in so doing. Howell's writings earned him the title 'the dean of American letters.'

Washington IRVING (1783–1859)

Short Stories
Often called the father of American fiction, his best work is in the collection *The Sketch Book of Geoffrey Crayon*, 1820. In 'Rip Van Winkle' an indolent hen-pecked man falls asleep for twenty years. On returning to his native village he finds his wife dead and all changed, but, now cheerful and benign, he lives happily ever after with his daughter. 'The Legend of Sleepy Hollow' concerns the terrifying apparition which thwarts the marriage hopes of Ichabod Crane, a schoolteacher from the North.

Henry JAMES (1843–1916)

The Europeans 1878
The relationship between penniless cultured Europe and industrious, ingenuous America is depicted with beautiful economy of style and introduces one of James's major themes.

Daisy Miller 1879
The girl of the title is an innocent young American set loose in Europe to encounter the censure and prejudice of its inhabitants.

The Portrait of a Lady 1881
One of the great novels of the nineteenth century and probably the most satisfying of James's work for those who find James's later, baroque prose style too much and the stories too little. In a world bent on greed and corruption Isabel Archer's youth, energy and idealism are sapped by the collaboration of her wordly husband Gilbert Osmond and the sinister Madame Merle.

Washington Square 1881
A miniature Jamesian novel, this is a good first taste of the 'Master'.

The Bostonians 1886
As a book on feminism, it may disappoint if not infuriate modern readers, since the movement is mocked and the reactionary young man wins the heroine from the arms of another woman. But the novel mixes a Dickensian sense of character and place with a Conradian understanding of the many motives and obsessions which come together in any 'movement of ideas'.

The Spoils of Poynton 1897
The beautiful furniture and art objects of an English country house manipulate the emotions and inclinations of the people concerned with their possession.

What Maisie Knew 1897
Maisie as a child of six is subjected to the malevolence and corruption created by the divorce of her immoral and thoughtless parents. Written from the innocent viewpoint of Maisie, this is a remarkable technical achievement.

The Turn of the Screw and Other Stories 1898
James wrote many fine short stories. The most famous of ghost stories dominates this collection and is a subtly awesome construction. The others are 'The Pupil' and 'Third Person' which help to demonstrate James's careful observation and skilful delineation in an easily readable form. A long short story is the very enjoyable 'Aspern Papers'.

An Awkward Age 1899
Written largely in dialogue, the 'awkward age' is the transition from girlhood to adulthood for Nanda and her cousin Aggie, each of whom experience initiation in a different way and with different results. A novel full of nasty people.

The Wings of the Dove 1902
Perhaps the best balance between style and substance in the later novels is achieved in this story of passion, intrigue and tragic retribution. The innocently attractive but fatally-ill American millionairess, Milly Theale, comes to London to live before she dies. The brilliant and corrupt Kate Cory uses her to further her love affair with Merton Densher.

The Ambassadors 1903
The Ambassadors of the title are emissaries sent to Paris by the wealthy Mrs Newsome, who believes her son, Chad, is languishing in an affair. Lambert Strether – the rather pompous New Englander sent to retrieve him – is the first emissary but he becomes tangled up in the romantic plot. A subtle blend of the 'old' and 'new' world values, which James himself thought was 'quite the best "all round" of my productions'.

The Golden Bowl 1904
A story of betrayed relationships, exploited innocence and the struggle for money and comfortable surroundings is focused through the lives of four intertwined characters.

The elaborate prose style and the insistence on the superiority of European art and culture are not easy to take at this length. The punishment for the erring characters – to be sent back to America.

James JONES (1921–)

From Here to Eternity 1951
A large, raw novel about the brutality of army life in Hawaii on the eve of the Japanese attack on Pearl Harbour.

Jack KEROUAC (1922–69)

On the Road 1957
An episodic book which attempts to construct a new American mythology. It describes the author's journey across America, his jobs, friends and companions. Kerouac was a member of the Beat Generation of writers who wished to escape from the conventional forms of life and literature, often with the aid of drink and drugs.

Ken KESEY (1935–)

One Flew over the Cuckoo's Nest 1962
The narrator is 'Chief Bromden' a catatonic Red Indian. The novel is set in a mental hospital and concerns the dehumanization of the Indian's close friends and ultimate destruction of his ally, the violent McMurphy. The pressure on everyone is to conform, in spite of the apparent 'liberalism' of Big Nurse's regime.

Jerzy KOSINSKI (1933–)

Being There 1971
Chance, the mentally retarded gardener, who can only re-iterate television chat, is hailed as a sage and a candidate for the Vice Presidency of the USA. A subtle, satirical story from a Polish emigré author whose work is usually more complex.

Elmore LEONARD (1925–)

Probably the best current exponent of American hard-boiled crime fiction as created by Hammett and Chandler. His backgrounds are usually Detroit as in *The Switch* (1978), *City Primeval* and *The Bounty Hunter* (1953) or the blue-rinse and Cuban crime world of Florida, as in *Stick* (1983) and *La Brava* (1983).

Sinclair LEWIS (1885–1951)

Babbit 1922
Realtor Babbit has come to epitomize the life and success-oriented values of middle America – at least as they were for many years.

Jack LONDON (1876–1916)

The Call of the Wild 1903
This famous story of the dog that reverts to the wild is often published with its mirror image, *White Fang*, where a wild dog is tamed by kindness. London's short, tough life and socialist beliefs provide the material for many of his short stories.

Alison LURIE (1926–)

The War Between the Tates 1974
A sad-comic, campus novel which creates a strong sense of its Nixonian period and New England location.

Carson McCULLERS (1917–67)

The Heart is a Lonely Hunter 1940
An unusual, compassionate first novel. It describes the lot of a deaf mute who becomes a hero, despite his own inner solitude, emanating a kind of calmness needed by the frustrated individuals whose lives he touches.

The Ballad of the Sad Cafe 1951
The title piece of this book of stories is about a woman whose great physical and emotional strength is finally broken by the collaboration of two men once close to her.

Norman MAILER (1923–)

The Naked and the Dead 1948
One of the best novels to come out of the Second World War. At one level it is a naturalistic portrayal of the ordinary soldiers' war in the Pacific. At another, it is a commentary on society as much as on war through the power games played by the General, the Sergeant and their victim, the liberal-minded Lieutenant.

An American Dream 1965
A picture of corruption in American society through the breakdown of a marriage and the subsequent reckless and violent behaviour of Rojack, the husband who can finally live only on dreams.

Why Are We in Vietnam? 1967
A good question, unintentionally answered in this later novel by a Texan disc-jockey who recounts the story of a bear-hunt in his youth. This may be the best and – given the date it was written – most courageous of Mailer's amalgams of mood, journalism and autobiography which have formed most of his writing since *An American Dream*.

The Executioner's Song 1979
This is a prime example of 'faction'. A long novel about the case of the executed murderer Gary Gilmore. A horribly real picture of the modern West (Salt Lake City) emerges and Gilmore's own extensively quoted writings are disturbingly vivid.

Bernard MALAMUD (1914–)

The Fixer 1966
A novel based on fact, about a Jew in Tsarist Russia who is imprisoned for a murder he has not committed. The resultant persecution of all Jews in the country leads the hero to believe in 'no such thing as an unpolitical man, especially a Jew'. Also to be recommended are *The Assistant*, set in Jewish New York, *Dubious Lives*, about middle aged America, and *God's Grace*, about the end of the world. See also the collection of some of his short stories in *Stories* (1983).

Herman MELVILLE (1819–91)

Moby Dick 1851
More honoured by reference than by reading, a wealth of scientific knowledge and allegory convert this sea-adventure story about a whaling-shipful of strange characters into a massive classic of educational, philosophical, and sociological depth.

The Confidence-Man 1857
This 'Masquerade' aboard a Mississippi steam boat is a pessimistic satire which just fails at a high level of both philosophical debate and narrative form.

Billy Budd 1924
Left in manuscript at Melville's death, this fine short novel tells the story of the wrongful accusation and inevitable execution of a sailor at the time of the Spithead Mutiny.

Henry MILLER (1891–1980)

Tropic of Cancer 1934
Long famous as a 'dirty book', this autobiographical novel of bohemian life in Paris was later celebrated as a textbook for the irresponsible 'innocence' of the 1950s Beat Generation. Today, the repetitive sexual couplings may seem less like liberation for the hero than enslavement for the women.

Vladimir NABOKOV (1899–1977)

The Real Life of Sebastian Knight 1945
Sebastian is a successful novelist and brother to the narrator who in turn attempts to discover something about the 'real' character behind the fictional one he is creating. It can be seen as a novel about the problems of writing a novel.

Pnin 1957
A short, accessible novel made up of a series of tragi-comic incidents about Timofey Pnin, an eccentric emigré professor in an American college.

Lolita 1955

Humbert Humbert tells the story of his disastrous love-affair with a twelve year old girl. Satire and parodies of everything American add humour to the pathos. If its original notoriety drew more readers to a novelist who, through his immense gifts, too easily falls between the categories of nationality and literary type, then justice has been done.

Pale Fire 1962

A wonderful joke against modern literary scholarship – and Man's pretensions generally. The reader is presented with the text of a long poem which has been annotated by a dotty editor – a visiting professor in Zemblan at Wordsmith College – so as to wrench its meaning around to his own obsessions.

Ada 1969

An incestuous passion is harboured by Van Veen for his sister Ada. A difficult, inventive, sensual work involving various of the author's techniques built up through the years.

Frank NORRIS (1870–1902)

The Octopus 1901

'The Octopus' of the title is the railroad, pushing its way through California and attempting to squeeze the life out of anyone who opposes it. The ranchers of San Joaquin valley, typified by Magus Derrick, fight against the company bosses. A novel of great emotional force and one which attempts to be both 'realistic' and 'epic' at the same time.

Dorothy PARKER (1893–1967)

Here Lies 1939

These are Parker's collected stories, famous for their author's cynicism and pointed irony which cuts through any sentimentality or idealism.

Edgar Allan POE (1809–49)

Poe is *the* exponent of the 'tale of terror'. His *Tales of Mystery and Imagination* (1840–45) are full of insights into the darker recesses of the mind. 'The Fall of the House of Usher' presents a debilitated 'hero' facing a crumbling world while 'The Pit and the Pendulum' is a tale of suspense which keeps the readers guessing about the eventual fate of the main character. *The Narrative of Arthur Gordon Pym* (1838) is Poe's only attempt at longer fiction and concerns the tales of a returning mariner; many find the book confusing in tone but it is full of suspense and adventure.

Thomas PYNCHON (1937–)

V. 1963
A long and complex science fiction-cum-mystery story; erudite, parodying literary styles and containing allusions and philosophical investigations. Two characters crossover on their respective quests; one of them, Stencil, searching for the mysterious woman V., who is at various stages – Venus, Virgin and Void.

The Crying of Lot 49 1966
A similar, but shorter novel.

Philip ROTH (1933–)

Portnoy's Complaint 1969
Some may find Portnoy's sexual troubles and his archetypal Jewish mother too repulsive for enjoyment – but it does say something funny about something sad.

The Ghost Writer 1979
Nathan Zuckerman seeks critical praise for his writing while at the same time, he tries to escape from his very conventional middle-class home background. He meets the eccentric Lonoff who seems to be able to fulfil both needs, but Zuckerman has to discover for himself what being 'a writer' really means.

Damon RUNYON (1884–1946)

Guys and Dolls 1936
Here and in other later collections, are the stories of Harry the Horse, Nathan Detroit, Little Isadore, Nicely-Nicely Jones, Big Nig, Miss Hilda Slocum and such other citizens of New York as you would not wish to know in real life.

J D SALINGER (1919–)

The Catcher in the Rye 1951
Holden Caulfield is the celebrated adolescent hero who appealed so strongly to the disillusioned youth of the 1950s. Holden explores the New York world of 'phoneys'. He is asking for honesty and love – a remarkable, gentle protest at the grown-up life awaiting the child.

For Esme – With Love and Squalor and Other Stories 1953
Members of the Glass family who live in New York and comprise a Catholic woman, her Jewish husband and their seven children are the characters for most of these stories and those in the subsequent collections.

Franny and Zooey 1961
The two youngest members of the Glass family have a section devoted to each of them in this book which pursues the religious problems created by their brother Seymour and his suicide. Some kind of solution is hinted at in Salinger's fusion of Eastern and Western religion.

Issac Bashevis SINGER (1904–)

The Family Moskat 1950
Living in New York since the 1930s, Singer is a Polish born Yiddish writer. His works have been translated some time after their initial production, and now reach an appreciative non-Jewish public. His stories have a strong mystical element and describe the many conflicts in Jewish life and culture. *The Family Moskat* covers the dramatic years 1914–39 in the life of a Jewish family in Warsaw. See also *The Manor*, *The Estate* and *The Slave*. Short stories containing some of Singer's finest writing are in a number of volumes, including *Collected Stories* containing 47 tales.

John STEINBECK (1902–68)

Of Mice and Men 1937
A short novel concerned with the working-class and its constant, fruitless yearning for a home of its own. Two farmhands are the victims of poverty and their own brute strength in this moving tragedy.

The Grapes of Wrath 1940
The story of the Joad family driven West by the Oklahoma dust bowl of the 1930s and seeking work in a California only too willing to exploit them. The narrative is interspersed with essays on the problems of migrant labourers. A successful film added to the impact of this novel which may now seem to be close to sentimental oversimplication.

Cannery Row 1945
A return to the matter of his first successful novel, *Tortilla Flat*. An assorted mixture of characters live on Cannery Row in Monterey, California, in happy idleness and attempt to throw a party for their biologist friend, Doc.

East of Eden 1952
A long chronicle of two Californian families which parables the fall of man and the story of Cain and Abel. The ex-prostitute Cathy Ames and her son Caleb are doomed to set in motion a tragic sequence of events which can finally be dissipated by a particular interpretation of the Biblical story.

Paul THEROUX (1941–)

Picture Palace 1978
The 'autobiography' of Maude Pratt, photographer, who claims D H Lawrence and Marilyn Monroe amongst her subjects, as well as more mundane, but prize-winning subjects.

The Mosquito Coast 1982
The 'Father', Allie Fox, removes the whole of his family from the decadence of modern society and sails downstream into the heat of the jungle, where they all learn to cope with both the climate and Allie himself.

James THURBER (1894–1961)

The Beast in Me and Other Animals 1948
Thurber's distinctive elegant prose tells tales of humour and fantasy, illustrated by his own drawings. Essays and short stories are also in *Alarms and Diversion*, and *The Thurber Carnival* is a useful selection from his work over the years.

Mark TWAIN (Samuel Langhorne Clemens) (1835–1910)

The Adventures of Huckleberry Finn 1884
This is Mark Twain's best novel, the hero first appearing in the children's book *The Adventures of Tom Sawyer* (1876). The episodic adventures are narrated in South-Western dialect by Huck himself, a fourteen year-old who is more of an outlaw than his friend, Tom, who wants to escape the constraints of civilization. Hemingway saw this novel as the starting-point from which all later American fiction proceeded.

A Connecticut Yankee in King Arthur's Court 1889
The high spirits disguise the serious criticism intended of the romanticization of the Middle Ages. A Yankee finds himself transported back to the time of King Arthur, and his story exposes the limitations of the society, whilst Twain exposes the limitations of the Yankee himself.

John UPDIKE (1932–)

Rabbit, Run 1960
Harold 'Rabbit' Angstrom is introduced in this first novel in a series which continues with *Rabbit Redux* and *Rabbit is Rich* and chronicles domestic life in a small town in America. Rabbit is ruled by fear of death and compulsion for sex, and in his escape from the one and search for the other he is on a desperate quest for some kind of perfection.

Couples 1968
In the permissive age of the 1960s, the fashionable game of swapping sexual partners hits the little town of Tarbox and ten couples indulge in its ritualistic mysteries.

The Coup 1978
A brilliant – perhaps too brilliant – 'autobiography' of an American-educated African dictator. The tragi-comedy of modern African politics in some ways provides a more unrestrained opportunity for Updike's rich imagination and word power than the consumer society of middle America. Updike is also a prolific writer of short stories, as in such collections as *The Same Door*, *Pigeon Feathers*, *The Music School* and *Museums and Women*.

Gore VIDAL (1925–)

The City and the Pillar 1948
One of the first novels to deal frankly with homosexuality.

Myra Breckinridge 1968
A small landmark of wit and bad taste, dealing with a sex change operation and the main character's unconventional attitudes towards pleasure.

Burr 1973
A brilliant historical novel set among the founding fathers of the Republic, which is told from the point of view of one of America's anti-heroes, Aaron Burr. Jefferson and Washington appear in less than flattering portraits. Historical novels seem to give more scope to Vidal's strength of intellect and imagination than contemporary novels where the demands of plot produce rather cardboard characters, as in *Washington DC*.

1876 1976
A successor to *Burr*, it captures the Republic at its next high point – the centenary of Independence. President Grant is the main victim of Vidal's satire.

Kurt VONNEGUT Jr (1922–)

Player Piano 1952
The first of Vonnegut's popular but pessimistic novels, set in a near future when automation reduces the masses to a life of futility. They revolt, but in so doing destroy necessary machines along with the unnecessary.

Cat's Cradle 1963
A science-fiction novel wrought with dry irony in the suggestion that we should live by 'foma' – lies that allow people happiness. The religion Bokononism and the lethal crystal 'ice-nine' are two of Vonnegut's nihilistic inventions. *God Bless You, Mr Rosewater* is in a similar vein.

Slaughterhouse Five 1969
A powerful work inspired by Vonnegut's own experience on emerging from an underground slaughterhouse after the horrific bombing of Dresden in World War II. Bill Pilgrim comes to see the tragic absurdity of life, a feature of all Vonnegut's novels, but seldom realized by his characters.

Robert Penn WARREN (1905–)

All the King's Men 1946
Based on the political career of the populist southern leader Huey 'Kingfish' Long, its theme is the corruption of the 'abstract passion for power'.

Nathaniel WEST (1903–40)

The Day of the Locust 1939
This is as much about the disillusionment and misfits of the 'new' California as it is specifically about the Hollywood film world. This empty, lonely world is the opposite of glamourous. See also the earlier *Miss Lonelyhearts* about the sad world of the agony column, and the comic send-up of the Horatio Alger myth, *Cool Million*.

Thornton WILDER (1897–1975)

The Bridge of San Luis Bay 1927
When five disparate people die in the collapse of a bridge in Peru, a Franciscan monk strives to place the event as an act of Providence, researching each of their lives. The story brought fame to Wilder for its delicate irony and clear execution.

Owen WISTER (1860–1938)

The Virginian 1902
This proved to be the classic novel of the mythical West, with its stereotyped, handsome, brave and upright hero, who defeats a villain and marries the woman who loves him.

Thomas WOLFE (1900–38)

Look Homeward, Angel 1929
A vast, vivid novel based on his own family's life in North Carolina which was carved into shape by the famous New York editor, Maxwell Perkins. An unmanageable mixture of good and bad lyric prose, romantic autobiography and a romanticized embrace of American experience. The autobiographical story continues in *Of Time and the River* (1935).

WORLD LITERATURE IN ENGLISH

It was entirely predictable that such countries as Australia, New Zealand, South Africa and Canada, where English is in large part the home language, and the population in large part of European descent, would eventually produce great literature in English. In other cases, there could be no such certainty. India, the West Indies, and the African countries have their own languages and story-telling traditions through which to express themselves. Their experience of colonial government has been entirely different, and in many ways humiliating. In India, for example, resistance to the English language is associated with a positive rejection of imperialist values.

However by its usage, English is the most international and multicultural of languages. It offers not just overseas markets and an international reputation for non-English writers, but for some it is the only common language through which they can communicate with the majority of their own people. As a result, English literature has become the beneficiary of new talents from old and very different cultures. The only real connection between the works in this section is that they are written in English by authors whose imaginative world is neither in the British Isles nor America.

The selection of works for inclusion in this section is further complicated by the phenomenon of the expatriate writer. Some highly distinguished non-English writers, such as Doris Lessing and V S Naipaul, settled in England at an early stage of their careers and their work reflects the experience of living in England. The works of such authors are included in the English fiction section. On the other hand, authors who work in England or America but write in and about their home culture are included here. It is a distinction without firm frontiers. Those who are interested in exploring specifically black literature writers in Britain will be helped by Prahbu Guptara's *Black British Literature*.

Literature in English was first enhanced by the contribution of writers from the 'Old Commonwealth'. From this source, Patrick White's work is the towering achievement. His first major novel, *The Aunt's Story*, appeared in 1948. Since then he has produced a body of literature equal to that of any other author working in fiction. In 1973 he was awarded the Nobel Prize for literature.

Perhaps second only to White is the Nigerian, Chinua Achebe, whose *Things Fall Apart* astounded the literary world on its first appearance, not only for the vividly imagined picture of tribal life before the white man came but for the accomplishment of the writing. Throughout the next decade Achebe produced several other excellent works – the above mentioned novel is the first of a trilogy – which describe the development of life in his country from its tribal days through to the conflicts and dreams of independence, and the inevitable disillusionment that followed. These three divisions of historical development have been crucial subject matter for the emergent African writer. Kenya's Wa Thiong'o Ngugi has covered them in his own trilogy. *A Grain of Wheat*, the last of these, is one of the finest novels to come out of Africa. Armah's *The Beautiful Ones Are Not Yet Born* is an excellent post-revolution novel from Ghana. There are also several early works that centre on childhood reminiscence. George Lamming's *In The Castle of my Skin* is recognized by many as the first truly West Indian novel. It is an account of his boyhood in Barbados.

Early Australian, Canadian and South African literature deals with early colonial days from a different perspective. Olive Schreiner's *Diary of an African Farm* is a famous example, as is Henry Handel Richardson's *The Fortunes of Richard Mahoney*, which uses Australian history as a framework for the narrative development of the hero's rise and fall. Finally, Amos Tutuola's *The Palm Wine Drinkard*, has been greeted both as the ramblings of a madman and as a work of genius. What Tutuola offers us in this and his later works are the great myths, fables and folklore of his native land, Nigeria, taken from the oral tradition and written down in English.

These same images, symbols and their accompanying rituals strongly influenced the famous Nigerian dramatist Wole Soyinka. Much of his work employs them as a means of exploring the morals of current political life and the path to personal regeneration, invariably the prominent themes in his plays. Soyinka is without doubt the most significant playwright to come out of Africa. J P Clark and Athol Fugard are other important contributors to the art. Over the years Fugard has, like Soyinka, produced a body of work of considerable value. However, unlike Soyinka, Fugard has no past tradition to fall back on other than the European. His early works borrow heavily on Beckett and Pinter. In his *Three Port Elizabeth Plays* he reveals the implausibility, inhumanity and history of the apartheid system. Of the three plays in *Statements, Sizwe Bansi is Dead* is the most successful and popular. Using workshop methods Fugard and the two African actors, John Kani and Winston Ntshona, devised this moving, funny and vivid drama about life for the urban African under apartheid.

The world of poetry has been steadfastly served by writers from the 'Old Commonwealth' without any particular poet creating a sustained international reputation. In Canada, Margaret Atwood's *The Circle Game* indicated the possibility that she would inherit E J Pratt's mantle as Canada's most distinguished poet. In Australia the works of Brennan, Fitzgerald and Stow have been important. In the West Indies Edward Braithwaite and Derek Walcott have achieved great popularity with their poems, and in Africa, Kofi Awoonor and Soyinka stand out.

The countries and cultures from which these works have been chosen are all young in terms of their artistic contribution to world literature in English. Almost all the truly major works have come since the end of the Second World War, and it is certain that there is much more yet to come.

Peter ABRAHAMS (1919–)

Mine Boy 1946
This novel concerns work in the South African gold mines and life in the black urban slums of Johannesburg. As with Paton's *Cry the Beloved Country* it shares the post-war optimism for racial harmony.

Chinua ACHEBE (1930–)

Things Fall Apart 1958
The tribal life of the Ibo and the disastrous impact of the white man's arrival. The best possible introduction to African literature.

No Longer at Ease 1960
The youthful idealism of the main character, Obi, is shown to be totally unrealistic in modern Lagos. The crisis of a rootless culture is brilliantly portrayed through the hero's adventures.

The Arrow of God 1964
A tragedy set in the traditional culture of the old days and dealing with human and superhuman power and their use; the novel deals with the effect on the priest Ezeula and his people of his particular struggle.

A Man of the People 1966
A biting, satirical farce and attack on the corruption in Nigeria between Independence and the military coups as told by the anti-hero Odile.

Timothy ALUKO (1920–)

Kinsman and Foreman 1966
Aluko's style is lightly satirical, poking fun at a world of corruption rather than attempting to protest seriously through his writing. This novel looks at the problems of a Nigerian engineer sent to work in his own town.

His Worshipful Majesty 1973
The world of the petty bureaucrat is the object of ridicule in this story about an established governor having to come to terms with the new rules created by colonialism.

Elechi AMADI (1940–)

The Concubine 1966
An admirably convincing portrayal of a tribal village community in pre-colonial Africa, in which age-old customs are challenged by the aspirations of individuals.

The Great Ponds 1969
The harmony of the villagers is here shattered by the eruption of warfare. Their suffering does not alienate them from their belief in the gods but rather ennobles them through their acceptance.

Mulk Raj ANAND (1905–)

Untouchable 1935
Written with zest and indignation at the plight of the poverty-stricken villages of India and their much-maligned inhabitants. This novel concerns the events of one fateful day which began with a disastrous accidental 'touching'.

Ayi Kwei ARMAH (1939–)

The Beautiful Ones Are Not Yet Born 1968
The title is a slogan written on the back of a Ghanaian bus. The integrity of the hero is set against the corruption of post-revolutionary Ghana. A powerful first novel.

Margaret ATWOOD (1939–)

The Journals of Susanna Moodie 1970
Selected Poems 1976
The Handmaid's Tale 1985
Atwood is strongly committed to Canadian themes and life as witnessed, for example, in the Susanna Moodie collection. Her poetry and fiction is probably the most impressive body of work to issue from Canada for some while. She has also written novels and an excellent criticism of Canadian Literature, *Survival: A Thematic Guide to Canadian Literature* (1972)

Kofi AWOONOR (1935–)

Night of My Blood 1971
The second of Awoonor's three major collections of poems. Born in Ghana he has utilized with great power and skill the vernacular oral tradition of the Ewe tribe.

This Earth, My Brother 1971
Described as 'an allegory' by the author, this is a stylish and poetic novel using daring and evocative language to analyse the problems of a newly-independent African state.

Rolf BOLDERWOOD (Thomas Alexander Brown) (1826–1915)

Robbery Under Arms 1888
Originally published in serial form in *The Sydney Mail* this is the story of Captain Starlight and his gang as told by a repentant and converted bushranger.

Edward BRAITHWAITE (1950–)

Rights of Passage 1967
Masks 1968
Islands 1969
Rootlessness, not only of the past but also of the present; the culture of the Africans used as a means to an identity; a new view of the West Indian individual – these are just some of the themes in these extremely complex but powerful poems. They were re-published as *The Arrivants: A New World Trilogy* in 1973.

Christopher BRENNAN (1870–1932)

Poems 1914
Seventeen poems which explore the search for the lost Eden through empire, civilization, and sex, while recognizing the inevitable failure of such a quest. Brennan was very influential in introducing non-English poetic traditions into Australian poetry.

Martin CARTER (1927–)

Poems of Resistance 1954
Carter is a Guyanese poet concerned with social, historical and political situations. These themes are expanded through the means of vision, dream and a particularly effective use of local language.

John Pepper CLARK (1936–)

Three Plays 1964 – *Song of a Goat, The Masquarade and the Rafts*
Ozidi 1966
Although Clark has written poetry and criticism his reputation is based most strongly on these four verse dramas which witness his primary fascination with the rituals and myths of the Ijaw tribe.

Marcus CLARKE (1846–81)

For the Term of his Natural Life 1870
This is a tale of convict days in nineteenth century Tasmania.

Anita DESAI (1937–)

Cry, the Peacock 1963
Desai's first novel has a heroine dominated and culturally educated by her beloved Brahmin father. An unsuccessful marriage leads to her going mad and finally killing her insensitive husband.

Fire on the Mountain 1977
A group of women, each individually lonely, struggle to cope with their desolation.

G V DESANI (1909–)

All About H Hatterr 1948 (revised 1970)
The one revered book by this author celebrates life in exuberant, vivacious, original style. Hatterr narrates his spiritual self-education achieved through the use and abuse of Indian sages.

Geoffrey DUTTON (1922–)

Tamara
An Australian scientist falls in love with a Russian poetess and views the contradictions of Soviet society with a sympathetic mixture of comic perception and social concern. Dutton's work invariably explores the conflicting values within and between various societies.

Robert David FITZGERALD (1902–)

The Wind at my Door 1959
Using the flogging of Irish convicts in New South Wales in 1904 as its focal point this excellent poem explores past and present, both on the national and personal level.

Athol FUGARD (1932–)

Three Port Elizabeth Plays – The Blood Knot 1961, *Hello and Goodbye* 1965, *Boesman and Lena* 1969,
Statements – Sizwe Bansi is Dead 1972, *The Island* 1973, *Statements after an Arrest under the Immorality Act* 1974
Three Port Elizabeth Plays represent the best of Fugard's early work; each deals with a different aspect of South African society. *The Blood Knot* presents two non-white (coloured) brothers; *Hello and Goodbye*, an Afrikaans brother and sister sorting through their past for meaning; *Boesman and Lena*, two 'married' coloured people living amongst the rubbish on the city outskirts. The plays are strongly derivative of Beckett and Pinter, employing small casts, little action, and a threatening background.

Sizwe Bansi and *The Island* were created employing improvisation methods and deal with the pass laws and Robben Island prison.

Joseph FURPHY (1843–1912)

Such is Life 1903
'Being certain extracts from the diary of Tom Collins', the sub-title runs. An evocation of bush life in early Australia which at the time was original in form and subject matter, as well as very funny.

Nadime GORDIMER (1923–)

Livingstone's Companions 1972
A collection of some of her best short stories; an excellent introduction to her work.

The Conservationist 1974
Winner of the Booker Prize, this subtle work analyses exploitation of land and people and brilliantly evokes an historical perspective for the fantasies and behaviour of the white capitalist, Mehring.

Berger's Daughter 1979
The Treason Trials of 1976 are the background for an examination of the South African political left through Rosa Burger, the daughter of Afrikaner-descendent Marxists who have died in prison.

F P GROVE (1879–1948)

The Master of the Hill 1938
This is the best of several works of a similar kind by this author. He combines his evolutionary myths with the representation of Canadian rural life and values.

Wilson HARRIS (1921–)

Palace of the Peacock 1960
The Far Journey of Oudin 1961
The Whole Armour 1962
The Secret Ladder 1963
Many now regard Harris as a great novelist whose reputation continues to grow. *Palace of the Peacock* is the first of a series known as the 'Guiana Quartet', all of which are listed above, and is probably the best introduction to Harris's world.

Bessie HEAD (1937–)

When Rain Clouds Gather 1968
A black South African activist escapes to Botswana where he and others join to create a new self-sufficient community.

Maru 1971
Two men, Maru and Moleka, become enemies over their love for Margaret, an outcast. Renouncing political power, it is Maru who wins her.

A Question of Power 1974
The best of the three novels. This tells of a coloured South African woman, Elizabeth, who becomes mentally ill whilst she is working in a farming cooperative. In all three books Head links the individual to the political to establish an ethic for development.

John HEARNE (1926–)

Strangers at the Gate 1956
Set in the Caribbean island of Cayuna (the author's own invention) the novel explores the social relations of Jamaica while keenly evoking a sense of place.

Voices Under the Window 1955
In the aftermath of a riot in Kingston, Jamaica, the hero lies dying; he relives his past, revealing the desperate social plight in which he and his fellows found themselves.

Ruth Prawer JHABVALA (1927–)

Heat and Dust 1975
Upper middle-class Europeans in India trying to understand their native neighbours are lightly satirized, but warmly portrayed, by one of the best writers of Indian fiction in English at present. Her book of short stories, *How I Became a Holy Mother and Other Stories*, 1976, is also excellent.

Thomas KENEALLY (1935–)

Bring Larks and Heroes 1967
Keneally's novel is a recreation of the convict period which is regarded as a milestone in Australian fiction.

Schindler's Ark 1982
Winner of the 1982 Booker Prize, this novel tells of Oskar Schindler's defiance of the SS in Poland and his persistence in the protection of his fellow Jews.

Henry KINGSLEY (1830–76)

The Recollection of Geoffrey Hamlyn 1859
This is a classic adventure story of the early settler days. The author is the brother of Charles Kingsley; he was born in England but lived in Australia from 1853 to 1858.

Alex LA GUMA (1925–)

A Walk in the Night 1962
Published in Nigeria, this novel is set in the District Six slum area of Cape Town and explores the life of the coloured people living there in poverty and under apartheid.

George LAMMING (1927–)

In the Castle of My Skin 1953
A major West Indian novel. It tells the story of young boys growing up in Barbados as well as registering the changes taking place in the islands.

Ray LAWLER (1913–)

The Summer of the Seventeenth Doll 1955
The play is about two Queensland sugarcane cutters in perhaps the only significant dramatization of Australian life and values, until the recent wave of films.

Stephen LEACOCK (1869–1944)

Sunshine Sketches of A Little Town 1912
Arcadian Adventures with the Idle Rich 1914
These are vivid and amusing portraits of Canadian small town and city life by one of the great humourists and supporters of the British Empire.

Roger MAIS (1905–55)

The Hills Were Joyful Together 1953
Plain prose is combined with passionate remonstrance in this depiction of the slums of Kingston, Jamaica, and its inhabitants who are caught in the trap of poverty and crime. An important work by an important writer of West Indian fiction.

Brother Man 1954
A folk-preacher and his wife suffer public failure, but manage to survive privately through their individual resourcefulness and their love for one another.

Hugh MacLENNAN (1907–80)

Each Man's Son 1951
Probably the author's best work to date, it deals with the effects of puritanism in a Cape Breton mining village.

Edgar MITTELHOLZER (1909–65)

A Morning at the Office 1980
A prolific writer, Mittelholzer was the first West Indian novelist to gain an international reputation. Set in a Port of Spain office where the messenger boy anonymously declares his love for the manager's secretary, this is one of his best works. He was also successful with the sequence of novels known as *Children of Kaywana*.

Es'Kai MPHAHLELE (1919–)

Down Second Avenue 1959
This novel is a classic of its kind. It is an autobiographical account of growing up under apartheid, strong on its account of village life and the urban ghetto.

V S NAIPAUL (1932–)

See the Fiction Section.

R K NARAYAN (1907–)

The Financial Expert 1952
Narayan is Indias's most successful novelist. All his works are set in the fictional town of Malgudi. Here, Margayya, a money-lender, makes and loses a fortune through a series of accidents.

Waiting for the Mahatama 1955
This is a fictional study of the responses to Ghandi's Quit India Campaign.

The Guide 1958
A confidence trickster after a spell in jail is mistaken for a holy-man. It is perhaps Narayan's most accomplished novel.

Wa Thiong'o NGUGI (formerly James) (1938–)

Weep Not Child 1964
The first East African novel in English, is set around the Mau Mau wars in the 1950s.

The River Between 1965
Tells the story of two villages during the arrival of the British colonials in the form of educationalists and missionaries.

A Grain of Wheat 1967
Set at the time of Independence this presents the view of several characters, especially of their pasts and what they bring with them for the new country.

Petals of Blood 1977
This is one of the best post-Independence novels to come out of Africa.

Abiosech NICOL (1924–)

The Truly Married Woman and Other Stories 1965
Both Africans and Europeans are pictured at the time of the colonial shift in this volume of excellent stories. The problems of the era are described with gentle satire and great compassion.

Gabriel OKARA (1921–)

The Voice 1964
A melancholic piece written as a parable in a strange style resulting from the author writing in the language of Ijaw before translating it into English. The effect is at times poetic and at times absurd.

Vance PALMER (1885–1959)

The Rainbow Bird and Other Stories 1957
The title story is a piece about childhood and contains subtle and sympathetic insight
into immature feelings. These short stories indicate that Palmer's expression is more
suited to this form than that of the novel.

The Big Fellow 1960
The last of a trilogy set in his birthplace of Queensland, Australia, *The Big Fellow*
traces the rise of Macy Donovan to the position of State Parliament leadership. The
style is documentary in a conscious attempt to distinguish it from the English
'literary' style. The others of this trilogy are *Golconda* and *Seedtime*.

Alan Stewart PATON (1903–88)

Cry the Beloved Country 1948
A Zulu priest attempts to find his son in Johannesburg in this most famous of white
South African novels.

Too Late the Phalarope 1953
A much better novel than the above, this deals with the relations of an Afrikaner
family; and through it the problems of Afrikanerdom as a whole.

William PLOMER (1903–73)

Turbott Wolfe 1926
First published by the Hogarth Press, this is one of the first white South African
condemnations of colour policy. Plomer also wrote good light and more serious
poetry: see his *Collected Poems*.

Edwin John PRATT (1882–1964)

Brebeuf and his Brethren 1940
Towards the Last Spike 1952
Collected Poems 1958
Regarded as Canada's greatest poet, Pratt has gained surprisingly little recognition
outside his own country. His contribution to both narrative poetry and to the epic
vision of his country is of considerable importance.

Raja RAO (1908–)

Kanthapura 1938
The village of Kanthapura, its history, its religious life, and the life of the villagers are
recounted at the time of the Quit India Campaign.

The Serpent and the Rope 1960
Rao's most important and possibly most complex novel to date, this is often
considered 'difficult' for Western readers. Superficially it is a re-working of the
legend of Satyavan and Savithri through the modern marriage of the Indian Rama
with Madelaine, his French wife.

Mary RENAULT (1905–)

The Last of the Wine 1956
After her popular success, *The Charioteer*, with its heavy homosexual content set against the Second World War, her best work was produced in the form of historical novels. *The Last of the Wine* is set in Athens at the time of Socrates. *The Mask of Apollo* returns to the same period.

Henry Handel RICHARDSON (Ethel Florence Richardson) (1870–1946)

The Fortunes of Richard Mahoney 1930
This famous Australian saga, based on the life of the writer's father, was originally published in three volumes: *Australia Felix*, *The Way Home* and *Ultima Thule*.

Mordecai RICHLER (1981–)

The Apprenticeship of Duddy Kravitz 1959
Set in Montreal this book explores the life of a young Jewish boy growing up in modern Canadian society.

Frank SARGESON (1903–)

I For One... 1954
A short novel written most effectively in the form of diary entries by a schoolmistress after the death of her father. A sensitive understanding of her predicament is conveyed by an apparent lack of authorial intrusion.

I Saw in My Dreams 1949
A short story (entitled 'When the Wind Blows') extended into a novel on the theme of a boy's revolt against his bourgeois background.

Collected Stories 1965
A fine set of stories using satire to point to what is seen as the harshness and artificiality of typical New Zealand life.

Olive SCHREINER (1855–1920)

The Story of an African Farm 1883
The land and the experience of living are the subjects of this classic pioneering novel, the first truly South African work.

Khushwant SINGH (1915–)

Train to Pakistan 1955
A fable set in Mano Majra, a fictional village where a railway line crosses from India into Pakistan. The inadequacy of law and intellect alike is demonstrated in the face of the violent and/or loving passions of the peasants. See also stories in *Black Jasmine* 1971.

Wole SOYINKA (1934–)

The Lion and the Jewel 1959
A Dance of the Forests 1960
The Road 1965
Kongi's Harvest 1967
Madmen and Specialists 1970
Soyinka is the most famous of all African playwrights, although he has also written
poetry and a novel – *The Interpreters* (1965). The conflict between traditional rural
life and modern life is often the centre of the action. He also concisely uses and blends
the traditions of both African and European culture. Soyinka was detained during the
Biafran war and spent two years in prison, mostly in solitary confinement; his book
The Man Dies (1972) gives an account of his experiences. He won the 1986 Nobel
Prize for literature.

Randolph STOW (1935–)

To the Islands 1958
This novel about Hariot, a failed missionary, was compared with Patrick White's
Voss on its first appearance. Despite the similarity in themes, this is an excellent
work.

Outrider 1956–62 1962
A collection of Stow's early poems. A further connection with White is that Sidney
Nolan (to whom White's *The Vivesector* was dedicated) illustrated the first editions.

The Merry-go-round in the Sea 1965
Set in Australia in the period before and during the Second World War, this fine
novel, perhaps Stow's best to date, traces the growth from boyhood to adolescence of
both its hero and Australia itself.

Amos TUTUOLA (1920–)

The Palm Wine Drinkard 1952
My Life in the Bush of Ghosts 1954
Tutuola, in his curious English, retells in these two works, and in others he has
produced since, various Yoruba tales (used also by Soyinka). He is not so much a
novelist as one who continues the oral tradition and who has helped to keep the
Yoruba culture alive.

Derek WALCOTT (1930–)

In a Green Night: Poems 1948–60 1962
Walcott has established an international reputation as a poet. This is an excellent
collection of his early work.

The Dream on Monkey Mountain and Other Plays 1971
Walcott's theatre uses West Indian dances, songs, and folklore which he combines with his own strong dialogue and verse. Although he has produced several volumes of plays, *Monkey Mountain* remains the most successful to date.

Patrick WHITE (1912–)

The Tree of Man 1955
Voss 1957
In these early novels, the pioneer's life in the great Australian outback is portrayed with a spiritual intensity that raises the content to the level of myth. *The Tree of Man* is a realistic story of a husband and wife building a farm and a family at the beginning of the century. *Voss* is a big resonant novel that creates a legend from the life and death of a nineteenth century explorer into the interior.

Riders in the Chariot 1961
The Solid Mandela 1966
These novels are set in the imagined Sydney suburb of Sarsaprika and have echoes of Dostoevsky, both in their characterizations and in the struggle between good and evil. A group of extreme characters in *Riders in the Chariot* – a lovely old lady, a refugee from Nazi Germany, an aborigine – are realistically observed in an emigrant society living at the extremity of the world. *The Solid Mandela* tells the story of twins from the point of view of each one.

The Vivisector 1970
A novel about the life of an artist, in this case a painter. Patrick White's works listed here, together with later novels, plays, poems, short stories and a painfully honest autobiography, *Flaws in the Glass*, form the most important contribution to literature to come out of Australia, if not the whole field of white commonwealth literature.

CHILDREN'S LITERATURE

Britain is rich in books for children and young people. There are over 35,000 children's books in print in Britain and about 2,500 new titles are published each year. Amongst all these there are many of high literary and artistic quality, particularly in the two themes in which British writers excel: fantasy and the historical novel.

During the last 100 years there has developed a range of books from those for the very young to teenage reading. The themes mirror most aspects of imagination and reality, and the formats use all the available art, design and printing technology.

More than a dozen children's book awards, for merit of one kind or another, have helped to maintain the high standards; the development of paperback publication for both junior novels and picture books, has made possible the widespread ownership of books. Public libraries, school libraries, organizations such as the Federation of Children's Book Groups and the School Bookshop Association, have spread information, interest and the experience of reading. Children's book programmes and the televising of so many stories and picture books have added another dimension to the printed word and picture.

It has been more than usually difficult in this section to keep a constant historical perspective, since so much recently published work seems so very good. We have attempted to do justice to the historical spread, the range of sub-genres and age appeal, to 'literary quality' and to reader popularity. Some titles have been included as representatives of current popular genres of children's fiction. Their literary merit may be less than the classics and some are unlikely to survive into future editions of this work. But their appeal to children is a cherishable value since it starts and encourages the habit of reading.

In this section of the Library the listed titles usually carry a recommendation on the particular edition, as indicated by the imprint which follows the title listing. This recognizes the importance of design and illustration in children's literature. The selection of the edition takes into account its suitability as a book which will be read and re-read by a child-owner and perhaps even handed down to the next generation. Where a suitable paperback edition is available this is indicated. The dates given are the publication dates of the edition cited. The annotation usually mentions the actual or approximate date of original publication.

The literature that has been selected is on the whole that which is especially suitable for readers up to about the age of 14 years. There are several works of 'adult' fiction which are particularly popular among late teenagers and these can be found in the section on English and American fiction. These include such works as *Catcher in the Rye*, *The Lord of the Flies*, and the Sherlock Holmes stories.

Richard ADAMS (1920–)

Watership Down (Puffin) 1973
A band of rabbits, in danger on the Berkshire Downs, search for safety. The 480 page saga is interspersed with myths from rabbit folklore. Originally published by Rex Collings, an illustrated edition was published by Kestrel in 1976.

AESOP

Aesop's Fables (Macmillan) 1981
Here large format re-tellings of a selection of the fables are accompanied by full-colour, full-page pictures by American artist Heidi Holden.

Janet and Allan AHLBERG (1944–) and (1938–)

Each Peach Pear Plum (Fontana) 1978
Janet Ahlberg illustrates the books and her husband writes the stories and the rhymes. This book is a combination of familiar nursery rhyme and fairy tale characters into a story. Aimed at 5–7 year olds.

Joan AIKEN (1924–)

Kingdom under the Sea (Puffin) 1973
A collection of simple Eastern European tales, including Baba Yaga, with superb black/white silhouette drawings. It has all the narrative qualities needed for reading aloud, and is illustrated by Jan Pienkowski.

Louisa M. ALCOTT (1832–88)

Little Women (Puffin) 1970
Published in USA in 1868 the story of Jo, Beth, Meg and Amy has been translated into more than twenty languages and remains one of the best known children's books. The story of the March family continues in the less popular sequels, *Good Wives*, *Little Men* and *Jo's Boys*.

Hans Christian ANDERSEN (1805–75)

Hans Andersen Fairy Tales translated by Naomi Lewis (Puffin) 1981
Over 100 translations and re-tellings have been made with varying degrees of fidelity to the original tales. This collection of twelve tales has accuracy, sympathy and freshness.

Rev. Wilbert AWDRY (1911–)

Thomas the Tank Engine (Ladybird) 1974
Humanized engines such as Thomas the Tank Engine, fussed over by the Fat Controller, are shown in these tiny format books: 32 titles are available.

Enid BAGNOLD (1889–1981)

National Velvet (Pan) 1978
First published in 1930, this is the story of a 14 year old girl, Velvet Brown, who buys a horse for a shilling and wins the Grand National.

R M BALLANTYNE (1825–94)

Coral Island (Hamlyn) 1858
The tale of shipwrecked mariners, Ralph Rover and his friends, which combines realism and romanticism.

James M BARRIE (1860–1937)

Peter Pan and Wendy re-told by May Byron for boys and girls with the approval of the author, (Puffin) 1970 and (Hodder) 1976
Originally a play, this was first published in story-form in 1911 and Peter Pan, Wendy, Captain Hook and Tinker Bell are now part of British folklore. The paperback Puffin version is illustrated by Richard Kennedy with an introduction by Naomi Lewis. The Hodder version is small format and illustrated by Shirley Hughes.

Frank L BAUM (1856–1919)

The Wizard of Oz (Armada) 1969
The fantasy adventures of Dorothy, the Lion, the Scarecrow and the Tin Woodman have made this an American classic with a world-wide readership. The modern full-colour detailed illustrations are by Michael Hague in the Methuen hardback edition, with very clear print. Originally published in 1900.

Nina BAWDEN (1925–)

Carrie's War (Puffin) 1973
An adventure story set in World War II, this concerns Carrie, an evacuee sent from London to live in Wales. A realistic account of the traumas involved.

Quentin BLAKE (1932–)

Mister Magnolia (Armada) 1980
Quentin Blake began his career as an illustrator of children's books but soon moved to creating his own picture books, of which this is one. Amusing text and drawings for 3–7 year olds. Winner of the Kate Greenaway medal in 1980.

Michael BOND (1926–)

A Bear Called Paddington (Armada) 1971
Illustrated by Peggy Fortnum, the bear from Darkest Peru, with marmalade sandwiches under his hat, goes from one misdemeanour to another in this and the many subsequent books. The humour and indefinable age of Paddington enable the stories to be enjoyed by a wide age range.

Lucy M BOSTON (1892–)

The Children of Green Knowe (Puffin) 1975
Superb writing evokes ghostliness at the house called Green Knowe where Tolly goes to holiday with his grandmother. There are five titles in the series; the fourth, *A Stranger at Green Knowe*, won the Carnegie Medal in 1961.

Raymond BRIGGS (1934–)

Father Christmas (Picture Puffin) 1975
Picture strip illustration and balloon talk depict, with dry humour, Father Christmas doing his job. Briggs's other work in similar style includes *Fungus The Bogeyman* (Hamilton, 1979) and *When the Wind Blows* (Penguin, 1986), the former becoming a cult amongst teenagers and the latter dealing with the theme of nuclear war.

Jean de BRUNHOFF (1899–1937)

The Story of Babar (Methuen) 1977
The baby elephant runs away from the forest, adventures in the city, returns to the jungle and is made king. This and other Babar stories are classic French picture books, fully accepted by children all over the world. A A Milne wrote the introduction to the first English translation in 1934.

Frances Hodgson BURNETT (1849–1924)

The Secret Garden (Puffin) 1983
By the author of *Little Lord Fauntleroy*, this is the story of an orphaned girl who helps herself, two boys and an abandoned garden to grow. The enchanting background enhances the secret part of the plot.

John BURNINGHAM (1936–)

Mr Gumpy's Outing (Puffin) 1970
This is the story of a punting expedition that goes wrong – and right. A gently humorous novel, and a good read for 5–8 year olds.

Eric CARLE (1929–)

The Very Hungry Caterpillar (Hamish Hamilton and Picture Puffin) 1974
Clever visual and tactile effects bring to life the story of a caterpillar who eats his way
through the pages to become a technicolour butterfly. The holes in the pages help
towards a feeling of accuracy: the paperback version is slightly less effective.

Lewis CARROLL (Charles Lutwidge DODGSON) (1832–98)

Alice's Adventures in Wonderland and *Through the Looking Glass* (Macmillan) 1980
This two-volume edition has the Tenniel line drawings which so perfectly depict
Alice and her fantasy worlds. Since its original publication in 1865, Alice's
popularity has spread to all age groups and cultures to become, possibly, the best
known children's book in the world.

Angela CARTER (1940–)

Sleeping Beauty and Other Favourite Fairy Tales (Gollancz) 1985
Strikingly illustrated by Michael Foreman and translated by an imaginative modern
writer, the old tales have fresh appeal for all ages.

John CHRISTOPHER (1922–)

The Sword of the Spirits (Puffin) 1972
After a volcano and earthquake have destroyed the world a few groups of people
remain. In this and Christopher's many other science fiction works the future is
clearly rooted in the present. *The Guardians* (1970) is also recommended.

Richmal CROMPTON (1890–1969)

Just William (Macmillan) 1983
This tells the first tale of one of William's many scrapes resulting from his very
disorganized approach to life. William began his 40-year career as an anarchic
11-year old in 1922.

Helen CRESSWELL (1934–)

Lizzie Dripping (BBC Jackanory Book) 1973
Humour is the appeal of many of Cresswell's books. Lizzie is shadowed by a witch
whose inappropriate appearances cause problems. In the Bagthorpe series
(Faber/Puffin), an idiosyncratic family lives life to the full as in the stories *Ordinary
Jack* and *Bagthorpes Unlimited*.

Kevin CROSSLEY HOLLAND (1941–)

Beowulf (OUP) 1982
The author, an Anglo-Saxon scholar, has retained the energy and excitement of the
old story, extended superbly by the sepia pictures of Charles Keeping.

Roald DAHL (1916–)

Charlie and the Chocolate Factory (Puffin) 1979
The acquisition of a golden ticket entitles Charlie to visit Mr Wonka's factory with its inventive and amusing characters and events. All Dahl's work has either humour or suspense, e.g. *James and the Giant Peach, The BFG, Danny Champion of the World* and the collection of stories *The Wonderful World of Henry Sugar*.

Eleanor FARJEON (1881–1965)

The Little Bookroom (OUP, new ed.) 1979
The author wrote over 70 books for children, including *Martin Pippin in the Apple Orchard* and (with Edward Ardizzone) *The Old Nurse's Stocking Basket*. *The Little Bookroom* is a collection of her tales and was first published in 1955.

Wanda GAG (1893–1946)

Millions of Cats (Picture Puffin) 1977
This tale has an excellent oral quality which inspires children to ask for it again and again. An old couple who wanted a cat end up with 'millions and billions and trillions of cats'. Black and white pictures give emphasis to the crisp economy of the words.

Leon GARFIELD (1921–) and Edward BLISHEN (1920–)

The God Beneath the Sea (Kestrel) 1976
Elemental human emotions in the re-telling of the Greek myths are depicted in vital language and are powerfully illustrated by Charles Keeping.

William GOLDING (1911–)

Lord of the Flies (Faber) 1954
Ralph, Jack and Piggy are marooned on a desert island; how will they survive? Often cited as a study of how people – not just children – would really behave if left in such circumstances.

GOSCINNY and UDERZO (1926–77)

Asterix the Gaul (Hodder) 1973
One of the many examples of picture strip art combined with witty text from the Belgian writer/artist duo, this depicts the small Gaul taking on the Roman Empire.

Kenneth GRAHAME (1859–1932)

Wind in the Willows (Methuen) 1971
This well-loved story of Ratty, Mole and Toad, the river bank and the Wild Wood, is here presented with E. M. Shepard's illustrations in a Methuen classic version. A paperback version, with illustrator John Burmingham's interpretation, is an alternative (Kestrel 1983).

J GRIMM (1765–1863) and W. GRIMM (1786–1859)

The Brothers Grimm: Popular Folk Tales translated by Brian Alderson (Gollancz) 1978
Of the many versions available this is a good modern translation of the tales, with harmonious line drawings and water colours from Michael Foreman. The first English translation of the classic German folk-stories and fairy tales was published in 1823 and illustrated by George Cruickshank.

Rider HAGGARD (1856–1925)

King Solomon's Mines (Puffin) 1958, (Dent) 1963
She (Macdonald) 1969
These are two good yarns, with an African setting, by a master of narrative with a highly-charged imagination.

Roger HARGREAVES (1930–88)

Mr Men 1971 onwards
A series of simply illustrated stories featuring such characters as Mr Tickle, Mr Bump and Mr Greedy. A popular TV cartoon series emerged; Hargreaves creates 'types' and relates them to their names.

Chandler HARRIS (1848–1908)

Uncle Remus (Puffin) 1886
Uncle Remus is series of linked tales 'recounted' by a black southern American. The tales had been absorbed by Harris during his work on folk-tales.

Virginia HAVILAND (1911–)

Fairy Tales Treasury (Hamish Hamilton and Young Puffin) 1974
A large selection of familiar tales by Virginia Haviland which has full-colour, lively illustrations in large format, making it the kind of book that children pore over and pass on from one generation to another.

Faber Book of North American Legends (Faber) 1979
An excellent edited collection of tales from Indian, Eskimo, Black American and European immigrant cultures, plus some American tall tales, for reading or telling. This book includes notes on their origins and the complementary illustrations by Ann Strugnell are in black and white.

Nathaniel HAWTHORNE (1804–64)

Tanglewood Tales (Gollancz) 1963
Eustacia Bright presents the 'editor', Hawthorne, with a series of tales based on Greek myths, suitably reworked (and sanitized) for children. Edward Dulac illustrated the 1911 edition.

Shirley HUGHES (1919–)

Here Comes Charlie Moon (Armada) 1980
This novel describes the antics of Charlie, a young boy who stays with a relative who just happens to run a joke shop. Shirley Hughes began her career as an illustrator, turning to children's fiction later. Suitable for children up to 7 years.

Ted HUGHES (1930–)

The Iron Man (Faber) 1968
Adults may recognize certain themes from Ted Hughes here: a huge man, made of iron, suddenly appears and begins to destroy machinery – by eating it.

Thomas HUGHES (1822–96)

Tom Brown's Schooldays (Dent) 1976
The most famous of school stories with Tom, East and bully Flashman at Dr Arnold's Rugby in 1857, it helped to create the 'public school ethos'.

Pat HUTCHINS (1942–)

Rosie's Walk (Penguin) 1968
This is a wordless story about a hen who spends her time wandering around her farmyard home. Suitable for ages 3–4.

Gene KEMP (1926–)

The Turbulent Term of Tyke Tyler (Puffin) 1977
This is the first of two 'Cricklepit' novels, set in the school of that name, dealing with schoolboy activities – and not always innocent ones at that. Straightforward prose, depicting realistic schoolchildren.

Clive KING (1924–)

Stig of the Dump (Puffin) 1970, (Kestral) 1980
King's novel is a strong candidate for classic status. Barney finds a caveman in a local quarry and through various ways of communicating learns of Stig's inventive use of other people's rubbish. This warm and curious friendship is illustrated by Edward Ardizzone.

Charles KINGSLEY (1819–75)

The Water Babies (Gollancz) 1961
Black and white drawings by Harold Jones complement this version of the classic story. Kathline Lines has edited it to remove some of the parts that confuse the child reader. A basic text of 'victorian values'.

Rudyard KIPLING (1850–94)

Stalkey & Co (Macmillan) 1977
'Stalkey' is the nickname of Corkran, leader of a small group of boys who are being educated at 'the College' and who display cunning in the face of the short-sightedness of the masters. First published in 1899.

The Just-So Stories (Piccolo) 1975
These original, timelessly amusing stories with a clever vocabulary give answers to such questions as how the leopard got its spots and the elephant its trunk. In *The Jungle Book* (Pan, 1975) the characters Mowgli, Bagheera and Akela also live on in the memory. Kipling's other works, including *Kim*, are listed in the Fiction Section.

Andrew LANG (1844–1912)

The Blue Fairy Book (Kestrel) 1975
One of several 'colour' books of Lang's collections of fairy tales, each book has a different, first-class illustrator and all are excellently edited with additional notes and introductions.

C S LEWIS (1898–1963)

The Complete Chronicles of Narnia (Macmillan) 1950 – 56, (Puffin, 7 volumes) 1965
A series of seven books starting with *The Lion, the Witch and the Wardrobe* (1950), where children enter the land of Narnia through a wardrobe door. There begins and ends the battle between good and evil. Illustrations by Pauline Baynes convey the mood throughout the series.

Penelope LIVELY (1933–)

The Ghost of Thomas Kempe (Puffin) 1973
This novel deals, like many of Penelope Lively's writings, with the relationship between the past and the present and shows that 'people evolve during their own lives'. Winner of the 1973 Carnegie Medal for children's fiction.

Hugh LOFTING (1886–1947)

The Story of Dr Dolittle (Puffin) 1967
The Doctor gives up treating people and turns to animals instead who are more appreciative of his efforts. Triggered by Lofting's experience of the First World War.

Carlo (COLLODI) LORENZIN (1826–90)

Pinocchio (Puffin) 1974
The tales of a small boy (actually a puppet come to life) who must never tell lies or, if he does, he is reminded in a clear and decisive fashion.

George MACDONALD (1824–1905)

At the Back of the North Wind (Puffin) 1984
First published in serial form then as a book (1871) with illustrations by Arthur Hughes, this tells of the love by Champion for the North Wind – which appears as a powerful and sometime destructive 'character' in the story.

A A MILNE (1882–1956)

Winnie the Pooh (Methuen) 1979
Multi-level humour for all ages in the story of the doings of a 'bear of very little brain'. With *The House at Pooh Corner* as a sequel or a separate book, Christopher Robin's humanized toys remain favourites from generation to generation. E H Shepard's illustrations have complemented the text since first publication in 1926.

L M MONTGOMERY (1874–1942)

Anne of Green Gables (Puffin) 1977
One of a series of gentle family chronicles set in Canada, *Anne* has spoken to the hearts of girls for many years. The author's series about *Emily* are similarly popular.

Jill MURPHY (1949–)

The Worst Witch (Puffin) 1974
Miss Cackle runs an Academy for Witches. One of the pupils, Mildred Hubble, turns a fellow pupil into a pig. Ethel – the pupil – extracts revenge.

Bill NAUGHTON (1910–)

The Goalkeeper's Revenge (Puffin) 1970
Thirteen realistic stories about boys who do the things that good and bad boys do, are written in a crisp, concise, effective style. A potential classic.

Edith NESBIT (1858–1924)

Five Children and It (Puffin) 1959
Magic powers, via the Psammead, take the children into another time. Other books follow up with other talismans, e.g. *The Phoenix and the Carpet, The Story of the Amulet*. The books blend realism with fantasy and humour.

The Railway Children (Puffin) 1983
Temporarily fatherless children work hard at keeping the family together in the house beside the railway track. The emotional impact of both book and film has kept the story alive since first publication in 1906.

John NEWBERG (1713–67)

The History of Little Goody Two-Shoes 1765
Newberg was the pioneering publisher of children's books and is probably also the author of this story.

Philippa PEARCE (1920–)

Minnow on the Say (Puffin) 1955
Tom's Midnight Garden (Puffin) 1976
The Elm Street Lot (Kestrel) 1969
Philippa Pearce is one of the leading contemporary writers of works for children. She deals with fantasy worlds (*Tom's Midnight Garden*), adventure (*Minnow on the Say*) and is an able short story writer, as shown in the last-named work which deals with a street and the working-class children who live in it.

Beatrix POTTER (1866–1943)

The Tale of Peter Rabbit (Warne) 1902
The first of the classic series of stories which extended to 20 books, through to *Johnny Town Mouse* in 1918. The small format and gentle water colours depict the simple adventures of the humanized animals. The illustrations, with Lake District backgrounds, are now valued as much as the stories. The books are available individually or boxed as a set.

Arthur RANSOME (1884–1967)

Swallows and Amazons (Puffin) 1962
Ransome's tale of messing about in boats, strongly-drawn characters and evocative scenery capture the feeling of the early 1900s. In this and his other holiday adventure books the children are active, resourceful and free from adult interference.

Frank RICHARDS (Charles Hamilton) (1876–1961)

Billy Bunter at Greyfriar's School (Granada) 1947
Born in *The Magnet* comic and derided for its low literary style, the stories about Billy and his chums still survive. 'Yaroo' and 'squelch' to the critics!

John RUSKIN (1819–1900)

King of the Golden River (Dover, paperback) 1975
Gentleness in story and pictures make this a deeply affecting picture book. Pale water colours animate a beautiful friendship between an almost human bear and a tenderly affectionate mouse.

Maurice SENDAK (1928–)

Where the Wild Things Are (Picture Puffin) 1963
A twentieth century classic from the American illustrator whose every book is a worthwhile experience. Young Max, sent to bed without supper as a punishment for wild behaviour, journeys to where the wild things are, tames them and returns to his supper. Psychologically and visually satisfying.

Ian SERRAILLIER (1912–)

The Silver Sword (Puffin) 1970
Set in war-torn Europe a group of children travel to find their parents and in the course of the journey learn much about themselves. The book has long been used in classrooms for its action packed account of war and its effects.

Anna SEWELL (1820–78)

Black Beauty (Puffin) 1971
Written at the end of the nineteenth century, the style and language are of that period, but the emotions are not dated in this classic story of trials and pleasures 'straight from the horse's mouth'. Line drawings are by Charlotte Hough.

Johanna SPYRI (1827–1901)

Heidi (Puffin) 1983
Although written over a century ago, the story of the Swiss orphan, in this book and the sequels, is so skilfully told that the modern reader is carried along by the events.

Robert Louis STEVENSON (1850–94)

Treasure Island (Gollancz) 1983
For the centenary of the first publication a reprint of the edition containing N C Wyeth's pictures shows that the American artist's dramatic illustrations are colourful and bold and entirely in keeping with the strong story. Stevenson's historical romances *Kidnapped* and *Catriona* may now be losing some of their appeal.

Catherine STORR (1913–)

Marianne Dreams (Puffin) 1968
Whatever Marianne draws with her magic crayon when she is awake comes to life in her dreams. She is responsible for a sick boy, hostile objects and menacing effects.

Noel STREATFIELD (1895–)

Ballet Shoes (Dent) 1977
The story that has launched many fantasy stage careers.

Rosemary SUTCLIFF (1920–)

Eagle of the Ninth (Puffin) 1977
The foremost contemporary writer of historical fiction for young people conveys in each of her 30 books the events and the flavour of the chosen period with a consistent quality of writing. In this book Marcus attempts to recover the lost standard of the legion in Roman Britain. Also recommended are *The Lantern Bearers* (Penguin, 1981) and *Warrior Scarlet* (Puffin, 1976).

Barbara Euphan TODD (1890–1976)

Worzel Gummidge (Puffin) 1969
In this facsimile of the original text and illustration the eponymous scarecrow and his friends, Earthy Mangold and Hannah Harrow, share adventures with children John and Susan. The successful translation to the television screen has ensured a place in classic children's literature.

J R R TOLKIEN (1892–1973)

The Hobbit (Allen & Unwin) 1975 (paperback) 1981
First published in 1925 the book is intended for young people though there is appeal for both child and adult. A strong relationship to *The Lord of the Rings* is seen in Bilbo Baggins, the Hobbit, and his battles with giant spiders, a meeting with Gollum in a subterranean lake, and the safety of the Ring.

Geoffrey TREASE (1909–)

One for Treason (Puffin) 1970
A Tudor spy story in which a band of travelling players plans to assassinate Queen Elizabeth. The book is notable for its grasp of the period and its pace.

Mark TWAIN (1835–1910)

The Adventures of Tom Sawyer (Puffin) 1970
Written in the nineteenth century, the events in the life of a Mississippi boy are told in action-packed episodes with a keen eye for adult absurdities. *The Adventures of Huckleberry Finn* (Penguin, 1966) depicts Tom's friend and a runaway slave in what is possibly an even better book. Twain's historical fantasy, *The Prince and the Pauper*, in which Edward VI changes place with a beggar boy, is still read.

Alison UTTLEY (1884–1976)

Tales of Little Grey Rabbit (Piccolo Pan) 1982
Four stories, with attractively detailed pictures, depict the doings of Hare, Young Squirrel, Fuzzypeg the Hedgehog and Little Grey Rabbit in a comfortable and amusing style.

Robert WESTALL (1929–)

The Machine Gunners (Puffin) 1975
Westall's first novel tells of the theft of a machine gun from a crashed aircraft in World War II and shows the rivalries between gangs in Newcastle.

Elwyn Brook WHITE (1899–)

Charlotte's Web (Picture Puffin) 1982
A little girl and a spider save Wilbur the pig from death. Young readers' emotions have been stirred by the book for many years and in many countries, making it a modern classic.

Oscar WILDE (1854–1900)

The Fairy Stories of Oscar Wilde (Gollancz) 1985
Black and white drawings by Harold Jones and an introduction by Naomi Lewis add to the collection of tales that include *The Happy Prince, The Selfish Giant* and *The Young King*.

Laura Ingalls WILDER (1867–1957)

The Little House on the Prairie (Puffin) 1969
Laura and family pioneering in the American West find an equal measure of hardship and joy in everyday life. This and the many other titles in the series form a classic family chronicle which was first published in 1935.

John WYNDHAM (1903–69)

The Day of the Triffids (Penguin) 1970
For 30 years the story of the plants taking over the world has gripped the imagination of young people and adults and is now studied in schools.

ed. Jack ZIPES (1937–)

Don't Bet on the Prince (Wildwood) 1987
An anthology of modern fairy stories told by women writers with a critical introduction by the editor.

CHILDREN'S POETRY

Raymond BRIGGS (1934–)

The Mother Goose Treasury (Picture Puffin) 1973
A wide range of familiar and unfamiliar nursery rhymes in large format is set amid a wealth of Briggs's superb illustrations.

Charles CAUSLEY (1917–)

Dawn and Dusk; poems of our time (Hodder) 1972
This selection of poems enjoyable to children includes amongst many others some from Graves, Auden, Hughes, Betjeman and Ruth Pitter.

T S ELIOT (1888–1965)

The Illustrated Old Possom (Faber, 2nd edition paperback) 1975
Illustrations by Nicholas Bentley perfectly complement the humour and place of the poems. Among the most memorable are 'Macavity the Mystery Cat' and 'The Railway Cat' but all have a life of their own.

Kate GREENAWAY (1846–1901)

A Selection from Marigold Garden (Collins) 1971
The original editions of Greenaway's works are collectors' items, particularly her *Mother Goose* and *Under the Window*, but her unique style of illustration is available in this modern version, retaining the Greenaway pictures.

eds Seamus HEANEY (1939–) and Ted HUGHES (1930–)

The Rattle Bag: an anthology of poetry (Faber) 1982
This presents a rich mix of old and new English and American poetry of all kinds for children and adults.

Heinrich Struwwelpeter HOFFMAN (1809-94)

Cautionary Tales (Piccolo Pan) 1972
First published in 1845, the German doctor's cautionary verse stories of 'Shockheaded Peter', 'Little Sucka-Thumb' and 'The Dreadful Story of Harriet and the Matches' have become familiar to children in many countries. The apparently frightening pictures are accepted by most children as morally apt and funny.

Ted HUGHES (1930–)

Moonbells and Other Poems (Chatto) 1978
With powerful imagery the poet forces the reader to see life his way and the poems produce fresh insight with each reading. Other volumes include *Under the North Star* (Faber, 1981), *Season Songs* (Faber, 1985) and *Wodwo* (Faber, 1987).

Charles KEEPING (1924–)

The Highwayman (OUP) 1981
Dramatic illustrations complement the atmospheric poem from endpaper to endpaper in this picture book version of the well-known ballad by Alfred Noyes.

Edward LEAR (1812–88)

The Complete Nonsense of Edward Lear (Faber) 1947
The collection of verse and Lear's illustrations, edited by Holbrook Jackson, gives full rein to humour based on incongruity, nonsense and the play on words, ranging from 'There was an old man with a beard' and 'The Owl and the Pussycat' to nonsense stories.

Spike MILLIGAN (1918–)

Silly Verse for Kids (Puffin) 1970
These nonsense rhymes are on a par with Lear's 'bosh' and equally memorable. Modern children find them hilarious.

A A MILNE (1882–1956)

When We Were Very Young (Methuen, paperback) 1963
Buckingham Palace, the King's breakfast and Vespers, plus the 'hums' of Pooh, are part of British folklore. E H Shepard's illustrations capture the essence of childhood. *Now We Are Six* (Methuen, 1965) is equally desirable and Milne's poems in general can be read in *The Christopher Robin Verse Book* (Methuen, 1969).

Iona and Peter OPIE (1923–) and (1918–82)

The Oxford Book of Children's Verse (OUP) 1973
A well-produced volume of poetry written for children from earliest times to the present day, this provides a standard by which to assess both the poetry and the changes in society over the years.

Michael ROSEN (1946–)

You Can't Catch Me (Puffin) 1982
This humorous modern poet colloquially depicts childhood fears and pleasures with the help of the exactly harmonizing illustrations of Quentin Blake.

R L STEVENSON (1850–94)

A Child's Garden of Verses (Gollancz) 1985
To celebrate the centenary of the collection's first publication the poems are beautifully illustrated by Michael Foreman and there is an explanatory foreword by Mary Thwaite. The edition will surely last another 100 years.

'YOUNG WRITERS'

Young Writers (Heinemann) annual
Children's own writing varies from the derivative to the original. This W H Smith
competition attracts 35,000 entries each year and produces a large amount of fresh,
imaginative poetry. This selection testifies to the place of poetry in the life of a child.

BOOKS ABOUT CHILDREN'S BOOKS

F J Harvey DARTON

Children's Books in England (CUP, 3rd revised edition) 1982
This is a survey of children's literature from the Middle Ages to the end of the
nineteenth century, edited by Brian Alderson. The most authoritative description and
discussion of the development of children's literature, this is the standard work on the
children's section of English literature.

Margery FISHER

Intent Upon Reading: a critical appraisal of modern fiction for children
(Brockhampton) 1964
The author is an experienced critic and reviewer and has brought her perception and
knowledge to this detailed study of much of the large range of children's books,
arranged in thematic sections.

The Bright Face of Danger; an exploration of the adventure story (Hodder &
Stoughton) 1986
Intended to be read as a whole, the book is a detailed study of the subject, covering
both adult and children's literature, in style similar to *Intent on Reading*.

Who's Who in Children's Books: a treasury of familiar characters of childhood
(Weidenfeld and Nicholson) 1975
An alphabetical encyclopaedia of characters in children's books through the ages,
with illustrations from the sources, this text enables the reader of any age to identify
the half remembered person and book.

D L KIRKPATRICK

Twentieth Century Children's Writers (Macmillan, 3rd revised edition) 1983
Signed critical essays on English-language authors of fiction, poetry, and drama for
children, arranged alphabetically, Kirkpatrick's book provides information on the
life and works of major writers internationally.

Robert LEESON

Reading and Righting (Collins) 1985
The author of *The Third Class Genie* (Collins, 1981) and *Grange Hill Rules – OK?*
(Fontana, 1980) assess the political, social and educational influences on children's
reading and children's literature, past, present and future.

Margaret R MARSHALL

An Introduction to the World of Children's Books (Gower, 2nd edition) 1987
Intended for people new to the subject, the book draws together themes usually
separated in books – contemporary trends in publishing, the book trade, children's
reading interests, criteria, guidance and an international viewpoint.

John Rowe TOWNSEND

Written for Children (Penguin, 3rd edition) 1987
A good paperback survey and assessment of the development of children's literature.

POETRY

English poetry is one of the great literary traditions of the world. The selection here is an attempt to choose, from the perspective of 1990, a library of British poetry that would give the general reader varied enjoyment, an awareness of the range and significance of our poetry, and an understanding of its historical development.

Each part of this definition of aim is troublesome. First, the perspective of 1990 or 2090 may be radically different. The prominence of Donne and the Metaphysical poets in our contemporary assessments may be as startling to future generations as our misgivings about some of the great Victorians or as Donne's nineteenth century eclipse is to us. Additionally, we must recognize that our 1990 sense of the corpus of English poetry is partly determined by the work of contemporary poets. Their preoccupations and techniques place in the foreground particular aspects of the tradition. For example, the way in which Seamus Heaney's *North* (1975) confirmed Wordsworth and Yeats as living influences or the slight, but complex, difference made to an understanding of the Metaphysicals by a reading of Craig Raine's poetry.

Secondly, 'British' has been construed to include not only a handful of writers in Scotland, but also Irish poets who wrote in English and a small number of the nineteenth and twentieth century American writers whose work is an indispensable part of the canon of English poetry read (and taught) on this side of the Atlantic. The claims for inclusion in the library of some of the latter are reinforced by periods of residence in England.

Thirdly, there is no such thing as a 'general' or a 'common' reader. Every individual's taste is based on experience and personality. Most people who read poetry will develop specialist interests on one hand and leave large gaps in their reading on the other. The writers included here are selected on the basis of those who are personally valued and supplemented by those whose importance cannot be denied.

Fourthly, 'enjoyment' is a term that can slip easily between discriminating appreciation and rank hedonism. Its merit is that it allows a catholic list that will give the general reader moments of unbuttoned pleasure in the company of Calverley or Betjeman that would be denied him by unambiguous reliance on a strict criterion and a searching scrutiny. It is nearer the mark to say that great poetry has the power to excite the feelings, the imagination or the intellect of the reader.

108

The resulting selection has produced a list of poets which can be variously classified as *germs, touchstones, representatives, links* or *isolated peaks*. The *germs* have influenced other poets, of their own times or of ours. The *touchstones* are poems in their way perfect, a standard by which other similar, productions are to be judged. The *representatives*, while making no decisively original contribution, are important for embodying the interests, merits (and limitations) of their age; and the *links* are the means by which we get from one mountain peak to the next. Finally *isolated peaks* are poems of some length and distinction from authors who wrote little else that is memorable and which cannot, because of their length, be adequately represented by excerpts in anthologies. From a general view the inclusion of every name in this list can be justified by one or more of the above criteria, but any individual reader may find some who do not measure to any of these criteria, or some who do but are absent.

A particular difficulty in this poetry section is that, whereas in most other sections of this *Library* the annotations to the entries can usefully describe a particular work, books of verse do not invite this treatment. However, in some cases specific poems are mentioned in the annotations which are either central to the poet's achievement or an illuminating introduction to it.

A further challenge is to strike a balance between individual poets and anthologies of poets. There are, perhaps, some forty standard poets whose works a reader might wish to have on the shelf either complete or in generous selection; to this can be added another twenty or so which are personal favourites of different types of reader. But there are many poets whose work may be adequately gauged in anthologies, including the authors of celebrated individual poems like Rupert Brooke, or Arthur Clough or G K Chesterton.

Books of poetry are among those few books which Bacon said are 'to be chewed and digested'. They read well when they look well, when a 'neat rivulet of text shall meander through a meadow of margin'. The first recommendation as to any edition is therefore on the basis of an attractive handbook to permanent reference, but where available a paperback edition is also mentioned. Secondly, single-volume selections have been chosen if the collected works comprise of more than one volume. Except for the one or two early texts, attractive lay-outs have been chosen in preference to scholarly annotation.

Finally, a personal observation about two classes of poets; a classification which gives rise to both a hope and a fear. *Class I is the accessible*: Chaucer, Henryson, Spenser, Milton, Dryden, Tennyson. They tell stories and express ideas rather than registering complicated states of mind. They write at greater length than those in Class II, often in a more relaxed way, and are much simpler to understand at every level, although they can only be fully understood with reference to their contemporary systems of thought. The irony is likely to be incidental and evident rather than central and baffling. *Class II is the difficult*: Wyatt, Donne, Marvell, Hopkins, Eliot, Yeats. Their poems tend to be short, intense and complex in tone, diction, syntax, content or allusion. They require the close reading and, in some cases, moral earnestness associated with I A Richards, F R Leavis, William Empson and other Cambridge critics and with American New Critics such as Cleanth Brooks. Their poems are ideally suited to the hour-long seminar because although they are short, there is much to be unpacked, much to disagree over and much to enable the critic to display his cleverness and sensitivity.

The hope is that, as critical methods are developed which permit attention to larger structures and to social meanings, the tyranny of 'the teachable poem' will be ended. When that happens, the general reader will come into his or her own and it may become possible for modern poets to do what is now, notoriously, impossible: write long poems.

The fear is that the critical methodologies of structuralism, deconstructionism and Marxism will drive even bigger wedges between professional critics and general readers, the dying life of pure mind and the living death of pure pleasure.

ANTHOLOGIES

Al ALVAREZ

The New Poetry (Penguin)
First published in 1962 this influential anthology represented 'British poets who began to come into their own in the fifties'. The anthology's aim 'Beyond the Gentility Principle', is to exalt the energy characteristic of Ted Hughes rather than the tamer virtues of the Movement poets.

Kingsley AMIS

The New Oxford Book of Light Verse (OUP)
This anthology aims 'to raise a good-natured smile'. It covers a lot of ground and has a very interesting introduction.

W H AUDEN and N H PEARSON

Poets of the English Language (Penguin)
Vol. I   Langland to Spenser
Vol. II   Marlowe to Marvell
Vol. III   Milton to Goldsmith
Vol. IV   Blake to Poe
Vol. V   Tennyson to Yeats
Each volume contains about 700 pages, which is long enough to give an appropriate taste of both major and minor figures. It is probably the best anthology of its kind but at the moment only volumes II and IV are in print.

T CLAYTON

The Cavalier Poets (OUP)
A valuable anthology for those attracted to these graceful, witty, occasionally licentious poets, Herrick, Carew, Suckling and Lovelace, but who do not wish to buy the complete works of each.

V H COLLINS

A Book of Narrative Verse (OUP)
A wide range of comfortingly traditional material from some of the Canterbury Tales to Alfred Noyes's 'The Highwayman'.

B GARDNER

Up the Line to Death: The War Poets 1914–18 (Methuen), *The Terrible Rain: The War Poets 1939–45* (Methuen)
Two anthologies of verse from the two World Wars. Excellent selections, providing an insight into the different views of war poets; sentimental, intensely sad and moving, even humourous verse is included here.

Helen GARDNER

New Oxford Books of English Verse 1250–1950 (OUP)
Anyone buying all the other anthologies recommended here will not need this one.
For readers with more limited purses this is an indispensable book.

H J C GRIERSON

Metaphysical Poetry: Donne to Butler (OUP)
First published in 1921, this anthology was a major influence on the Modern
Movement in poetry and on a generation of critics. It remains, with Grierson's
lengthy introduction, an excellent approach to the metaphysicals.

G GRIGSON

The Oxford Book of Satirical Verse (OUP)
The heart of this anthology is, inevitably, the period from Dryden to Johnson.
Grigson does his best to give the nineteenth and twentieth centuries a decent showing.

Seamus HEANEY and Ted HUGHES

The Rattle Bag: an anthology of poetry (Faber)
This splendid anthology is included for the general readers as well as for their teenage
children. The poems are arranged in alphabetical order of first line or title so that each
takes its own chances in the world. The range is enormous and includes poems from
oral cultures as well as traditional favourites. Modern poetry is strongly represented.

P JONES

Imagist Poetry (Penguin)
A fine collection of the work of T E Hulme, H D, D H Lawrence, Amy Lowell, Ezra
Pound and others, arranged so as to form, with the introduction and extracts from
letters and manifestoes, the history of a vital aspect of the Modern Movement in
poetry.

J KINGSLEY

The Oxford Book of Ballads (OUP)
An anthology of 150 traditional ballads of Scotland and England with tunes. Kingsley
tried to get back beyond literary 'mending' to the oral tradition.

Philip LARKIN

The Oxford Book of 20th Century English Verse (OUP)
This anthology, published in 1973, deliberately favours poems that are short,
comprehensible, rational, crafted and felt. Hardy stands first because of the
chronological ordering but no doubt Larkin was pleased to give him primacy.

B D Wyndham LEWIS and Charles LEE

The Stuffed Owl (Everyman)
This was the pioneer *Anthology of Bad Verse*. How the mighty are fallen, Keats lying side by side with Cornelius Whur. The title is from a sonnet of Wordsworth, who is one of the book's heroes.

Roger LONSDALE

New Oxford Book of 18th Century Verse (OUP)
Published in 1984, but already this looks like widening our vision of eighteenth century poetry, giving an earthly context for the familiar satire.

Blake MORRISON and Andrew MOTION

The Penguin Book of Contemporary British Poetry (Penguin)
Published in 1982 this anthology aims to mark a 'decisive shift of sensibility' since Alvarez's *New Poetry*. It includes no poets from that book or from an older generation, and it favours the group of Northern Ireland poets and Martian School of poetry associated with Craig Raine. It prefers linguistic craftsmanship to 'walking naked' and deliberately gives pride of place to Seamus Heaney.

F T PALGRAVE

The Golden Treasury of Songs and Lyrics with a 5th book selected by J Press (OUP)
This is the standard nineteenth century (1861) anthology. Still a delight, though modern tastes are very different.

J REEVES and M SEYMOUR-SMITH

A New Canon of English Poetry (Barnes & Noble)
This anthology aims 'to offer a substantial body of poems, mostly short, both English and American, which deserve to rank in the canon' but are not in 'oxgrave' (the *Oxford Book of English Verse* and Palgrave's *Golden Treasury*). Apart from the editors' admiration for Trumbull Stickney this aim is fulfilled.

R SKELTON

Poetry of the Thirties (Penguin), *Poetry of the Forties* (Penguin)
The thematic arrangement is artificial but the flavour of the period comes over strongly. 'Even before they were quite new, the thirties took on the appearance of a myth'.

M R TURNER

Parlour Poetry (Michael Joseph)
'101 Improving Gems' for recitation by the kind of well-brought up Victorian child who, playing up and playing the game, standing on the burning deck and being wrecked in the 'Hesperus', would himself have experienced not Christmas Day in the Workhouse but a breathless hush in the Close.

WAVELL, Lord Archibald Percival

Other Men's Flowers (Cape)
The classic anthology 'to go with thee, and by thy guide, In thy most need to go by thy side' compiled by the Field Marshall and penultimate Viceroy of India.

F WOODS

The Oxford Book of English Traditional Verse (OUP)
'A genre that ranges from the high drama of the classic ballads to the more unassuming but revealing minor songs'.

INDIVIDUAL POETS

Matthew ARNOLD (1822–88)

Poetical Words (ed. Tinker et al., OUP)
Arnold's best poetry is distinguished by the high seriousness of its themes (the crumbling of accepted values, as in 'Dover Beach' and 'The Scholar Gipsy'), of its subject matter (the unwitting slaying of his own son, Sohrab, by the Persian warrior, Rustum, in *Sohrab and Rustum*) and of its emotions (as in the sequence, 'Switzerland', about his unconsummated passion for Marguerite).

John ASHBERY (1927–)

Self-Portrait in a Convex Mirror (Carcanet)
Ashbery is a difficult, allusive, discursive poet whose work has articulated, for many critics at least, the pain of living in an unknowable world. Perhaps his most influential poem has been 'Self Portrait in a Convex Mirror'.

W H AUDEN (1907–73)

Collected Poems (Faber)
Auden's poetry was open to many of the intellectual and political influences of the middle years of this century. It is distinguished by intelligence, wit, metrical subtlety and variety of subject matter and treatment. Too cool and casual for some tastes, the best poems speak from real emotion and the experience of his particular age like the love poems ('Lay Your Sleeping Head, My Love', 'O Tell Me the Truth About Love') and the subsequently rejected 'September 1st 1939', – which is not in this collection – or the fine elegy for Yeats.

William BARNES (1801–86)

The Dorset Poet (ed. C Wrigley, Dovecote Press)
Poems of Rural Life in the Dorset Dialect is precisely that. Barnes's work is metrically subtle and was a great influence on Hopkins and Hardy.

Hillaire BELLOC (1870–1953)

Cautionary Tales (Duckworth)
The light verse of the Cautionary Tales – Lord Lundy and his friends – will last for a good while yet.

The BEOWULF POET (c. 750)

Beowulf (ed. M Swinton, Everyman) Text with facing prose translations
The greatest of Old English poems tells the story of Beowulf. The monsters, Grendel and his den, devour the Danes who sleep in the court of Hrothgar at Heorot. Beowulf slays them and, years later, is himself killed by a monster. Much of the poem's power lies in the conflict between the kindness and courtesy of Heorot and the unreasoning evil of the monsters.

Sir John BETJEMAN (1906–84)

Collected Poems (Murray)
Betjeman's love of English people, English places, English buildings and the felicitous comprehensibility of his verse made him an ideal choice as Poet Laureate. His mood runs from light occasional through satirical to nostalgic and compassionate.

William BLAKE (1757–1827)

Complete Writings of William Blake (ed. Geoffrey Keynes, OUP)
Songs of Innocence and of Experience, two groups of lyrics 'shewing the Two Contrary states of the Human Soul', radiant childhood and repressed adulthood, have an unique visionary intensity. Blake illustrated the poems himself. They contain some of the best lyrics in the language ('The Lamb', 'The Tyger', 'The Sun Rise'). The later, longer poems are full of allegory and elaborate symbolism and require the dedication and moral earnestness associated with F R Leavis for the reader to extract full meaning and enjoyment. Longer, even more complex, are the 'Prophetic Books' including *Urizen* and *Visions of the Daughters of Albion* which develop Blake's very personal vision of the state of the human condition.

Robert BRIDGES (1844–1930)

The Shorter Poems (OUP)
Selected Poems (OUP)
Bridges wrote a number of fine short poems (such as 'Low Barometer' and 'Awake, My Heart') and an intermittently excellent long poem, *The Testament of Beauty*. He experimented, not always fortunately, with classical metre.

Emily BRONTE (1818–48)

Poems by the Bronte Sisters (OUP)
Emily wrote 193 poems. Some of them, like the famous 'No Coward Soul is Mine' are as compelling and expressive as *Wuthering Heights*.

Elizabeth Barrett BROWNING (1806–61)

Selected Poems (ed. Malcolm Hicks, Fyfield, 1983)
The best of her work is in the sequence of *44 Sonnets from the Portuguese* celebrating her love for her husband, Robert.

Robert BROWNING, (1812–89)

Poeticals 1833–64 (ed. Ian Jack, OUP)
Browning's greatest contribution both in itself and in its influence (Eliot's 'Prufrock', Pound's 'Hugh Selwyn Mauberley') was the development of the dramatic monologue. Among the best are 'My Last Duchess', 'Fra Lippo Lippi', 'Audrea del Sarto', 'Bishop Blougram's Apology', 'How it Strikes a Contemporary'. He is remarkable also for his insight into the feelings of men and women in and out of love ('Two in the Campagna', 'Any Wife to Any Husband' etc.). Fashion and the poetry's own faults have diminished Browning's reputation, but there is much enjoyment to be had in his best work.

Basil BUNTING (1900–85)

Collected Poems (OUP)
Bunting is at once English and Internationalist, deeply influenced by his Northumbrian background, by the symbolists and by writers he knew, above all Pound. His finest work is *Briggflatts*, a kind of autobiography in five (musical) movements.

Robert BURNS (1759–96)

Poems and Songs (ed. James Kingsley, OUP)
Burns is at his best, whether in social satire (e.g. 'Holy Willie's Prayer') or in love songs (e.g. 'Corn Riggs', 'John Anderson', 'My Jo'), when he writes in Scots. Burns Night Suppers remind us that his poetry has helped to define Scottishness.

George Gordon, Lord BYRON (1788–1824)

Poetical Works (OUP)
A relatively small amount of Byron's work has filtered through the notoriety of his life and death. His robustness can often flatten into coarseness, but he wrote some exquisite lyrics ('She Walks in Beauty Like the Night', 'So We'll Go No More a Roving'), several long satiric and comic poems (*The Vision of Judgement, Don Juan, Beppo*), and one thrilling poem about a Byronic hero *(Childe Harold's Pilgrimmage)*.

Charles Stuart CALVERLEY (1831–84)

The English Poems (ed. H D Spear, Leicester UP)
Calverley is one of the great parodists in English. *The Cock and the Bull*, a brilliant parody of Browning's *The Ring and the Book*, is a good place to start.

Thomas CAMPBELL (1777–1844)

Complete Poetical Works (ed. J L B Robertson, Haskell House Publishers, US)
Campbell is not a great poet nor indeed was he influential. But, as the author of 'Ye Mariners of England', 'Hohenlinden', 'The Battle of the Baltic' and 'Lord Ullin's Daughter', he has made an indelible mark.

Thomas CAMPION (1567–1620)

Ayres and Observations, Selected Poems and Prose (ed. J Hart, Carcanet)
Campion's poems and lute songs are, in their kind, perfect. He is inventive and self-assured. His finest poems include 'Follow your Saint', 'When Thou Must Home', 'Thrice Toss These Oaken in the Air' and 'Sleep, Angry Beauty'.

Thomas CAREW (c. 1595–1640)

Poems with his Masque 'Coelum Britannicum' (ed. Rhodes Dunlap, OUP)
Carew was one of the many very talented poets at the court of Charles II. 'An Elegie upon the death of the Deane of Pauls, Dr John Donne' is a moving tribute, not least because it is also acute literary criticism. He also wrote some fine love poetry.

Lewis CARROLL (Charles Lutwidge Dodgson) (1832–98)

The *Alice* books contain excellent nonsense, fantasy and parodic poems: 'You Are Old, Father William', 'How Doth the Little Crocodile', 'Jabberwocky'. 'The Hunting of the Snark' is a later, darker nonsense ballad.

George CHAPMAN (c. 1559–1634)

Selected Poems (ed. W L Phelps, Unwin)
Chapman rightly described his translations of the *Iliad* and the *Odyssey* as 'the Works that I was borne to doe'. One may also dip with profit into allegorical poems such as 'The Shadow of Night' and 'Orid's Banquet of Sense'.

Thomas CHATTERTON (1752–70)

Poems Supposed to Have Been Written at Bristol by Thomas Rowley (Gregg)
'The marvellous boy' imitated many styles of English poetry, notably from the
fifteenth century, in work he attributed to a Bristol priest, Thomas Rowley. His work
is of little intrinsic merit but the pastiche is dazzling and, as a sport, it will survive.

Geoffrey CHAUCER (c. 1340–1400)

Works of Geoffrey Chaucer (ed. F N Robinson, OUP)
Chaucer's two greatest works, *Troylus and Cryseyde* and *The Canterbury Tales*,
establish him as one of the supreme English poets in their narrative sweep,
psychological insight, social understanding and complexity of tone. Among the best
of the Tales are those of the Franklin, the Nun's Priest, the Knight and the Pardoner,
while the Wife of Bath is one of the great comic characters of English fiction. In
Troylus and Cryseyde the night of love in Pandarus's house (Book III) is just one
example of the sensitivity of which Chaucer was capable, and there are many other
passages which can be read without any great difficulty with the language.

John CLARE (1739–1864)

Selected Poems and Prose of John Clare (ed. Eric Robinson and Geoffrey
Summerfield, OUP)
Clare's poems are remarkable for their observation of the most detailed sights and
sounds of the English countryside. He continued to write even during the
twenty-seven years he spent in lunatic asylums; his most powerful poems (such as 'I
am') spring from his madness.

Samuel Taylor COLERIDGE (1772–1834)

Poems (OUP)
Coleridge, with his manifold interests and influences was 'one of the two great
seminal minds of the England of their age' (John Stuart Mill). As a poet, his
contribution to the epoch-forming collection of poems by himself and Wordsworth,
Lyrical Ballads, was directed 'to persons and characters supernatural or at least
romantic'. But 'The Rime of the Ancient Mariner' will move the most prosaic
rationalist with its visionary story of a soul in agony expressed in direct ballad form.
Other excellent poems are the opium-influenced 'Khubla Khan', the beautiful 'Frost
at Midnight' and the unfinished Christabel. 'Dejection: an Ode' is a record of his
personal unhappiness.

William COLLINS (1721–59)

Poems (ed. R Lonsdale, Everyman)
Collins wrote a few fine odes in the pastoral tradition or expressing his melancholia:
'Ode to Evening', 'Ode to Fear' and 'Ode on the Poetical Character'.

Abraham COWLEY (1618–67)

Poetry and Prose (ed. L C Martin, OUP)
Cowley is a polished, if unmoving, imitator, notably of Donne, sometimes of Jonson. He is of interest because he is, in sensibility, at once the last of the Metaphysicals and a forerunner of the Age of Enlightenment.

William COWPER (1731–1800)

Choice of Verse (ed. N Nicholson, Faber)
The jog-trot insipidity of 'The Diverting History of John Gilpin' is a less reliable guide to Cowper's real merits than is the luminous riddling of the hymn 'God Moves in a Mysterious Way'. Cowper was 'a stricken deer', afflicted by melancholia and madness, and seriousness is evident in all his finest work (e.g. 'The Task', 'The Castaway', 'Epitaph on a Hare', 'Yardley Oak').

George CRABBE (1754–1832)

Selection (ed. John Lucas, Longman)
Crabbe, who was a clergyman, describes the miseries and characters of his parishioners in poems such as 'The Village' and 'The Borough', a series of twenty-four verse letters, of which the best are perhaps those of 'The Parish Clerk', 'Peter Grimes' and 'Blaney'. His narrative methods influenced Victorian novelists.

Richard CRASHAW (1613–49)

The Poems (ed. L C Martin, OUP)
Crashaw became an ardent convert to Catholicism and spent the last years of his life in Rome. His poems are passionate, extravagant and baroque in spirit; 'Hymn to Saint Teresa' is typical.

E E CUMMINGS (1894–1962)

Selected Poems 1923–58 (Faber)
Cummings is significant for his assault, for expressive effect, on typographical conventions. His poems, from the collection *XLI* onwards, are witty and enjoyable while reflecting all the discords of the age.

Donald DAVIE (1922–)

Collected Poems 1950–70 (Routledge)
Collected Poems 1970–83 (Carcanet)
Davie is an outstanding critic and a gifted poet. Since his move to America his early elegant and precise poems have loosened up in various ways.

Emily DICKINSON (1830–86)

Complete Poems (ed. T H Johnson, Faber)
Her characteristic poems are brief, rapt versions of some moment of experience or of
some idea, and they are oddly expressive in diction and syntax. Her intensity and
honest oddity have made her influential and admired in our own times.

John DONNE (1572–1631)

Complete English Poems (ed. A J Smith, Penguin)
Donne was obsessed with physical love and with death. Hardly an English poet of the
first half of the seventeenth century was uninfluenced by some aspect of Donne's
style with its dramatic openings, witty images, frequently colloquial tone,
conversational rhythms, and awareness of variety in experience and in ideas. Because
of the necessary obscurity of some of his metaphors and references, the individual
poems are too often anaesthetized upon the table for student dissection.

Gavin DOUGLAS (c. 1474–1522)

Virgil's Aeneid *translated in Scottish Verse* (ed. D F Coldwell, Blackwood)
Douglas translated the twelve books of Virgil's *Aeneid* and added an original
Prologue to each. The Prologues ranged from discussions of his literary aims to
astonishingly fresh nature poetry. Ezra Pound thought the translation better than the
original. A modern reader would have no more difficulty with Douglas's Middle
Scots than with Chaucer's Middle English.

Keith DOUGLAS (1920–44)

Complete Poems (ed. Desmond Graham, OUP)
The most talented of the poets of the Second World War, Douglas combined technical
accomplishment and fluency with great honesty.

Ernest DOWSON (1867–1900)

Poems (ed. Desmond Flower, Cassell)
While much of Dowson is world-weary, *fin-de-siécle* preciousness, his best lyrics
have great beauty of sound and honesty of sentiment e.g. 'Vitae Summa Brevis'
('They are not long, the days of wine and roses').

Michael DRAYTON (1563–1631)

Selected Poems (ed. Vivien Thomas, Carcanet)
Drayton is one of the most varied and accomplished of the Elizabethan poets. He is at
his best in the sonnet sequence *Idea* (which includes 'Since there's no help, come let
us kiss and part'); other works worth dipping into include *Polyolbion* and *England's
Heroicall Epistles* (verse letters exchanged by historical lovers).

Liam DRUMMOND, Laird of Hawthornden (1585–1649)

Poems and Prose (ed. R H MacDonald, Scottish Academic Press)
Drummond established the new Renaissance (Italian) forms in Scottish poetry. He wrote a fine Petrarchan sonnet sequence (on the death of the woman to whom he was engaged) as well as other works of a religious and satirical character.

John DRYDEN (1631–1700)

Poems and Fables of John Dryden (ed. James Kinsley, OUP)
Dryden, the greatest poet of the late seventeenth century, is at his most accessible in *MacFlecknoe*, a robust satire on a contemporary poet, and in the incisive character portraits of Charles II, Buckingham, Shaftsbury, Monmouth etc. in his political satire, *Absalom and Achitophel*. His translations of Virgil are, arguably, the finest in the language.

T S ELIOT (1888–1965)

Collected Poems 1909–62 (Faber)
Eliot is one of the key figures for the understanding of English poetry in this century. Early doubt and humour ('The Love Song of J Alfred Prufrock') darkened into tragic despair ('Gerontian') and into the fragmented, meaningless world of 'The Waste Land' and 'The Hollow Men'. A growing religious conviction signalled by the ever-popular 'The Journey of the Magi' lead to high Anglican certainties, more or less provisional, of *Four Quartets*. It is in the nature of our times that the poet, critic, dramatist and publisher should be most widely known as the unintentional lyricist of a hit musical: *Cats* is the 1980s show built around his pre-war book of children's poems, *Old Possum's Book of Practical Cats*.

Edward FITZGERALD (1809–83)

Selected Works (ed. Joanne Richardson, Hart-Davis)
Rubaiyat of Omar Khayyam is a free translation of the work of a Suni mystic of the eleventh century. Fitzgerald memorably transforms the original into a bitter attack on God and a defence of hedonism.

Robert FROST (1874–1963)

Selected Poems (ed. Ian Hamilton, Penguin)
Frost's carefully casual manner and gnomic wisdom are not to every taste but in many poems (e.g. 'Birches', 'The Death of the Hired Man', 'After Apple-Picking', 'Mending Wall') he creates memorable and resonant scenes. His period in England from 1912 to 1915 enabled him to get his first two books published and to influence, among others, Edward Thomas.

Roy FULLER (1912–)

Individual and His Times, A Selection of the Poetry of Roy Fuller (ed. V J Lee, Athlone)
Fuller is a skilful poet who has treated a largely traditional subject matter (the individual's fears and problems) with elegance and accuracy.

David GASCOGNE (1916–)

Collected Poems (ed. R Skelton, OUP)
Gascogne's finest work is probably contained in *Poems 1937–42*. His best poems are surrealist, intense and rhapsodic, a contrast to much poetry written at the time.

The GAWAIN POET (c. 1350–1400)

Sir Gawain and the Green Knight (ed. W R J Barron, Manchester UP)
This edition has old-spelling text with facing prose translation. The alliterative poem, written in a Cheshire dialect, tells the story of Gawain's response to the challenge of the Green Knight and his seduction by the Knight's lady. The poem wonderfully captures both the desolation in the forest and the delights in court and castle.

Allen GINSBERG (1926–)

First Blues: Rags, Ballads and Harmonium Songs (Full Court Press, U S)
Ginsberg's poetry is marked by syntactical ellipsis and by variety in register and line-lengths. In scope and energy, at least, it is like Whitman's poetry. With Kerouac he helped to create and define the Beat Generation.

Oliver GOLDSMITH (1728–74)

Poems and Plays (ed. Tom Davis, Everyman)
Goldsmith's major achievement in poetry was *The Deserted Village*, inspired by the action of a landowner who moved a whole village in order to undertake some landscaping. Goldsmith's social criticism is all the more effective for the calm tone of much of his writing.

John GOWER (c. 1330–1408)

Selected Poetry (ed. J A W Bennett, OUP)
Confessio Amantis is a poem of over 30,000 lines in octosyllabic rhymed couplets. The frame of the story provides a setting for tales, many of them touching, about people who have been deceived in love.

Robert GRAVES (1895–1985)

Collected Poems (Cassell)
The most prolific love poet of recent times, Graves combines intensity, strangeness and verbal felicity. His poems are influenced by his profound understanding of myth.

Thomas GRAY (1716–71)

Selected Poems (ed. A Johnson, E Arnold)
Dr Johnson said of Gray's 'Elegy Written in a Country Churchyard' that it 'abounds with images which find a mirror in every mind, and with sentiments to which every bosom returns an echo'. This could equally be said of the handful of poems on which his fame rests, such as 'Ode on a Distant Prospect of Eton College' and 'The Progress of Poetry'.

Sir Fulke GREVILE (1554–1628)

Selected Writings (ed. Joan Rees, Athlone)
Greville is the author of a powerful sequence of poems, *Caelica*, about love, religion and politics. There is fine verse too, in his play *Mustapha*, notably the much anthologized chorus of priests: 'Oh Wearisome Condition of Humanity!'.

Thom(son) GUNN (1929–)

Selected Poems 1950–75 (Faber)
Gunn moved from England to San Francisco in 1954. His subject matter, the mind's relation with the body and the individual's relation with the world, has had different pretexts, just as his technique has evolved from constraint to apparent freedom.

Thomas HARDY (1840–1928)

Complete Poems (Macmillan)
Hardy is one of the few 'double firsts' in English literature: he is in the front rank as both a novelist and poet. Whether serious or humorous, his poems often have complex and haunting rhythms, and they combine in a remarkable way idiosyncracy of phrasing with an ear for the speech of the people. The Wessex country life gives both a precision and an universality to the emotion in many of the best poems such as 'Channel Firing', 'Wessex Heights' and 'Afterwards'. *Poems 1912–13*, written after the death of his first wife, expresses, like much of his verse, an intensely moving agony at the thought of missed opportunities.

Seamus HEANEY (1939–)

North (Faber)
Selected Poems (Faber)
Described as 'the best Irish poet since Yeats', Heaney displays insight, intelligence and intensity in finely wrought poems.

Robert HENRYSON (c. 1430–1506)

Poems (ed. Charles Elliott, OUP)
Selected Poems (ed. Barron Ray, Carcanet)
Henryson was the greatest of the 'Scottish Chaucerians' and in some ways the greatest of Scottish poets. His finest poems include *The Testament of Cresseid* and *The Moral Fables of Aesop in Eloquent and Ornate Scottish Metre*.

George HERBERT (1593–1633)

English Poems (ed. C A Patrides, Everyman)
The Temple is the collection of poems on which Herbert's reputation rests. In its significant arrangement, its careful choice of titles, its variety of stanza form, its delight in verbal adroitness coupled with a yearning for simple sincerity and its religious feeling, deep but unfrenzied, this is a profoundly moving volume.

Robert HERRICK (1591–1674)

Selected Poems (ed. David Jesson-Dibley, Carcanet)
Herrick's poetry combines acute responsiveness to sensuousness, often erotic, and beauty with sense of morality. His poems often have song-like rhythms.

Geoffrey HILL (1932–)

King Log (Deutsch)
Mercian Hymns (Deutsch)
Hill's poetry sets modern anguishes in historical and mythical contexts (the Wars of the Roses, Offa's Mercia). It is difficult, allusive, tightly organized, and rewarding. The *Collected Poems* are available in a Penguin edition.

Thomas HOOD (1799–1845)

Hood Winked, Poems by Thomas Hood (Chatto)
Hood wrote comic ballads full of incongruities in subject and rhymes and, above all, full of puns. In 'The Song of the Shirt' and 'The Bridge of Sighs' he turned those gifts, with great popular success, to social protest.

Gerard Manley HOPKINS (1844–89)

Poems (ed. W H Gardner and N H Mackenzie, OUP)
Hopkins was a Jesuit priest who made his poems out of his loving quarrel with God. They are marked by thrilling technical innovations (sprung rhythm, dense alliteration, compression of syntax) as well as by terrifying senses of ecstasy, urgency and despair. 'Pied Beauty', 'The Windhover', 'Binsey Poplars', 'Spring and Fall': these short poems might be read before 'The Wreck of the Deutschland'. Perhaps most moving are the last poems written in frustration, exile and near-collapse of faith.

A E HOUSMAN (1859–1936)

Collected Poems (Cape)
In *A Shropshire Lad* and two other volumes, Housman expressed, in occasionally deeply thrilling verse, banal thoughts about misery and hopelessness and loss: 'The land of lost content', 'Those blue remembered hills'.

Ted HUGHES (1930–)

Selected Poems 1957–1981 (Faber)
Hughes was the rather unexpected choice as Poet Laureate in succession to John Betjeman. He is the poet of animal violence and of the bleakness of impersonal Nature. Whatever the subject, his verse has energy, seen at its most effective when it is controlled, as in the admirable 'Hawk Roosting'.

Samuel JOHNSON (1709–84)

Complete English Poems (ed. J D Fleeman, Penguin)
Johnson's greatest poem is 'The Vanity of Human Wishes' based on the Tenth Satire of Juvenal, a powerful statement of the value of Christian stoicism in the face of universal adversity, while 'London' is a condemnation of metropolitan society in Sir Robert Walpole's time.

David JONES (1895–1974)

Anathemata (Faber)
The *Anathemata* celebrates the history of Britain from the earliest times to the Anglo-Saxon settlement and also deals with such great themes as incarnation and salvation. Its allusive techniques derive from Eliot and Pound. All of Jones's work refracts the past to illuminate the present, obliquely and powerfully.

Ben(jamin) JONSON (1572–1637)

Poems (ed. G B Johnston, Routledge)
Some of Jonson's greatest poetry is to be found in his plays (e.g. the sensuous speeches of Sir Epicure Mammon in *The Alchemist* and of Volpone in his attempt to seduce Calian), but he wrote many fine poems ranging from the moving sonnet on the death of his son ('Farewell, Thou Child of My Right Hand ...') to the praise of the aristocratic tradition in 'To Penshurst'.

John KEATS (1795–1821)

Complete Poems (ed. Miriam Allott, Longman)
Between October 1818 and October 1819 Keats wrote 'Lamia', 'Isabella', *The Eve of St Agnes*, 'Hyperion', 'La Belle Dame Sans Merci' and the great Odes. These poems unite an astonishing sensuous vitality with an awareness of the deepest issues about creativity, art and love. Too often force-fed to school-chidren, they should be read for enjoyment.

Henry KING (1595–1669)

Poems (ed. J Baker, Denver)
King was a bishop and a friend of Donne. His elegy to his wife, 'An Exequy to his Matchlesse never to be forgotten Friend', is deeply moving. He also wrote some effective satirical verse and some very attractive love poems.

Rudyard KIPLING (1865–1936)

Choice of Verse (ed. T S Eliot, Faber)
Kipling wrote in a wide variety of popular forms – ballad, hymn, dramatic monologue – and few writers have as many of their lines and tags in general usage. At its best, it is poetry not verse: 'Danny Deaver', 'McAndrews Hymn', 'Gethsemane'. New readers will be surpised how often the sentiment is anti-establishment rather than jingoistic.

Walter Savage LANDOR (1775–1864)

Poems (ed. Geoffrey Grigson, Centaur)
Landor is a minor poet, but some of his epitaphs and epigrams are, of their kind, perfect. He has been much admired by other poets, notably Pound and Yeats.

John LANGHORNE (1735–79)

Poetical Works (Gregg)
Langhorne is a minor poet but it is well worth reading 'The Country Justice' to see how deep is the continuity between the eighteenth century and Wordsworth's character portraits. Wordsworth described it as 'the first poem ... that fairly brought the Muse into the company of common life'.

William LANGLAND (c. 1332–1400)

Piers Plowman (ed. A V C Schmidt, Everyman)
Piers Plowman, read in the B-Text, is a poem of over 7000 lines which, in a series of dream-visions, condemns the iniquities of a world rooted in money, and asks what we must do to be saved. Its greatest passages, e.g. the Harrowing of Hell and the Coming of Antichrist, have tremendous power. This edition has old spelling but modern letters with word meanings at the end of the lines.

Philip LARKIN (1922–86)

Whitsun Weddings (Faber)
Collected Poems (ed. Anthony Thwaite, Faber)
Larkin's three principal collections (*The Less Deceived, Whitsun Weddings* and *High Windows*) defined the attitudes of a generation: the sense of small aspirations and small achievements. At its best (as in such piercing lyrics as 'Coming', 'Going', 'Days') his verse escapes these limitations.

David Herbert LAWRENCE (1885–1930)

Complete Poems (ed. V de Sola Pinto and F W Roberts, Penguin)
In free verse Lawrence found an ideal form for the expression of his delightful and sensitive apprehension of life and of the natural world. This is displayed in such poems as 'Snake', 'Kangaroo' and 'The Mountain Lion', where Lawrence the preacher is subservient to Lawrence the artist.

Sir David LINDSAY (c. 1490–1555)

Poems (ed. Maurice Lindsay, Everyman)
Lindsay was a widely popular and powerful poet. His reputation today rests on *Ane Pleasant Satyre of the Thrie Estatis*, a morality play in verse, depicting typical contemporary villains.

Henry Wadsworth LONGFELLOW (1807–82)

Poetical Works (OUP)
'Evangeline', 'The Wreck of the Hesperus', 'Excelsior', 'The Song of Hiawatha': Longfellow combined jog-trot metre with emotional uplift in a way that proved irresistible in his own time and, in some quarters, ever since.

Richard LOVELACE (1618–58)

The Poems (ed. G B Wilkinson, OUP)
Lovelace was a Cavalier poet. His best poems (e.g. 'Lucaster, Going to the Warres' and 'Gratiana Dancing and Singing') are not only light and graceful in manner but represent a perfect balancing of widely different tones or of complex subject matter.

Robert LOWELL (1917–77)

Poems: A Selection (ed. J Raban, Faber)
Lowell's work reflects tensions and problems of an exceptional and disturbed individual. Between the magnificent rhetoric of the early poems (such as 'The Quaker Graveyard in Nantucket') and the loosely structured, later collections of verse that attempt to find order and to celebrate domestic life ('Notebook', 'For Lizzie and Harriet', 'The Dolphin'), there were the profoundly influential autobiographical 'confessional' poems included in 'Life Studies', 'For the Union Dead' and 'Near the Ocean'. An American, some of the best poems draw directly on the New England people and places, such as the Boston Common Monument in 'For the Union Dead'.

Norman MacCAIG (1910–)

Old Maps and New: Selected Poems (Hogarth)
Norman MacCaig is a fine poet, insufficiently known, writing powerfully of Nature and how 'dreadful alienations bring you down into proper loneliness'.

Hugh MacDIARMID (Christopher Murray Grieve) (1892–1978)

Complete Poems 1920 – 1976 (ed. H Grieve and W R Aitken, Martin Briaa and O'Keefee)
Selected Poems (ed. Craig and Manson, Penguin)
MacDiarmid wrote many excellent poems both in Scots and in English. His work included lyrics, satires, poems of political inquiry and statements deriving from his communism.

Louis MacNEICE (1907–63)

Collected Poems (ed. E R Dodds, Faber)
'World is crazier and more of it than we think'. MacNeice's poetry catches much of
the world's craziness and diversity, its excitement and sadness.

Christopher MARLOWE (1564–93)

Poems (ed. M MacLure, Methuen/Manchester UP)
Much of Marlowe's greatest poetry is to be found in the 'mighty line' of *Tamburlaine*
and in the wonderfully expressive dramatic verse of *Dr. Faustus*, which prepared the
ground for Shakespeare. His most famous lyric is 'The passionate Sheepheard to His
Love'; the long poem *Hero and Leander* is erotic and often beautiful.

Andrew MARVELL (1621–78)

Complete Poems (ed. E S Donno, Penguin)
Marvell is one of the greatest of love poets ('To His Coy Mistress'), nature poets
('Upon Appleton House', 'The Garden'), religious poets ('A Dialogue Between the
Resolved Soul and Creative Pleasure', 'The Coronet'), political poets ('An Horation
Ode upon Cromwell's Return from Ireland') and satirists in English. His best work
has a uniquely daring variety and felicity of tone.

John MILTON (1608–74)

Complete Poetry and Selected English Prose (ed. E H Viseak, Nonesuch)
If Milton's greatest work, *Paradise Lost*, attempts to 'justify the ways of God to men'
(new readers might start with Books I, II, IX, X), much of the rest may be seen as a
perennially contemporary conflict between sensuous enjoyment and austere
philosophy. His achievement is monumental but, to many today, uninspiring in its
dependence on received systems of thought (Christianity, neo-Platonism, classical
mythology) and on Latinate use of English. Milton has sustained critical attacks from
equally big names such as Johnson and Eliot, but this should not obscure the sheer
verbal delights of the earlier works such as 'L'Allegro', 'Il Penseroso', and the
magnificent elegy, 'Lycidas'.

Marianne MOORE (1887–1972)

Complete Poems (Faber)
Marianne Moore was an influential writer of syllabic verse. She was clear-eyed,
brisk, unassuming – virtues that are aimed at by many contemporary writers.

Thomas MOORE (1779–1852)

Life and Poems (ed. Brendan Clifford, Athol)
Moore is in this list because he enjoyed in his own time an enormous popularity based
on a long oriental poem, *Lalla Rookh*, and on the lyrics he wrote for traditional
melodies. Neither appeals much to modern critical interests.

William MORRIS (1834–96)

Selected Writings (ed. G D H Cole, Nonesuch)
Selected Writings (ed. Asa Briggs, Penguin)
The Defence of Guenevere and Other Poems is PreRaphaelitish, vivid in details but
often unreal and archaic; even so, poems like 'The Haystack in the Floods' are still
disturbingly powerful. As Morris moved towards socialism, his poetry became more
realistic and optimistic, as may be seen in *The Earthly Paradise* and *Socialist Chants*.

Edwin MUIR (1887–1959)

Collected Poems (Faber)
Muir is a heartening case of a poet who started writing really well when nearly 40. His
best poems are fables developing out of remembered experience, for example on the
Orkneys.

Ogden NASH (1902–71)

Collected Verse (Deutsch)
Nash is neither a great poet nor a great influence. His best poems, however, with their
sophisticated indifference to all aesthetic laws, are entirely distinctive. Seduction
could not be more tellingly summed up than; 'Candy is dandy/ But liquor is quicker'.

Wilfred OWEN (1893–1918)

Collected Poems (ed. C Day Lewis, Chatto)
'The subject is war, and the pity of war'. Owen is the most widely admired of the
poets of the First World War. His poems range from the elegiac 'Anthem for Doomed
Youth' to the satirical 'The Dead-beat' – their richness of sound and imagery owes
much to Keats.

Sylvia PLATH (1932–63)

Collected Poems (introduction by Ted Hughes, Faber)
Plath's poems are about her sense of herself and her alienation from the world. She
found her distinctive voice, grieved, terrified and private, in *Ariel*, a collection
published posthumously.

Alexander POPE (1688–1744)

Poetical Works (ed. H Davis, OUP)
Pope is the greatest poet of the eighteenth century and the most deadly satirist in
English, whether in the light-fantastic, mock-heroic vein of 'The Rape of the Lock',
the mature vision of the 'Moral Essays', the forthright onslaughts of the 'Epistle to Dr
Arbuthnot' or the desolate vision of Book IV of 'The Dunciad'. In his hands the

heroic couplet is a subtle and varied weapon of ridicule, which can also match the scope of Shakespearian blank verse, e.g. in the passage from *An Essay on Man*: 'placed on this isthmus of a middle state, A being darkly wise, and rudely great ...'.

Ezra POUND (1885–1972)

Selected Poems 1908–1959 (Faber)
A great influence on his contemporary poets (e.g. T S Eliot), Pound has less for the general reader today. He was a translator of genius ('The Seafarer', 'Homage to Sextus Propertius') and, in *Hugh Selwyn Mauberley* and the *Cantos*, the author of two of the most allusive and technically original works of modernism.

Winthrop Mackworth PRAED (1802–39)

Praed was a most accomplished writer of light verse, particularly of *vers de société*. He is represented in, for example, the *New Oxford Book of Light Verse*.

Matthew PRIOR (1664–1721)

Literary Works (OUP) 1971
Prior was an accomplished, witty, minor poet, who shared the values of his age and reflected them in relaxed, often octosyllabic verse. He gives some indication of the nature of English poetry between the death of Dryden and the maturity of Pope.

Francis QUARLES (1592–1644)

The Complete Works (ed. A B Grosart, AMS Press, US)
Emblems is a series of 75 allegorical engravings about the soul's struggle for salvation, each engraving being accompanied by an explanatory poem. Enormously successful in its own time and now fascinating as a guide to a vanished way of thinking.

Sir Walter RALEIGH (1552–1618)

Choice of Verse (ed. Robert Nye, Faber)
'He was sometimes a Poet, not often' wrote John Aubrey. When he was, as in 'The Nymph's Reply to the Shepherd', 'The Passionate Men's Pilgrimage' and parts of 'The Ocean to Cynthia', he was so unquestionably.

Craig RAINE (1944–)

A Martian Sends a Postcard Home (Faber)
Rich (Faber)
Raine has been influenced by such diverse poets as Dante, Rimbaud, Ford Madox Ford as well as Anglo-Saxon poetry. He writes tight but sensuous verse full of the imagery of everyday life, but put together so as to make the reader view it differently.

John Wilmot, Earl of ROCHESTER (1647–80)

Complete Poems (ed. D M Veith, Yale)
'A Satyr against Mankind', 'The Maxim'd Debauchee' and 'Upon Nothing' are intelligent poems in which Rochester scathes the frivolous life he himself led. His attitudes are to be compared with those of the Restoration playwrights.

Christina ROSSETTI (1830–94)

Selected Poems (ed. C H Sissen, Carcanet)
For some, her work is adequately available in anthologies ('When I am Dead My Dearest – Sing No Sad Songs for Me' or 'Remember Me When I am Gone Away') but others will want to explore one of the relatively rare women's voices in literature for many of the conflicts and problems of the nineteenth century. Her work ranges from the carol 'In the Bleak Midwinter' to the ambiguously allegorical 'Goblin Market'.

Dante Gabriel ROSSETTI (1828–82)

Collected Works (World Classics)
Today the poetry is less well known than Rossetti's life as a painter. The Medievalism of 'The Blessed Damosel' is less interesting than the monologue over the sleeping prostitute 'Jenny' or the best sonnets in *The House of Life* sequence.

Siegfried SASSOON (1886–1967)

Collected Poems (Faber)
Sassoon's best poems are cannon fired against the stupidity and jingoism of the First World War.

Sir Walter SCOTT (1771–1832)

Selected Poems (ed. Thomas Gawford, OUP)
Scott's own poetry developed out of *The Minstreling of the Scottish Border*, the collection of Border ballads he assembled in his youth. 'The Ley of the Last Minstrel' and 'Marmion', narrative poems of chivalry, are the best of his original work along with some of the songs he wrote for his novels.

William SHAKESPEARE (1564–1616)

Poems (ed. F T Price, Methuen)
If Shakespeare had written nothing else, his *Sonnets*, addressed to a patron and a mistress, real or imaginery, would still be recognized as probably the greatest sequence of poems in English. In their approach to the mutability of human relationships they have a ruthless immediacy and honesty. The songs from the plays rightly appear in most anthologies of English verse where the celebrations of youth, love, life and death lose nothing by being short and sweet.

Percy Bysshe SHELLEY (1792–1822)

Poetical Works (ed. T Hutchinson, OUP)
Although Shelley's visionary idealism now often seems to be windy rhetoric, few readers will resist the energy or poignancy of his poems; 'Ode to the West Wind', 'Adonais', 'To A Skylark', 'When the Lamp is Shattered', and 'Ozymandias'.

Sir Philip SIDNEY (1554–86)

Selected Poems (ed. Katherine Duncan-Jones, OUP)
The sonnet sequence *Astrophel and Stella* is one of the most remarkable in the language, dramatizing the characters (perhaps based on Sidney and Penelope Devereux, just after her marriage to Lord Rich) and their relationship. The sequence influenced all subsequent Elizabethan poets.

Charles Hubert SISSON (1914–)

Selected Poems (Carcanet)
'A few verses that would outlive the century': Sisson's description of Catallus's self-appraisal might be his own. Sisson is, like Eliot, a conservative, a classicist, and a Christian and his poems are often concerned with religion and lust and have had a significant influence on younger poets.

Edith SITWELL (1887–1964)

Collected Poems (Macmillan)
Recommended here less for the later, clever poetry, and the well known war poem 'Still falls the rain', than for the funny verbal pyrotechnics of the *Facade* lyrics.

John SKELTON (c. 1460–1529)

Complete English Poems (ed. J Scattergood, Penguin)
The most important poems ('Phylyp Sparowe', 'The Tunning of Elynor Rumming', 'Colyn Cloute', and 'Why Come Ye Nat to Courte?') are written in Skeltonics, short lines with, usually, three stresses rhyming up to four lines or more at a stretch. Skelton's work has been vigorously championed by Robert Graves and others but for some Skelton's 'artlessness' remains artlessness.

Christopher SMART (1722–71)

The Poetical Works of Christopher Smart (ed. K Williamson, OUP)
The finest poetry of 'mad Christopher Smart' ('Jubilate Agnus, A Song to David') is a burst of praise to God and to his Creation. Sometimes apparently naive, it is in fact learned and complex in organization.

Stevie SMITH (1902–71)

Selected Poems (ed. J MacGibbon, Penguin)
Stevie Smith's poems are like no-one else's. They can seem inconsequential and yet they remain to trouble the mind. 'Not Waving, But Drowning' is already a part of the common culture.

Edmund SPENSER (1552–99)

Poetical Works (ed. J C Smith and E de Selincourt, OUP)
The Faerie Queene is a heroic poem in seven Books; in each Book a Knight, champion of a virtue, rides out from the court of Gloriana, Queen Elizabeth, to do battle with that virtue's enemies. It is a work of great decorative beauty, rising at times to grandeur, an importantly bold manifesto for the Tudor nation-state. Spenser's other poems include *Prothalamion*, *The Shepheardes Calendar* and *Amoretti*, a sonnet sequence.

Wallace STEVENS (1879–1955)

Collected Poems (Faber)
Stevens is one of the masters of blank verse. In thought, phrasing and syntax his work powerfully combines austere purity with memorable extravagance and mannerism. From his first collection, *Harmonium*, onwards his poetry was about the relation between the world and the creative imagination.

Henry Howard, Earl of SURREY (c. 1516–47)

Poems (ed. E Jones, OUP)
Surrey was Wyatt's pupil and wrote a fine elegy to him. His most impressive work is his translation of Books II and IV of the *Aeneid*; its successful use of blank verse influenced the whole development of Elizabethan tragedy. He also invented the English sonnet form: three quatrians and a couplet.

Jonathan SWIFT (1667–1745)

Complete Poems (ed. Pat Rogers, Penguin)
Swift is a master of light,but not wholly unserious, verse, much of it in informal octosyllabic couplets. His most famous poem is, 'Verse on the Death of Dr Swift'.

Algernon Charles SWINBURNE (1837–1909)

Selected Poems (ed. L M Finlay, Carcanet)
Swinburne's work seemed thrilling to an age with stricter religious and sexual conventions and reticences than our own. *Atlanta in Calydon* and *Poems and Ballads*, which includes 'Hymn to Prosperine', may be enjoyed. Swinburne's gift for rhyme and assonance produces some fine lines but too much was written on automatic pilot.

Alfred, Lord TENNYSON (1809–92)

Poems (ed. C Ricks, OUP)
The solemn image of the Great Victorian – the beard, the Peerage, the Laureatship and the enormous success – keeps many readers at bay. But Tennyson was only too aware of the uncertainty of religious belief, the confused values of industry and science and the transience of life and beauty. Few English poets have been as well equipped by ear and technique to express these feelings in poetry. 'In Memoriam' is uneven but it is one of the big poems of English literature. The early 'Lady of Shalott', and 'The Lotos Eaters' celebrate the attractions of art and youth, while the later, magnificent 'Ulysses' and 'Tithonus' achieve a kind of heroic reconciliation with life's inevitable end.

Dylan THOMAS (1914–53)

Collected Poems 1934–52 (Dent)
Thomas's poetry is rapturous and intense, the work of a Welsh bard. In the later poems he was beginning to control his lyrical gifts in the interests of making sense.

Edward THOMAS (1878–1917)

Collected Poems (ed. R G Thomas, OUP)
Thomas's poetry celebrates with moving precision the English countryside and its people but it is often crippled by a peculiarly English nostalgia and tentativeness.

Ronald Stuart THOMAS (1913–)

Selected Poems 1946–68 (Hart-Davis)
Later Poems 1972–82 (Papermac)
Thomas served as an Anglican priest in Welsh country parishes. His brief, austere poems grow out of the religious and moral difficulties encountered by an educated man in that situation.

Francis THOMPSON (1859–1907)

Hound of Heaven (OUP)
The *Hound of Heaven* is a definitive rendering of the terror of the soul's flight from God and the immediacy of God's pursuit. Thompson also wrote some 'goodish' love poems.

James THOMSON (1700–48)

The Seasons and Castle of Indolence (OUP)
The author of 'Rule Britannia' should be better remembered for *The Seasons*, a long blank verse poem influenced by Milton and by Virgil's *Georgics*. Its descriptions of nature, here and in other countries, and its account of a mind responding to Nature influenced Wordsworth and all subsequent English nature poetry. *The Castle of Indolence* and 'Hymn in Solitude' are also well worth reading.

James (B V) THOMSON (1834–82)

Poems and Letters (ed. A Ridler, Centaur)
Thomson's inclusion in this selection is based on one poem 'The City of Dreadful Night', a nightmarish description of the city which alienates and destroys men.

Charles TOMLINSON (1927–)

Selected Poems 1951–74 (OUP)
Charles Tomlinson on his own poems: 'They are about seeing and saying, and about the body's sense of the physical world through which we move.' Whether about England, New Mexico or the United States, the poems are marked by craftmanship and intelligence.

Thomas TRAHERNE (1638–74)

Selected Writings (ed. Dick Davis, Carcanet)
Traherne's poetry was lost until 1895. He is a poet who unforgettably celebrates moments of enjoyment and of innocence.

Henry VAUGHAN (1622–95)

Complete Poems (ed. A Rudrum, Penguin)
Vaughan's greatest poems are contained in the volume *Silex Scintillans*. They combine a delight in nature with a horror of man's 'hard, stonie heart'. He owes much to Herbert and, in some surprising ways, prefigures Wordsworth.

Edmund WALLER (1606–87)

Poems (ed. G T Drury, Greenwood)
Waller is not now read extensively but he was, with Denham, the pre-cursor of Augustan poetry. His principal innovation was the development of the rhymed complet. The poems that still have power are, however, entirely Caroline in manner and sentiment (e.g. 'Go Lovely Rose' and 'It is Not That I Love You Less').

Walt WHITMAN (1819–92)

Complete Poems (Penguin)
Between 1855 and 1870 Whitman brought out five editions of *Leaves of Grass*; each edition included new poems and worked towards a significant ordering. In these poems Whitman celebrated himself and America; they are long, repetitive, energetic, unashamed, and they create an American Poetry. They include 'Song of Myself', 'Out of the Cradle Endlessly Rocking', 'Vigil Strange I Kept in the Field One Night', 'I Sing of the Body Electric' and 'When Lilacs Last in the Dooryard Bloom'd'.

Oscar WILDE (1854–1900)

The Ballad of Reading Gaol (Journeyman Press)
Most of Wilde's poems are awful but his personal experience of prison and the use of the popular ballad form, combine to express the humanity and the horror of one of the basic dramas of popular culture – the execution of a convicted murderer.

William Carlos WILLIAMS (1883–1963)

Selected Poems (ed. C Tomlinson, Penguin)
Williams tried to include ordinary characters and speech in his poems. His most important early volume was *Spring and All* containing 'The Red Wheelbarrow'. Later he wrote *Paterson*, an epic poem in five books.

William WORDSWORTH (1770–1850)

Complete Works (ed. T Hutchinson, OUP)
Too easily identified with the Lake District and wooly sentiment, Wordsworth is not, in the usual limiting sense of the term, a nature poet. He writes about the influence of nature on 'the Mind of Man', 'the main region of my song', and, in particular, its influence on himself. The best introduction is through the 1800 edition of *Lyrical Ballads*, which includes the Lucy poems, and the first two books of his intellectual autobiography, *The Prelude*. 'Resolution and Independence' and 'Ode: Intimations of Immorality' are among the finest medium length poems in the language. Although there is much, much else that is unread and unreadable, Wordsworth is a great poet.

Sir Thomas WYATT (1503–42)

Complete Poems (ed. R A Rebholz, Penguin)
Wyatt wrote some of the finest of our love poems ('They flee from me that sometyme did me seke', 'My lute, awake!'). He is historically important for developing the English sonnet.

William Butler YEATS (1865–1939)

Collected Poems (Macmillan)
Possibly the greatest twentieth century poet in the English language, Yeats now commands a world wide readership and much scholarly attention. His poetry developed from the beautiful but insubstantial fantasies of the Celtic Twilight ('The Lake Isle of Innisfree', 'He Wishes for the Cloths of Heaven') to a profoundly troubled awareness of his social responsibilities, ('Easter 1916', 'Nineteen Hundred and Nineteen'), the relationship between life and art, ('The Fascination of What's Difficult', 'Lapis Lapzuli', 'Byzantium') and the varied limitations of his own body and personality ('Sailing to Byzantium', 'The Tower', 'The Circus Animals' Desertion'). By the later poems he had an enormous range of poetic utterance from the complex and symbolic to the direct casual statement.

Edward YOUNG (1683–1765)

Selected Poems (ed. B Hepworth, Carcanet)
Young's most famous poem 'The Complaint; or Night-Thoughts on Life, Death and Immortality', is a long blank verse poem springing, like Tennyson's 'In Memoriam', from bereavement. It is Augustan in much of its phrasing but points to the Romantics in its emphasis on feeling.

DRAMA

A selection of the finest plays in the English language written and performed over a period of some five centuries inevitably contains some of the greatest writing in all literature. Yet drama is the most fleeting, as well as the most social, of the arts. In addition, many of the plays listed here enjoyed a mere handful of performances in their own time before giving way to new productions. Several failed to achieve either the success or the acclaim we now feel they deserve. In many instances modern revivals have helped to correct these factors, as indeed has the vast distribution of these works in book form.

Witnessing a live performance in the company of others is an entirely different experience from reading: much is lost, but often something is gained through reading. The poetic language, the depth of thought, the pleasure of a well-constructed plot can be appreciated, enjoyed and studied in less pressing and electric circumstances than those of a live performance. It is worth emphasizing however, that performance is the prime medium through which dramatic writing achieves its effect.

The plays listed have largely been written for performance in a theatre. Yet drama has been, and continues to be, presented in a variety of settings. Consequently there are certain representatives from other media, as with the radio plays of Giles Cooper and Dylan Thomas's *Under Milk Wood*. In fact so successful has radio been as a medium, and so large its demand for material that most of the plays included will have been performed at one time or another in this medium. Television offers yet another means through which the playwright can develop and explore his or her art. Television is frequently unsuccessful in its translations of drama from the stage into its altogether more 'naturalistic' and 'cinematic' medium. But many of the new playwrights such as Pinter, Stoppard and Griffiths have been keen to explore this new means of expression and relish its vast audiences.

In chronological order the selection commences with the great medieval religious works – *The York Mystery Plays* (see Cawley), *The Chester Mystery Plays* (see Hussey). These works, which represent the beginnings of the English dramatic heritage, were not designed for performance in a theatre. They were conceived as local, usually annual, events performed in the open air on religious feast days as an integral part of the community's celebrations. Alongside the Mystery Plays, another form of religious drama was developed in the form of the Morality Play, the most famous examples of which are *Everyman* (see Cawley) and *The Castell of*

138

Perservance (see Franklin). If the Mysteries attempted to dramatize the significant events in Christian mythology, the Moralities employed allegory to demonstrate the moral struggle of mortal man which, according to the Christian religion, each individual must recognize as his or her lot.

By the end of the fifteenth century the main thrust of this religious drama began to weaken, but it was not until the 1570s that theatres were built on the outskirts of London, and the great plays of the late Elizabethan and Jacobean period began to be produced. There are few plays of any great merit that survive from this interim period but F. S. Boas's edition of *Five Pre-Shakespearian Comedies*, which features *Ralph Roister Doister* (1553) and *Fulgens and Lucrece* (c. 1486), the latter being the earliest example of a fully secular English play in existence, is included as representative of some of the important developments that were taking place.

Late Renaissance England produced one of the greatest periods in the history of drama anywhere. Shakespeare's universal tragedies, history plays, comedies and his problems plays are sufficient to establish any period as a golden age. However, there are also the earlier innovative blank verse dramas of Christopher Marlowe – *Tamburlaine the Great* and *Doctor Faustus* – and are great moral satires of Ben Jonson – *Volpone*, *The Alchemist* (said by Coleridge to have one of the three best plots of all time), and *Bartholemew Fair*.

In addition to these three acknowledged giants there are the prodigious talents of Thomas Middleton and John Webster. The latter's dark tragedies – *The Duchess of Malfi* and *The White Devil* – are masterpieces of the more extreme dramas that developed toward the end of the period when the world seemed less optimistic and more troubled than it had been but a decade earlier. Middleton's *A Chaste Maid in Cheapside* is the best of the Jacobean City comedies, while *The Changeling*, part tragedy, part psychological thriller written jointly with William Rowley, is increasingly recognized as a play for all ages. There are also included several playwrights who produced single excellent plays within the body of their works: John Marston's *The Malcontent*, Tourner's (attributed) *The Revenger's Tragedy*, and Heywood's domestic tragedy *A Woman Killed with Kindness*.

The excessively visible and social nature of drama singled it out for attention by Protestant divines and moralists. It was not until the Restoration of Charles II that drama was again possible in London. For the first time women were allowed on the stage, and this doubtless contributed to the somewhat lascivious nature of the drama for which this period is most famous – Restoration Comedy. Certainly in the witty dialogues and complex plots of disguise and sexual intrigue by such exponents as Etheridge with *The Man of Mode* and Wycherley with *The Country Wife* and *The Plain Dealer*, the Court and its hangers-on saw its morals and behaviours represented with devastating if perhaps exaggerated accuracy. Many of these plays are now recognized to be of the highest quality and in William Congreve's *The Way of the World* there is an undoubted masterpiece.

The success of Restoration Comedy overshadowed the heroic drama of the age, as represented by the romances and tragedies written by the poet John Dryden. A selection of his works, in particular *All for Love* (a reworking of *Antony and Cleopatra*), is included in this list as an example of this kind of drama.

The worthwhile work during the eighteenth century is mainly in the satirical tradition. In particular the burlesque plays which were initiated with the Duke of Buckingham's *The Rehearsal* (see Hampden), a wonderful send-up of the romances and tragedies mentioned above, and which has long outlived them. The tradition was extended by Pope, Gay and Fielding amongst others. A selection is collected in Simon Trussler's *Burlesque Plays of the Eighteenth Century*. Closely related to this particular genre is Sheridan's *The Critic*. Two other Sheridan plays – *The Rivals* and *The School of Scandal* – and Goldsmith's *She Stoops to Conquer*, all of which are moving toward the sentimental tradition, more or less exhausts the list. However special mention must be given to John Gay's ballad opera *The Beggar's Opera*, a masterpiece that is often revived and much adapted.

An emasculating blow to satirical comedy was dealt by the Licensing Act of 1737 which effectively censored plays before they were performed. Thus sentimental comedy, and later melodrama, were the two forms that dominated popular, dramatic entertainment during this period. They provided morally acceptable conclusions no matter how inappropriate these may be to the preceding action. The best example are the early ones by George Farquar – *The Beaux' Strategem* and *The Recruiting Officer*.

Most plots of nineteenth century melodrama were taken from continental plays, as with Taylor's *The Ticket of Leave Man* (reputed to feature the first stage detective), or from books, or occasionally from real life as in Latimer's *The Red Barn Murder*. The chief ingredients of melodrama are plenty of action, simple characters (types), and the espousal of simple conventional virtues. As the century wore on they also became more elaborate and spectacular in presentation, as in the works of Boucicault.

In the second half of the nineteenth century the theatre (along with the music hall) was the country's chief form of entertainment. But there was little serious content in the dramas performed. It was not, in fact, until 1889 that Ibsen's *The Doll's House* was performed in London. Around the same time the home grown works of Jones and Pinero, particularly with *The Second Mrs Tanqueray*, proved to London theatre management that there existed an audience for a more serious drama. Yet it was in the newly formed theatre clubs and independent theatres, particularly the (Royal) Court Theatre and the Abbey Theatre in Dublin, that the drama was to make its real progress. Galsworthy, and in particular Shaw had their works presented at the Court. Whatever his artistic faults, Shaw almost single-handedly transformed the face of British theatre with a body of plays of considerable variety and excellence. The Abbey Theatre was run by W B Yeats, who continued to produce work well into the thirties. The theatre also premiered the works of Synge and O'Casey.

Yeats tried to revive verse drama, combining it with classical and religious forms and the appeal to myth. This concept of drama was again attempted in the thirties and forties in the works of Auden and Isherwood (*Ascent of F6*), T S Eliot (particularly successful in *Murder in the Cathedral*) and Christopher Fry. Apart from the works of Eliot and John Whiting the post-war period was essentially bland, e.g. Noel Coward and Terence Rattigan. The revival, when it came, once more centred around the independent theatres, the Royal Court and the Theatre Workshop in particular. The arrival of Beckett's *Waiting for Godot* popularized the bleak tragi-comic view and techniques of Absurd Theatre. They were surprise popular successes, but the real breakthrough was with John Osborne's *Look Back in Anger* and *The Entertainer*.

Osborne in these two plays challenged the accepted value of a country clinging to its past and achieved a notoriety that in itself helped add impetus to a new British theatre. The arrival of Pinter's *The Birthday Party* and *The Caretaker*, John Arden's *Serjeant Musgrove's Dance*, and Arnold Wesker's *Western Trilogy* produced one of the most fruitful periods of drama since the first Elizabethans.

And so it has proved to be. From the early sixties onward conditions were exceptionally favourable for such development. The site of the National Theatre was chosen and the building finally completed in 1976. In 1968 censorship was finally withdrawn. Perhaps even more significant was the establishment of regional theatres, funded by the Arts Council in an attempt to bring quality theatre to the provinces. While the London circuit continued to provide brilliant new writers, such as Edward Bond, Tom Stoppard and David Storey, the regional theatre developed such talents as David Hare, Howard Brenton and Trevor Griffiths. In addition many talented touring companies produced their own work, in particular John Macgrath's 7:84 Company.

Many of these writers have not confined their drama to the stage. Pinter, Stoppard, Beckett, Hare, Brenton, and Griffiths have all written for radio or television or both. In some cases, especially Griffiths, the benefit of reaching a larger and more diverse audience has been paramount in influencing this choice of medium. This list of British drama includes plays by three American dramatists: Eugene O'Neil, Arthur Miller, and Tennessee Williams. The plays of O'Neil and Miller are already 'set texts' whose work is as commonly read and performed in Britain as that of many British writers. Tennessee Williams' status is more difficult to assess as his work has probably travelled outside the USA more by successful film adaptations than by reading off the page.

ANTHOLOGIES

F S BOAS

Five Pre-Shakesperian Comedies 1934
Classified as 'early Tudor', the five plays are significant in the development of the richness of the English stage.

A C CAWLEY

Everyman and Mediaeval Miracle Plays 1956
Contains fourteen biblical pageants from five different medieval towns, accompanied by the moral play *Everyman*.

Alexander FRANKLIN

Seven Miracle Plays 1963
Seven biblical plays which reflect the story of man, from the creation to the final judgement.

John GASSNER

Elizabethan Drama 1967
Eight non-Shakespearean plays which cover the reign of Elizabeth I, from *Arden of Feversham* to *A Woman Killed with Kindness*.

Brian GIBBONS

Five Restoration Comedies 1984
Elizabethan and Jacobean Comedies 1984
If drama reflects the times in which it was written then Restoration London must have been the jolliest place around: fops, beaus, distraught and distracted lovers abound as do wit and jocularity.

John HAMPDEN

The Beggar's Opera and Other Eighteenth Century Plays 1928
Gay's famous play is accompanied by now mostly unperformed pieces, including Addison's *Cato*, Fielding's *Tom Thumb* and *The West Indian* by Richard Cumberland.

Maurice HUSSEY

The Chester Mystery Plays 1957
A book for every reader who wishes to follow the mystery plays as enacted in one town.

A N JEFFARES

Restoration Comedy 1981
A representative selection from Wycherley, Congreve, Etherage and Farquhar.

Tom MASCHLER

New English Dramatists 1960

A K McILWRAITH

Five Elizabethan Comedies 1934
Shakespeare and Jonson are deliberately omitted making room for Lyly, Peele, Greene and Dekker.

J S PURVIS

The York Cycle of Mystery Plays 1957
Like Hussey's volume, this one enables the reader to see a complete cycle from one town.

Gamini SALGADO

Three Restoration Comedies 1968
A further selection of plays from this most lively of periods.

Simon TRUSSLER

Burlesque Plays of the Eighteenth Century 1969
The Age of Satire produced some notable hits, largely against the prime minister, Walpole. Fielding takes centre stage.

INDIVIDUAL DRAMATISTS

ANON

Arden of Feversham c. 1592
This unusual play, a domestic tragedy concerning the murder of a man by his wife and her lover, is sometimes attributed to Thomas Heywood or even to Shakespeare. It is based on an actual murder case of 1551.

John ARDEN (1930–)

Serjeant Musgrove's Dance 1959
Subtitled *An Un-historic Parable* this is an epic drama, much influenced by Brecht, using verse, song, and prose. Set in a nineteenth century mining town it involves three

deserters from a colonial war who bring back their dead comrade to his home-town and attempt to confront the locals with their shared responsibility.

Island of the Mighty 1972 (with Margaretta D'Arcy)
This is a complex trilogy of plays that re-explore the Arthurian legends.The plays are an attempt to emphasize the peasant background of the people who worked and fought for Arthur. The first two parts recount Arthur's decline and fall while Part III centres on Merlin (an artist figure) and his role. Arden's work has tended to become less objective and more openly committed since his collaboration with D'Arcy.

W H AUDEN (1907–73) and Christopher ISHERWOOD (1904–)

The Dog Beneath the Skin 1935
The Ascent of F6 1937
On the Frontier 1938
These are interesting but not entirely successful attempts to create a form of theatre using verse, music (Benjamin Britten collaborated), and the techniques of classical theatre in the shape of monologues and chorus interludes. Both Auden and Isherwood were strongly committed to radical politics in the Thirties.

Alan AYCKBOURN (1939–)

The Norman Conquests 1974
Comprises three full length plays (*Table Manners; Living Together; Round and Round the Garden*) the action of which all take place at the same time and in the same house over one weekend. The plays are however set in differtent rooms: dining-room, living room and garden. At his best, Ayckbourn is a very funny and accurate writer about the stresses and strains of British middle class life.

J M BARRIE (1860–1937)

Peter Pan 1904
Barrie's most popular play about the famous boy who would never grow up and his visit to the Never Never Land with the Darling children. A favourite alternative to pantomine as a children's Christmas entertainment.

The Admirable Crichton 1914
Shipwrecked on a desert island, survival depends on Chrichton, the butler, taking control. When the party is rescued he once more becomes a servant.

Francis BEAUMONT (1584–1616) and John FLETCHER (1579–1625)

Best Plays (2 vols, 1904)
Dramatic Works in the Beaumont and Fletcher Canon (ed. Bowers, 1966)
Reputed to be the most popular playwrights of the Jacobean period, together they produced a large body of work. Fletcher also collaborated with Rowley, Massinger,

and possibly Middleton and Shakespeare and wrote a good number of plays on his own. It is possible that Beaumont wrote *The Knight of the Burning Pestle* (1609), a satire on the audiences of the popular romances, and he collaborated with Fletcher in the writing of *Philaster, or Love lies a-bleeding* (1611).

Samuel BECKETT (1906–)

Waiting for Godot 1955
All that Fall 1957
End Game/Action without Words 1958
Krapp's Last Tape 1958
Embers 1959
Happy Days 1962
Words and Music 1962
Play 1963
Cascando and Other Short Dramatic Pieces 1966/7
Ends and Odds (Not I; That Time; Footfalls) 1977

Beckett, an Irishman living in France and writing his original scripts in French, is one of the most outstanding and influential playwrights of the post-war years. He is influenced by French symbolism and existentialism and uses symbolic backgrounds, situations and minimal collections of characters who are usually outcasts (the tramps in *Waiting for Godot*) or maimed (as in *End Game*) or buried up to the neck (*Happy Days; Play*). Beckett deprives the audience of conventional plot development, dialogue, or character. The human condition is seen as rootless, meaningless, and without dignity: humankind has no control or understanding of its place in the universe. The early plays spiced this vision with humour, particularly *Waiting for Godot*, but Beckett's work has become progressively bleaker. *Breath* (1969) lasts 30 seconds: it opens with a child's cry and ends with a man's dying gasp. Beckett has also written several plays for radio, notably, *All That Fall*.

Brendan BEHAN (1923–64)

The Quare Fellow 1956
An unnamed murderer is to be executed. The action of the play over a period of twenty-four hours preceding this event, offers a compelling evocation of prison life and an anti-capital punishment moral.

The Hostage 1958
Set in a Dublin brothel, the hostage, an English soldier, falls in love with one of his captors. He is being kept to trade for the life of an IRA man who is due to be hanged. He is accidentally killed when the police raid the house to rescue him.

Alan BENNETT (1934–)

Forty Years On 1968
Using flashbacks, a retiring headmaster at a British public school sees important scenes of his life at the annual school play as Bennett satirizes the ruling class ideology throughout its years of crisis.

Getting On 1971
A middle-aged Labour MP, whose strength and idealism have been reduced by experience to rhetoric, reflects on the 'old days' as his only solace from the present.

An Englishman Abroad 1982
With wit and economy the cultures of Soviet Russia and Old Etonian England are brought together in the brilliant television play about an encounter with Guy Burgess in Moscow. Subsequently adapted for the stage in the double bill *Single Spies*.

Edward BOND (1934–)

Saved 1965
Set in South London this is a study of the aimless lives of unemployed youths. Its most famous scene is the stoning of a baby in its pram, simply for amusement.

Lear 1971
An horrific parable on how power corrupts, this is a rewriting of Shakespeare's famous tragedy in an attempt to give it contemporary relevance.

Bingo 1973
An imagined account of Shakespeare's last years in Stratford wherein he becomes involved in a dubious land transaction, refuses to have anything to do with his dying wife (who is never seen) and tells his daughter that he hates her.

Dionysius Lardner BOUCICAULT (1822–90)

London Assurance 1841
His first play (he wrote over 200), this was recently revived in London with considerable success. It is a comedy of manners and, as such, constitutes something of a link between Goldsmith and Wilde, two other Irish playwrights.

The Shaughraun 1874
Shanghraun is a charming version of the stage Irishman.

Howard BRENTON (1942–)

Brassneck 1973 (with David Hare)
Three generations of a Midlands family are examined in the epic style, highlighting their general greed and corruption. Highly polemical, it was written for performance at the Nottingham Playhouse and is an excellent example of the work produced in the seventies for the provinces.

The Churchill Play 1974
Set in Britain in the future (1984) it recounts how a coalition government deals with militant trade unionists by bringing in the army.

Epsom Downs 1977
Derby day – a panoramic and occasionally celebratory view of English society seen through a variety of groups and a loosely woven plot.

Caryl CHURCHILL (1938–)

Cloud 9 1979
Cloud 9 is an interesting socio-comic study of two separate generations. The first part is set at the turn of the century and the latter in the present.

Light Shining in Buckinghamshire 1976
Written for the Joint Stock Company with which the author is closely associated, this play is set in seventeenth century England at the time of the Civil War and deals with the revolutionary longings of the people who fought for Cromwell in the belief that they fought for the coming millennium.

William CONGREVE (1670–1729)

Love for Love 1695
Valentine feigns madness to escape his financial problems and is rescued by the independently minded Angelica. A fine play with a superb prose style.

The Way of the World 1700
This is the greatest of all Restoration Comedies, and possibly the best comedy of manners in the language. Although often revived it is notoriously difficult to stage successfully. Millamant is one of the great classic parts for an actress and a precursor of modern women in her refusal to 'by degrees dwindle into a wife'. For Congreve's four comedies and one heroic tragedy, see *Complete Plays* (ed. Davis, 1967).

Giles COOPER (1918–66)

Four Radio Plays (including *Under the Loofah Tree; Unman, Wittering and Zigo*) 1965
Giles Cooper plays were very important in drawing attention to the radio as a serious dramatic medium. *Unman, Wittering and Zigo*, is set in a boys' school.

Everything in the Garden 1964
This is an attack on sixties materialism wherein suburban housewives, bored and desiring more join a brothel to boost their resources and create interest. An examination also of the lengths people will go to maintain respectability.

Noel COWARD (1899–1975)

Hay Fever 1925
Retired actress Judith Bliss and her family invite guests for a weekend in the country and proceed to bewilder them by acting out scenes from her plays during their conversations. Hilarious comedy.

Private Lives 1930
Perhaps his most famous play, two honeymooning couples are lodged in adjoining hotel suites. The bride of one pair and the groom of the other discover that they knew

each other only too well in the past. After many complications and much hesitation they run away with each other.

Thomas DEKKER (1570–1632)

The Shoemaker's Holiday 1600
This is Dekker's most famous work. An early Romantic Comedy it tells of a shoemaker who becomes Lord Mayor.

Shelagh DELANEY (1939–)

A Taste of Honey 1958
This play by the then teenage Delaney was first produced at Joan Littlewood's Theatre Workshop, and alerted the public to a growing swell of 'provincial' talent awaiting its chance. It is the story of a young girl and her illegitimate pregnancy.

John DRYDEN (1631–1700)

A prolific writer for the Restoration Theatre – comedies, tragedies (heroic and neo-classicial) and operas – his work today is more studied than performed. Dryden, a great poet, was also a pioneer of dramatic criticism.

Marriage-à-la-Mode 1672
This is a Restoration battle-of-the-sexes comedy.

Aureng Zebe 1675
Aureng Zebe's famous speech 'When I consider life, 'tis all a cheat...' reflects the plot and is an example of Dryden's mastery of the heroic couplet.

All For Love, or the World Well Lost 1678
A classically proportioned blank verse drama based on the downfall and deaths of Anthony and Cleopatra.

The Spanish Fryar 1681
'An unnatural mingle' in this tragi-comic-pastoral play, containing the undoubtedly corrupt Friar Dominic and the beautiful song 'Farewell Ungrateful Traytor'.

T S ELIOT (1888–1965)

Murder in the Cathedral 1935
The Family Reunion 1939
The Cocktail Party 1950
The Confidential Clerk 1954
The Elder Statesman 1958
Eliot was the most successful exponent of twentieth century verse-drama. *Murder in the Cathedral*, performed at Canterbury, is a classic of the genre. Its combination of history, morality play, and ritual as well as the strong poetical language was perfectly

suited to the subject. In his later plays Eliot continued to explore the use of verse and serious problems, often religious in treatment, but tended towards a lighter format, a type of sophisticated comedy. Neither the verse nor the drama have encouraged many revivals of the later works.

Sir George ETHEREDGE (1635–91)

The Man of Mode 1676
Etheredge's best and most famous play, this is a wonderful evocation of Restoration life featuring Sir Fopling Flutter, a man totally overcome by fashionable affectations.

George FARQUHAR (1678–1707)

The Recruiting Officer 1706
The Beaux' Stratagem 1707
Farquhar's tragic death deprived the drama of a rare talent. He represents a major shift to the more sentimental eighteenth century comedy. Both plays listed above have been frequently revived with considerable success.

John FLETCHER (1579–1625)
See under **Francis BEAUMONT**

John FORD (1586–1640)

'Tis Pity She's a Whore 1633
Ford was almost obsessively concerned with the situation where a normally expressed love is forbidden by society and its laws. This, his most famous play, deals with the theme of incest.

Brian FRIEL (1929–)

The Freedom of the City 1975
An unauthorized Civil Rights march is dispersed and three demonstrators – two young men and a mother of eleven – take refuge in the mayor's parlour. They are surrounded, and when they give themselves up, shot.

Translations 1980
Set in a hedge-school in County Donegal in 1883 this confronts local people with Royal Engineers carrying out an ordinance survey with the intention of changing the names of the places. A far reaching comment of Anglo-Irish history.

Christopher FRY (1907–)

The Lady's Not for Burning 1948
The most famous of a series of verse plays which took their thematic connections from *The Seasons*. Set in Elizabethan times this play is 'spring'. *A Yard of Sun* (1970), the last to be written is summer, *Venus Observed* (1950) and *The Dark is*

Light Enough (1954) are autumn and winter respectively. Subsequently eclipsed by the post-Osborne generation, the language and settings reflect the general attempt of their times to escape the drabness of post-war Britain.

John GALSWORTHY (1867–1933)

Strife 1909
Strife deals with a major coal dispute and the larger context of capital versus labour. Galsworthy was an exponent of the naturalist theatre and in many ways his play is an investigation of Darwinism – 'the survival of the fittest' – applied to the economy.

Justice 1910
The story of a solicitor's clerk who forges a cheque to get money for a poor family. One of the few works of literature that can claim to have changed the law of the land: this tale of the clerk's subsequent imprisonment and suicide so influenced Churchill that he acted upon it.

John GAY (1685–1752)

The Beggar's Opera 1728
A light hearted combination of political satire and burlesque of Italian Opera (then very popular) set amongst the whores and thieves of Newgate. The idea was suggested to Gay by Swift.

Oliver GOLDSMITH (1730–74)

She Stoops to Conquer 1773
A comedy that has been deservedly popular since its first performance, when it was hailed as a laughing antidote to the Sentimented Comedy of the time. Marlow and Hastings mistake Mr Hardcastle's house for an inn and his daughter for the bar-maid.

Harley GRANVILLE-BARKER (1877–1946)

The Voysey Inheritance 1905
Edward Voysey inherits the family business – a flourishing firm of solicitors – only to find that its success is based on misappropriated funds.

Waste 1910
Henry Trebell, an up-and-coming politician with radical ideas for the reform of society finds himself and his career compromised by a sexual relationship he had in the past. No public performance was allowed until 1936 by the Lord Chamberlain.

The Madras House 1907
A social comedy involving early feminism, business and high fashion. It was first produced by Shaw at the Royal Court and can be read (or seen) as a companion piece to Shaw's *Misalliance*.

Robert GREENE (c. 1558–92)

Complete Plays
All Greene's plays were published after his death. *Friar Bacon and Friar Bungay* (1594) is the best known of his plays being a comic treatment of the Faust theme. *Pandosto* (1588) is regarded as the basis for Shakespeare's *A Winter's Tale*.

Trevor GRIFFITHS (1935–)

The Party 1973
Set in 1968 in the house of a successful television producer a group meets to discuss socialism, its implications and how it can be achieved. The discussion is contrasted with the producer's own story and his relationship with his wife and brother.

Comedians 1975
This is serious play about laughter, why we laugh and what we laugh at. A group of budding comedians meet at nightschool for a final briefing before going on to audition before a London manager.

David HARE (1947–)

Knuckle 1974
This play uses the format of the detective thriller as a vehicle for staging a serious examination of international capitalism.

Teeth 'n Smiles 1975
A pop group prepares to stage a performance at an established university and raise the question of the value of their existence and the purpose of the music they play. The concert is a riot and all except the female lead singer join the establishment.

Thomas HEYWOOD (1553–1641)

A Woman Kilde with Kindnesse 1607
Like *Arden of Feversham*, with which Heywood has sometimes been linked, this is a domestic tragedy and Heywood's best play. A country gentleman takes revenge on his wife's unfaithfulness by killing her with kindness.

Christopher ISHERWOOD
See under W H AUDEN

Ben JONSON (1572–1637)

Volpone 1605
Epicene 1609
The Alchemist 1610
Bartholomew Fayre 1614
The most influential artist of his day, even more respected than Shakespeare himself, Jonson is now often regarded as one of the most famous, but least seen or read,

playwrights of English drama. This is a great loss since his works, particularly *Volpone* and *The Alchemist* are extraordinarily effective in performance. Jonson is also historically important for his espousal of the classical tenets of the drama and the shaping of the dramatic work over the next two centuries.

Thomas KYD (1557–95)

The Spanish Tragedy, with the First Part of Hieronimo 1592
This is considered to have been an important influence on Shakespeare when he came to write *Hamlet*. One of the first important Revenge Tragedies, the 'play within a play' ending was extremely popular and influential.

George LILLO (1693–1739)

The London Merchant, or the History of George Barnwell 1731
Lillo's plays are important early examples of 'middle class' domestic tragedies. Barnwell is an apprentice who, having been seduced by a courtesan, robs his employer and murders his uncle.

Joan LITTLEWOOD (1914–)

Oh! What a Lovely War 1963
This is the most famous play to come from the enormously influential Theatre Workshop. The First World War is seen largely from the perspective of the lower classes at home and in the trenches, and presented through the use of popular songs.

Christopher MARLOWE (1564–93)

Tamburlaine the Great 1587
Marlowe's life was short and the circumstances of his death mysterious. Primarily a great poet he forged a dramatic language that benefited all who followed him. *Tamburlaine* is Marlowe's first essay on the theme of power which occupies all his plays. This is also the first major verse drama.

Doctor Faustus 1588
The Faust myth and the limits of power and knowledge are the themes of Marlowe's greatest play.

The Jew of Malta 1592
This is a grotesque comedy seen as a satire of religious hypocrisy, and even of the Christian state. The main character is a Machiavellian outsider figure, and there is an outrageous plot of multiple poisonings.

Edward II 1593
A chronicle play concerning the failure of Edward to satisfy the lords of the land and his eventual ghastly murder.

John MARSTON (c. 1576–1634)

The Malcontent 1604
The Malcontent is a comedy, at least in tone, around the theme of revenge.

The Dutch Courtesan 1605
Another comedy, this concerns a young man's love for a courtesan and her revenge on her jilting lover. Not as successful as *The Malcontent*, it is often funny, and like his other plays, it holds the potential to turn into tragedy at any moment.

Philip MASSINGER (1583–1640)

A New Way to Pay Old Debts 1633
Massinger was principal playwright to the King's Men (Shakespeare's company) from 1625. *A New Way to Pay Old Debts* is a City Comedy.

Thomas MIDDLETON (1570–1627)

Michaelmas Term 1607
A Mad World My Masters 1608
A Trick to Catch the Old One 1608
A Fair Quarrel 1617 with William Rowley
The Changeling 1623 with William Rowley
A Chaste Maid in Cheapside 1630
Women Beware Women 1657
Middleton's fame as an important Jacobean dramatist continues to grow apace as more of his works are studied and performed. The first three plays listed are of the type known as Jacobean City Comedies – plays about the urban middle class. *A Chaste Maid in Cheapside* is the classic of the genre. The later works are tragedies and the strong characterization of the female characters is an added interest to modern readers. *The Changeling* is an undoubted masterpiece both in the psychological realism of the central relationship and the direct power of the dramatic verse.

Arthur MILLER (1915–)

The Crucible 1953
Death of a Salesman 1949
Miller is one of the best dramatists – not just 'American' dramatists – of this century. He was intensely concerned with what constituted modern America, both politically and socially. In his play *The Crucible* he examines the nature and origins of the McCarthy era in America while at the same time setting the play in seventeenth century New England. In *Death of a Salesman* he creates the character of Willy Loman, the sad figure who still clings closely to the ideals of the 'American Dream'. *The Collected Plays* were published in 1958 but Miller is still producing interesting work.

Peter NICHOLS (1927–)

A Day in the Life of Joe Egg 1967
This powerful and moving play is based on autobiographical material. It concerns two people who have a spastic child who is so damaged she is almost a vegetable.

Sean O'CASEY (1884–1964)

The Shadow of a Gunman 1925
An ironic tragi-comedy set against the background of the British Army hunting an IRA gunman, it combines knockabout comedy with serious events.

Juno and the Paycock 1925
Juno concerns the changing fortunes of an Irish family against the background of the Civil War in Ireland. Possibly O'Casey's best play.

The Plough and the Stars 1926
Set against the background of the 1916 Easter Rising, O'Casey here contrasts the fanatical idealism of revolutionaries against the sufferings of their women.

Eugene O'NEILL (1888–1953)

Mourning Becomes Electra 1931
A successful post-Freud 'modernization' of the classic Greek three-part tragedy, the Oresteia. In the aftermath of the American Civil War, the returning general's family destroys itself in a conflict between puritan guilt and sensual passion.

Long Day's Journey into Night 1941
A family tragedy in which a drug addict, Mary, her husband James and sons Jamie (an alcoholic) and Edmund act out destructive and soul-destroying relationships. *Long Day's Journey into Night* is a long play full of talk which none the less has enormous dramatic power. The father, who is modelled on O'Neill's actor father, has provided triumphs for two of Britain's great actors: Ralph Richardson and Laurence Olivier.

The Iceman Cometh 1946
This is a naturalist play, set in Harry Hope's bar, about a group of 'no-hopers' who drunkenly pass the time dreaming and talking of better things.

Joe ORTON (1933–67)

Entertaining Mr Sloane 1964
This is a very successful black comedy in which a young man lodges at what appears to be a normal family house but soon becomes party to sinister happenings. An extraordinary contrast is achieved between the outrageous violence of the action and the pretentions of the participants.

Loot 1965
Using the conventions of detective fiction to satirize police corruption this anarchic farce centres around coffins, dead bodies and money.

What the Butler Saw 1969
A parody of a farce set in a psychiatrist's office. Orton offers a black comedy view of modern day psychology and authority figures.

John OSBORNE (1929–)

Look Back in Anger 1956
Jimmy Porter rages about life with his long suffering wife and a friend – a play more famous for what it achieved in the theatre than for its actual quality.

The Entertainer 1957
Osborne's best play uses three generations of the Rice family, who are music hall entertainers, to show the decline of Britain – 'don't clap, lady, it's a very old building' – and the contrast between personal values (or fantasies) and reality.

Thomas OTWAY (1652–85)

Venice Preserv'd 1682
A play of political and sexual betrayal. Along with Dryden, Otway is the major tragedian of the Restoration period – and this is the best play of the genre.

Arthur Wing PINERO (1855–1934)

The Magistrate 1885
This is the first of Pinero's farces and superb entertainment in performance.

The Second Mrs Tanqueray 1893
A serious play concerning 'a woman with a past', this was very influential in alerting theatre management to the potential for 'serious' drama.

Trelawny of the Wells 1898
Set around the stock theatres where Pinero began his career this splendid comedy continues to grace the stage in frequent revivals.

Harold PINTER (1930–)

The Birthday Party 1958
The Caretaker 1960
The Collection/The Lover 1961/3
The Homecoming 1965
Old Times 1971
No Man's Land 1975
Betrayal 1978
Pinter is perhaps the most established and influential of modern British playwrights. Using small casts, minimal action and an accurate representation of everyday speech he succeeds in creating an atmosphere of threat and distrust. Comedy is laced with

potential, or actual, violence. Audiences are left in the dark, as the characters often seem to be, as to what (if anything) is happening. Pinter has also produced work for radio and for the cinema, usually adaptations. *The Collection* and *The Lover* were written for television.

James Robinson PLANCHÉ (1796–1880)

The Vampyre; or the Bride of the Isles 1820
Planche adapted many melodramas for the theatre, often translating them from French, Italian and Spanish. *The Vampyre* is a good example of the genre, while technically it introduced the 'vampire trap' to the English stage.

J B PRIESTLEY (1894–)

Time and the Conways 1937
This is one of Priestley's 'Time' plays wherein he uses different perspectives in time to illuminate character and situation.

An Inspector Calls 1945
Priestley's most famous play. A rich and influential family in a Northern town is torn to pieces by the persistent attempts of the Inspector to solve a murder.

Terence RATTIGAN (1911–)

The Winslow Boy 1946
Based on the true story of an Edwardian naval cadet who was unjustly accused of theft and the fight to clear his name. Rattigan's great success in providing well made plays for 'Aunt Edna' meant that she watched a series of studies in loneliness such as *The Burning Vision, Separate Tables* and *Ross*.

Thomas William ROBERTSON (1829–71)

Caste 1867
In his most famous play Robertson introduced realistic settings and a studied naturalism unusual for the time. Here he condemns the class system through the story of a young girl whose fiancé's family rejects her because of her background.

Nicholas ROWE (1674–1718)

The Fair Penitent 1703
Rowe was one of the foremost tragedians of his period and *The Fair Penitent* is his most famous work. It gave a type a name in the character of the 'gay Lothario'.

Peter SHAFFER (1926–)

The Royal Hunt of the Sun 1964
This tells the story of the conquest of Peru. It is an attempt to use 'not only words but rites, mimes, masks and magics'.

Equus 1973
A stable boy blinds six horses with a metal spike – the play explores the question 'why?' through the intervention of a psychiatrist.

Amadeus 1980
The brilliant idea of Salieri's quarrel with God over the genius of Mozart is rather better presented in the excellent film version than on the stage where Shaffer's tendency to tell rather than show weakens both the drama and the arguments.

William SHAKESPEARE (1564–1616)

Complete Works (ed. Peter Alexander, 1961)
Complete Works (ed. C J Sisson, 1963)
The Complete Pelican Shakespeare (ed. A Harbage, 1969)
The Complete Works of Shakespeare (ed. Gary Taylor and Stanley Wells, 1988)
There are single-play editions available in *The New Arden Shakespeare*, *The New Swan Shakespeare*, *The New Cambridge Shakespeare*, and the *Penguin Shakespeare*. Each play has a separate editor and the texts are annotated, with introductions and glossaries.

'He was not of an age, but for all time!': Ben Jonson said it first and simplest. Between about 1588 and 1613 Shakespeare wrote the 37 plays generally accepted as his. It is neither a perfect or sacred body of work. In performance, the texts are often cut or expanded in order to clarify the sense or improve the dramatic impact. But taken all in all, he is England's greatest creative genius, who has left a legacy of fiction, drama and poetry which is probably unsurpassed in world literature. It has inspired great work in other languages and other arts, and, by providing the classic challenges in dramatic performance, is one of the main avenues through which the theatre itself evolves.

For convenient reference, the plays are divided into Comedies, Histories, Tragedies, Problem Plays and Romances. Such categorization is inevitably a travesty of work which could encompass different moods and modes of expression in one play. Similarly the citing of certain plays as representatives of their category leaves unmentioned works which, if written by a less prolific author, would be featured as excellent examples. In each category the plays are listed in the order in which they were written.

Comedies

The Comedy of Errors 1592–3, *The Taming of the Shrew* 1593–4, *The Two Gentlemen of Verona* 1594–5, *Love's Labour's Lost* 1594–5, *A Midsummer Night's Dream* 1595–6, *The Merchant of Venice* 1596–7, *Much Ado About Nothing* 1598–1600, *As You Like It* 1598–1600, *Twelfth Night* 1598–1600, *The Merry Wives of Windsor* 1600–1601
Many of the comedies belong to Shakespeare's 'early' period as a dramatist and involve such things as dual plots, mistaken identities and the contrast between the courtly and the ordinary life. Several of them, such as *Love's Labour's Lost* and

Twelfth Night contain hints of the darker themes of the tragedies, while *The Merchant of Venice* is close to a problem play, in the moral ambiguity with which it treats Shylock and his claims for justice. *A Midsummer Night's Dream* contains most of the elements of early comedies. The plot is a mixture of farce and down-to-earth observations as Quince, Snug and Bottom contrive to produce an entertainment for Theseus, the Duke, while Hernia, Helena, Lysander and Demetrius show us the agonies of love. Magic conspires with sense to bring about a happy resolution.

   Twelfth Night, a work of Shakespeare's maturity, is probably the most frequently studied and performed of the comedies. There is a wide range of character parts, both male (Malvolio, Feste, Sir Toby Belch, Sir Andrew Aguecheck) and female (Olivia, Viola, Maria), liquid verse speeches and colloquial prose dialogue, farcical complications and cruel disappointments and the haunting epilogue of Feste's song.

Histories

Henry VI (Parts 1,2 and 3) 1590–91, *Richard III* 1592–3, *Richard II* 1595–6, *King John* 1596–7, *Henry IV (Parts 1 and 2)* 1597–8, *Henry V* 1598–1600, *Henry VIII* 1612–13

With the exception of *Henry VIII*, which was Shakespeare's last play, the histories are works of his early career. The history cycle is that of the turbulent years of usurpation, revolt and civil war which starts with the overthrow of Richard II, moves through Henry V's victory in France, to the chaos of the Wars of the Roses and the eventual replacement of the murderous Richard III by the first Tudor king. The plays explore such issues as the nature of kingship, the personal qualities of rulers and revolutionaries, the corruption in the state and the justification for overthrowing lawful government. The central achievement in this genre is *Henry IV, Parts 1 and 2*, in which Prince Hal, son of Henry IV, is shown as an irresponsible youth who prefers the company of Sir John Falstaff to the attendance at court, but who is preparing himself nobly for the demands of leadership. The plays contain political awareness, comedy, conflict and action as the head battles with the heart. The character of Falstaff is one of the great creations of English literature. The modern tendency to stage the two parts of *Henry IV* and *Henry V* in sequence allows for the full portrait of Hal to be drawn: from spoilt brat to the magnanimous victor of Agincourt.

Tragedies

Titus Andronicus 1593–4, *Romeo and Juliet* 1594–5, *Julius Caesar* 1598–1600, *Hamlet* 1600, *Othello* 1604–5, *King Lear* 1605–6, *Macbeth* 1605–6, *Anthony and Cleopatra* 1606–7, *Coriolanus* 1607–8, *Timon of Athens* 1607–8

These plays can be sub-divided into the 'Roman Plays' and the 'Great Tragedies'. In style and characterization the Roman Plays are very different: the brutal savagery of *Titus Andronicus*; the sparse verse and real-politic of *Julius Caesar*; the sensuous language and self-deceit of *Anthony and Cleopatra*. They are linked histories in their exploration of the nature of leadership and mob rule. 'Conspiracy' is never far from the lips of those in power or those who seek it. In *Coriolanus* the hero is a brave man, with a strong sense of personal honour but his contempt for the 'ordinary citizen' and his refusal to compromise on any issue makes us question the nature of his leadership.

The Great Tragedies of *Hamlet, Macbeth, Othello* and *King Lear* continue the examination of a great man's downfall. The hero is destroyed by a fatal flaw in his character which either spurs him on to an unreasonable action or which prevents him from acting when he should. Hamlet is tortured by doubts about his mother and determined to revenge his murdered father, but prolongs his own agony and creates fatal crises in the lives of other people and for the state itself.

King Lear is the most powerful evocation of a man confronted by evil and good at the same time, an act of misjudgement unleashes the forces of nature against him. Macbeth is a murderous dictator with a vigorously ambitious wife: types that make today's headlines. Yet the power of the play's poetic language and imagery, especially in its illumination of the inner tensions of the Macbeths, is such as to create an excitement and understanding rather than disgust and condemnation. In all these plays, arguably the greatest ever written, Shakespeare examines the nature of good and evil, but in doing so the artist and humanist takes precedence over the moralist or political philosopher.

Problem Plays

Troilus and Cressida 1602–3, *All's Well That End's Well* 1602–3, *Measure for Measure* 1604–5

In previous ages these three plays tended to be classified as comedies and little performed because of their partial or uncomfortable fulfilment of the expectations of comedy. In them, Shakespeare grapples with the perennial, personal problems of love, fidelity, justice, and forgiveness and acknowledges the contradictory nature of man's reponses to these issues. They are difficult works, combining gloom with humour, base instincts with high feelings. In dramatic terms, the problems are resolved with obvious difficulty and with a different 'message' in each play: *Measure for Measure* offers a religious resolution, *All's Well That Ends Well* finds a kind of nobility in the individual will, while *Troilius and Cressida* offers little hope that people can live by any man or god-given code of conduct.

Romances

Pericles, Prince of Tyre 1608–10, *Cymbeline* 1608–10, *The Winter's Tale* 1608–10, *The Tempest* 1611–12

Often referred to as the 'Last Plays', the alternative categorization of 'Romances' is here preferred because it avoids the inference that Shakespeare himself saw them as his last works at the time of their writing. The assumption that Shakespeare portrayed himself as Prospero putting aside his magic is neither a good interpretation of the meaning of *The Tempest* or of Shakespeare's biography. He went on to write another two works by himself (*Henry VIII*) and in collaboration (*The Two Noble Kinsmen*, with J Fletcher, 1634). These plays are fashioned from story-book romances in which potentially tragic events and violent emotions are held within a framework of fable. This allows for an ultimate reconciliation of the characters and motives. They are built around the ancient themes of loss and rediscovery, the protection of innocence and beauty and the healing power of time and natural renewal.

The Winter's Tale recounts the reconciliation of Leontes, King of Sicily, with his wife Hermione. Leontes' fit of sudden passionate jealousy, which precipitated their separation, is expressed in vivid, fractured verse which marks another level of achievement on Shakespeare's poetic expression. The renewal theme is carried by the love story of the lost daughter, Perdita, and Florizel, which flourishes away from the traumas of court in the innocent pastoral world of shepherds and clowns. *The Tempest* focuses on the final processes of reconciliation. Prospero regains his Dukedom with the help of magic but not before all the characters – including Prospero himself – have been tested and their fitness for a 'brave new world' established. As in the other romances the reconciliation of the quarrelling rulers is achieved through the love of the younger generation.

George Bernard SHAW (1856–1950)

Works (26 vols, Penguin Shaw Plays, 1930–50)
The Complete Plays 1934
The Complete Prefaces 1934
Shaw was almost forty when *Widower's Houses*, his first play was produced. It was a further ten years before he was established as the leading playwright in the English language. His plays tackle controversial social and political subjects and, as there were early difficulties getting them performed, he had them published with introductory prefaces which are well worth reading in their own right. In all, he wrote more than 50 plays.

Arms and the Man 1894
In this play Bluntschli goes to war with chocolate rather than a pistol in his holster – an anti-romantic comedy.

Man and Superman 1903
This is a comedy of manners about the battle between the sexes which also carries on Shaw's arguments – especially in the intermediary 'Don Juan in Hell' Act – about the lifeforce and the nature of progress.

Major Barbara 1907
A Salvation Army daughter and her arms-manufacturing father are subjected to paradoxical dilemmas and propositions.

Pygmalion 1912
Henry Higgins teaches Eliza Dolittle in a comic masterpiece that has now re-emerged from the shadow of the successful but saccharine musical version.

Heartbreak House 1917
Written in the Chekhovian manner, a house full of attractive dreamers, misfits, eccentrics and lay-abouts talk through the countdown to the violence of the First World War. Good talk and strong symbols, but the message remains obscure.

Saint Joan 1924
Saint Joan contains a great part for an actress and some good arguments as the Church and the Law strive for a burning. Perhaps it says something about the relative merits of Shaw as a serious playwright and as a writer of comedies that in the theatre one can feel at least as much for the predicament of Eliza Dolittle as for that of Saint Joan.

Richard Brinsley SHERIDAN (1751–1816)

The Rivals 1775
A high-spirited comedy verging on farce, *The Rivals* is famous for Mrs Malaprop's legendary scrambling of the English language.

The School for Scandal 1777
A salon's gossip causes no end of trouble to young lovers in one of the greatest English comedies. An instant 'hit' when it was first performed, its frequent revivals owe as much to its humanity as to its wit.

The Critic 1779
Similar to Buckingham's 'The Rehearsal' in its sending up of theatrical genres *The Critic*'s satire is more generalized in not having a specific target.

R C SHERRIFF (1896–1975)

Journey's End 1928
One of the most successful of the middle class 'serious' dramas of the period between the wars, this is centred around the meeting of two men in the First World War trenches. One (now an alcoholic and broken man) had been the hero of the other.

Tom STOPPARD (1937–)

Rosencrantz and Guildenstern are Dead 1967
The Real Inspector Hound/After Magritte 1968
Jumpers 1972
Travesties 1974
Professional Foul 1977
The Real Thing 1982
Stoppard's plays use wit and comic invention to probe intellectual situations with perception and agility. *Rosencrantz and Guilderstern are Dead* has the brilliant idea of putting the bit-part players in *Hamlet* in the centre of a drama that they cannot understand. *Jumpers* is about philosophers, while *Travesties* combines both literary parody and parallels with philosophical debate. *Professional Foul*, his first television play, deals with a philosophy professor's visit to Prague at the same time as an England *v.* Czechoslovakia football match.

David STOREY (1933–)

The Restoration of Arnold Middleton 1966
Storey's first play is a comedy dealing with the family life of a school teacher who continues to behave like one at home.

The Contractor 1969
The building and taking down of a tent for the wedding reception of the contractor's daughter forms the focus for an examination of this fascinating play's characters and their backgrounds.

Home 1970
Greatly influenced by Pinter and Beckett, *Home* is set in an asylum garden and centres around the conversations of two old men and two women who eventually and briefly meet.

J M SYNGE (1871–1909)

Riders to the Sea 1904
Regarded by some as the best short play in the language this tells of a mother who has lost all but one of her sons to the sea and now has to say farewell to the last one.

The Well of the Saints 1905
A dark, almost savage comedy of two blind beggars who regain their sight and then, given the opportunity, reject it, as blindness seems preferable.

The Playboy of the Western World 1907
In a village near Mayo, Christy Mahon boasts how he has killed his father. It is something of a shock when his father appears to challenge him. In a good performance it can be one of the funniest of twentieth century plays.

Deidre of the Sorrows 1910
Doomed to bring disaster on all who love her Deidre and her lover attempt to avoid their fate, unsuccessfully, by living apart. Written in a high style of lyric prose.

Tom TAYLOR (1817–80)

The Ticket of Leave Man 1863
A famous melodrama, important for its use of realistic contemporary detail, this includes what is believed to be the first stage detective.

Dylan THOMAS (1914–53)

Under Milk Wood 1954
Subtitled 'A Play for Voices' this offers a day in the life of an imaginary Welsh fishing village (Llareggub – try it backwards). The static nature of the narrative, the comic

vignettes and the poetic language were perfectly suited to radio. It continues to be immensely popular.

Cyril TOURNEUR (1575–1626)

The Revenger's Tragedy 1607
Sometimes claimed to be the work of Middleton, partly because it is so good, this is a revenge tragedy very closely patterned around a morality play framework. Vendice exposes corruption in court but in doing so becomes corrupted himself.

Ben TRAVERS (1886–1981)

A Cuckoo in the Nest, 1925
Rookery Nook 1930
The Aldwych Farces, of which these are two excellent examples, are sometimes called Bedroom Farces as so much depends on falling trousers and ladies in underwear being confronted at inappropriate moments.

John VANBRUGH (1664–1726)

The Relapse, or Virtue in Danger 1696
This should be read (or seen) in relation with Cibber's *Love's Last Shift* of which this is a continuation and a criticism, featuring many of the same characters, including Lord Foppington and Sir Novelty Fashion.

John WEBSTER (1580–1625)

The White Devil 1608
A story of love and revenge, this is a tragedy that is in many ways comparable to Shakespeare's *Anthony and Cleopatra* in its theme of personal and political tragedy.

The Duchess of Malfi 1613–14
The Duchess marries secretly for love and sets in train a series of revenge plots and murders, including her own by a hired killer obsessed with extracting a confession of guilt from her. One of the most famous and best of late Jacobean tragedies it is often revived with success. In both plays, Webster's language and imagery matches the macabre plots in their concern with 'the skull beneath the skin'.

Arnold WESKER (1932–)

The Western Trilogy – Chicken Soup with Barley 1957, *Roots* (1959), *I'm Talking about Jerusalem* 1960
These plays examine the life of an East End Jewish family over the thirty years up to 1960 against their social background, contemporary events, and the decline of socialist commitment.

Chips with Everything 1962
As with all Wesker's plays, a mixture of realism, naturalism and symbolism is combined. A pacifist RAF recruit is eventually made to conform.

John WHITING (1917–63)

Marching Song 1954
An intelligent play in which a defeated German general attempts to understand the motives for his actions in the past and comes to a grim solution.

The Devils 1961
Based on Aldous Huxley's *The Devils of Loudon*, this is a dark epic tragedy of love, religion, and political persecution in seventeenth century France.

Oscar WILDE (1854–1900)

Lady Windermere's Fan 1892
A Woman of No Importance 1893
An Ideal Husband 1895
The Importance of Being Earnest 1895
During the brief period of writing these plays Wilde was the most successful playwright in the country, and his popularity shows no sign of waning. *Lady Windermere's Fan* initiated a series of social comedies which not only offered situations that were familiar in the 'serious' plays of Jones or Pinero, but mocked Victorian morality through the witty dialogue and the deliberately contrived mechanisms of the plots. *The Importance of Being Earnest* is the finest comedy of manners since Congreve: sustained and brilliant wit, absurd plot, and the monstrous Lady Bracknell.

Tennessee WILLIAMS (1914–83)

The Glass Menagerie 1945
The play is set in the home of Laura and her mother in St Louis, Mississippi, and tells of the mother's frustrated reasons for attempting to provide a good marriage for her daughter.

A Streetcar Named Desire 1947
The Williams' themes of self-deceit and sexual frustration first achieved an international audience in this New Orleans drama about the would-be refined schoolteacher, Blanch Dubois, and her violent clash with her working-class brother-in-law.

Cat on a Hot Tin Roof 1955
It is Big Daddy's birthday, but the family gathering reveals the tensions and potential violence which simmer under the surface as his son, Brick, drinks himself into melancholia despite the attempts of his wife, Maggie, to save him.

William WYCHERLEY (1640–1716)

The Country Wife 1675
In this famous Restoration Comedy Horner cuckolds the town by having it put around that he is no longer capable of sexual encounters. A strong attack on social hypocrisy.

The Plain Dealer 1677
This is another excellent comedy considered by some to be superior to *The Country Wife*. The plot is an adaptation from Moliere's *Le Misanthrope*.

William Butler YEATS (1865–1939)

The Countess Cathleen 1892
The Countess, representative of the spirit of Ireland, must sell her soul to save her country. Yeats's first contribution to verse and symbolist drama was not performed until 1899 and then amidst church condemnation, student demonstrations and watchful police: 'I forgot that in Ireland there are not symbols but realists.'

Cathleen ni Houlihan 1902
'Did that play of mine send out certain men the English shot'. Perhaps not the play, but Maud Gonne's performance in it. It marks the highpoint of Yeats's involvement in Irish nationalism.

On Baile's Strand 1904
Yeats's many interpretations of the Cuchulain legends and myth were part of his attempt to forge a drama which spoke of Ireland to the Irish and made the past relevant to the present. This one concerns Cuchulain's meeting with an overlord, King Conchubar. It is partly dramatized through the technique of an old man telling the story to a younger man.

Purgatory 1938
Purgatory was much admired by Eliot who felt it successfully solved the problems of verse drama. Here Oedipus (the man who killed his father) meets Cahulica (the man who killed his son). This emphasizes Yeats's preoccupation with cyclical history and the returning journeys of restless souls.

BIOGRAPHY

Biography caters for several very strong and persistent interests: curiosity, admiration for the great, a desire to experience vicariously the surroundings of the famous, a sense that lessons of particular moral value inhere in the lives of such people. It has thus always held out a particularly faithful reflection of the times in which it was produced. In the Middle Ages, the lives of Saints offered examples of individual virtue and the beneficent workings of Divine Providence. In the Renaissance, collections of exemplary political careers such as *The Mirrour for Magistrates* or North's highly influential English rendering of Plutarch's *Lives* catered to a fascination with the rise and fall of princes and statesmen bound on Fortune's Wheel. The seventeenth century liking for antiquarianism combined with enthusiasm for the new science and its first explorers found its most attractive expression in Aubrey's *Brief Lives*.

In the eighteenth century, Dr Johnson perceived a special moral value in biography's service to a curiosity which had become more widespread and explicit in his time:

> 'I have often thought that there has rarely passed a life of which judicious and faithful narrative would not be useful .... There is such a uniformity in the state of man ... that there is scarce any possibility of good or ill but is common to human kind.' (*The Rambler*, No. 60)

Later, Carlyle was to reflect a typical Romantic sense of the pivotal role of the heroic figure in human affairs in his assertion, 'What is history but the essence of innumerable biographies?' In the 1920s an approach suggested by the new insights of psychology reinforced the impulse given to biography by Lytton Strachey's *Eminent Victorians*, which vividly epitomized a disillusion with Victorian complacency and hypocrisy.

Desmond McCarthy defined the biographer as an artist, but an artist on oath. He is faced with a quest for all possible evidence relating to his subject; Boswell drew on half-a-dozen different accounts to compose the scene where Dr Johnson is interviewed by George III. The biographer's oath also enjoins scepticism in sifting often unreliable evidence. For example, much of the correspondence of Victorian notables was silently censored by relatives before being published. Again, Robert Gittings has described how Cabinet minutes during the Second World War were rewritten twice by civil servants, first to give to them the coherence and logic of what the participants should have said, secondly to reintroduce enough colloquialism and informality to make them acceptable to participants as what they might in fact have said.

Frequently the biographer's respect for truth has had to cope with deliberately placed barriers. The subject himself may have harboured a strong desire for privacy and the relatives a desire to suppress everything detracting from a purely commemorative image. Victorian biographers felt very intensely the claims of privacy and decorum. Lockhart, at one point in his great biography of Scott, expressed the dilemma succinctly; to report conversations fairly, one must be on intimate terms with all the parties; those intimate terms impose in turn a duty of discretion. Furthermore, many Victorian biographies were virtually commissioned as memorials; Dr Arnold's biographer, Arthur Penrhyn Stanley, was charged with writing the official life by Arnold's widow while in attendance at the family's mourning. Thus a major task of many twentieth century biographers has been to unearth long-suppressed evidence, to revise legends which originated as pious falsifications on the part of earlier biographers, and have now solidified into the acceptable, traditional face of their subject.

Leon Edel, the biographer of Henry James, has said that the biographer 'must judge the facts, but he must not sit in judgement', yet some of the finest English biographies have exhibited widely varying proportions of sympathy and judgement. Elizabeth Gaskell's study of Charlotte Bronte was impelled by a passionate admiration for a friend; Lytton Strachey's portraits of eminent Victorians by an intense scorn for hypocrisy and complacency. Sometimes the reader may feel that the power of a portrait is drawn from the biographer's own experience of a life like that of his subject. Dr Johnson expresses a clear-eyed assessment of the many faults of Richard Savage, but the vividness of his *An Account of the Life of Mr Richard Savage* stems from his memory of his own tribulations as a struggling hack-writer at a time when he and Savage met on equal terms.

Johnson himself asserted; 'Nobody can write the life of a man, but those who ate and drank and lived in social intercourse with him.' This dictum, when enthusiastically put in practice by Boswell, produced the masterpiece of English biography. However, the twentieth century has also been a rich period in biography and its best work has arisen as often from the objective judgement and painstaking investigation of a more academic approach. Among the distinctive qualities of the best twentieth century biographies has been the insight into the inner man offered by a sensitive application of psychoanalytic concepts, though this always requires caution, and a weighing of its testimony in the context of all the other evidence; the availability of more reliable texts of letters and other papers (sometimes previously edited by the biographer himself) has been an advantage which has often been exploited to good effect. Another strength of twentieth century biography has frequently been a deftness in narrative technique, which may avoid a strictly linear treatment of time, or apply skilful variation in the point of view from which the subject is seen. The best 'artists on oath' have combined something drawn from the art of the novelist with a scrupulous concern for the truth.

Although most critical acclaim is based on scholarly thoroughness, perception and integrity, the books included here have the essential merit of being good to read. There is a conscious bias towards 'style', and for being entertained in works like these, either by the *mot juste* or the trenchant judgement, or even the doubtfully relevant diversion. Massive tomes crammed with meticulous reference do not necessarily make the most lucid portraits.

The problem dealt with in meeting the demands of such a concern for the truth are interestingly described by J L Clifford in *From Puzzles to Portraits*. He has also edited an anthology of views on biography from 1560 to 1960 in *Biography as an Art*. A very stimulating history of literary biography in England and America is to be found in R D Altick's *Lives and Letters*. In addition to Clifford, two other distinguished contemporary biographers have written illuminating studies of the form, Leon Edel in *Literary Biography* and Robert Gittings in *Nature of Biography*. Sir Harold Nicolson's *The Development of English Biography* is interesting in that it conveys very clearly the attitudes prevalent at the moment when biography was taking a decisive turn away from nineteenth century models. Virginia Woolf's two essays, *The Art of Biography* and *The New Biography* (reprinted in *Collected Essays*, ed. L Woolf, vol. iv), are of interest, firstly as a theoretical consideration of biography to consider alongside her close friend, Lytton Strachey's practice, and secondly, as indicating the higher status accorded in the twentieth century to biography as a branch of literature.

These selection criteria mean that certain biographies, especially those of eminent political figures, have been excluded as have 'potted' aids for the student in a hurry, encomiums by close relatives or sycophants, diatribes of hostility, highly derivative 'commissioned' works and 'character pictures' in which politics are not in the foreground. On the other hand, a case for inclusion is made by studies of figures whose careers impinge on the political world or who move, however uneasily, in and out of it: interesting and ambitious lawyers, military men and trades unionists – these have been included if they have also been fortunate enough to attract the attention of a real writer. The main bias, however, is towards literary biography, i.e. biographies of literary figures because these are the lives which are most likely to interest the readers of *An English Library*.

Peter ACKROYD (1917–)

T.S. Eliot 1984
It has so far been impossible to produce a definitive biography of T S Eliot. Access to Eliot's unpublished work or correspondence has always been withheld. Drawing on other evidence, Ackroyd presents a thoughtful portrayal of the complex man who lay behind some of the most important poetry of the twentieth century.

John AUBREY (1626–97)

Brief Lives 1669–96
Dick's excellent 1949 edition (republished by Penguin in 1972) presents the first coherent rendering of Aubrey's fragmentary papers. Though his sketches of so many of the prominent figures of the seventeenth century dwell often on the humanly revealing rather than the decisive moments of their lives, his verve as a raconteur and delight in the variety of human behaviour convey the spirit of his age.

Jocelyn BAINES (1925–73)

Joseph Conrad: a critical biography 1960
The first full biographical and critical study of Conrad and his work, throwing much new light on his career and character. Shows how Conrad transmuted much of his own experience in his novels.

Quentin BELL (1910–)

Virginia Woolf: a biography 1972
A lucid and sensitive two-volume study of a great writer whose personal sufferings were as intense as the imaginative life so coloured by them. The biography draws not only on the intimacy possible to the author as Woolf's nephew, but also on his tact and skill in deploying his knowledge.

Eileen BIGLAND (1898–1970)

The Indomitable Mrs Trollope 1953
Frances Trollope was the mother of Anthony, and herself a novelist. She is best remembered for the *Domestic Manners of the Americans*, the most vivid – if highly disillusioned – account by an English writer of the United States in its early years. An interesting study of a courageous, energetic and lively character.

Robert BLAKE (1916–)

The Unknown Prime Minister 1955
A celebrated life of Andrew Bonar Law: the paradox of 'power through self-effacement' is explained in sympathetic terms, and offers a valuable insight into Conservative politics during a long period first of opposition and then of coalition.

Disraeli 1966
This is a scholarly and entertaining life of the Tory legend by the foremost historian of the Conservative Party. It supercedes the classic multi-volume Moneypenny and Buckle: as the author says in his preface: 'the reader will console himself with the thought that it is not as long'. A masterpiece of condensation, re-appraisal and wit.

2nd Earl of BIRKENHEAD (1907–75)

The Life of F E Smith, First Earl of Birkenhead 1933–5, 1959
A filial offering but the 2nd Earl was a skilled biographer. This is an authorative study of a remarkable man of fabled ambition and brilliance: it demonstrates the close ties that bind politics and the law in England.

James BOSWELL (1740–95)

The Life of Samuel Johnson 1791
This is the most famous literary biography in English. Modern scholarship provides more details about Johnson's life and attitudes, but Boswell brings his friend alive and – above all – lets him speak to us. The first edition was re-edited by Birkbeck Hill and published in 1887 and a revised edition by L F Powell was brought out between 1939 and 1950. Several inexpensive abridgements are available such as that in Everyman's Library, Oxford University Press's Worlds Classics, and the Penguin edition.

Andrew BOYLE (1919–)

Poor Dear Brendan 1974
This presents political biography as detective story, and is as compulsively readable. Brendan Bracken's misty origins and his closeness to Churchill prompted the rumour that he was the leader's natural son. The author does not conclude that he was, but the raffishness and mystery of his subject makes for a splendid yarn.

John BUCHAN (1875–1940)

The Marquis of Montrose 1913
Montrose was one of the great seventeenth century generals. Buchan unfolds the major events of his life with an undisguised admiration, but one which convinces the reader. Well documented with illustrations and maps of campaigns.

Alan BULLOCK (1914–)

The Life and Times of Ernest Bevin 1960–83
The definitive three-volume study of Ernest Bevin, dealing with his career as a Trade Union leader, Minister of Labour, and Foreign Secretary.

Hitler: A Study in Tyranny 1952 (revised 1964)
The most highly regarded biography of this century's Lucifer in any language, this large volume brings dispassionate scholarship to a figure inevitably surrounded by wild passions. A classic.

Gilbert BURNET (1643–1715)

Some Passages of the Life and Death of John Earl of Rochester 1680
This includes a first-hand account of the death-bed repentance and conversion of the famous libertine and poet. Burnet, as a friend and clergyman, attended Rochester during his last illness. Burnet's *History of My Own Times* (see the History section) contains many biographical sketches of the leading personalities of his day.

David CARLTON (1938–)

Anthony Eden 1981
The first major biography from David Carlton, who has interested himself in the international politics of the twentieth century. Although the reader is spared Eden's formative influences (into Parliament in eight pages), he is drawn towards his pre-Suez career by the author's devotion of four-fifths of the book to his life before becoming Prime Minister – a valuable corrective.

Thomas CARLYLE (1795–1881)

Life of John Sterling 1851
For Carlyle, as the most energetic proponent of the nineteenth century's enthusiasm for the heroic figure, biography was an especially significant activity. His largest works in this field were the *History of Frederick the Great* (1858–65) and his compilation of the *Letters and Speeches of Cromwell* (1845). However, his account of John Sterling, written in defence of a close friend against a highly critical study by Archbishop Hare, is perhaps the most attractive of his biographies for its avoidance of strident advocacy and its sympathy and sharpness of observation.

Humphrey CARPENTER (1946–)

W H Auden: a biography 1981
Although Carpenter's study was published only eight years after the poet's death, it had already been preceded by a flood of memoirs and a couple of full-length biographies. Carpenter's stands out in having had access to most of Auden's letters,

and the cooperation of his friends. A thorough and sympathetic biography, though taking full account of Auden's frailties.

George CAVENDISH (c. 1500–62)

The Life and Death of Cardinal Wolsey 1641
Cavendish was Wolsey's gentleman-usher and he writes largely from personal knowledge. As with Thomas More, the theme of the fall of a great man is a conventional one, but the vividness of description, the convincing background detail and the feeling for the character make this a striking early experiment in biography.

Margaret CAVENDISH, Duchess of Newcastle (c. 1624–74)

The Life of the Thrice Nobel Prince William Cavendish, Duke Marques and Earl of Newcastle 1667
An affectionate biography of the Royalist poet and playwright by his second wife, who also wrote poems and plays. One of Charles Lamb's 'jewels' of literature.

Lord David CECIL (1902–86)

Melbourne 1955
This is the combination of two books: *The Young Melbourne* (1939) and *Lord M* (1954). In prose as elegant as the author, this unsurpassed picture of Victoria's first and favourite PM is written with sympathy for a languid, disinterested figure.

R W CHAMBERS (1874–1942)

Thomas More 1935
A standard work on the only person to be both canonized by the Roman Catholic Church and made a Hero of the Russian Revolution.

W S CHURCHILL (1874–1965)

Lord Randolph Churchill 1906
Notwithstanding that Winston Churchill stood too close to his subject, and that Robert Rhodes James draws fascinatingly on material not admissable in 1906 in his study of the author-son, the magnificence of the Churchillian prose remains intoxicating and compelling.

Marlborough, His Life and Times 1947
The author's love of the subject – a soldier-statesman and a family mentor across 250 years – is evident on every page. Churchill's broad brush is appropriate for this epic figure, striding across Europe and re-drawing the map with panache and excitement.

James L CLIFFORD (1901–78)

Young Sam Johnson 1955
Dictionary Johnson 1980
Clifford's aim in the two parts of his biography was to present an account of Johnson's life up to 1763 that would approach the fullness of Boswell's portrayal of his later years. Recognized as one of the greatest achievements of twentieth century biography, it traces very fully the influence of Johnson's native setting in Lichfield on the development of his character and the dramatic fluctuations of his fortunes during the most productive period as a writer.

G G COULTON (1858–1947)

Chaucer and His England 1908
Although not enough was known at the time to write a fully-fledged biography of Chaucer, the author manages to combine an account of Chaucer's life in England with his voyages to the continent and shows the influence of contemporary poets on him. Social history is blended in for good measure.

Edward CRANKSHAW (1909–84)

Bismark 1981
This single volume biography, which tends to concentrate on the earlier and less celebrated phase of the Iron Chancellor's career, will become the most widely read English life of the man. Crankshaw has been praised for his study of Krushchev.

Bernard CRICK (1929–)

George Orwell: A Life 1980
A deliberately 'external', factual, honest biography of an elusive figure.

Helen DARBISHIRE (1881–1961) (ed)

The Early Lives of Milton 1932
Six accounts of Milton's life which were written by acquaintances of the poet or by writers who had contact with contemporary witnesses.

Ernest De SELINCOURT (1870–1943)

Dorothy Wordsworth 1933
This is possibly the best biography of Dorothy Wordsworth, by a scholar who also edited the letters of Dorothy and William, and Dorothy's journal.

Bernard DONOUGHUE (1934–) and G S JONES (1936–)

Herbert Morrison 1973
Students of Labour Party politics, of London government, and of the art of in-fighting, will find this indispensable to their libraries. The subject's ill-concealed ambition for power, and his bitterness on his disappointment, are fully traced. The authors are themselves familiar with many of the corridors tramped by Morrison.

Leon EDEL (1907–)

Henry James: The Untried Years 1843–70 1953
Henry James: The Conquest of London 1870–83 1962
Henry James: The Middle Years 1883–94 1963
Henry James: The Treacherous Years 1895–1901 1969
Henry James: The Master 1901–16 1972
Edel's work is probably the greatest twentieth century literary biography. James's career touched the literary world of America, England and France at almost every point, and Edel displays a complete knowledge of his life, a penetrating understanding of the man and a sensitive insight into his work. James was a highly industrious letter writer and one of the finest features of Edel's biography is his use of this mass of correspondence gradually to reveal the man.

Richard ELLMANN (1918–1987)

James Joyce 1959
A very full and illuminating life of Joyce, which draws on all the published and unpublished work of the author. A particular concern is to find in the details of Joyce's life the material which was to go into the composition of *Ulysses*.

Yeats: the Man and the Mask 1948 (revised 1979)
The definitive biography of Yeats has still to be written, but this is a scholarly and sensitive account of his life and work.

Oscar Wilde 1988
A detailed life of Wilde which shows signs of not having been completely finished before its author's death.

Geoffrey FINLAYSON (1927–)

The Seventh Earl of Shaftesbury 1801–1885 1981
Based on manuscript archives, this authorative and scholarly book traces Shaftesbury's commitments to the great reform issues of the day and examines his relationship with Cobden, Peel, Gladstone and Disraeli among others.

Michael FOOT (1913–)

Aneurin Bevan 1962, 1973 (vols I, II)
This massive book must be treated with caution – Michael Foot carried on the Bevanite tradition in Labour politics. Yet his admiration for the man illuminates rather than obscures his career, his background and more significantly, his mind. A joy to read for lovers of the English language.

John FORSTER (1812–76)

Life of Dickens 1872–4
There have been several important later studies of Dickens, of which the most distinguished is perhaps Edgar Johnson's. Forster's work, however, based on years of close friendship, and making good use of a very large correspondence between the author and Dickens remains indispensable.

James Anthony FROUDE (1818–94)

Thomas Carlyle: History of the First 40 Years of his Life 1882
Thomas Carlyle: History of his Life in London 1884
Froude was a close friend and disciple of Carlyle, and was given access to his private papers. In its frankness about Carlyle's frailties and the strains in his marriage it marks a significant move away from the conventional eulogy and discreet evasions of the typical Victorian biography. The controversy it aroused was unprecedented in its length and bitterness.

Thomas FULLER (1608–61)

The Worthies of England 1662
Well worth dipping into for its prose style and for a seventeenth century view of what and who made England 'worthy'.

J L GARVIN (1869–1947) and Julian AMERY (1919–)

The Life of Joseph Chamberlain 1935–69
Garvin, a long-serving editor of *The Times*, spent thirty years on this extraordinary figure, but left an incomplete work. Julian Amery, whose father carried Radical Joe's imperial message into the 1950s, has brought this massive life to its final six volumes.

Norman GASH (1912–)

Peel 1975
A condensed version of the author's two-volume definitive life: *Mr Secretary Peel* and *Sir Robert Peel*. Acclaimed as a major contribution not only to political biography but also to our understanding of early nineteenth century politics.

Elizabeth GASKELL (1810–65)

The Life of Charlotte Bronte 1857
Elizabeth Gaskell was a close friend of Charlotte Bronte and knew intimately the landscape where Charlotte grew up. Her biography is marked by an intense loyalty to its subject, sympathy for her sufferings, admiration for her selflessness, and understanding of her art. Possibly the finest biography of the nineteenth century.

Winifred GERIN (1901–81)

Anne Bronte 1959
Branwell Bronte 1961
Charlotte Bronte: the evolution of genius 1967
Emily Bronte: a biography 1971
Gerin is the only writer to have produced studies of all four members of the Bronte family, the first to have written the biography of Anne, and the first to have analysed sympathetically the character of the black sheep, Branwell. The setting of Haworth draws on the writer's familiarity as a resident of the place itself and her research throws much new light on Charlotte. The tetralogy was completed by a fine portrayal of Emily, one of the hardest challenges possible to any biographer in combining an almost totally uneventful external life with an inner life of extreme intensity. See also her biography *Elizabeth Gaskell*.

Martin GILBERT (1936–)

Finest Hour: Winston S Churchill 1939–1941 1983
Never Despair: Churchill 1945–1965 1988
The first volume covers the most apocalyptic years of Churchill's vast career, and is conceived in suitably epic proportions, drawing on a very wide range of sources, and written in prose which matches the excitement of the times. The second covers the years of victory – in war to defeat at the hands of the electorate and his subsequent parliamentary career and death.

Alexander GILCHRIST (1828–61)

Life of William Blake, 'Pictor Ignotus' 1863
Of the two volumes, the first is biographical, while the second contains a selection from his poetry and artistic work. As Gilchrist died before its completion, contributions to the work were made by Rossetti and other members of the Pre-Raphaelite circle. Though rather slanted by a number of anecdotes tending to fix the image of Blake as a saintly eccentric, this work was the beginning of a sympathetic and informed understanding.

Robert GITTINGS (1911–)

John Keats 1968
Before this full study, Gittings had written *John Keats: the Living Year*, which had followed in unprecedented detail the most productive period of Keats' life from 1818 to 1819. With comparable detail this work establishes the external facts of Keats' experience and the relation between his inner life and his poetry. Gittings has used his own exploration of the actual landscapes Keats knew to throw light on descriptive passages in his poetry.

Young Thomas Hardy 1975
The Older Hardy 1978
Hardy's attempt to protect his life from biographers has been singularly ineffective.
He has been portrayed in fact and fiction and the obscurities of his early life and loves
are a source of fascination. Gittings two-volume biography is thorough and unsparing
in its exposure of the sadness and guilt of the last years.

G R GLEIG (1796–1888)

The Life of Arthur, Duke of Wellington 1862
Rather heavy for many twentieth century readers, this book also contains a message,
that of following duty 'as the great duke did'. However, the biography is interesting in
that Gleig was Wellington's subaltern and he had first-hand experience of the man.

William GODWIN (1756–1836)

Memoir of Mary Wollstonecraft Godwin 1798
Mary Wollstonecraft, author of *The Vindication of the Rights of Women* was a highly
significant figure in the emergence of feminism. The memoir is a very valuable
first-hand testimony by an important writer of the period, who was her husband
during the last year of her life.

John GRIGG (1924–)

Lloyd George: The People's Champion 1978
This book is the companion volume to Grigg's earlier *The Young Lloyd George*
(1973) and completes the survey and study of this most renowned of politicians.

Gordon S HAIGHT (1901–85)

George Eliot: a biography 1968
Haight previously edited George Eliot's letters and this work is the result of a
profound immersion in the subject, and throws much new light on Eliot's life. The
way in which Haight, wherever possible, allows the central figures to speak for
themselves is especially welcome.

Nigel HAMILTON (1944–)

Monty: The Making of a General, 1887–1942 (vol. 1); *Master of the Battlefield,
1942–1944* (vol. 2); *The Field Marshall, 1944–1976* (vol. 3) 1978–83
This huge three-volume study of Field Marshall Montgomery has received wide
critical acclaim. The second volume is concerned entirely with the years 1942–44.
The author draws on Montgomery's private papers and treads a careful path between
the heroic legend and any preconceived attempt to destroy a reputation.

J L HAMMOND (1872–1949) and B HAMMOND

Lord Shaftesbury 1923
Shaftesbury entered Parliament in 1826 and became involved in the great domestic reforms of the nineteenth century, including those in public health, mines and factories. The 'Hammonds' biography is a highly readable account, sympathetic yet critical at the same time.

Nicholas HARPSFIELD (c. 1519–75)

Life of Sir Thomas More c. 1557
First published in 1932 this is an early example of the art of the biography – and the art of writing English prose.

Kenneth HARRIS (1856–1931)

Attlee 1982
A sympathetic treatment of a statesman who has had to wait too long for an assessment of appropriate stature. One of the most important recent political 'lives'.

Roy HARROD (1900–78)

John Maynard Keynes 1950
The nearest thing to an 'official life', this study by a distinguished pupil of Keynes and contributor to economic debate in his own time, sets the subject in the political background against which he propounded his principal arguments on economic management. The authorative life, even if the author is too close an admirer.

Christopher HIBBERT (1924–)

Benito Mussolini 1962
A feat of concision, this is the most popular and direct study of Mussolini, capturing the crazed mixture of high drama and low farce. Anecdotal and racy, it is nonetheless well-researched and worthy of a successful writer of historical narrative: his book on Lord Raglan preceded this study.

Michael HOLROYD (1935–)

Lytton Strachey: A Critical Biography 1967–8
Holroyd's two-volume biography exemplifies the candour which Strachey himself enjoined. Unsparing in its view of its subject's failure in personal relations, it nevertheless does full justice to the many facets of Strachey's talents and presents a vivid and comprehensive picture of many of the Bloomsbury figures.

Bernard Shaw: The Search for Love 1988
The first of a multi-volume biography currently in the process of publication. It reveals the young, passionate Shaw that preceded the aged sage.

Richard HOUGH (1922–)

First Sea Lord 1969
Richard Hough is an immensely readable naval historian whose almost racy prose raises the immediate excitement of sea stories. His account of Russia's naval humiliation by the Japanese in 1904–5 will prepare many readers for this study of Admiral Lord Fisher, one of the navy's most brilliant and idiosyncractic figures.

Donald R HOWARD (1927–)

Chaucer and the Medieval World 1987
A fully documented yet readable account of Chaucer's career as a diplomat and a poet. This traces Chaucer's voyages in Europe and shows the influences that European poets had on him. An excellent survey of the poet and his time; illustrated with contemporary portraits and documents.

H Montgomery HYDE (1907–)

The Unexpected Prime Minister 1973
This study of Baldwin, together with his life study of Edward Carson, is the author's major excursion into large scale political biography. Erudite and entertaining.

Lord Reading 1967
Montgomery Hyde has taken a special interest in major politico-legal figures of recent British history, and his life of Rufus Isaacs, first Marquess of Reading, is the acknowledged definitive study of this remarkable liberal lawyer who was at different times Lord Chief Justice, Viceroy of India and Foreign Secretary.

Christopher ISHERWOOD (1904–)

Kathleen and Frank 1971
Isherwood's final tribute to the parents who had furnished him with material for fiction in many of his works. As well as an exploration of his own past, it conveys a fascinating picture of middle-class life at the turn of the century and of army life in the years leading up to the First World War.

Roy JENKINS (1920–)

Asquith 1964
Readable perhaps because the author finds his subject (and his period?) so congenial, this single volume life encompasses momentous periods in British history. With Jenkins' relish for a telling phrase and an illuminating anecdote, this briskly covers ground covered more ponderously by the official biography of 1932. *Mr Balfour's Poodle*, shows the author on no less familiar territory.

Edgar JOHNSON (1901–)

Charles Dickens: His Tragedy and Triumph 1952
In spite of much writing on Dickens this two-volume work is the only biography since Forster to be able to claim plausibly the 'definitive' tag. For all the attempts to kidnap Dickens – as George Orwell put it – for the purposes of political or pyschological study and argument, he has eluded most of his biographies.

Samuel JOHNSON (1709–84)

The Lives of the English Poets 1779–81
These brief biographies were originally commissioned by a consortium of London booksellers as prefaces to a series of editions of English poets. Many of their critical observations have formed a starting point for later discussions of the writers concerned. The merit of the best of these as biography lies in a fine balance between sympathetic understanding and clear-eyed judgement, so trenchantly conveyed in the terse, epigrammatic quality of Johnson's style. There are 52 lives covering the period from Milton to Johnson's own time and including *An Account of the Life of Mr Richard Savage*, which was written earlier. This was Johnson's first major work: a landmark in biography and a moving portrait of a gifted, charming and self-destructive man. There is a selection of the lives in the Everyman Library.

Ernest JONES (1897–1958)

Sigmund Freud: Life and Work 1953–9
Jones was a close friend of Freud and his family, and himself a distinguished contributor to psychoanalysis. In spite of the differences on scientific questions that existed between Jones and Freud, this extensive biography presents a very clear and objective study of the development of Freud's views. It also successfully penetrates the reticence of its subject to provide a frank, but warm and sympathetic portrait of the private man. Jones's work is outstanding among scientific biographies. An abridgement of the three-volume work is available in the Penguin edition.

John Maynard KEYNES (1883–1946)

Essays in Biography 1933
Divided into two sections 'Sketches of Politicians' and 'Lives of Economists', the essays are based mainly on people with whom Keynes had direct acquaintance. They include Lloyd George, Winston Churchill and Alfred Marshall. Their stated aim is 'to bring out the solidarity and historical continuity of the High Intelligentsia of England who have built up the foundations of our thought'.

Sydney D KITSON (1871–1937)

Life of John Sell Cotman 1937
A fascinating study of an important English artist whose talent was perhaps never fully realized because of poverty and ill-luck. This biography is written with

enthusiasm and a knowledge enhanced by acquaintance with the settings of Cotman's life and access to many hitherto unseen letters.

Basil Henry, LIDDELL HART (1895–1970)

Sherman 1959
Liddell Hart clarifies the complexities of military conflicts without compromizing the integrity of the military historian. This study of a major figure of the American Civil War is a useful and concise introduction to the art of the military historian.

Jack LINDSAY (1900–)

J M W Turner: a critical biography 1966
Lindsay's is the best and most reliable biography of Turner. A very sympathetic study is made of his painting and a particularly clear and understanding account is offered of his complicated and difficult character. A new edition with the title *Turner* was published in 1973.

John Gibson LOCKHART (1794–1854)

Memoirs of the Life of Sir Walter Scott 1837–8
Lockhart was Scott's son-in-law and literary executor, and therefore uniquely placed to write an account of his life. The vividness of observation and fullness of portrayal make it one of the very greatest of English biographies. Lockhart's other works include a highly regarded biography of Robert Burns.

Edward LOCKSPEISER (1905–73)

Debussy 1962–5
A cumulative picture of the composer emerges from an unusual narrative method in which Debussy's relations are described with each one of a wide range of significant musical, artistic and literary figures.

Elizabeth LONGFORD (1906–)

Wellington: The Years of the Sword 1969
Wellington: Pillar of State 1972
The second volume of this major biography of the soldier/statesman, is perhaps the more generally interesting and illuminating. It deals with his later life (the last 37 years of it) as a key figure in the turbulent politics of Britain after the Napoleonic wars. Scholarly research is combined with an incisive style and perception.

F S L LYONS (1923–83)

Charles Stewart Parnell 1977
The Provost of Trinity College, Dublin, Lyons is the leading authority on Irish politics in the second half of the nineteenth century, in which Parnell is the most important character. The prose is fluent and persuasive.

J W MACKAIL (1859–1945)

Life of William Morris 1899
As a son-in-law of Edward Burne-Jones, Morris's life-long friend and collaborator, Mackail had the advantages of first-hand testimony and access to papers. His work remains probably the best portrayal of the many facets of Morris's character. It is supplemented, but not supplanted, by G P Thompson's study in which the emphasis falls on Morris's intellectual development and his place within the history of socialist ideas in England.

Maynard MACK (1909–)

Alexander Pope: A Life 1985
A labour of love from a man who has dedicated most of his life to writing and teaching about Pope. Some readers feel the opening chapters to be a little sentimental but perservance pays a reward as Mack unfolds the intrigue which surrounded Pope and shows the continuing relevance of his poetry.

Iain MACLEOD (1913–70)

Neville Chamberlain 1961
Perhaps this book suffers from its author's overt sympathy for a man to whom history has not been kind, and it should be read in conjunction with Keith Feiling's sterner life of 1946, itself written when the memory of Munich was too close.

Sir Philip (Montefiore) MAGNUS-ALLCROFT (1906–)

Gladstone 1954
Not a tribute, as was Morley's 'life', but an engaging assessment of the G O M's personality, drawing heavily on papers at Hawarden Castle. The spirit of nineteenth century parliamentary government is skilfully evoked in direct and economical prose.

Kitchener – Portrait of an Imperialist 1958
A study of a remarkable and complex man: the author's familiarity with Kitchener's period of British history is probably unsurpassed.

King Edward VII 1964
Filling a need for a dispassionate assessment of this popular monarch, this book superseded the official biography. It gives no more than proper weight to the indiscretions of the Prince of Wales, and admirably demonstrates how the King gave his name not merely to a style but a period.

David MARQUAND (1946–)

Ramsay MacDonald 1977
Himself no stranger to the contortions of Labour Party politics, David Marquand tries
to fill the gap between the 'eulogistic' and the 'obsessionally hostile' books about a
man who still stirs violent passions on the left. Based on hitherto unused MacDonald
papers, this is the definitive study.

Michael MEYER (1921–)

Ibsen: The Making of a Dramatist 1828–1864 1967
Ibsen: The Farewell to Poetry 1864–1882 1969
Ibsen: The Top of a Cold Mountain 1971
Fully documented from Isben's letters, his speeches and the writings of
contemporaries, this is a monumental biography of a complex but rewarding
dramatist and an example of thorough and painstaking research. All events and plays
are discussed in depth.

Keith MIDDLEMAS (1935–)

Baldwin 1969
The definitive scholarly study of this most representative figure of Britain between
the wars, brings a much-needed objectivity to a subject who has suffered equally from
the hostile G M Young and the apologia from his own son. (A W Baldwin, *My father;
the true story*). Some might prefer Montgomery Hyde's life (see above).

Thomas MOORE (1779–1852)

Life, Letters and Journals of Lord Byron 1830
Byron has attracted the attentions of biographers to a greater extent than any other
English poet. Beginning with Leigh Hunt and John Galt, the tradition has extended to
such modern examples as Leslie Marchand's very substantial work and Iris Origer's
illuminating study. Moore's account still deserves prominence as it combines the
advantages of a contemporary witness with a greater candour than other biographers
of the time, and a skill in the gradual unfolding of Byron's complex character.

Thomas MORE (1478–1535)

The History of King Richard III 1543
This work has a fair claim to be regarded as the first biography in English. The theme
of the downfall of a wicked prince was a commonplace of its time, but More's
treatment was original in seeking first-hand testimony from the generation which had
experienced Richard's rule. Some of the testimony is challenged by those historians
who class the work as Tudor propaganda.

Kenneth O MORGAN (1934–)

Keir Hardie: Radical and Socialist 1975
The author is interested in radical politics, and here provides a much-needed study of a political legend. Precisely because he is a legend, the biographer is faced with the challenge of separating reality from the myth.

John MORLEY (1838–1923)

Voltaire 1872
Rousseau 1873
Morley is best known as the biographer of Gladstone and the author of studies of Burke and Walpole. His studies of Voltaire and Rousseau are of interest as biography conceived primarily in terms of the development of the subject's ideas, and the interplay between this development and contemporary climates of opinion.

ed. Edward NEHLS

D H Lawrence: a composite biography 1957
A strictly chronological compilation of extracts from reminiscences of Lawrence interspersed with his own letters, this is generally regarded to be the fullest and most just account. Its success comes partly from the richness of available memoirs and partly from the formidable effort of the compiler in tracing hitherto unpublished obscure reminiscences.

Ernest NEWMAN (1868–1959)

Life of Richard Wagner 1933–7
Possibly the greatest musical biography of the twentieth century, this four-volume work presents the composer's life comprehensively and frankly.

Harold NICHOLSON (1886–1968)

King George V: His life and reign 1952
This is not merely a biography, but a manual of constitutional monarchy. Extensive use of documents makes this a widely-quoted work of reference.

Curzon – the Last Phase 1934
Strictly speaking, not a biography – the author's own sub-title is 'A study in post war diplomacy' – but this is still a much valued assessment of a creative Foreign Secretary (1918–24) and extraordinary man.

Nigel NICHOLSON (1917–)

Portrait of a Marriage 1973
A short account of the remarkable marriage between the writer–diplomat Sir Harold Nicholson and the gardener–writer Vita Sackville West by their son. Both appear frequently as characters in several contemporary novels thanks to their social standing and sexual ambiguity.

Sir Thomas NORTH (1535–1601)

Lives of the Noble Greeks and Romans 1579
North's version of Plutarch's *Parallel Lives* is a fine example of Tudor prose and is often cited as a source for Shakespeare's Roman plays.

Frank OWEN (1907–79)

Tempestuous Journey 1954
A genius with words, Lloyd George has not unnaturally inspired many more, most of them devoted to his personal life and to particular aspects of his enormous political achievement. Frank Owen is a persuasive recorder, writing in places with appropriate Celtic lyricism.

George PAINTER (1914–)

Marcel Proust: a biography 1959, 1965
A very full and enlightening life of Proust; this is noteworthy for sensitive use of a psychoanalytic approach to a writer where the relation between life and work makes it perhaps particularly apt.

William Riley PARKER (1906–68)

Milton: a biography 1968
Detailed analysis of Milton's involvement in poetry and politics from a man who 'likes Milton as a person'. Parker's work is essential reading for anyone wishing to penetrate the mind of England's most intellectual poet.

Sir Charles PETRIE (1895–1977)

The Life and Letters of Sir Austen Chamberlain 1939–40
'Austen always played the game – and always lost it'. This is a two-volume study by a much-respected historian.

J H PLUMB (1911–)

Sir Robert Walpole 1956, 1960
This is a magisterial work, by possibly the most distinguished historian of eighteenth century England.

A F POLLARD (1869–1948)

Thomas Cranmer and the English Reformation 1904
Cranmer has been termed the most mysterious figure in the English reformation. Both delighted at Henry VIII's success at breaking with Rome, yet fearful of the man himself, he played a foremost role in the divorce of Catherine of Aragon, the Reform itself and the writing of the first book of Common Prayer. Pollard's study explains the intricacies of court politics in a clear and factual manner.

James POPE-HENNESSY (1916–74)

Robert Louis Stevenson 1974
Stevenson has been the subject of a quite voluminous library of commemoration and reminiscence. This biography makes good use of this abundant documentation and of the author's own knowledge of the Samoan setting of Stevenson's final years.

Trollope 1971
A thoroughly researched and documented book; supplies much information about the writing of Trollope's novels and about his contemporaries.

Peter QUENNELL (1905–)

Hogarth's Progress 1955
This is a full a portrait of Hogarth as the fairly modest information available will allow, together with an informed assessment of his art and a vivid recreation of Hogarth's London. In addition to this work, Quennell has also written biographical studies of Byron and Ruskin.

Robert (Vidal) RHODES JAMES (1933–)

Churchill – A Study in Failure: 1900–1939 1970
When this book appeared, Churchill had yet to be encompassed by a single study of sufficient gravity to match the man. This fascinating exception dwells on Churchill's earlier career in politics and explains why, in the wilderness years of the '30s, he was written off severely as a failed politician, a caged lion or a burnt-out case. Written by a leading historian of modern British political history.

Roseberry 1963
This book rehabilitated one of the most enigmatic figures ever to enter Downing Street; Archibald Philip Primrose was the 'coming man' who arrived only just in time, promptly to depart the scene in a state of mind seldom explained until this rich study arrived. Excellent reading, even if Roseberry himself still eludes us.

Jasper RIDLEY (1920–)

Lord Palmerston 1970
This is the most scholarly and comprehensive of several studies – weighty in size, judgements and documentation. A sharp contrast with Ridley's previous biographical excursions, which are mainly concerned with reformation divines.

Garibaldi 1974
Few Europeans have had such an influence on English emotions as this celebrated and almost mythical Italian soldier and revolutionary leader. Arguably the most complete life in any language.

L T C ROLT (1910–)

Isambard Kingdom Brunel 1957
Thomas Telford 1958
George & Robert Stevenson 1960
Rolt was an engineer by training and one with a special gift for clear and interesting exposition of the technicalities of the subject. He intended these three books as a chronicle of the revolution in our civilization carried out by the engineers of the Industrial Revolution. His study of the Stevensons is probably the best of the three.

William ROPER (1496–1578)

Mirror of Vertue in Worldly Greatness; or the Life of Sir Thomas More 1626
A short, first-hand account of More's struggle with his king and his conscience by his son-in-law. One of the first biographies.

Stephen ROSKILL (1903–82)

Hankey: man of secrets 1974
A portrait of the celebrated *eminence grise* of British defence and foreign policy in the first half of the twentieth century, this study is the product of the meticulous scholarship and lucid writing by one of the foremost authorities on war strategy.

A L ROWSE (1903–)

Shakespeare the Man 1973
This is a literary biography told by an historian. Lively and entertaining and occasionally provocative: not everyone will agree with Rowse's discovery of the identity of the Dark Lady.

J J SCARISBRICK (1928–)

Henry VIII 1968
Scarisbrick looks closely at the King himself, he discusses the complexities of the man, the political decisions he made and analyses the schism with Rome and his hatred of France. An interesting study of one of England's awesome sons.

Geoffrey SCOTT (1885–1929)

The Portrait of Zelide 1925
Zelide (Isabelle van Tuyll) was a very minor novelist, who found a place in literary history for her brief friendship with Benjamin Constant. Geoffrey Scott's work is a minor classic in its suggestive use of a minimum of detail, the wit and economy of its style and its vivid recreation of the times and setting of its heroine.

Sir Walter SCOTT (1771–1832)

Life of John Dryden 1808
Scott's work first appeared as the 'Memoir to John Dryden' appended to his great edition of the works, and had immediately to stand comparison with Dr Johnson's study and Malone's voluminuous account. He placed Dryden in the context of the intellectual, cultural and social life of his age and along with his understanding of the man and his shrewd appraisal of his works, contributed to a study still often regarded as the best critical biography of his subject.

George SHERBURN (1884–1982)

The Early Career of Alexander Pope 1934
This remains outstanding among biographical treatments of Pope; it finds, with the aid of a carefully-weighed mass of evidence, a balance between the Victorian denunciation of Pope's character and the passionate partisanship of Edith Sitwell's study published only two years before this work.

David SHUB (1877–1973)

Lenin 1948
David Shub escaped to the United States in 1908, having been an active participant in the 1905 revolution in Russia, and became an authority on Soviet politics. His study of Lenin is penetrating and authentic.

Robert SKIDELSKY (1939–)

Oswald Mosley 1975
Mosley was the 'hero' of this author's definitive study of the second Labour government, *Politicians and the Slump*, and this authorative life sprang from Mosley's radicalism on unemployment, which drove him from the Labour party into the wilderness of British fascism. It has been accused of 'glossing over Mosley's inherent evil', but it is the most objective assessment of a notorious figure.

Robert SOUTHEY (1774–1843)

The Life of Horatio, Lord Nelson 1813
Southey is remembered as the associate of Wordsworth and Coleridge and a voluminous author. This is probably, however, his best work. A lucid style, narrative drive and enthusiasm for his subject make this a very readable account of Nelson.

Philip Henry STANHOPE (1805–75)

Notes of Conversations with the Duke of Wellington, 1831–1851 1886
This is an interesting source of anecdotes about the Iron Duke by a founder of the National Portrait Gallery.

Lytton STRACHEY (1880–1932)

Eminent Victorians 1918
Strachey's studies of General Gordon, Cardinal Manning, Florence Nightingale and
Dr Arnold perfectly catch the contemporary mood with their irreverent irony and the
verve of their attack on Victorian decorum and hypocrisy. Strachey's work is
sometimes criticized as being as one-sided in its urge to caricature as the typical
Victorian biography in its tendency to eulogize. Nevertheless the elegance of style,
the deft irony, the eye for the telling detail, all provide evidence in support of
Strachey's own claim that the biographer could be an artist rather than a mere
compiler. His later study *Queen Victoria* shows the same wit and elegance, but the
sharpness of his irony gives way to a much more sympathetic view.

A J A SYMONS (1900–41)

The Quest for Corvo: an experiment in biography 1934
Frederick Rolfe was totally unsuccessful in acquiring any reputation as a writer within
his own lifetime; his arrogance, aloofness and unreliability in money matters made all
his friendships precarious and short lived, and the evidence of his life is sparse and
scattered. Instead of attempting to construct a conventional biography from the slight
remains, Symons contrives to allow a portrayal of this highly talented and enigmatic
man to emerge from a highly entertaining account of the search for the evidence itself.

Edward John TRELAWNY (1792–1881)

Records of Shelley, Byron and the Author 1858
Originally envisaged as the second part of an autobiography, of which the first part
Adventures of a Younger Son had appeared in 1831. Trelawny was a constant
companion of Shelley in the last few months of his life and later accompanied Byron
to Greece to take part in the War of Independence. Although autobiographical in
context and not entirely reliable in matters of fact, the vividness of his first-hand
testimony make this a uniquely interesting study.

G M TREVELYAN (1876–1962)

Lord Grey of the Reform Bill 1920
Grey was in office during one of the most exciting times in English history: while
attempting to become involved in the reformation of parliament, he was also aware of
the threat of Napolean abroad and revolution at home. A lucid account of a complex
interwoven series of events.

John WAIN (1925–)

Samuel Johnson 1974
Not simply a factual account of Johnson's life, this biography contains discussions
about his ideas, his literary criticism and his 'Dictionary' work, as well as giving a

detailed description of eighteenth century England. An immensely enjoyable book about one of the largest of English figures.

Graham WALLAS (1858–1932)

The Life of Franci Place 1771–1854 1898
This is the standard life of a great social reformer, whose ideas on the control of population were some generations in advance of his time.

Izaak WALTON (1593–1683)

Lives of Donne, Wootton, Hooker, Herbert & Sanderson 1640–78
Each of Walton's lives is concerned to fulfil an exemplary purpose – to illustrate a beneficent Providence. He reduces all his subjects to a like image of placid and resigned piety – very little is conveyed of their literary achievements – but the seasoning of lively anecdote and a warm sympathy for his subjects make this work outstanding among earlier English biographies.

Laurence WHISTLER (1912–)

Sir John Vanbrugh: architect and dramatist 1938
Whistler's is the first full-length biography of a man who was involved with the life of his times at many points. Vanbrugh is vividly and attractively portrayed, and his dramatic writing is placed in context; however, the emphasis falls on his career as an architect, and especially on the fascinating story of the building of Blenheim Palace.

Philip WILLIAMS (1920–84)

Hugh Gaitskell 1978
A diligently documented study of a controversial figure in recent Labour Party history, this large scale, sympathetic biography is compelling reading.

John WILSON (1924–)

'C.B.' Campbell Bannerman 1973
This is a highly readable and even-handed assessment of a little-known Prime Minister, who has been buried under the reputations of Asquith and Lloyd George.

Cecil WOODHAM-SMITH (1896–1977)

The Reason Why 1953
This double study of Lords Lucan and Cardigan does not aim to be a fully exhaustive portrait of its central figures; rather it shows how a series of crucial experiences in their lives reinforced the influences of their background to make inevitable the tragedy of the Light Brigade at Balaclava. The book offers both a penetrating study of the mentality of the nineteenth century aristocrat, and a very vivid account of the Crimean War.

Kenneth YOUNG (1916–85)

Balfour 1963
Keynes said that Balfour 'was the most extraordinary "objet d'art" our society has produced', and this book savours the phenomenon of a civilized mind among politicians.

AUTOBIOGRAPHY

In one sense, nothing could be easier to define than an autobiography: a first-person account of one's own life. But if we then go on to ask what it is we look for when we read an autobiography, we realize that such a definition is at best disingenuous. Samuel Pepy's *Diary* and Cardinal Newman's *Apologia Pro Vita Sua* are both, by this definition, autobiographies, but we will hardly find the same kinds of things in the one and in the other. This is not only because they were very different men living in different times, but also because they chose to concentrate on widely disparate aspects of their experience of life and to express these in radically dissimilar ways. A definition which can accommodate such differences is really not very useful at all.

Most literary genres can be analysed in terms of 'schools' or 'traditions', within which some governing characteristics may be observed. But not autobiography – possibly because it is one form where authors rarely seem to be influenced by what others have done in this way before. Each autobiography seems to dictate its own form, to an extent which is not true of novels, poems and plays, or even of biographies. Some categorization is possible, of course. Many autobiographies, for example, focus on the spiritual experiences of their authors, to the virtual exclusion of mundane considerations such as family, friends, work and current affairs; these would include the *Confessions of St Augustine* the *Revelations of Divine Love* of Dame Julian of Norwich, John Bunyan's *Grace Abounding to the Chief of Sinners* and Newman's *Apologia*. But these texts are more striking in the end for the differences between them than for what they have in common. At another extreme are works like Pepy's *Diary*, James Boswell's *Journals* where there is a minimum of personal reflection and an apparent intention simply to record daily events and impressions as fully as circumstances permit. Even here, however, differences of motive (circumspection, ego, political conviction), as well as of emphasis and style, make it difficult to claim any real school or tradition.

Moreover, as the historical spread of these examples may suggest, we cannot confidently ascribe the disparities between autobiographies to the differences in style and outlook of the ages that produced them. It has been variously held that autobiography was a characteristic response: to the spirit of Renaissance individualism (The *Autobiography* of Bevenuto Cellini, and the *Essays* of Montaigne, are often cited as evidence); to the habits of introspection fostered by Protestantism and its Puritan outgrowths (e.g. Richard Baxter's *Reliquiae*

Baxterianae, and Jonathan Edward's *Personal Narrative*; to the intensified sense of the self that characterized Romanticism (e.g. the *Confessions* of Jean-Jacques Rousseau, William Wordsworth's *The Prelude*); to the American frontier, and so on. There is obviously some truth in all of these claims, but it is salutory to remember that works as different as Bunyan's *Grace Abounding* and Pepy's *Diary* were written at the same time as each other: and that Wordworth's autobiographical poem is paralled by the journals of his sister, Dorothy, which are far from obviously Romantic in either style or content.

In this refusal to be pigeon-holded, the autobiography may be seen as a triumph of the individuality of experience over the conformist pressures with which literature is normally beset. But one price the form has paid for being so awkward to classify has been to be widely ignored *as literature*. Some autobiographies, like Pepy's *Diary* and Boswell's *Journals* have been heavily mined by social historians, while others, like Sir Thomas Browne's *Religio Medici* and John Stuart Mill's *Autobiography*, have acquired some kind of status as 'representative documents' of their age. But, for all their obvious popularity with the reading public, they have attracted relatively little scholarly attention as an art form in themselves.

Strikingly, this seems to be changing just at the time when the nature of literary scholarship – with its traditional classifications and syllabuses – is itself being radically questioned. Works such as James Olney's *Metaphors of Self* and *Autobiography: Essays Theoretical and Critical*, William Spengemann's *The Forms of Autobiography* (with an excellent Bibliographical Essay), John Pilling's *Autobiography and Imagination* and A O J Cockshut's *The Art of Autobiography in 19th and 20th Century England* all testify to an intensified interest in the form – often precisely *because* it defies the conventional categorizations of literature and is strikingly amenable to new critical formulations. It is noticeable, for example, that Black Autobiography and Women's Autobiography are already distinct and flourishing scholarly fields.

Perhaps most interestingly in this regard is the respect now accorded to autobiography precisely because it challenges our usual notions of what is 'real' and what is 'unreal'. Autobiographies used to be suspect on the one hand because they were, by definition, 'subjective' and therefore liable to be 'untruthful'; or, on the other hand, because they were too closely tied to 'factual' material and so could not have the imaginative integrity deemed necessary for true art. In the post-structuralist world, in the era of the 'faction' novel, all these distinctions are meaningless: all writing is a fable, a metaphor for experience rather than a mirror of it, and autobiography is to be valued for the opennesss with which it admits to presenting a partial view of life. There is no way that it can be mistaken for that mythical beast, an objective record.

In this context, the last vestiges of our initial definition disappear: 'one's own life' is not a collection of facts to be catalogued, but whatever one makes of it, an act of creative selection and structuring, only one of any number of possible versions. If that is so, it is unrealistic to insist even that the narrative be in the first-person: the 'I' is only a trick of art or style (see, for example, Vladimir Nabokov's *Speak, Memory*) and in no way a guarantee of authenticity. So authors may choose to write about their lives obliquely, through the medium of what we used confidently to categorize as 'fiction', and this has just as much claim to be considered autobiography as less disguised forms. So we now find 'novels' such as Dicken's *David Copperfield*, Samuel Butler's *The Way of All Flesh*, D H Lawrence's *Sons and Lovers* and James Joyce's *A Portrait of The Artist as a Young Man* discussed, without reservations, as autobiography. The genre has even been pushed so far as to include T S Eliot's complex late poems, *Four Quartets*.

Given the problems of definition outlined here, it has not been easy to settle on the list of texts that follows. The guiding principle has been to try to indicate the sheer variety of forms that successful autobiography may take, rather than to impose arbitrary definitions on this most Protean of forms. A few classic American autobiographies have been included where they have made outstanding contributions to the development of the autobiographical form.

Henry ADAMS (1838–1918)

The Education of Henry Adams 1907
Subtitled *A Study of Twentieth Century Multiplicity*, Adams takes himself as a 'manikin' on which to test methods of education and his own ideas of the dynamic theory of history and the law of acceleration. An American classic, which is less well known in Britain than it should be.

Richard BAXTER (1615–91)

Reliquiae Baxterianae 1696
This is the autobiography of a Presbyterian Civil War minister who contributed to the Restoration but suffered considerable ill-treatment under Charles II and James II.

Arnold BENNETT (1867–1931)

Journals 1932–3
Bennett had a journalist's obsession with realistic details and an eye for the unusual or 'newsworthy' in everyday life, qualities also found in his novels.

Wilfred Scawen BLUNT (1840–1922)

My Diaries 1919–20
Poet, rebel, wealthy diplomat and sportsman, Blunt opposed British imperialism and, in this 'personal narrative of events 1888–1914' pleaded 'the case of the backward nations of the world, and especially those of Africa, Asia, from their slavery to Europe'.

James BOSWELL (1740–95)

The Boswell Papers: The Yale Editions of the Private Papers of James Boswell (thirteen vols so far) – 1950
Boswell's remarkably frank and revealing journals of his life from 1762 onwards were only discovered and published this century. Their chief virtues are 'articulateness, fidelity to experience, sensitiveness to small currents of feeling, and, above all, curiosity' (Cockshut). Boswell himself reflected: 'It is unpleasant to observe how imperfect a picture of my life this journal presents. Yet I have certainly much more of *myself* thus preserved than most people have'.

Sir Thomas BROWNE (1605–82)

Religio Medici 1643
'The Religion of a Physician' is a revealing document of the mid-seventeenth century, charting the pressures that Baconian methods of empirical enquiry imposed on a conventional Anglican faith. The style, which fluctuates from witty, colloquial familiarity to sonorous eloquence, used to be held up as a model.

John BUNYAN (1628–88)

Grace Abounding to the Chief of Sinners 1666
A narrative of Bunyan's search for the conviction that he has been saved by God's grace; this forms an interesting parallel to the fictional *The Pilgrim's Progress*.

Fanny (Madame D'Arblay) BURNEY (1752–1840)

Diary and Letters 1842–6
A lively and detailed account of life in intellectual and court circles in the late Georgian and Regency period. The author of *Evelina*, she knew Dr Johnson, Queen Charlotte and, via her husband, many French emigrées.

Samuel BUTLER (1835–1902)

The Way of all Flesh 1903
Though written as a novel, this is now recognized as an intensely autobiographical work, a remorseless indictment of family tyranny and in many ways a repudiation of 'typical' Victorian values.

George Gordon, Lord BYRON (1788–1824)

Journals 1830
The *Journals* reflect all the paradoxes of the most Augustan of the Romantics: 'it is difficult to distinguish the actual vagaries and inconsistencies of character from his delight in presenting himself as the most fascinatingly inconsistent of men' (Cockshut). The *Letters* are also self-revealing and are edited in 11 volumes by Leslie Marchand.

Thomas CARLYLE (1759–1881)

Sartor Resartus 1833–4
A baffling, often outrageous work by one of the most influential of Victorian thinkers: 'the tailor retailored' or 'reclothed' has been described as 'by turns a treatise on sociology, a discourse on philosophy, a sentimental novel, a series of sermons, a satire on pedantic scholarship, a biography, a cryptic autobiography'.

Reminiscences 1881
Much more conventional and accessible than *Sartor Resartus*, this is notable for Carlyle's accounts of contemporaries like De Quincey.

Margaret CAVENDISH, Duchess of Newcastle (c. 1624–74)

A True Relation of My Birth, Breeding and Life 1656
This is an early example of woman's autobiography in which religious experience is not the dominant issue.

Gilbert Keith CHESTERTON (1874–1936)

Autobiography 1936
The mixture of wit, shrewdness, paradox, tolerance and a light-heartedness which nevertheless insists upon Christian values will be familiar to anyone who knows Chesterton's other writings.

Colley CIBBER (1671–1757)

An Apology for the Life of Mr Colley Cibber, Comedian 1740
An informative account of the state, life and times of the much-maligned actor/playwright/poet laureate which helps balance the picture familiar from Pope's *The Dunciad*.

Edward Hyde, Earl of CLARENDON (1608–74)

The Life of Edward, Earl of Clarendon 1759
Written in the third person for his children, this is a self-justifying account of the life of one of the key figures of the Civil War and Restoration period.

Samuel Taylor COLERIDGE (1772–1834)

Biographia Literaria 1817
'The least of what I have written concerns myself personally.' However there are wedges of autobiography in this work of philosophy and literary criticism (see the Literary Criticism section).

Robin George COLLINGWOOD (1889–1943)

An Autobiography 1939
This is a vigorous personal statement by a philosophical historian and archaeologist of his intellectual development and political ideals.

Joseph CONRAD (1857–1924)

The Mirror of the Sea 1906
A Personal Record 1912
Some Reminiscences 1912
The Arrow of Gold 1919
Conrad drew heavily on his own experiences in his writings; these four works (the last in novel form) are the closest he came to 'pure' autobiography.

Thomas CREEVEY (1768–1838)

The Creevey Papers 1903
Creevey was an indefatigable gossip and man of fashion, whose combined diaries and correspondence provide a good deal of inside information about the politics of the late Georgian and Regency period.

Richard CROSSMAN (1907–74)

The Diaries of a Cabinet Minister (3 vols, 1975, 1976, 1977)
This is Crossman's prodigious attempt – running to over 1,500,000 words – to describe the business of Cabinet government from the inside, in all its personal and institutional intricacies.

William Henry DAVIES (1871–1940)

The Autobiography of a Super-Tramp 1908
This presents life 'on the road' in America by the hobo-turned-poet.

Thomas DE QUINCEY (1785–1859)

Confessions of an English Opium Eater 1821 (enlarged edition 1856)
The title is more titillating than the substance of the book, which is really an account of the lost and unattainable things in life; the addiction to opium and the dreams to which it gave rise are only one facet of this broader theme in De Quincey's life.

Autobiographic Sketches (also known as *Recollections of The English Lake Poets*) 1834
Here autobiography mingles with impressions of the Wordsworths, Coleridge and Southey.

Charles DICKENS (1812–70)

David Copperfield 1849–50
It has long been recognized that the book which Dickens called his 'favourite child' has strong autobiographical elements; with current definitions of autobiography, it is possible to argue further: 'Like Rousseau, Dickens saw in his past experience not the tangled root system of a single self but the seeds of many separate selves, all of whom had some ineffable kinship with each other but could be brought together only upon a fictive stage' (Spengemann). Another closely related self is Pip in *Great Expectations*, a novel which might almost be subtitled 'The Education of Charles Dickens'.

Keith DOUGLAS (1920–44)

Alamein to Zem Zem 1946
Douglas was called up in 1940 and joined the Notts Sherwood Rangers Yeomanry, serving as a tank commander in the Middle East and taking part in the battle of Alamein. This account records his experiences in the desert and evokes the atmosphere of battle and the emotions it aroused in Douglas and his comrades.

Jonathan EDWARDS (1703–58)

A Personal Narrative written c. 1740
Brief but powerful spiritual 'confession' of the leading figure in the New England
religious movement known as the 'Great Awakening'.

John EVELYN (1620–1706)

Diary 1818 (full edition 1955)
Less personal in tone than Pepys, but this presents a more balanced and complete
account of the life of a cultured and well-travelled gentleman in the second half of the
seventeenth century.

Lady Anne FANSHAWE (1625–80)

Memoirs 1829
An account of Carolean life by the wife of a committed Royalist, Sir Richard
Fanshawe, who was latterly ambassador in Lisbon and then Madrid.

E M FORSTER (1879–1970)

Commonplace Book 1985
Letters, dreams, news, personal agonies, jokes – a fascinating, often trivial but
ultimately sad, reflection of Forster's 45 years from the last novel to shortly before his
death.

George FOX (1624–91)

Journal 1694
A narrative of the spiritual experience, and later persecution of the founder of the
Society of Friends. Its simplicity and directness must owe to the fact that Fox could
not write; he dictated his reminiscences, which were later edited by a committee of his
followers.

Benjamin FRANKLIN (1706–90)

Autobiography 1867
A sadly unfinished account of the life of the self-educated natural philosopher,
diplomat and politician, this work reveals the rational and pragmatic character of one
of the most interesting of the founding fathers of the United States.

Edward GIBBON (1737–94)

Memoirs of My Life and Writings 1796
One of the 'classic' autobiographies, most interesting for its account of Gibbon's
motives and feelings while writing *Decline and Fall of the Roman Empire*.

Eric GILL (1882–1940)

Autobiography 1940
This is an outspoken *apologia* on sexual, political and religious matters by an artist
and sculptor who influenced a whole generation.

Sir Edmund GOSSE (1849–1928)

Father and Son 1907
Gosse presents a classic account of a grim unbringing by the son of a Plymouth
Brother zoologist who fiercely resisted the evolutionary theories of Charles Darwin.

Robert GRAVES (1895–1985)

Goodbye to All That 1929
This is Graves's remarkable attempt to make a new beginning in life, putting behind
him his upbringing, schooling and, most particularly, the First World War, in order to
follow his vocation as a poet and classical scholar.

Charles Cavendish Fulke GREVILLE (1794–1865)

The Greville Memoirs 1874, 1885, 1887
Greville was intimate with a number of statesmen, including Wellington and
Palmerston, in the first half of the nineteenth century, and his gossipy memoirs are a
gold-mine for historians. The complete edition was published in 1938.

Thomas HARDY (1840–1928)

The Early Life of Thomas Hardy, 1840–91 1928
The Later Years of Thomas Hardy, 1892–1928 1930
These volumes are officially credited to Hardy's second wife, Florence, but it is clear
that they are based on Hardy's own journals and notebooks and were composed under
his direction. They remain indispensable for what they include and intriguing for
what they leave out.

Augustus John Cuthbert HARE (1834–1903)

The Story of My Life 1896–1900
An immense and, some would say, tedious work which is perhaps valuable for the
insight it allows into the life and turn of mind of a Victorian worthy.

Frank HARRIS (1856–1931)

My Life and Loves 1922–7
'Frank has been received in all the great houses – once!' said Oscar Wilde. A
mish-mash of literary anecdotes (true and false) and sexual autobiography (probably

similarly divided) forms the least reliable but not the least valuable exercises in autobiography of its period. First published in Britain only in 1964 because of the explicit depictions of sexual activity.

Benjamin Robert HAYDON (1786-1846) (1786–1846)

Autobiography and Journals 1853
In many ways a sad monument to a man convinced of his own genius as a classical painter, this is now read far more for its account of his friendship with Wordsworth, Keats, Lamb, Hazlitt and other literary figures than for its author's sake.

William HAZLITT (1778–1830)

Liber Amoris 1823
Hazlitt's 'Book of Love' tells of his miserable infatuation for his landlady's daughter and offers an unusual insight into this quarrelsome man of letters.

Edward HERBERT, Lord Herbert of Cherbury (1583–1648)

Autobiography 1764
This is a vigorous self-portrait by a philosopher, historian, diplomat, soldier and poet which unfortunately stops before his experience of the Civil War.

John HERVEY, Lord Hervey of Ickworth (1696–1743)

Memoirs 1848
Memoirs is a lively, if often spiteful account of manners and morals in the court of George II by the man Pope attacked as 'Sporus' and 'Lord Fanny'.

William HICKEY (c. 1749–1830)

Memoirs 1913–25
Racy and frank accounts of voyages to India and elsewhere, of Hickey's chequered career as an attorney and of his weaknesses for women and claret.

Lady Margaret HOBY (1571–1633)

Diary, 1559–1605 1930
The earliest extant diary by an Englishwoman, this is interesting for its portrait of the domestic life of an Elizabethan gentlewoman.

William Henry HUDSON (1841–1922)

Far Away and Long Ago 1918
A naturalist's account of his early upbringing on the pampas of South America.

James Henry Leigh HUNT (1784–1859)

Autobiography 1850
Hunt's friendships formed a stimulating background to his own creative writing and they are reflected in this work which is also an interesting read in its own right.

Henry JAMES (1843–1916)

A Small Boy and Others 1913
Notes of a Son and a Brother 1914
The Middle Years 1917
The novelist James turned increasingly towards autobiography in his last years: the first two works describe his early years in America and Europe, the last is a fragment, to which he gave the title of one of his own short stories.

Richard JEFFERIES (1848–87)

The Story of my Heart 1883
This is the spiritual autobiography, over-sensitively written for some tastes, of an author whose other works are currently enjoying something of a revival.

James JOYCE (1882–1941)

A Portrait of the Artist as a Young Man 1916
An autobiographical fiction which needs to be read alongside Richard Ellman's classic biography, *James Joyce* and Stanislaus Joyce's *My Brother's Keeper* (1958) for a more 'objective' view of what it records.

Julian of Norwich (c. 1342–1413)

Revelations of Divine Love 1393
This is an account of the 16 visions experienced by Dame Julian in 1373 and her meditations in them. She became an anchoress and her work is one of the classics of medieval mysticism in which profound ideas are expressed with remarkable clarity.

Margery KEMPE (c. 1373–c. 1440)

The Book of Margery Kempe 1940
The earliest autobiography in the English language which was written in its final form around 1436 but was lost until 1936. The narrative – which she had to dictate, being illiterate – tells of her travels to Italy, Jerusalem, Compostella and Germany on her spiritual quest. She records her meetings and conversations with mystics and divines, including Dame Julian of Norwich, but also tells frankly of her marital relations, sexual temptations, and her frequent quarrels with fellow travellers and representatives of the Church. It is an unwitting self-portrait of a woman who is as energetic and distinctive as her fictional contemporary, the Wife of Bath.

Francis KILVERT (1840–79)

Diary, 1870–79 1938–40
The diary of a young curate and vicar in rural Wales and the Wye country, these are simple, unaffected accounts of country life and descriptions of the countryside.

Rudyard KIPLING (1865–1936)

Something of Myself 1937
An unfinished fragment, but an interesting insight into the man and his work. The title is deliberately evasive, reflecting a determination to 'deal with his life from the point of view of his work' – not to be too personal or confessional.

Charles LAMB (1775–1834)

Christ's Hospital Five and Thirty Years Ago 1820
A brief but fascinating autobiographical essay: the 'I' at the beginning relates to Lamb's school-friend, Coleridge, and only later refers to Lamb himself.

David Herbert LAWRENCE (1885–1930)

Sons and Lovers 1913
An autobiographical fiction, recording Lawrence's early years in Eastwood/ Nottingham and the struggle to escape his mother's influence. This should be read alongside *D H Lawrence, A Personal Record* by Jessie Chambers – the Miriam of Lawrence's story – (originally published in 1932 as by 'E.T.').

T E LAWRENCE (1888–1935)

The Seven Pillars of Wisdom 1926, 1935
The scholar and man of action of Lawrence of Arabia legend is also the confused victim of political compromise and private neurosis. If *The Seven Pillars of Wisdom* is a glamorized account of the Arab revolt against the Turks during the First World War, its literary as well as psychological antidote is his subsequent picture of his life in the ranks of the Royal Air Force, *The Mint*, which was written under his enlisted name of 'A/C Ross'.

Laurie LEE (1914–)

Cider with Rosie 1959
A modern classic of the nostalgia-for-rural-England school of autobiography (c.f. Flora Thompson and the recent enthusiasm for Francis Kilvert) which presents episodes from a Gloucestershire childhood. *As I Strode Out One Midsummer Morning* tells of Lee leaving Gloucestershire, making for London and a career.

William LOVETT (1800–1887)

The Life and Struggles of William Lovett 1876
This is the personal narrative of a notable Chartist and his struggles 'in pursuit of bread, knowledge and freedom'.

Edmund LUDLOW (c. 1617–92)

Memoirs, 1625–72 1698–9
An autobiographical narrative of a Puritan and regicide who, as Lieutenant-General in the army of the Commonwealth was right at the heart of the key events of his day.

Harold MACMILLAN (1894–1987)

The Winds of Change 1914–1939 1966
Political memoirs of the turbulent inter-war years; this book is not a history, but more a record of personal responses to the times.

Katherine MANSFIELD (1888–1923)

Journal 1927
An account of a literary career dogged by ill-health which was posthumously edited by her husband, John Middleton Murray.

John Stuart MILL (1806–73)

Autobiography 1873
A classic Victorian autobiography, which describes the young Mill's rigorous education by his Benthamite father and subsequent mental breakdown and restoration through the humanizing power of poetry.

Jan MORRIS (1926–)

Conundrum 1974
'Jan' was formerly 'James', married with children but who felt 'trapped' inside the wrong body; the original sensationalized newspaper story never gave a proper account and the first-person narration is both witty and sensitive.

Edwin MUIR (1887–1959)

An Autobiography 1940
This is the poet's account of his intellectual development, against the background of his life on the Continent, and of his work as a critic and translator of Kafka.

Vladimir NABOKOV (1899–1977)

Speak, Memory 1966
A complexly self-conscious, post-modernist exercise in autobiography, such as we might expect from the Russian emigré author of *Lolita* and *Pale Fire*.

Cardinal John Henry NEWMAN (1801–90)

Apologia Pro Vita Sua 1864
A clear and impassioned account of Newman's spiritual development including his conversion to Roman Catholicism, this was occasioned by an apparent attack on his integrity by Charles Kingsley.

Sir Harold NICHOLSON (1886–1968)

Some People 1927
Diaries and Letters 1966–68 (3 vols, ed. Nigel Nicholson)
The whole story about himself and his life does not emerge from these works but they are rich sources on the personalities and politics covering Britain's last years as a superpower.

Sean O'CASEY (1884–1964)

I Knock at the Door 1939
Pictures in the Hallway 1942
Drums under the Window 1944
Inishfallen 1947
Fare Thee Well 1949
Rose and Crown 1952
Sunset and Evening Star 1954
These are seven volumes of autobiography by one of the great dramatists of the century.

George ORWELL (Eric BLAIR) (1903–50)

Down and Out in Paris and London 1933
Orwell's vivid account of the lower depths in these two famous cities is compulsive and illuminating reading. How factual the account is, and how dependent it is upon William Davies' *Autobiography of a Super-Tramp* (1908) are points open to question but do not detract from the pleasure it offers.

Homage to Catalonia 1938
Orwell's autobiographical account of the Spanish Civil War and its role in determining his view that totalitarianism of any kind is the chief political enemy.

Mark PATTISON (1813–84)

Memoirs 1885
Memoirs is a deeply introspective account of a scholarly life and the shifts in religious conviction that ran through it.

Samuel PEPYS (1633–1703)

Diary 1970–83
For many people the definitive diary, though it only covers ten years of Pepys's life, from 1660–69. It stops before Pepys became secretary to the Admiralty. The lack of inhibition is engaging, as is the mixture of trivia and major events like the Great Plague and the Great Fire of London. Originally written in cypher and first published in 1825, it was only recently published in full, because of its sexual frankness.

John Cowper POWYS (1872–1963)

Autobiography 1934
A self-absorbed narrative of one of the most eccentric of modern novelists – something of a neo-pagan – and his struggle with sadistic sexual tendencies.

Kathleen RAINE (1908–)

Farewell Happy Fields 1973
The Land of the Unknown 1975
The Lion's Mouth 1977
Three volumes of what are already recognized as classic autobiography: a poet in search of esoteric wisdom and religious truth.

Forrest REID (1875–1947)

Apostate 1926
The Irish novelist's account of his spiritual and sexual development through boyhood, an age which in many ways he never came to terms with leaving behind; greatly superior to the sequel *Private Road*.

John RUSKIN (1819–1900)

Praeterita 1885–9
A powerful but unfinished autobiography of the Victorian art critic and sage. Written on the brink of madness, it contains a strong recreation of Ruskin's precious childhood in the household of his father, a successful wine merchant.

Bertrand RUSSELL 3rd Earl Russell (1872–1970)

Autobiography – I (1872–1914), 1967; II (1914–44), 1968; III (1944–67), 1969
'Bertrand Russell's autobiography is one of the finest and most satisfying of this century .... By showing an irreconcilable conflict between the thoughts and the feelings of a highly intellectual and extremely emotional man, it shows life ... in a grand symbolic attitude' (Cockshut).

Mark RUTHERFORD (William Hale WHITE) (1831–1913)

The Autobiography of Mark Rutherford 1881
Mark Rutherford's Deliverance 1885
Semi-fictional works of intense spiritual self-revelation, marked by a depth of feeling
and ironic humour. Should be read alongside his *Pages From a Journal* (three series,
1900, 1910, 1915).

Siegfried SASSOON (1886–1967)

Memoirs of a Fox-Hunting Man 1928
Memoir of an Infantry Officer 1930
Sheraton's Progress 1936
Collectively known as *The Complete Memoirs of George Sheraton*, these belong to
the grey area where fiction and autobiography merge, focusing most memorably on
the poet Sassoon's experience of the First World War.

Sir Walter SCOTT (1771–1832)

Journal 1890
Rather overshadowed by John Gibson Lockhart's classic early biography of Scott but
an effective and charming self-portrait.

George Bernard SHAW (1856–1950)

Sixteen Self Sketches 1949
A collection of autobiographical fragments from elsewhere in his writings rather than
a sustained piece of self-analysis; an odd light on a man who never had a small opinion
of his own talents.

Sir Osbert SITWELL (1892–1969)

Left Hand Right Hand 1945
The Scarlet Tree 1946
Great Morning 1948
Laughter in the Next Room 1949
Noble Essences 1950
A picture of a 'well-heeled' literary life-style now largely disappeared with a
memorable portrait of an eccentric father.

Alexander SOMERVILLE (1811–85)

The Autobiography of a Working Man 1848
A social document which successfully stirred liberal consciences when it was published, particularly in its account of savage punishments in the army.

Jonathan SWIFT (1667–1745)

Journal to Stella 1766–68
An unusually revealing document, never intended for publication. In the years 1710–13 Swift was parted from his friend (possibly wife), 'Stella' (Esther Johnson) and he sent these letters from London to Dublin, many of them written in baby-talk or 'little language', describing his life and thoughts during their parting.

Flora THOMPSON (1877–1947)

Lark Rise to Candleford 1945
A famous picture of English country life (North Oxfordshire) in the 1880s and '90s.

5th Viscount, John Byng TORRINGTON (1740–1813)

Diaries 1934–8
Basically travel diaries, full of invaluable information for historians of the early Industrial Revolution, but an entertaining self-portrait also emerges.

Anthony TROLLOPE (1815–82)

Autobiography 1883
A typically robust account of the author's rise from genteel poverty, through work for the General Post Office to fame and fortune as a novelist. His depiction of novel-writing as a money-making business offended many readers who preferred to think of literature as an art rather than a profession.

Booker Taliaferro WASHINGTON (1856–1915)

Up from Slavery 1901
The story of a man who was born the son of a black slave and a white man and went on to become a leading early educator of black people.

Evelyn WAUGH (1903–1966)

The Diaries of Evelyn Waugh 1976
A selection of diaries which cover Waugh's whole life from school days. Witty and self-revealing they also form a parallel text to the novels: many individuals and characters jumping from one track to the other.

Beatrice WEBB (1858–1943)

My Apprenticeship 1926
Our Partnership 1948
A leading figure in the world of economic and social theory, these two volumes
interestingly convey the relationship between the inner person and the public works.

Herbert George WELLS (1866–1946)

Experiment in Autobiography 1934
This reveals more than it intends, as the world-famous author reviews his
development and maturity with a self-confidence always bordering on conceit.

John WESLEY (1703–91)

Journal 1849
The journal of the founder of Methodism, which covers the years 1735–90, records,
as one might expect, his intense spiritual experience and tireless activity in its cause;
but it also has moments of pathos, humour and shrewd human observation which
make it particularly memorable in its kind.

Oscar WILDE (1854–1900)

De Profundis 1905
'From the depths': the long and bitter letter to Lord Alfred Douglas that Wilde wrote
in Reading Gaol, reviewing his life and beliefs after his conviction for
homosexuality.

Harriet WILSON (1789–1846)

Memoirs of Herself and Others 1825
Entertaining and often outrageously frank memoirs of a fashionable courtesan; the
tone is caught in a famous first sentence: 'I shall not say why and how I became, at the
age of fifteen, the mistress of the Earl of Craven'. Perhaps best known for
Wellington's reaction to the suggestion that his liaison with Harriet could be left out
of the work on payment of a suitable fee – 'publish and be damned!'.

Anthony À WOOD (1632–95)

The Life and Times of Anthony À Wood 1891–1900
Part informal autobiography, part notes and jottings, this is a store of anecdotes and
racy episodes from the reign of Charles I to William and Mary.

James WOODFORDE (1740–1803)

The Diary of a Country Parson 1758–1802 1924–31
A vivid picture of life both at an Oxford college and in a country parish; Woodforde
was particularly fond of his food and drink.

Leonard WOOLF (1880–1969)

Sowing 1960
Growing 1961
Beginning Again 1964
Downhill All the Way 1967
The Journey Not the Arrival Matters 1969
A life at the centre of 'Bloomsbury' reflected in a five-volume autobiography which copes honestly with the achievements and disappointments in the pursuit of Bloomsbury ideals and the tragedy of his wife's death.

Virginia WOOLF (1882–1941)

A Writer's Diary 1953
Edited by her husband, Leonard, from the novelist's journal, to include everything (after 1915) relating to the conception and execution of her published works.

Dorothy WORDSWORTH (1771–1855)

Journals 1896, 1904
Journals written between 1798 and 1828 record her life, and several tours, with her brother, William. Long valued for the light they cast on his poetry, they have only recently come to be valued in their own right.

William WORDSWORTH (1770–1850)

The Prelude, or Growth of a Poet's Mind 1850 .
The only poem in the language which is indisputably also an autobiography, a map of the poet's developing consciousness, and exploration of subjectivity. It was begun in 1798 but not published until after Wordsworth's death. It is an enormous achievement: one of the very successful long poems in the language.

Elizabeth WYNNE (1779–1857)

The Wynne Diaries, 1789–1820 1935–40
This is a spontaneous picture of life in the Napoleonic period, with interesting details of naval affairs.

Thomas WYNTHORNE (1528–96)

Autobiography 1961
Discovered in manuscript in 1955, this is the earliest autobiography in the language which is not devoted primarily to spiritual experience. Not only does it offer a fascinating insight into wealthy Elizabethan society but, being written in Whythorne's own phonetic 'orthografye', also provides many clues to the pronunciation of the day.

William Butler YEATS (1865–1939)

Autobiographies 1955
A collection of Yeat's autobiographical writings, including *Reveries Over Childhood and Youth* (1916), *The Trembling of the Veil* (1922) and *Dramatis Personae* (1936).

ESSAYS AND OTHER PROSE WRITINGS

The plain and simple form of the essay is a short piece of prose writing (usually about five hundred words and upwards) with observations appropriately linked and elegantly expressed: the sort of thing that Bacon wrote; the sort of thing we try to produce in examinations. When we look more closely at the essay form, however, we find it less simple. It has a disconcerting habit of running into other forms.

One difference is of degree, not kind. What distinguishes the essay from journalism? Meeting a daily, weekly, or monthly deadline is something of a hit-and-miss affair. Most pieces so produced, even by the gifted writer, will remain in the journal only. A few, dignified by the name of essay, will aspire to books. Thus it is that we have the 'essays' of Addison, Steele, Johnson, Hazlitt, Hunt, de Quincey and Lamb.

One of the things most valued in the essayist is personal reflection. Charles Lamb, Sir Thomas Browne and Izaak Walton make pleasant companions for their charm of spirit. In this area, personal reflection merges most easily into poetry. More people, no doubt, know Edward Thomas as a poet than as a writer of prose, but the subtle rhythms of his poetry grew out of his long experience as a prose writer.

Personal reflection of this kind is sometimes, more ambitiously, developed into a model of the working of an entire culture. In *A Vision* Yeats sought to give prose form to mythological structures like those of his poems. Continual speculation about society led George Orwell and Aldous Huxley to create works like *1984* and *Brave New World*. Like the parable *Animal Farm* these are extended essays on their authors' cultures. Through the essay Cauldwell explored art in relation to the economics of his society. In *The Dyer's Hand*, Auden explores the relationship of poetry with other aspects of his society.

Character may be considered the special preserve of the novelist and dramatist, but it has also been found necessary to the essayist. Greene, Nashe, and Dekker, the foremost of the Elizabethan pamphleteers, made great use of irony by speaking in two voices. When Dekker instructs his gull how to behave he seems to be encouraging him to show off and thus make a fool of himself. The voice of the instructor conceals the satirist. Sometimes the essayist makes the ambiguity of his discussion plainer by presenting it in a form of a dialogue, such as in the work of Prior or Landor. In some sense the plays of Shaw can be seen as the argument contained in their prologues or epilogues continued in many voices.

Many essayists have found it convenient to create characters for sustained irony and ambivalence. Addison and Steele created the country gentleman Sir Roger de Coverley for use in *The Spectator*. Steele borrowed Issac Bickerstaffe from Swift and gave him Jenny Distaff as co-editor. Sterne invented Mr Yorick; Defoe signed his *Journal of the Plague Year* 'H.F.'. The greatest creation in this vein is Lemuel Gulliver. His subtlety lies in his varying relations with the reader. We share his disgust at Lilliputian vanity, perceive the same vanity in himself in Brobdingnag, and endorse his common-sense view of intellectual excess and hypocrisy. All is prepared for the fourth book, where the butt of the satire is human reasoning itself. We dissent from Gulliver's enthusiasm for theoretical horse sense. Swift is using fictional disguise for an extended satirical essay.

The essayist also strays into the territory of the sociologist and the philosopher. Deep personal reflection leads to engagement in the great debates of the age. Milton defended the freedom of the press, Arnold his view of culture and Carlyle the poor in the face of a complacent Victorian commercialism. Many essayists joined in the debate of the respective claims of religion and science at the same period. In the twentieth century Virginia Woolf took up the cause of women, Bertrand Russell defended and was imprisoned for his view of individual freedom against the authority of the state.

The essay has changed its nature in response to the demands of its age. The Elizabethan pamphleteers, moralists like Stubbes or anti-moralists like Greene, found a market and established a tradition. Later classics of it are Milton's *Areopagitica* and Defoe's *The Shortest Way with Dissenters*. Addison and Steele created the perfect medium for polishing the refinement of the middle classes. In the early nineteenth century by vigorous expression of personal points of view, Hazlitt, de Quincey, Hunt, and Lamb all contributed to the ideal of individual development. Carlyle, Arnold, Macaulay, and Newman were among the great debaters of their century. In the first half of the twentieth century, while the written word was still the main vehicle of the public exchange of ideas, essayists proliferated. In *The Modern Age* (vol. 7 of *The Pelican Guide to English Literature*) they are listed in droves; from *The Present* (vol. 8 of the same) they have been driven away. Has our age really dispensed with them?

Certainly, in public debate, the spoken word now prevails over the written. Radio and television have taken over from newspapers as the main channel of news. But specialization has been as powerful a force, as the essayist has been eclipsed by the the expert. Artists are expected to work in oils, *or* etching, *or* engraving, *or* some other form of printing; the media have correspondents in specialized areas – industry, the city, foreign affairs, parliament, music, art, and so on. We no longer expect a single voice to speak with authority on all subjects.

Essays which are largely concerned with travel or literary criticism are to be found in those sections.

ANTHOLOGIES

ed. Kenneth ALLOT

The Pelican Book of English Prose 1956 (5 vols)
Each volume covers a separate age from 'Elizabethan and Jacobean' to 'Victorian' arranging its material under four main headings; 'The Picture of the Age', 'The Movement of Ideas', 'The World of Imagination, Feeling and Comic Invention', and 'The Criticism of the Arts'. Extracts in all from some 350 writers.

ENGLISH ASSOCIATION

English Essays of Today 1936
An anthology compiled by the English Association at a time when essayists were much admired, this covers acknowledged masters of the art as well as others who have a place in the history of the essay but are on the borderline of pure journalism – Neville Cardus, for example, whose work sticks closely to cricket and music.

ed. Daniel GEORGE

A Peck of Troubles 1936
A splendid compendium of complaints – not a complete essay among them, but the perfect bedside book.

ed. Gamini SALGADO

Cony-Catchers and Bawdy Baskets 1972
'An Anthology of Elizabethan Low Life', as its sub-title suggests, but also an interesting selection of the art of the Elizabethan pamphleteer. Contains work by Gilbert Walker, John Audelay and Thomas Hardane as well as the Greene cony-catching pieces.

ed. James SUTHERLAND

The Oxford Book of English Talk 1953
Not strictly essays, the entries are compiled as a record of English talk, but they cover an astonishing range of material and characters. Likely to be of interest to the specialist linguist as well as the general reader.

ed. John Dover WILSON

Life in Shakespeare's England 1911
This is an anthology of contemporary accounts of Shakespeare's England. Besides throwing light on many aspects of the life of the times it is also an excellent introduction to the essayists though it prints extracts rather than complete works.

INDIVIDUAL AUTHORS

Joseph ADDISON (1672–1719) and Sir Richard STEELE (1672–1729)

The Spectator 1711–12
An astonishing range of social comment, often through the opinionated Sir Roger de Coverley, the perfect satirical vehicle for the dissemination of cultivated values to the growing middle classes. The essays on Milton reflect Augustan literary Feste.

Robert ARMIN (c. 1568–1611)

A Nest of Ninnies 1608
A Nest of Ninnies is an enlarged edition of *Foole upon Foole; or Six Sortes of Sottes*. Six accounts of natural fools in a creaking philosophical framework by the original Feste of *Twelfth Night* throw interesting light on the way a professional fool collected his material.

Mathew ARNOLD (1822–88)

Culture and Anarchy 1869
Arnold's pursuit of an ideal of culture through his analysis of society into barbarians, philistines and populace. Arnold's gospel of 'the progress of humanity towards perfection' may carry diminished authority as the philosophy of 'meritocracy' is increasingly under attack, but his analysis and prose style are still worth reading.

Literature and Dogmas 1873
This is a discussion of biblical truths in a 'scientific' age. Still of value when the common discussions of theologians intermittently shock the general public.

W H AUDEN (1907–73)

The Dyer's Hand & Other Essays 1963
This represents a wide-ranging and radical appraisal of his art by a practising poet. Auden regards poetry as a social and a psychological phenomenon and the volume thus becomes reflections on art and society rather than 'lit. crit'.

Francis BACON (1561–1626)

Essays or Counsels, Civil and Moral 1597 (enlarged 1612 and 1625)
The arche-type of English essays: rational, subtle, and polished; required reading for anyone interested in the essay or the Renaissance and eminently quotable.

Henry C BARKLEY (c. 1874–1945)

Studies in the Art of Rat-Catching: a Manual for Schools 1891
A spoof primer: the experiences of a rat-catcher are presented here as though the subject had become part of the school curriculum. The joke is quite jolly, and the experiences are vigorously presented.

Max BEERBOHM (1872–1956)

The Incomparable Max 1962
A selection of his essays, parodies and reviews containing amongst others: a study of dandies, a brilliant parody of Henry James, and some of the late broadcasts, by which time the brilliance of his earlier writing had declined into mere elegance.

Brendan BEHAN (1922–64)

Island, An Irish Sketch Book 1962
Hold Your Hour and Have Another 1963
Colloquial bar-room chat of an *enfant terrible*. Are we surprised to learn that Yeats could put salt in his coffee and mistake parsnips for pudding?

Hilaire BELLOC (1870–1953)

Belloc: a Biographical Anthology
This work contains a wide selection from his over 150 works. Not surprisingly, Belloc has a prose style of absolute clarity and assurance – a delightful raconteur, a wit, a man of very pronounced sympathies, a joy to read. *The Path to Rome* is the account of his pilgrimage on foot.

George BOURNE (1863–1927)

The Bettesworth Book: talks with a Surrey peasant 1901
Change in the Village 1912
The Wheelwright's Shop 1923
A Small Boy in the Sixties 1927
Technical comment in *The Wheelwright's Shop* is interspersed with reflections on village life. These are the records of a man who knew well a life he sought to understand in his writing.

Rupert BROOKE (1887–1915)

The Prose of Rupert Brooke 1956
A useful cross-section of Brooke's work: extracts on literature, travel, and the cultural issues of his time give a much more convincing picture of Brooke than the popular roseate poet-hero.

Thomas BROWNE (1605–82)

Religio Medici 1643
Written for his private pleasure and published without his consent, this is a winsome book, full of delights: the reflection of the form of creation in a beautifully framed and eccentric imagination. The Everyman edition also has a selection of his other works.

Robert BURTON (1577–1640)

The Anatomy of Melancholy 1621
An early attempt at a psychological treatise, especially notable for its treatment of the melancholies of love and religion. This is a storehouse of its author's wide reading, beloved of generations of writers.

Samuel BUTLER (1612–1680)

Prose Observations 1980
Butler had a fascinating mind. This collection contains witty and detached observations on major abstractions such as learning and knowledge, religion, wit, reason, and nature, besides a collection of aphorisms.

Samuel BUTLER (1853–1902)

Note-Books of Samuel Butler 1912
The arrangement of Butler's comments by the editor, Henry Festing Jones, reduces the encyclopedic interests to a manageable field, but he has been more concerned for his reader than meticulous towards his originals. In a later edition Geoffrey Keynes and Brian Hill (1951) are more careful of their sources, but less readable. Amongst other subjects, Butler wrote on religion, science, music, photography, natural history, painting and morality.

Thomas CARLYLE (1795–1881)

Sartor Resartus 1833–4
An imaginary professor of Things-in-General develops his philosophy of clothes: a loose vehicle for Carlyle's speculations, wit and great sincerity. 'It is in and through *symbols* that man, consciously, lives, works and has his being.'

Past and Present 1843
Carlyle's attack on the social evils of his day through comparison with the past.

Joyce CARY (1888–1957)

Selected Essays 1946
This work contains powerful evocations of childhood, subtle studies of his own developing understanding, besides literary, social and political comment.

Christopher CAUDWELL (1907–37)

Illusion and Reality 1937
Studies in a Dying Culture 1938
Romance and Realism 1970

Christopher St John Sprigg – Caudwell is a pseudonym – was equally interested in flying and the relationship between art and society. *Illusion and Reality* is a study of poetry in its social context which also examines the place of myth and the role of the individual psyche. A sensitive and penetrating study which led him to Marxism; *A Study in English Bourgeois Literature*. His beliefs cost him dear; he was killed on his first day of combat as a volunteer in the Spanish Civil War.

G K CHESTERTON (1874–1936)

All Things Considered 1908
Essays and Poems 1958

All Things Considered includes the classic essay 'On Running After One's Hat'. The whole volume reflects the distinction 'It is so easy to be solemn; it is hard to be frivolous'. Chesterton's sense of paradox allowed him to be brilliantly frivolous and wise at the same time. Much of his work should be read for its sheer intelligent fun.

Cyril CONNOLLY (1903–74)

The Condemned Playground: Essays 1927–44
The Unquiet Grave 1944
Previous Convictions 1963

Selected articles of a literary reviewer who edited the journal *Horizon* (1940–50), and was also interested in travel and animals. The reviews give a wide introduction to his literary scene and there are examples of his skill as a parodist.

Abraham COWLEY (1618–67)

Essays 1668

These are tranquil reflections on the main issues of any age – liberty, agriculture, and solitude among others: morality running to aphorisms with occasional charm.

Daniel DEFOE (1661–1731)

The Shortest Way With Dissenters 1702

An attack on the Tories in the form of an ironic appeal for the savage suppression of dissenters, at first taken at face value. Once his real intention was discovered, Defoe was imprisoned for publishing it.

A Journal of the Plague Year 1722
The *Journal* reconstructs the experience of the plague and is interlaced with anecdote, religous speculation, and comment.

Thomas DEKKER (1570–1632)

The Wonderful Year 1603
Lanthorne and Candlelight 1608
The Gull's Hornbook 1609
English Villanies Discovered by Candle-light 1616
An educated working dramatist with a hand in some sixty plays, Dekker spent several years in prison for debt. His biting satires of the clothes, behaviour and language of those seeking social success may be sour grapes but they give a vivid picture of London life in Elizabethan and Jacobean times. *The Wonderful Year* is a powerful account of the plague years.

Thomas DE QUINCEY (1785–1859)

The English Mail Coach and Other Writings 1863
The Everyman collection contains some of De Quincey's best prose pieces including 'On Murder, Considered as One of the Fine Arts' and the brilliant study of dreams, 'The English Mail Coach'.

John DONNE (1572–1631)

Paradoxes and Problems 1633
Donne may have been showing off when he wrote these prose works, but they are the work of a precise and intricate mind with a profound grasp of the possibilities of words. Of interest to readers of essays because the problem of paradox is fundamental to any kind of creative writing.

Norman DOUGLAS (1843–1926)

London Street Games 1916
Norman Douglas: A Selection from his Works 1955
A traveller given to rapid sketches, but his picture of teeming life is seen with an odd lack of curiosity suggesting complacency, despite the close detail.

T S ELIOT (1888–1965)

Notes Towards the Definition of Culture 1948
The 'Notes' spring from Eliot's reflections on the formation of UNESCO: an interesting analysis chiefly, perhaps, because of the view of culture reached by the culture that the author was so well qualified to represent.

Havelock ELLIS (1859–1939)

Views and Reviews 1932
Dance of Life 1936
Dance of Life has the particular value of presenting life as a work of art – a view inadequately aired nowadays. *Views and Reviews* are culled from his writings between 1884–1932 and reflect considerations of subjects literary, political, cultural, and psychological by an early guru of sex.

Sir Thomas ELYOT (1499–1546)

The Booke Named the Governour 1531
This discusses the authority of the state, and the education and qualities most praised in a governor. It finds room for dance, among other arts.

Ford Maddox FORD (1873–1939)

The Spirit of the People 1907
Reflections of varying perceptiveness on such main concerns as law, faith, and conduct, by a man who wrote with wit and clarity. At times he throws into clear focus what our society puts at risk.

E M FORSTER (1879–1970)

Abinger Harvest 1936
Two Cheers for Democracy 1951
An intriguing comparison: the earlier book begins with a cosy acknowledgement of bourgeois predilections; the later has at its centre a much more thoughtful discussion of 'what I believe'. The war intervened, but even so Forster's perceptiveness charts fundamental aspects of changing cultural assumptions in the mid-century. He moves from special confidence to troubled diffidence: 'two cheers', not three.

Eric GILL (1882–1940)

Essays 1947
Better known as typographer and sculptor, as essayist Eric Gill inherits the tradition of the cultivated mind reflecting on the issues of his day. His arguments, though clearly developed, start from first principles that beg all the questions.

George GISSING (1857–1903)

The Private Papers of Henry Ryecroft 1903
A hybrid work, neither essay nor novel: a writer of fiction uses a fictional writer to reflect, under the headings of the four seasons, on such disparate topics as the bells of Evesham, breakfasting on apples, and writing in a London garret.

Graham GREENE (1904–)

Collected Essays 1969
Lucidly perceptive on classics like Fielding and Henry James, but his reviews of contemporary writers urbanely conjure a literary scene: these are civilized comments on writers who may escape the academics.

Robert GREENE (1560–92)

A Notable Discovery of Cosenage 1591
A Groatsworth of Wit, Bought with a Million of Repentance 1592
The second of these works is a satire on the respective merits of wealth and learning; the other, while claiming to condemn cosening or confidence tricksters, treats them with considerable relish. Part of a recognizable tradition of sixteenth and seventeenth century prose where accounts of low life are ostensibly presented as moralizing.

Joseph HALL (1574–1656)

Character of Virtues and Vices 1608
In presenting his moral and social types, Hall is an effective satirist.

William HAZLITT (1778–1830)

Table Talk, or Original Essays on Men and Manners 1821–2
Probably the most vigorous of English essayists – everything is written with zest, whether he is expressing pleasure, close perception or sheer prejudice. *Table Talk* is the most wide-ranging of his collections.

Lectures on the English Poets 1818
The Spirit of the Age 1825
Published together in the Everyman edition, there are excellent commentaries on his contemporaries, whether literary (Wordsworth, Coleridge, Byron), political (Canning, Brougham) or philosophical (Malthus, Bentham).

Thomas HOBY (1530–66)

The Courtier 1561
A translation of Castiglione's *Il Cortegiano*, this handbook of polite behaviour for the renaissance man is a classic of its kind.

William Henry HUDSON (1841–1922)

A Shepherd's Life 1910
'His writing was like the grass that the good God made to grow and when it was there you could not tell how it came.' So said Joseph Conrad. *A Shepherd's Life* is a powerful evocation of men (particularly Caleb Bawcombe) and events in Wiltshire at the time of the agricultural riots and trials.

James Henry Leigh HUNT (1784–1859)

Selected Essays 1929
A prolific journalist, Hunt's attack on the Prince Regent landed him in jail. This work contains interesting discussions of contemporary theatre.

Aldous HUXLEY (1894–1963)

Collected Essays 1960
Huxley's most famous novel *Brave New World* is an extended essay on the implications of biological conditioning in a world where social values have been inverted. His best essays reflect rationalists' paradoxes: an excellent analyst of ambiguities deriving from given first principles without the profoundest examination of those first principles.

Henry JAMES (1843–1916)

The Painter's Eye 1868–97
The Scenic Art 1872–1901
The Art of Fiction 1884
Partial Portraits 1888
A Little Tour in France 1900
English Hours 1905
James was a prolific writer in many literary forms. Among the essay collections *A Little Tour in France* rapidly evokes scenes with customary urbanity; *English Hours* has a splendid description of Derby day, and claims to observe 'that inexorable gentility which the English put on with their Sunday bonnets and beavers'; *The Painter's Eye* which contains a full account of the Wallace collection among others and *The Scenic Art* (on drama) comments on European theatre, not merely British.

Richard JEFFERIES (1848–87)

The Open Air 1885
Jefferies' England 1937
Jefferies had not merely an eye which noted the English countryside, but an imagination to celebrate it.

Samuel JOHNSON (1709–84)

The Rambler 1750–52
Johnson writes with such lucid good sense that he seems to acquiesce in the authority of the age he helped to create; 'such is the certainty of evil that it is the duty of every man to furnish his mind with those principles that may enable him to act under it with decency and propriety'. Selections from *The Rambler* are published in a 1953 Everyman edition.

Arthur KOESTLER (1905–84)

Drinkers of Infinity: Essays 1955–67
Contains a representative range of Koestler's interests: science and the imagination, legal and political matters, socialism, and religion. Like all the best essayists, Koestler's achievement is rather to orchestrate the issues he discusses than to argue them out of existence. See also *The Sleepwalkers* and *The Act of Creation*.

Charles LAMB (1775–1834)

Essays Of Elia 1823
Last Essays Of Elia 1833
Sometimes 'desultory and unmethodical', but a man of warm sympathies and prejudices in a style flexible enough to conceal his art. The most gentle and sensitive of all English essayists, he recognized 'the fragility of life' and had the delicacy to capture it without damage.

Walter LANDOR (1775–1864)

Imaginary Conversation 1824
With ironic wit and shrewd characterization in these pieces Landor has found a convincing medium for making art form out of different points of view.

D H LAWRENCE (1885–1930)

Psychoanalysis and the Unconscious 1921
Fantasia of the Unconscious 1922
Selected Essays 1950
D H Lawrence: A Selection from Phoenix 1971
Lawrence's essays are a blunt analysis of moral pretentions and pretentiousness in a language that makes his criticisms challenging and simple. The vigorous colloquialism creates a powerful record of his deep feeling. The direct expression of his philosophical ideas in his essays and letters are often more convincing than when they are forced through the medium of his novels. *Phoenix* is a large posthumous collection of miscellaneous writings.

Percy Wyndham LEWIS (1886–1957)

The Art of Being Ruled 1926
Time and Western Man 1927
Paleface: The Philosophy of the Melting Pot 1929
Wyndham Lewis: An Anthology of his Prose 1969
Frighteningly convincing analysis of the democratic system as a sort of Narcissistic closed shop. In 'the melting pot' he advocated a new kind of fusion, a social symbol corresponding to the new images of contemporary art. The progression from his ideas on the supremacy of the life of intelligence to the embrace of fascism cost Lewis friends and serious critical attention. Lewis was an important painter and novelist.

John LYLY (c. 1554–1606)

Euphues: the Anatomy of Wit 1578
Euphues and his England 1580
'Delightful to be read, and nothing hurtful to be regarded; wherein there is small offence by lightness given to the wise, and less occasion of looseness proferred to the wanton'. His mannered style helped shape English prose.

Rose MACAULAY (1881–1958)

Personal Pleasures 1935
An extravaganza on daily life that makes excellent reading.

Thomas Babington MACAULAY (1800–59)

Critical and Historical Essays 1843
Delightful to those who seek magisterial exposition and an Augustan style; shallow to those who want analysis and ambiguity. 'Gladstone on Church and State' and his review of Leigh Hunt's edition of Wycherley, Congreve, Vanbrugh, and Farquhar are good examples of his style and sympathies.

Hugh McDIARMID (1892–1978)

Selected Essays 1969
The analysis is of a committed and sensitive poet, reflecting his interests in the art of literature, socialism and Scottish problems. See also *The Company I've Kept*.

George MEREDITH (1828–1909)

An Essay on Comedy 1897
Reprinted in *Comedy 1956*, this essay is a subtle analysis of the English comedy of manners in a European context by one of the most conscious stylists in the language.

John MILTON (1608–74)

The Reason of Church Government 1642
The Doctorine and Discipline of Divorce 1643
Of Education 1644
Areopagitica 1644
Milton's prose is masterly in its clarity and emotional power and his subjects – education of the young, freedom of the press, nature of marriage – are of abiding importance. His subjection of minor to major issues derives directly from the emotional precision of his words; his attack on his reader's sensibility is intense and unremitting. *The Portable Milton* contains a useful selection of the prose.

Mary MITFORD (1787–1855)

Our Village 1824–32
Exquisite vignettes of real charm, though suggesting the sensitivity of a literary ideal rather than direct involvement in rural labour.

William MORRIS (1834–96)

Hopes and Fears for Art 1882
Signs of Change 1888
Architecture, Industry and Wealth 1902
In his essays Morris writes as a visionary socialist who offers an analysis of the work which is still of value to our society.

Edwin MUIR (1887–1959)

Essays on Literature and Society 1965
An accurate title: the book offers an intriguing analysis of Panurge and Falstaff, Emma Bovary and Becky Sharp as symbols of national life.

Thomas NASHE (1567–1601)

The Anatomie of Absurditie 1589
Pierce Penilesse, his Supplication to the Divell 1592
A gifted satirist and pamphleteer, Nashe wrote the *Anatomie of Absurditie* as a counterblast to Stubbes's *Anatomie of Abuses*.

John Henry NEWMAN (1801–1900)

The Idea of a University Defined 1873
This contains both series of Newman's lectures on universities: 'The Scope and Nature of University Education' and 'Lectures on Universities'. The first rector of the Catholic University in Dublin, Newman believed in the importance of the educational role of universities, a view that is relevant to the current re-evaluation of universities and their funding. His concern with the training of the mind parallels his own search for acceptable ideals.

George ORWELL (1903–60)

Inside the Whale 1940
The Lion and the Unicorn 1941
The English People 1947
Shooting an Elephant 1950
England Your England 1953
Perhaps the most widely read and accomplished essayist of the mid-twentieth century, Orwell's close observations of himself led him to understand the paradoxes in his own received assumptions. A writer of great importance because his essays can

do the same for the reader. Amongst the subjects are capital punishment, the middle class murder, 'comic' postcards, and Dickens. The *Collected Essays* are available in four volumes (1970).

John Cowper POWYS (1872–1963)

Psychoanalysis and Morality 1923
The Meaning of Culture 1929
Obstinate Cymric: Essays 1935–47
'The whole wisdom of life is to distinguish between those illusions that carry with them the intentions and purposes of nature, and those others that either cramp and restrict us, or start us off on wildgoose chases down side-alleys and criss-cross vistas'. Powys's explorations of the contrary pulls of self and love which constitute his fundamental life-sensation help to illuminate his novels.

Llewelyn POWYS (1884–1939)

Black Laughter 1925
Impassioned Clay 1931
Dorset Essays 1935
Essays on country life and philosophical reflections, and expressed with a genuine relish for the world.

Matthew PRIOR (1664–1721)

Essays and Dialogue of the Dead 1907
Interesting examples of a form, also used by Lucian and Landor amongst others, that expresses ambivalence by casting opposing views into characters; another way of achieving the irony and ambiguity of more traditional essay forms.

Samuel ROGERS (1763–1855)

Recollections of the Table Talk of Samuel Rogers 1856
Amusing anecdotes with some more extended portraits, particularly of Porson, by the popular poet who refused the laureateship, which then went to Tennyson.

Bertrand RUSSELL (1872–1970)

Religion and Science 1935
In Praise of Idleness and Other Essays 1935
Authority and the Individual 1949
Russell was a mathematician and philosopher whose commitment to freedom of speech led to imprisonment through his belief in pacifism during World War I – the foremost popular philosopher of his age. The works given here reflect his writing on social issues.

George William RUSSELL (AE) (1867–1935)

Collections and Recollections 1903
Social Silhouettes 1906
AE's arguments in prose are liberally supported by anecdote – he was an excellent raconteur. *Social Silhouettes* presents an intriguing selection of social types – schoolboy, teacher, curate, candidate etc.

William SANSOM (1912–76)

Pleasures Strange and Simple 1953
Blue Skies, Brown Studies 1961
Away to it All 1964
His best work is in his short stories, but Sansom's essays are full of bustling detail and verve – a vigorous celebration of some of life's jolly absurdities.

George Bernard SHAW (1856–1960)

Selected Prose of Bernard Shaw 1953
Bernard Shaw: A Prose Anthology 1959
Shaw on Theatre 1960
Platform and Pulpit 1961
Shaw wrote voluminously on questions social, political, musical, and dramatic. His wide range of interest is best reflected in his prefaces to his various plays where he continues discussion of social issues raised in the plays themselves.

Sir Richard STEELE (1672–1729)

The Tatler 1709–11
Steele's editorial creations Isaac Bickerstaff (from Swift) and Jenny Distaff held up an ideal of taste for the age. Steele himself was a rake and, despite the success of his light satirical vein, the ideal of taste he sought gained some piquancy from the distance between it and his experience.

Laurence STERNE (1713–68)

A Sentimental Journey through France and Italy 1768
A book based on Sterne's travels, but consciously composed – 'my design in it was to teach us to love the world and our fellow creatures better than we do'.

Robert Louis STEVENSON (1850–94)

Travels with a Donkey in the Cevennes 1879
Virginibus Puerisque 1881
Familiar Studies of Men and Books 1882
An important essayist with the breadth of feeling to observe and the control of language to record his impressions: 'Our affections and beliefs are wiser than we; the

best that is in us is better than we can understand; for it is grounded beyond experience and guides us, blindfolded but safe, from one age to another'.

Lytton STRACHEY (1880–1932)

Characters and Commentaries 1933
Spectatorial Essays (ed. James Strachey, 1964)
These two posthumous volumes of selections of Strachey's essays reflect his interests: history, Shakespeare and the Elizabethans and the theatre, on which his comment is wide and perceptive.

Philip STUBBES (c. 1555–91)

The Anatomie of Abuses 1583
Shrill complaints of an encyclopedic list of vices, this is a fine example of vigorous pamphleteering and records a number of the popular amusements of London.

Jonathan SWIFT (1667–1745)

An Argument . . . 1708
Gulliver's Travels 1726
A Modest Proposal 1729
The basis of Swift's satirical method is to follow the implications of human desires with remorseless logic. *Gulliver's Travels* is a satirical exposition of the vanities – social, intellectual, and spiritual – of the human sensibility. It is the most thorough-going indictment of human failings. His more precise attacks, such as *A Modest Proposal* (to eat babies), are equally cogent. His use of irony remains a model of the form, as in *An Argument to prove that the Abolishing of Christianity in England may as things now stand, be attended with some Inconveniences, etc.* A great stylist and arguably our greatest satirist.

William Makepeace THACKERAY (1811–63)

The Book of Snobs 1848
Splendid satire of vulgarity and pretentiousness: 'I believe such words as Fashionable, Exclusive, Aristocratic, and the like, to be wicked, unchristian epithets, that ought to be banished from honest vocabularies'.

Dylan THOMAS (1914–53)

Quite Early One Morning 1954
A Prospect of the Sea 1955
These contain zest, vigour, and wit: reminiscences of childhood, the Festival of Britain Exhibition of 1951, and instructions on how to be a poet in Thomas's rich and inimitable style.

Edward THOMAS (1878–1917)

Edward Thomas on the Countryside 1977
Edward Thomas: Selected Poems and Prose 1981
Though better known as a poet, Edward Thomas earned his living as a writer from essays, reviews and travel books amongst the best of which is *The Icknield Way*.

Izaak WALTON (1593–1683)

The Compleat Angler 1653
A book to make us 'love all anglers, they be such honest, civil, quiet men'. The perennial charm of Walton's countryside is an idealized picture by a townsman. Nevertheless, a much treasured book.

Edward WARD (1667–1731)

The London Spy 1703
Mine host of the King's Head moralizes with gusto on the 'varieties and vices of the town' to a country tyro.

H G WELLS (1866–1946)

Mankind in the Making 1903
Socialism and the Family 1906
An Englishman Looks at the World 1908
The Work, Wealth and Happiness of Mankind 1931
The Fate of Homo Sapiens 1939
Wells was a prolific writer of essays, novels and other prose. The above are a few of Wells's publications, which number over 150 in all. There is a selection in: *Journalism and Prophecy* (ed. W Wager, 1966) George Orwell was surely right to believe that Wells was too sane to understand the world he analysed with such intelligence, so that the prophet of the Edwardian era became, somehow, out of touch for later generations.

Gilbert WHITE (1720–93)

The Natural History and Antiquities of Selbourne 1788
This work grew out of White's correspondence with two other naturalists of his age. Chiefly concerned with scientific observation, White's accounts are also laced with picturesque details of village life.

Oscar WILDE (1856–1900)

The Works of Oscar Wilde 1948
'All art is entirely useless'. Wilde's essays challenge the Victorian values of productivity and the tyranny of Public Opinion over art and individual freedom.

Expressed with paradoxes both playful and subversive the important essays are 'The Decay of Lying' and 'The Critic as Artist', published in *Intentions* (1891) with 'The Truth of Masks' and 'The Soul of Man under Socialism'. All are in Maine's edition of the works.

Virginia WOOLF (1882–1941)

Collected Essays 1966
Woolf is impressive in art and argument, whether she is making an exposition of the different attitudes towards men and women, or observing a world so full and intricate that it is beyond observation. Excellent command of the rapid sketch, and satirical approach, as in Judith Shakespeare – Will's frustrated sister – from the celebrated pioneering feminist essay, 'A Room of One's Own' (1929).

W B YEATS (1865–1939)

A Vision 1925
Essays and Introductions 1961
The *Essays* are a useful reflection of Yeat's various artistic interests. *A Vision*, which was much revised after first publication, is an attempt to imagine models by which to understand his world from a mixture of history and philosophy as well as more dubious manifestations of the occult.

TRAVEL

Travel literature is as diverse as the places there are to visit and the people who undertake to visit them. It offers the reader a variety of style and purpose, a rich assortment of experiences, feelings and psychological insights, philosophy, and, of course, adventure that would surprise an unsuspecting person who mistakenly believed that all this is only to be found in imaginative fiction. Indeed it is frequently difficult to distinguish travel literature from memoir, autobiography or fiction itself with any degree of confidence. Graham Greene's *Journey Without Maps* (1936) is at one level an account of a journey through an uncharted wilderness in Africa. At a deeper level, it is an account of Greene's own childhood memories, a fact that could easily place the work under autobiography or even fiction. However, although many of the works included in the following selection would not fit such categorization, it is possible to divide travel literature into the two separate phases of the 'tour' which was so popular in the late eighteenth and early nineteenth centuries, and the travel books that were produced in such great numbers from the end of the nineteenth century until the start of the Second World War.

One function of travel literature, and some might say its most important, is the historical account it offers of our changing relationship with the world we live in. As a consequence many of the earliest works in this list are devoted to exploration – in particular Richard Hakluyt's *Principal Navigations* and Purchas, his literary heir, with *Purchas His Pilgrimes*. In these collections (and Hakluyt's is considered a masterpiece of the genre) the major tales of Jacobean and Tudor seamen and explorers are recorded for posterity. Also included is Charles Ley's anthology of *Portugese Voyages* (1498–1663) which covers a similar period. In the same vein are Captain Cook's *Voyages of Discovery*. There are also the many and various records of the British love affair with Arabia and 'darkest Africa' in the nineteenth century. Travellers such as Sir Richard Burton, David Livingstone, and Sir Henry Stanley are still household names. Not only are some of their works included here but also a selection of anthologies of their writings and of the other major explorers. Of equal importance to the history of exploration are those twentieth century explorers Scott and Shackleton in their separate attempts to reach the South Pole.

A sub-species of the explorer's literature is that in which Nature is challenged to mortal combat. Typical examples would be Captain Joshua Slocum's *Sailing Alone Around the World* or Wilfred Noyce's *South Col*. The challenge is paramount and these works are almost as equally at home in the literature of sport.

It is not necessary to travel far or to such extremes to produce literature that contributes to our understanding of ourselves. The quest for knowledge as much as for adventure is the modification of several books which, taken as a whole, leave us with a detailed history of previous ages. Camden's *Britannia* and Stow's *Survey of London* provide the starting point for what has become, something of a great tradition in the literature of protest. Such famous works as Daniel Defoe's *A Tour Through the Whole Island of Great Britain* and William Cobbett's *Rural Rides* offer both social description and moral commentary about the state of Britain. They are complemented by similar works produced in the 1930s such as J B Priestley's *English Journey* and George Orwell's *The Road to Wigan Pier*.

Those works belonging both to the 'tour' and to 'travel' are not only the most numerous but the ones that most disturb the desire to classify. The closeness to autobiography and memoir emphasized in the Greene book already mentioned is equally apparent in D H Lawrence's *Sea and Sardinia*, Conrad's *Mirror of the Sea*, the works of George Orwell, Evelyn Waugh and Robert Byron. It is possible to read these books, and others of their kind as much for the light they throw upon the characters of their authors as for their various contributions to the literature of travel. Yet here there is the problem of falsification. How true, for example, is Orwell's account of his life of poverty in *Down and Out in Paris and London*, or again, how accurate a description of himself is the portrait offered in the final part of *The Road to Wigan Pier?* It is well known, for instance, that in *Labels: A Mediterranean Journal* Evelyn Waugh falsifies a considerable proportion of the events that touched upon his personal life. It is perhaps significant that most of the writers mentioned have established reputations in other areas of literature. It indicates the depth and wealth of material to be found in travel literature and points to the enduring significance of the genre as a medium of expression.

ANTHOLOGIES

ed. G R CRONE

The Explorers 1962
An anthology of first-hand accounts of adventures by famous explorers arranged in chronological order, and with maps of the routes taken.

ed. Charles David LEY

Portuguese Voyages 1498–1663
An anthology from the golden age of discovery, this includes Samuel Johnson's translation of Father Jerome Lobo's *A Voyage to Abyssinia (The Jesuits in Abyssinia) 1625–34* and an account of the colonization of Brazil. Translations by the editor.

eds Margery and Jack Simmons PERHAM

African Discovery 1942
Collects notable passages from the writings of the great British explorers. Commencing with James Bruce's *Ethiopian Journey* in 1769 to the death of Livingstone in 1878. It includes selections from Mungo Park, Burton, Baker and Stanley. Biographies are supplied by the editors as well as original illustrations and maps.

INDIVIDUAL AUTHORS

Hilaire BELLOC (1870–1953)

The Path to Rome 1902
The description of a walk from Lorraine taken at the turn of the century.

The Cruise of the 'Nana' 1925
Introduced by Lord Stanley and one of Belloc's best books, it describes his experiences with an old-fashioned 10-ton cutter.

On Sailing the Seas 1951
A selection from Belloc's several travel books including *The Cruise of the 'Nana'*.

James BOSWELL (1740–95)

Journal of a Tour to Corsica 1768
This was Boswell's first major publication. It includes an account of his support for Corsican independence.

Journal of a Tour to the Hebrides with Samuel Johnson 1786
This work is a companion piece to Dr Johnson's *A Journey to the Western Isles of Scotland* and the great doctor is the main subject.

Sir Richard Francis BURTON (1821–90)

Pilgrimage to El Medurah and Mecca 1855
Burton's most widely read book, probably a strong influence on future adventurers and explorers of Arabian lands.

First Footsteps in East Africa 1856
The account of the explorer's journey into the Somali country.

The Lake Region of Central Africa 1860 (ed. Alan Moorehead, 1961)
Considered to be one of the best explorer journals ever written, it gives an account of the first major penetrations of Africa.

Samuel BUTLER (1835–1902)

The Alps and Sanctuaries of Piedmont and the Canton Ticino 1881
Described by R A Streatfield, who edited and revised the work in 1913, as 'one of the wisest, wittiest and tenderest of Butler's books'.

Robert BYRON (1905–41)

The Station: Alhos – Treasures and Men 1928
This describes a visit to Mount Alhos to study Byzantine art and architecture, a subject on which Byron produced several interesting works.

The Road to Oxiana 1937
The road is through Persia to North-East Afghanistan. This is now regarded as one of the greatest of all travel books. Byron was killed during the Second World War.

William CAMDEN (1551–1623)

Britannia 1586 (translated from the Latin by Philemon Holland, 1610)
The first important survey of Britain. A further translation was made in 1789 by Richard Gough.

William COBBETT (1763–1835)

Rural Rides 1830 (ed. E W Martin, 1975)
An account of several tours of the country commencing in 1821, this is an important account of 'the state of the nation' during a period of considerable hardship and change by a leading campaigner for greater democracy.

Joseph CONRAD (1857–1924)

The Mirror of the Sea 1906
A series of 'memories and impressions' of Conrad's journey to Europe and a record of his romantic attachment to the sea and ships. Contains evocative descriptions of the people and the places he encountered.

Captain James COOK (1728–79)

The Journals of Capt. James Cook on his Voyages of Discovery (ed. J C Beaglehole and three others) Volume I: *The Voyage of the 'Endeavour' 1768–71* 1955, Volume II: *The Voyage of the 'Resolution' and the 'Adventure'* 1961
These volumes are accompanied by a *Portfolio of Charts and Views* drawn by Cook and his officers and reproduced from original manuscripts. This definitive edition is published by the Hakluyt Society.

Voyages of Discovery 1773, 1777, 1784
Written by Cook himself and Captain King these are accounts of the first voyage of 1771, the second voyage toward the South Pole and around the world, 1772–5, and the voyage to the Pacific Ocean, 1776–86.

Richard Henry DANA (1815–82)

Two Years Before the Mast 1840
A classic account of the author's personal experiences on board a merchant ship.

Charles DARWIN (1809–82)

Journal of Researches into the Geology and Natural History of the various countries visited by H.M.S. Beagle 1839
'Beagle' travelled to South America, Patagonia, Chile, Peru and the Pacific Islands. During this voyage Darwin made some of his most significant discoveries which led him to make important contributions to the theory of evolution.

Daniel DEFOE (1660–1781)

A Tour Through the Whole Island of Great Britain 1724–7
Defoe's record of the social and economic conditions is a justly famous work and invaluable to students of the eighteenth century.

Charles DICKENS (1812–70)

American Notes 1842
Pictures from Italy 1846
Written by the great nineteenth century novelist these works are filled with the insight and distortions of an imaginative artist.

Norman DOUGLAS (1868–1952)

Siren Land 1911
Fountains in the Sand 1912
Old Calabria 1915
One of the best of pre-war travel writers Douglas mixes evocation of landscape with essays on ethics, local folklore, food, etc., to create an invigorating account of his journeys through parts of Italy and Tunisia.

Lawrence DURRELL (1912–)

Prospero's Cell 1945
Reflections on a Marine Venus 1953
Bitter Lemons 1957
Durrell combines sharp observations of the physical details of landscape and the characters who occupy it with a poetic style that is a joy to read. The three books mentioned are all concerned with mediterranean islands: Corfu, Rhodes and Cyprus.

Henry FIELDING (1707–54)

Journal of a Voyage to Lisbon 1755
Suffering from gout and other terminal illnesses, this last work is a vivid account of a journey by this most famous of picaresque novelists. Fielding died soon after his arrival and was buried in Lisbon.

Peter FLEMING (1908–71)

Brazilian Adventure 1933
Perhaps the most popular travel book written between the wars. Amongst other things Fleming finds himself searching for a mountain range shown on the maps but actually non-existent.

GIRALDUS de BARRI ('Cambrensis') (1146–1220)

The History of Archbishop Baldwin through Wales 1585 (trans. Sir R C Hoare, 1806), *Description Cambriae* (Description of Wales)
Both works are important sources for the legends and topography of Wales in the twelfth century.

George GISSING (1857–1903)

By the Ionian Sea 1901
Sometimes described as Gissing's 'happiest work', this is much prized for its search for the emotional link between landscape and literature.

Graham GREENE (1904–)

Journey Without Maps 1936
An account of a trip made in 1934 with his cousin Barbara through part of West Africa. This is linked with an evocation of Greene's childhood experiences.

The Lawless Roads 1939
Greene's unhappy visit to Mexico produced this lesser work as well as his famous novel *The Power and the Glory*.

Richard HAKLUYT (1552–1616)

Principal Navigations 1589, 1599
Hakluyt collected and edited most of the famous narratives in his vigorous prose. They include Drake's voyage around the world, the defeat of the Spanish Armada, and many less known, but equally marvellous adventures.

Aldous HUXLEY (1894–1963)

Beyond the Mexique Bay 1934
The Olive Tree 1936
Huxley's travel books are interesting for the various philosophical essays that were inspired by his visits to Mexico and Tunisa.

Henry JAMES (1843–1916)

A Little Tour of France 1884
Parisian Sketches 1875 (ed. L Edel and Isle Dusoni Lind)
English Hours 1905 (ed. A L Lowe)
These are James' impressions of England and France. The last named is a collection of 'letters' to the *New York Tribune* from 1875 to 1876.

Samuel JOHNSON (1709–84)

A Journey to the Western Islands of Scotland 1775
A companion piece to Boswell's work. Johnson reflects on the habits and culture of the Scottish with more generosity than is present in his famous aphorisms.

Rudyard KIPLING (1865–1936)

From Sea to Sea 1899
A collection of various works including 'Letters of Travel' – 'Letters of Marque', and 'The City of Dreadful Night'.

D H LAWRENCE (1885–1930)

Twilight in Italy 1916
Sea and Sardinina 1923
Mornings in Mexico 1927
Etruscan Places 1932
D H Lawrence lived much of his life in exile after the First World War and his writings on the places he lived in or visited are not only an invaluable contribution to our understanding of Lawrence but also the places he describes. *Mornings in Mexico*, contains the famous essays on 'The Hopi Snake Dance'.

Patrick LEIGH FERMOR (1915–)

A Time of Gifts 1977
In 1933, at 18 years of age, Fermor decided to rebel and packed his bags with the intention of travelling to Turkey, taking in as many European countries as possible on the way. A refreshingly observed book capturing the panache of youth.

David LIVINGSTONE (1813–73)

Missionary Travels and Researches in South Africa 1857 (ed. James I Macnair, 1954)
A compilation of Livingstone's journals and diaries.

Sir John MANDEVILLE (c. 1300–1372)

Travels (modern facsimile edition, 1963) (trans. C W R D Moseley, 1983)
Translated from the French of Jean d'Outremonst and believed to be a compilation of several travel books the reader is taken to the Holy Land, Turkey, Persia, Egypt, India and Tartary and on the way introduced to all kinds of wonders, imaginary and otherwise. A remarkable and entertaining curiosity.

Jan (formerly James) MORRIS (1926–)

Venice 1960 (revised edition 1974)
Oxford 1965 (revised edition 1978)
These are acutely observed guides to the history and topography of two of the world's most famous cities. Full of information for the observing tourist.

H V MORTON (1892–1979)

A Traveller in Italy 1964
Morton can be annoying in that some of his observations assume the patronizingly old-fashioned air of the English tourist, but both the Italian people and the countryside are vividly described and the book is a pleasure to read.

Eric NEWBY (1919–)

A Short Walk in the Hindu Kush 1958
Newby sometimes gives the impression of being a pith-helmet and long white socks explorer, but he tells a good tale.

Wilfred NOYCE (1917–62)

South Col 1954
The famous successful 1953 Everest expedition described in vivid detail.

George ORWELL (Eric Arthur Blair) (1903–50)

The Road to Wigan Pier 1937
Cast in the mould of social and political writing as practised by Defoe and Cobbett, Orwell gives a classic account of the poverty of England during the Depression.

Homage to Catalonia 1938
In this powerful work, Orwell recounts his involvement in the Spanish Civil War. Like the work of Greene and Waugh it demonstrates the gradual movement in this period of the travel writer to the role of war correspondent.

Francis PARKMAN (1823–93)

The Oregon Trail 1849 (ed. H S Commager)
This account of the author's time spent with the Indians in 1846 is a vivid collection of 'Sketches of Prairie and Rocky Mountain Life'. It is still widely read today.

J B PRIESTLEY (1894–1984)

English Journey 1934
Sub-titled 'a rambling', this famous work is an account of what one man saw, heard, felt and thought on a journey through England during the autumn of 1933.

Samuel PURCHAS (1576–1626)

Purchas His Pilgrimes: Containing a History of the World, in Sea Voyages and Land Travels by Englishmen and Others 1625 (ed. H G Rawlinson, 1931)
A lesser collection than that of Hakluyt, but nonetheless a worthy and useful continuation. The standard edition of the complete Purchas narratives was published by Maclehose in 20 volumes, 1905–7.

Robert Falcon SCOTT (1868–1912)

The Voyage of the 'Discovery' 1905
An abridged, popular edition of the 1900–1904 Antarctic exploration.

Scott's Last Expedition: Journals and Reports
Scott's Last Expedition: The Personal Journals (ed. Leonard Huxley, 1913, 1923)
A popular edition of the two-volume work which records the journeys and the research undertaken. The tale of this ill-fated expedition continues to fascinate.

Sir Ernest SHACKLETON (1874–1922)

South 1919
An account of Shackleton's last expedition to the South Pole between 1914 and 1917.

Captain Joshua SLOCUM (1844–1906)

Sailing Alone Around the World 1900
An account of one of the most famous voyages ever undertaken. Slocum died when making a second attempt.

Captain John SMITH (1580–1631)

The Generall Historie of Virginia, New England and The Summer Isles 1624
True Travels and Adventures into Europe, Asia, Africa and America 1593–1629 1630
An early traveller, Smith colonized Virginia and became its president in 1608.

Tobias SMOLLETT (1721–71)

Travels Through France and Italy 1776
Shrewd and caustic commentary on the manners, customs, art and architecture of these lands.

Sir Henry Morton STANLEY (1841–1904)

How I Found Livingstone 1872
Through the Dark Continent (2 vols) 1878
In Darkest Africa 1890
Some of the most popular narratives of exploration and adventure including the myth-making tale of how he found Livingstone and how he rescued Emin Pasha.

Freya STARK (1895–)

The Journey's Echo 1964
Freya Stark has managed to travel almost everywhere in Africa and Asia. The recommended book is a selection of her writings.

John STEINBECK (1902–68)

Travels with Charley 1962
Steinbeck travelled throughout the United States with his dog; the observations combine the down-to-earth with the sentimental.

Robert Louis STEVENSON (1850–94)

Across the Plains 1892
An account of Stevenson's journey from New York to San Francisco.

Essays of Travel 1905
Eight essays which together offer examples from all Stevenson's travel essays. The account of a journey from Monastier is bound up with other popular essays: 'An Island Voyage', 'The Silverado Squatters' and 'The Amateur Emigrant'.

John STOW (c. 1525–1605)

A Survey of London 1598, 1603
The principle source of our knowledge of Elizabethan London, its people, places, and social conditions.

John Millington SYNGE (1871–1909)

The Aran Islands 1907
'In these pages I have given a direct account of my life on the islands... .' An invaluable introduction to the background and inspiration of much of Synge's dramatic works as well as a beautiful account of the islands and their peoples.

Paul THEROUX (1941–)

The Great Railway Bazaar 1975
Theroux is a traveller in the grand American tradition: determined to experience everything, meet everyone and stamp the scene with his own often too American observations. In this book he travels throughout Asia on the railway system; the people, the trains, the countries (including Vietnam at war) and Theroux himself are thoroughly observed.

Wilfred THESIGER (1910–)

Arabian Sands 1959
Thesiger undertook one of the most difficult and dangerous of journeys; he crossed the Arabian deserts and did so without the benefit of Western comforts, for he joined the Bedouins on their travels. His observations on their way of life are as interesting as the descriptions of the journey itself.

Edward THOMAS (1878–1917)

The Heart of England 1906
The South Country 1909
Two works by the Edwardian poet in which he explores England, particularly the area surrounding the North and South Downs.

Mark TWAIN (Samuel Loughorne Clemens) (1835–1910)

Life on the Mississippi 1833
An account of Twain's early life as a journeyman pilot.

The Innocents Abroad 1869
A journey through Europe, Egypt, and the Holy Land. This account established Twain as a brilliant humourist and it is still imensely popular. He later followed it up with *A Tramp Abroad* (1880) and *More Tramps Abroad* (1897) which are semi-fictional accounts of travel in Europe.

Evelyn WAUGH (1903–66)

Labels: A Mediterranean Journal 1930
The best of Waugh's several travel books and one of the most entertaining of the period between the wars.

William WORDSWORTH (1770–1850)

A Guide Through the District of the Lakes 1810, 1835
Of considerable interest to students of Wordsworth and also still of some practical use to fell-walkers.

LITERARY CRITICISM

'Literary criticism' covers a variety of enterprises, scattered along the spectrum between biography and text analysis: towards one end, John Middleton Murray's *Keats and Shakespeare*, towards the other I A Richard's *Principles of Literary Criticism*.

In making a selection of the more important contributions, we find ourselves concentrating on the development of literary theory; but not exclusively. A few items have been included because of the special interest of their author, as with Yeats' *Essays and Introductions*; others have been added as works for reference purposes, like Ann Jefferson and David Robey's *Modern Literary Theory* and George Saintsbury's *History of Literary Criticism*. Although this selection is based on criticism by British writers, a short listing with annotations of some major American works is appended. In recent years, literary criticism has become as transatlantic as much of the literature itself.

Theories of literature can be traced back to Aristotle's *Poetics* which still underlies much of the critical work in existence – as it is bound to do for its pure and logical statements, on the nature of tragedy in particular. The first true criticism from an English culture can be seen in the work of John Dryden in the seventeenth century. His descriptive and theoretical analyses are an effort to find the structural lines upon which he subconsciously based his poems and plays. The trend of poets becoming critics has continued with such figures as Arnold, Coleridge and T S Eliot. There is a variance of opinion on whether or not the 'creatively inspired' themselves are the best people to talk about their methods, but it is a fact that the critical works of these poets, not to mention the novelist Henry James, are amongst the most significant in the history of the subject.

Samuel Johnson's contribution is immense, his *Lives of the Poets* forming the foundation of historical criticism. He is dismissive of theoretical judgements and relies instead on the basic relationship between reader and work, his own assessments being based largely on what he intuitively likes or dislikes. Coleridge, on the other hand, makes little reference to his personal thought on the quality of a poem, although his 'romantic' approach, opposed to the neo-classical position of Johnson and Dryden, maintains that the ultimate aim of the poetry is to give pleasure 'through the medium of beauty'. His progression from Johnson can be seen in his consideration of the importance of historical details as fundamental, rather than incidental, to the criticism of a creative work.

It is with Matthew Arnold that the modern age of criticism begins. His intention was to move away from the analyses of authors' characters, which were encouraged in preceding historical criticism, and to formulate some kind of critical method. Whilst rejecting romanticism and the values of his time, Arnold was nevertheless reactionary in returning to classicism by way of resistance. He denounced the 'philistine' frame of mind he saw to be prevalent in his society with a didacticism which has evoked some hostility. His basic thesis is that poetry is a 'criticism of life' and that its importance will grow parallel with, but in opposition to, the provinciality of the times. The task of the critic was to spread 'culture' in an era when vulgarity was threatening to take over.

The aesthetics of the late nineteenth to early twentieth century believed in 'art for art's sake' and refused to attach any value to it other than its pleasure-giving qualities. Walter Pater and Oscar Wilde were its main exponents, Wilde doing his usual witty things with words so that statements like 'All art is immoral' and 'All art is useless' became widely known and almost accepted as true in the way of oft-heard slogans. Although neither would have welcomed the comparison, Wilde was in accord with Arnold, in the sense that literature and criticism were seen as free activities.

Whilst the aesthetes were denying any meaning in art, Henry James, as the first writer to attempt a serious analysis of the novel, was developing in prefaces, in his novels and in reviews his own profoundly moralistic criticism. Largely derived from French theorists – Gustave Flaubert in particular – James's aim was to exclude the author from the narrative so that the story seemed to be telling itself. He wanted the novel to have a form, so that it distinguished itself from the 'fluid puddings' of Tolstoy or Dostoyevsky; but the narrative should be an impressionistic representation of life, where action was not divided up into blocks of time but occurred as a continuous and simultaneous set of movements, like the movement of the mind itself.

T S Eliot is the major figure in creative and critical writing in the first half of the twentieth century. Following on from Arnold, Eliot suggested that criticism belonged to an élite few who were to lead a cultural revolution, or, more accurately, a cultural reaction. In the same way as Henry James proposed the novel as an art form in its own right, Eliot decided that poetry was not to be confused with its author – 'to divert interest from the poet to the poetry is a laudable aim' (from 'Tradition and the Individual Talent'). Poetry was conceived as a purveyor of universal truth and the poet, Eliot himself included of course, as a kind of divine figure with the ability to convey emotions common to human beings. The character of the individual artist therefore became irrelevant, a stance which was taken up more firmly by the New Critics.

T S Eliot's review of the literary tradition assesses poets (it is significant that he deals almost exclusively in poetry) according to how useful they are to later practitioners of the art. Milton is dismissed out of hand, Shelley and Keats are found wanting, whilst John Donne and the metaphysical poets of the seventeenth century are praised for being masters of the metaphor in their use of apparently incompatible comparisons or 'conceits'. For Eliot, metaphor is the ultimate method for creating impersonality in poetry, and it was an impersonal order that Eliot wished to see in his 'tradition'. Such a tradition sounds dangerously élitist and authoritarian and has been attacked, not least by the Marxists, although its influence on subsequent criticism has been remarkable.

F R Leavis placed Eliot at the end of his own highly selective tradition in *New Bearings in English Poetry* in 1932. Leavis's later interest moved towards the novel, more suited to his moralistic position. His *The Great Tradition* begins with Jane Austen and includes George Eliot, Henry James, Joseph Conrad and D H Lawrence on the grounds of their application to moral concerns. For nearly half a century as teacher and writer Leavis piloted the study of literature and those authors who made his first-class passenger list through the shallows of contemporary culture. Frequently claiming to be ignored but immensely influential on the post-war generations of students of literature and society, his strong and sensitive response to certain authors will probably outlast the accompanying messages, whether serious or silly.

Leavis and his wife Q D Leavis pioneered *Scrutiny* a quarterly review founded in 1932, the aim of which was to raise the cultural and critical consciousness of England. The Scrutineers, who included L C Knights and D W Harding, saw themselves as educators who could save society by spreading the literary word, or at least the particular words they had decided amongst themselves were worth spreading. The method of 'practical criticism' is closely associated with them although is has been pointed out, by George Watson, for example, that actual examples of it are difficult to find. The idea was that literature should be analysed by 'close reading' of the text without taking any account of its historical or political context, a position which had originated in I A Richards and was later developed by the New Critics.

I A Richards in his books *Principles of Literary Criticism* (1924) and *Practical Criticism* (1929) proposed a reading of the text without the irrelevant encumbrances of time, place and author, concentrating instead on the response of the reader. In this way Richards can be seen as an 'effectivist' critic, viewing the poems as a means of recreating in the reader's mind the psychological condition of the author. It seems paradoxical that Richards' interest in psychology as an addendum to criticism should be accompanied by a claim to 'dehumanize' poetry and treat it an an autonomous object to which 'scientific' principles must be applied to grapple with 'emotive' language. Poetry is 'emotive' and makes 'pseudo-statements', and it is to these that surgical instruments must also be applied to determine their literary 'value'.

The New Critics of the 1950s took Richards subtraction of external sources from the poem itself a step further, and took the reader away as well. The author's intentions and the reader's response were as irrelevant as the clothes the poet liked to wear. The American New Critics included W K Wimsatt and Munroe Beardsley, Cleanth Brooks and R P Blackmur. The Englishmen William Empson and Robert Graves preceded and in some ways anticipated the movement, but were less rigidly anti-historical in their approach.

Although they are are not included here, there were of course relevant developments in other countries which influenced the development of English Literary Criticism. A major movement was Russian Formalism, espoused most notably by Roman Jakobson and Rene Wellek in the 1920s. These theorists sought to establish literary studies as a discipline in its own right with its proper devices for analysing literary style. The later structuralists owed a lot to Formalism, as the structuralist founder, Ferdinand de Saussure, in his early *Course in General Linguistics* (1916) was also an influence on the formalists. Structuralism, an important influence on current critical trends, strove to define a 'poetics' which could clinically apply rules to a literary text. Again historicism was out of the window, and the words on the page reduced to a series of signs with long labels. This has been followed, naturally, by post-structuralism and the complex writings of Jacques Derrida.

Recent criticism has tended to concentrate more and more on the text itself. Certain British and American critics, however, have stuck to the old idea of looking at author, reader, social, political and historical contexts, and have challenged the very foundations of literary theory as it has come to be conceived. Thus, Marxist and feminist theories assist us in viewing literature from a politico-historical perspective; although reactionary in the sense that they refuse to take up the new linguistic approach, they are revolutionary in disputing the bases and value of literature. Feminists such as Elaine Showalter in *A Literature of Their Own* (1977) and Gilbert and Gubar in *The Madwoman in the Attic* (1979) seek to show the influences of a patriarchal society on the literature of women, and the consequent need to redefine 'literature' and 'literary theory', while the Marxist Terry Eagleton, after arguing that literature is an illusion, concludes that the whole concept of literary theory deserves 'less of an introduction than an obituary', being entirely defunct.

ANTHOLOGIES

eds D J ENRIGHT and E de CHICKERA (1920–)

English Critical Texts: 16th Century to 20th Century 1962
A good selection of the best known works of criticism through the ages, from Philip Sidney to F R Leavis. The editors supply a lively introduction, a glossary, and an appendix from classical sources.

ed. Roger FOWLER (1938–)

Style and Structure in Literature 1975
A collection of essays by a variety of eminent critics, which grew out of a conference aimed at airing views on the new stylistic method of analysing literature. The essays are relatively accessible.

ed. D C FREEMAN (1938–)

Linguistics and Literary Style 1970
A set of essays demonstrating the recent growth in importance of linguistics in the study of literary criticism. Each essay is preceded by a useful summary of the argument it contains and the whole book by a good general introduction by Freeman.

ed. Mary JACOBUS (1944–)

Women Writing and Writing about Women 1979
An enlightening collection of recent essays by feminist literary figures, covering a range of subjects from Feminist Poetics to twentieth century Russian women poets. One of the contributors is Elaine Showalter whose book *A Literature of their Own: British Women Novelists from Bronte to Lessing* is recommended.

eds. Glen A LOVE and Michael PAYNE

Contemporary Essays on Style, Rhetoric, Linguistics, and Criticism 1969
A collection of important and accessible essays on style from the 50s and 60s, from authors including Ian Watt, Northrop Frye, Richard Ohmann and Roger Fowler. Each essay is prefaced by a short and clear note on the author and his literary stance.

ed. James SCULLY (1937–)

Modern Poets on Modern Poetry 1966
Prose writings by a number of poets giving illumination to the critical theories that underly their own poetry. Included are essays, letters or interviews by Ezra Pound, W B Yeats, Marianne Moore, E E Cummings and Dylan Thomas among others.

INDIVIDUAL AUTHORS

Lascelles ABERCROMBIE (1881–1938)

Principles of Literary Criticism 1960
A lucid and manageable exposé of Aristotle's *Poetics* is the basis of this brief but compact book, arguing for criticism as a literary activity in its own right. A short, concise history of criticism follows, and a conclusion asking for the good critic to combine both objective rules and subjective judgement in his appraisal of literature.

Walter ALLEN (1911–)

The English Novel: A Short Critical History 1954
Allen claims not to espouse any particular formal theory of the novel, indeed it is difficult to do so when reviewing the life time of the novel. His lack of dogma and amiable style make for a very acceptable survey of literature. *Reading a Novel* (1949, revised 1963) is a more basic book for beginners.

Miriam ALLOTT (1920–)

Novelists on the Novel 1959
The idea that novelists are the best people to talk about fiction is the axis of this collection of writings by writers, including extracts from prefaces, letters and essays.

Matthew ARNOLD (1822–88)

Essays in Criticism (1st, 2nd and 3rd Series) 1865, 1888, 1910
Seen by many as the forefather of modern criticism, Arnold's intention is to collaborate with, rather than preach to, the reader. As in his poetry, underlying much of his critical writing there is a questioning of the values accepted by the society of his time. The most important of the essays included are 'The Function of Criticism at the Present Time' in the first volume, 'The Study of Poetry' in the second, and 'On the Modern Element of Literature' in the third. Remaining essays are on individual authors ranging from Milton to Tolstoy, and covering aspects of European literature.

Culture and Anarchy 1869
Arnold develops his theory of literature and culture in general which is, according to Arnold, an ideal state which enables man to see 'things as they really are'.

Patricia BEER (1924–)

Reader, I Married Him 1974
A study of the women characters of Jane Austen, Charlotte Bronte, Elizabeth Gaskell and George Eliot, Patricia Beer's book is a highly enjoyable examination of women characters drawn by women novelists of the Victorian era.

Frederick Samuel BOAS (1862–1957)

An Introduction to Tudor Drama 1977
A lucid description of Tudor plays associated with the Royal Court, and other facets of 16th century institutions. A helpful complement to the study of Shakespeare and his contemporaries, but not including Ben Jonson or Chapman.

Introduction to Eighteenth Century Drama, 1700–80 1978
Here Boas uses a simple and effective method: a chapter on each of twenty authors, assessing their influence and detailing their plots.

A C BRADLEY (1851–1935)

Shakespearean Tragedy 1904
Assuming that poetry is not an imitation of life but 'an end in itself', Bradley's criticism necessitates a complete immersion in the fictional world and deals with the plays primarily as dramas. Essays on the substance and construction of Shakespearean tragedy are followed by studies of each of the four major tragedies, with particular emphasis on the characters as being almost independent of the plays.

Anthony BURGESS (1917–)

Shakespeare 1982
A wide-ranging introduction, in Burgess's exuberant style, to Shakespeare's life and times. Highly recommended for its liveliness and beautiful illustrations.

Samuel BUTLER (1835–1902)

The Essential Samuel Butler (ed. G D H Cole) 1975
A selection of the eccentric criticism of Samuel Butler, in which his apparently preposterous theories are presented clearly and convincingly. His re-arrangement of Shakespeare's sonnets and his proposition that *The Odyssey* was written by a woman still provide interest and entertainment.

Samuel Taylor COLERIDGE (1772–1834)

The Portable Coleridge (ed. I A Richards) 1950
Coleridge: poems and prose (ed. Kathleen Raine) 1957
Coleridge is one of the greatest of English literary critics, for some *the* greatest. Yet his critical theory and descriptive criticism is scattered through lectures noted down by others, a preface written by someone else, a sort-of autobiography, and his nephew's record of his table conversation. Both the Penguin paperbacks cited above contain selections from the work listed below: *The Portable Coleridge* is the larger 'helping' with a longer introduction, although Kathleen Raine provides more of the Shakespeare criticism. Neither print the Preface to the second edition of *Lyrical Ballads*, which was written by Wordsworth but thought by Coleridge.

Biographia Literaria 1817
The 'practical' literary criticism is largely in the second part, an examination of the 'defects' and 'beauties' of Wordsworth's poetry (chapters 17–20 and 22). Earlier chapters (especially 4, 12 and 13) establish – often in fragmentary form – the philosophical basis for Coleridge's aesthetic, at the centre of which is his view of the creative act as a perpetual counteraction between the poet and his subject shaped by the spirit of imagination. There is an Everyman edition of the text by George Watson.

Coleridge's Shakespearean Criticism (ed. T M Raysor) 1930
The Shakespearean criticism is mostly in the 1811–1812 lectures. Shakespeare is seen as a great Romantic poet, the ultimate expression of Coleridge's view of the creative process: he is a natural force who becomes his own poetry rather than – in the neoclassical view of Johnson – a recorder of nature who should stick to certain rules of art and morality.

Coleridge's Miscellaneous Criticism (ed. T M Raysor) 1936
Non-Shakespearean criticism, including passages on Milton and Jonson, mostly from the 1818 lectures.

Gail CUNNINGHAM

The New Woman and the Victorian Novel 1978
The New Woman of the 1890s did not fulfil the roles assigned to her and thus became a figure of fear or of fun. Gail Cunningham examines women characters in novels of the nineteenth century – Hardy, Gissing and Meredith – in the context of their social position in the period.

Eneas Sweetland DALLAS (1828–79)

The Gay Science 1866
An oddly-named but important contribution to criticism for being an early attempt at formulating critical principles. Aristotle's view of art as imitation is disputed and art is seen instead as a representation of something perceived by the subconscious rather than by the eye.

John F DANBY

Wordworth's 'Prelude' 1960
Written for a series aimed at introducing students to close analysis and evaluation of texts, this brief study lucidly sets the poem in its age and surveys Wordworth's developing talents.

Shakespeare's Doctrine of Nature in 'King Lear' 1961
Lear is seen as a drama of ideas, with emphasis on the different meanings and connotations of the word 'Nature'. An excellent aid to the grasping of this difficult play.

Thomas DE QUINCEY (1785–1859)

Literary Criticism (ed. Helen Darbishire) 1909
De Quincey's enthusiastic criticism concentrates on Wordsworth and the Elizabethans. His essay 'On the Knocking at the Gate in Macbeth' expounds his method of working from fundamental 'feelings' about literature and arguing effectively (and affectively) through to a conclusion.

John DRYDEN (1631–1700)

Of Dramatic Poesy and Other Critical Essays (ed. George Watson, 2 vols) 1962
Dryden's dialogue essay has four characters arguing on the classical and the modern versions of drama, and includes Dryden's appraisals of his fellow English poets in defence of those who 'prefer the French'. The other essays are mostly prefaces to his own poems and plays and, although apparently unremarkable in themselves, can be seen as the first examples of comparative analysis and descriptive criticism.

Terry EAGLETON (1943–)

Literary Theory: An Introduction 1983
After convincingly arguing that literature is an illusion, Terry Eagleton surveys different forms of literary theory to reveal the political dimension of each.

T S ELIOT (1888–1965)

Selected Essays (enlarged edition) 1951
The first and most famous of these essays, 'Tradition and the Individual Talent', sets forth Eliot's classicist position, calling for a need for some order and authority in the arts. This stance colours the subsequent essays on drama, and his appreciations of individual artists, including Shakespeare, the Metaphysical Poets, and Baudelaire.

For later essays, including 'Poetry and Drama', see the collection *On Poetry and Poets* (1957), where it becomes clear, on his own admission, that his literary activity cannot be separated from his personal, political and religious beliefs. But the main relationship is with his own poetry and reading his critical writings often produces an effect closer to that of poetry than philosophy.

William EMPSON (1906–84)

Some Versions of Pastoral 1968
A study of great style and influence, giving a new gloss to the appreciation of the pastoral mode in verse.

Seven Types of Ambiguity 1973
An intellectual fire-cracker, thrown by I A Richards' brilliant pupil. He argues for the richness of meaning given by linguistic ambiguity, and analyses 'the modes of action of a poetical effect'.

E M FORSTER (1879–1970)

Aspects of the Novel 1927
This accessible and explicitly modest little book presents Forster's consistently sound and unpretentious opinions on the structure of the novel, the most dwelt-on aspect being 'people' and containing his famous distinction between 'flat' and 'round' characters. See also essays in *Two Cheers for Democracy* (1951), notably 'The Raison d'Etre of Criticism in the Arts' and 'Art for Art's Sake'.

Paul FUSSELL (1924–)

The Rhetorical World of Augustan Humanism: Ethics and Imagery from Swift to Burke 1965
Concentrates on six writers: Swift, Pope, Reynolds, Gibbon, Burke and particularly Johnson whom Fussell sees as forming the mainstay of eighteenth century values, and through their ethics and recurring imagery he investigates the humanist struggle against the new age of impersonality, disorder and technology.

Abroad: British Literary Travelling Between the Wars 1980
Fussell chooses D H Lawrence, Graham Greene, Norman Douglas, Evelyn Waugh and Robert Byron to illustrate his exploration of literature and culture between the wars, and the emphasis placed on travel during this period.

Helen GARDNER (1908–1987)

The Business of Criticism 1959
A volume including 'The Limits of Literary Criticism' which demonstrates the pause in the flood of literary criticism in the 1950s, a pause dictated by the need to re-evaluate the boundaries of criticism and question the authority of uncompromisingly assertive critics like Leavis. On a similar theme is John Holloway's 'The New Establishment in Criticism' in *The Charted Mirror*.

Sandra M GILBERT and Susan GUBAR (1936–) and (1944–)

The Madwoman in the Attic 1979
The biased and ultimately misogynist representation of women in literature is exposed in this study of major British and American writers. The authors examine the effects of a patriarchal literary tradition on writings produced by women.

Gilbert and Gubar are also the editors of *Shakespeare's Sisters: Feminist Essays on Women Poets* (1979).

Harley GRANVILLE-BARKER (1877–1946)

Prefaces to Shakespeare (2 vols) 1971
The emphasis in these prefaces is on detailed examination of individual plays as living works of drama and the challenge they present to a producer in the theatre company – Barker having been one of the great producers and a fine playwright.

Herbert GRIERSON (1866–1960)

Cross-currents in English Literature 1929
These lectures, delivered at Cornell University, on the evolution of civilization, consider the effect on creative achievement of the conflict between Renaissance and Reformation; 'humanism' and 'puritanism'. Very much for the student of the development of literary criticism in England.

Barbara HARDY (1924–)

The Appropriate Form: An Essay on the Novel 1964
A work defending the novel as an art form worthy of critical analysis despite its great variety and range. Her theories are illustrated by studies of individual authors including Henry James, D H Lawrence, and George Eliot.

William HAZLITT (1778–1830)

Characters of Shakespeare's Plays 1817
Hazlitt disputes Johnson's judgement that each of Shakespeare's characters is a species rather than an individual and instead agrees with Pope that each is 'as much an individual as those in life itself'.

Lectures on the English Poets 1818
Hazlitt's passionate love for literature suffuses all of these essays and their primary aim is to convey his enjoyment of the works of poets discussed, from 'Chaucer' to the 'Living Poets'.

The Spirit of the Age 1825
A famous series of benevolent essays on literary personages of the time, including Byron, Scott, Wordsworth and Coleridge.

Richard HOGGART (1918–88)

The Uses of Literacy 1957
An original study of the impact of popular mass publications on the oral traditions of the British working class. Setting a trend for sociological surveys of the media's influence, Hoggart's descriptions, insights and warnings are still valid.

Gerald Manley HOPKINS (1844–89)

A Hopkins Reader (ed. John Pick) 1953
This expedition into the mind of Gerald Manley Hopkins contains a selection of his diary entries and letters, both personal and critical, which serve primarily to illuminate his poems, some of which are also included.

Henry JAMES (1843–1916)

The Art of the Novel (ed. R P Blackmur) 1934
In these retrospective prefaces to six of his novels and nine shorter stories, written between 1906 and 1907, James 'invented' criticism of the novel. A literary form which had long since achieved maturity is here for the first time analysed in terms of its artistic integrity, moral seriousness and technical content. It is a wonderful bonus to the reader that he is writing about his own novels.

The House of Fiction (ed. Edel) 1957
A selection of much-quoted essays on the state of the novel, and on nineteenth century English and French novels asking always how each achieves its effects.

Selected Literary Criticism (ed. Shapira) 1973
These mostly short essays on a variety of French, American and English authors span forty years and provide a good first survey of James as critic, with a useful introduction by F R Leavis.
    See also: *Literary Reviews and Essays on American, English and French Literature* (ed. Mordell)

Samuel JOHNSON (1709–84)

The Rambler 1750–52
Johnson remains the plain man's champion in English literary criticism: say what you like and dislike about what you read and use (intelligently and selectively) the best examples of the past as your standard for comparison. For Johnson his 'best' meant the ancient writers of Greece and Rome and his neo-classical aesthetics are first stated in several of the issues of *The Rambler*, especially numbers 37, 92, 125, 156 and 158.

Johnson on Shakespeare (ed. W Raleigh) 1906, 1925
The 1756 *Proposals for Printing the Dramatic Works of Shakespeare* and the subsequent (1765) Preface to the edition and some of the editorial notes on individual plays are collected in this volume. The Preface contains many a half-remembered quote as Johnson dares to find fault with Shakespeare's lack of moral purpose and the construction of his plots. Nevertheless, his administration of his subject prevades the argument which is expressed with a wit and vigour which makes the work eternally readable.

The Lives of the Poets 1781
Originally commissioned as biographical prefaces to a new collection of works, these 52 essays constitute Johnson's finest written achievement, combining biography, character portraiture and descriptive criticism. The poets are almost all Augustans of Johnson's own life-time, with the work of two of the biggest names – Dryden and Pope – inspiring the best criticism. However, the exceptions are of almost equal interest: the life of Milton defines some of the limits of Johnson's own sensibilities and the life of Cowley contains the famous attack on the metaphysicals – 'Their thoughts are often new, but seldom natural, etc'.

Ben JONSON (1572–1637)

Timber; or Discoveries 1640–41 (ed. R S Walker) 1953
In these essays, collected after his death, Jonson may be seen as one of Bacon's disciples, commenting on man and nature, considering a writer's craft, praising his classical heritage but optimistic that Nature encourages each generation of artists to experiment.

Arnold KETTLE (1916–)

An Introduction to the English Novel (2 vols) 1951–3
An an exponent of the Marxist viewpoint on literature, Kettle asks why the novel came about, and why it emerged when it did. He traces the roots back to the English revolution of the seventeenth century, and charts its progress up to 1950 using a few representative works from each period.

G Wilson KNIGHT (1897–1985)

The Wheel of Fire 1930 (revised 1949)
The first of a series of symbolic readings of Shakespeare, in which the plays are seen as 'extended metaphors'. Knight's approach is to interpret rather than to criticize: 'Criticism is a judgement of vision; interpretation a reconstruction of vision'. G Wilson Knight is an important Shakespearean critic whose work had a marked effect on the critics writing for *Scrutiny*.

L C KNIGHTS (1906–)

Explorations 1946
Most famous for the essay included here, 'How Many Children had Lady Macbeth', in which he advocates a move away from traditional Bradlean forms of criticism, L C Knights attempts to stimulate and assist explorations into the work of Shakespeare, George Herbert and Yeats.

Charles LAMB (1775–1834)

Lamb's Criticism (ed. E M Tillyard) 1923
An 'amateur' critic compared to his friend Coleridge, Lamb's response to the Elizabethan and Jacobean playwrights makes some insightful connections, but he 'missed' the later Romantics like Byron and Shelley.

Philip LARKIN (1922–86)

Required Writing 1955–82 1983
A collection of brief reviews and essays, mostly on writers and writing. This contains much enjoyment and insight, especially in the pieces dedicated to writers and artists, such as John Betjeman, who resisted the modernist way of Parker, Pound and Picasso – the 'irresponsible exploitation of technique in contradiction to human life'.

D H LAWRENCE (1885–1930)

A Selected Literary Criticism (ed. Beal) 1967
A selection of writings on literature gleaned from letters, reviews and essays. The studies vary in length and standard but are always interesting for Lawrence's passionately held views, especially in regard to the attitudes and achievements of his contempories, such as Arnold Bennett.

F R LEAVIS (1895–1978)

New Bearings in English Poetry 1932
This work is the first of Leavis's attempts to establish a 'great tradition' of English poetry and fiction. Following I A Richards, Leavis sees the artist as 'the most conscious point of the race in his time', and his chosen poets for examination here are T S Eliot, Ezra Pound and Gerald Manley Hopkins.

Revaluation 1936
Published after *New Bearings* and before *The Great Tradition*, this book is closely connected with both and claims to give 'the main lines of development in the English tradition'. Here he deals with Milton, Pope, the Augustans, Wordsworth, Shelley and Keats, with a great deal of reference to T S Eliot along the way.

The Great Tradition 1948
Leavis opens this highly influential and controversial work with the proposition that 'the Great English novelists are Jane Austen, George Eliot, Henry James and Joseph Conrad'. His book concentrates on only the last three of these, with chapters on chosen works of each. Dickens is relegated to an analytical note on *Hard Times*, but a more generous re-appraisal is made in the later *Dickens the Novelist* (1970), written with his wife, Q D Leavis.

A Selection from Scrutiny (ed. F R Leavis, 2 vols) 1968
The essays contained in these two volumes are from a variety of authors, predominantly Q D Leavis, F R himself, D W Harding, and James Smith, and on a variety of writers, works and trends in criticism.

C S LEWIS (1898–1963)

Selected Literary Essays (ed. Walter Hooper) 1969
This volume contains almost all of Lewis's essays on a diverse collection of subjects. For him the job of the critic is to encourage good reading of good texts, and his essays aim to explain and enhance rather than to judge.

C S LEWIS (1898–1963) and E M W TILLYARD (1889–1962)

The Personal Heresy: A Controversy 1939
The record of a controversy between two important figures in literary criticism. A series of essays instigated by the production of C S Lewis's essay *The Personal Heresey in Criticism* written in order to clarify and elaborate their original statements.

Percy Wyndham LEWIS (1884–1957)

The Lion and the Fox 1927
A highly individual study by one of the leaders of the Vorticist movement of the role of the hero in Shakespeare, based on the conflict in Machiavelli's figures of the lion and the fox: the fool and the knave. A thought-provoking work.

David LODGE (1935–)

The Language of Fiction 1966
Having attacked exponents of the New Criticism for applying strenuous linguistic appraisal only to poetry, Lodge goes on to offer a series of fascinating dissections, drawing specimens from novels ranging from *Mansfield Park* to *Lucky Jim*.

Working with Structuralism 1981
The book is intended to show how structuralism 'works' i.e. what the method produces when applied to a series of texts. Readers may be put off by the title, which would be unfortunate since the book is a lively and provocative account of what this 'continental' literary theory has to offer.

J L LOWES (1867–1945)

The Road to Xanadu 1927
This rather imposing-looking book is an impressively deep search into the workings of the mind which produced *The Rime of the Ancient Mariner* and *Kubla Khan*, its prime interest being in Coleridge's poetic imagination rather than his critical activity.

Percy LUBBOCK (1879–1965)

The Craft of Fiction 1921
A disciple of Henry James, Lubbock advocates that the novel must represent life and must give form to the life it depicts. Nevertheless, he is somewhat more flexible than James in his outlook, and his personal insights are of interest in their own right.

Thomas Babington MACAULAY (1800–1859)

Critical and Miscellaneous Essays 1841–4
A collection of essays originally contributed to *The Edinburgh Review*, displaying Macaulay's easy enthusiastic appreciation of literature, combined with his own blend of history and biography.

Karl MARX (1818–83) and Frederick ENGELS (1820–95)

On Literature and Art 1976
A selection of writings on Marxist aesthetics taken from letters, articles and essays. Marx and Engels viewed art and literature as a part of the whole social system, and its changing patterns as traceable to the social existence of its creators.

Edwin MUIR (1887–1959)

The Structure of the Novel 1928
Not the easiest book to read, this is Muir's attempt, following Forster's and Lubbock's, to define principles for the creation of the novel. His division of 'novels' into the three categories – 'novels of character', 'dramatic novels', and 'chronicle novels' – reflects the Kantian categories of the mind – Time, Space and Causality.

Essays on Literature and Society 1949
A collection of notes, essays and lectures by a poet whose eye is always for the unusual (the evil in Jane Austen, for example). Mostly brief and general, the essays provide a good starting point for the exploration of writers who are not readily accessible: Holderlin, Kafka, Spengler.

Gilbert MURRAY (1866–1957)

Euripides and his Age 1911
Its modest, admiring tone and simple style make this a good starting point for the general reader.

Aeschylus: The Creator of Tragedy 1978
Self-confessedly 'popular' in style, this book aims at a greater understanding of Aeschylus's ideas, and examines the stage techniques of his time in some detail.

John Middleton MURRAY (1889–1957)

The Problem of Style 1924
An attempt to define style and reinstate it in literature, while disposing of today's jargon. Murray's aim is to keep good writing alive, and at the same time to make literature accessible to the ordinary reader.

Keats and Shakespeare 1925
If you agree with this author that 'to know a work of literature is to know the soul of the man who created it', this study is an excellent introduction to the poetry of Keats.

Selected Criticisms (ed. Rees, 1960)
These are lightweight, wide-ranging essays and extracts on literature, useful for the occasional striking idea rather than for any sustained critical judgements.

George ORWELL (1903–50)

Collected Essays (4 vols) 1961
The essays of George Orwell, both critical and otherwise, are written in his distinctive simple and unambiguous style. He deals with writers such as Dickens and Yeats primarily from a political point of view, his argument being that a writer's personal beliefs 'will leave their mark even as in the smallest detail of his work'.

Walter PATER (1839–94)

The Renaissance: Studies in Art and Poetry 1873
As an aesthete, Pater claimed for the critic, 'the power of being deeply moved by beautiful objects'. His highly-wrought essays describe Renaissance artists chosen to illustrate the beauties of their age. See also: *Essays on Literature and Art* (ed. Uglow).

V S PRITCHETT (1900–)

The Living Novel 1946 (revised 1964)
No particular critical doctrine dictates the progress of these essays on British, French and Russian novelists, but there is a great deal of common sense and a talent for apparently stating the obvious. See also: *Working Novelists* (1965)

Richard PUTTENHAM (c. 1529–90)

The Art of English Poesie 1589
The style is not so attractive as Sidney's *Apologie for Poetry*, but this is still of interest to the student of Elizabethan literary criticism for its references to many poets in the English tradition.

Sir Arthur QUILLER-COUCH (1863–1944)

Studies in Literature (3 series) 1918, 1922, 1929
From an 'art for art's sake' perspective, writings display abundant enthusiasm and a feeling that literature is there to be enjoyed by everyone. His lack of philosophical criticism can be seen as facile – or refreshing.

Sir Walter RALEIGH (1861–1922)

Six Essays on Jonson 1910
Raleigh in light-hearted vein as usual, but here at his best on the writings of Jonson. His work is an attempt at a reaction against romantic criticism. See also his *Shakespeare* (1907), brief but rich.

I A RICHARDS (1893–1979)

Principles of Literary Criticism 1924
This is the first serious attempt at establishing measurable criteria for the value judgement of works of art. Drawing on psychological method, Richards explores the nature of experience as a base for judging literature, painting and sculpture.

Practical Criticism 1929
Richards aims to formulate techniques for the judgement of poetry. Quoting extensively from the now-famous responses of Cambridge undergraduates, he

applies four elements of meaning to the minute details of a text. This attempt to focus judgement on the text itself, shorn of imported emotions and prejudices, launched the new criticism and still underpins current critical practice.

Elaine SHOWALTER (1941–)

A Literature of their Own: British Women Novelists from Bronte to Lessing 1977
A feminist interpretation of literary history, in which Showalter points out the need to create a female literary tradition independent of its male counterpart. She hopes the strength of women will be illuminated by the independence of the novelists.

Philip SIDNEY (1554–86)

An Apologie for Poetrie 1595
The Elizabethan era's most elegant work of literary criticism, defending lyric and dramatic poetry, with much classical reference. Sidney also reviews contemporary English verse, calling for energy to match the language's native flow. For the text see *English Critical Texts* (eds Enright and de Chickera).

Sir Leslie STEPHEN (1832–1904)

Hours in a Library 1874–79
A collection in three volumes of Stephen's rambling essays. A Victorian look at literature with Stephen's Bloomsbury liberalism and philosophical insight shot with flashes of inspired writing, especially on William Hazlitt and Thomas De Quincey.

Lytton STRACHEY (1880–1932)

Literary Essays 1948
Most famous for his *Eminent Victorians*. Strachey's essays on French and English literature displays some of the same sharpness of perception.

Arthur SYMONS (1865–1945)

The Symbolist Movement in Literature 1899
An important work for being the first attempt to assess the movement which was subsequently to undergo rapid changes. Symons's influence on Yeats was great.

Kathleen TILLOTSON (1906–)

Novels of the Eighteen-Forties 1964
As readable as the novels under discussion, this commentary wears its scholarship lightly. Partly devoted to the literary background of the period and partly to studies of *Dombey and Son*, *Mary Barton*, *Vanity Fair*, and *Jane Eyre*.

Dorothy VAN GHENT

The English Novel: Form and Function 1953
Using Cervantes's *Don Quixote* as a starting-point for prose fiction, Dorothy van Ghent analyses eighteen classic English novels, from *Pilgrim's Progress* to *A Portrait of the Artist*. She sees the novel as a record of life and accordingly balances her criticism between the values of art and experience.

Ian WATT (1917–)

The Rise of the Novel 1957
This book attempts to pinpoint the distinctive literary features of the novel as it developed in eighteenth century England. Defoe, Richardson and Fielding are proposed as the leaders who paved the way for the subsequent production of the paradigmatic novel by Jane Austen.

Oscar WILDE (1854–1900)

The Artist as Critic (ed. Richard Ellman) 1968
Edited and introduced by Richard Ellman this volume contains Wilde's critical articles, displaying his famous 'art for art's sake' theories. Included is the Preface to *The Picture of Dorian Gray* with its collection of quotable statements.

Raymond WILLIAMS (1921–88)

Culture and Society 1780–1950 1958
Perhaps the best known of modern British critics who approach literature from a Marxist standpoint, i.e. an interpretation based on its historical and economic context, Williams' views are further developed in such works as *The Long Revolution*, *The Country and the City* and *The English Novel from Dickens to Lawrence* – the latter being a rather too verbatim version of his lectures at Cambridge.

Drama in Performance 1968
An interesting investigation into the relationship between the text of a play and the drama enacted on the stage. Individual plays are studied to explore the possibilities of a method of dramatic analysis.

Virginia WOOLF (1882–1941)

The Common Reader 1925
A collection including the classic essay 'Modern Fiction', in which Virginia Woolf attempts to discover the quality in Joyce which is lacking in the popular work of Wells, Bennett and Galsworthy. The latter deal in trivia and materialism, while Joyce pursues truth.

William Butler YEATS (1865–1939)

Essays and Introductions 1961
A selection of lyrical, intensely personal narrative essays on poetry and related subjects in which the poet plants ideas in a garden of luxurious prose. Yeats often tells us more about himself than about the artists he discusses.

SOME AMERICAN WORKS

M H ABRAMS (1912–)

The Mirror and the Lamp 1953
This important and learned book deals with the shift from the kind of criticism practised from Aristotle onwards to the 'Romantic' theory of criticism developed during the first half of the nineteenth century. Abrams gives valuable explanations of the various theories and their main exponents.

Wayne C BOOTH (1921–)

The Rhetoric of Fiction 1961
Booth clarifies and expands terms such as 'telling and showing', 'realism', and 'objectivity', building on the examples of Henry James and his followers. In the second part he examines the various methods of narration.

A Rhetoric of Irony 1974
In this text Booth distinguishes between 'stable' and 'unstable' ironies, and the extent of uses to which irony can be put by authors. His Aristotelian view that art is a method of communication and sharing is expanded by his clear argument.

Cleanth BROOKS (1906–)

The Well Wrought Urn 1949
In his attempt to ascertain the characteristic structure of poetry, Brooks examines a number of well-known poets from Donne to Yeats, studying primarily their use of irony, paradox and wit. Persuasively written.

R S CRANE (1886–1967)

The Languages of Criticism and the Structure of Poetry 1953
For Crane, criticism should focus on the work itself, but its complexities require a set of different 'languages', one for each aspect of the subject matter. Fundamentally Aristotelian, the implications of this work are far-reaching and important. See also: *Critics and Criticism: Ancient and Modern* (ed. R S Crane and others).

Northrop FRYE (1912–)

Anatomy of Criticism 1957
After the American New Criticism which concentrated on literature as an aesthetic object, Northrop Frye saw the need to convert criticism into a science, and this book sets about formulating a cyclical theory of literary history, encompassing the 'total structure' of literature. See also *Fables of Identity: Studies In Poetic Mythology*.

Murray KRIEGER (1923–)

The New Apologists for Poetry 1956
A comprehensive survey of the theories behind the works of exponents of New Criticism, particularly of T S Eliot and I A Richards.

Vladimir NABOKOV (1899–1977)

Lecture on Literature (ed. Fredson Bowers) 1980
Resurrected from notes to lectures given at Wellesley and Cornell in the 1940s, these presentations of, and commentaries on, specific works by Austen, Dickens, and Joyce among others hum with enthusiasm for the novelist as story teller making fables rooted in imaginative detail and structural plot. A novelist's view of novelists. See also: the companion volume, *Lectures on Russian Literature*.

John Crowe RANSOM (1888–1974)

The New Criticism 1941
Ransom was the American inventor of the name 'New Criticism' for the movement which gave literature, or more specifically poetry, an existence independent of any author, reader, or ideology.

Allen TATE (1899–1979)

Collected Essays 1959
A pupil of John Crowe Ransom, Allen Tate's essays also espouse the American New Criticism, disregarding history and biography in the appraisal of poetry.

Lionel TRILLING (1905–75)

The Liberal Imagination 1951
In an always readable selection of articles, this eminent critic examines the limiting effects of contemporary 'liberalism' on life and letters. Worth reading if only for the hilariously destructive review of the Kinsey Report (on sexual behaviour) and the society which made its publication both possible and necessary.

The Last Decade: Essays and Reviews, 1965–1975 (ed. Diana Trilling) 1979
A collection of pieces from the last ten years of Trilling's life, after the publication in
1965 of *Beyond Culture*. The 'liberalism' apparent in his book-length studies of
Matthew Arnold (1949) and *E M Forster* (1943), is still a pervasive influence, as is his
admiration for Freud. His concern for education and culture is apparent in the essay
'The Uncertain Future of the Humanistic Educational Ideal'.

Rene WELLEK (1903–) and Austin WARREN (1899–)

Theory of Literature 1949
The authors are agreed that 'literary study should be specifically literary' and are
therefore in favour of the autonomy of literature. Rather a difficult book, relying on
an assumed knowledge of Kant. Rene Wellek has also produced four volumes of *A
History of Modern Criticism 1750–1950*.

Jessie L WESTON (1850–1928)

From Ritual to Romance 1980
A classic work of practical scholarship, used by T S Eliot for the symbolic framework
of *The Waste Land*, it applies the anthropological insights of Frazer's *The Golden
Bough* to the Grail legend, tracing the development of archetypal events and symbols
from ancient rites to medieval romantic legend.

Edmund WILSON (1895–1972)

Axel's Castle 1931
The Wound and the Bow 1941
Wilson, in these classic works, traces the development of contemporary literature
through the 'symbolist' work of Yeats, Valery, Eliot, Proust, Joyce and Stein. His
approach is from a historical perspective, regarding literary criticism as 'a history of
man's ideas and imaginings in the setting of the conditions which have shaped them',
while he also includes Freudian interpretations in his late work.

W K WIMSATT (1907–75)

The Verbal Icon 1954
As eloquent spokesman for the American New Critics, in the first and most renowned
of this collection of essays Wimsatt proposes that criticism should deal with a work of
literature as an autonomous object, regardless of the intentions of the author or the
mind of the reader.

WORKS OF REFERENCE

Raymond CHAPMAN

Linguistics and Literature 1973
An introduction to the subject of literary stylistics and its relation to literature. A
useful bibliography concludes each chapter together with notes on the content and
accessibility of the books mentioned.

Jonathan CULLER

On Deconstruction: Theory and Practice after Structuralism 1985
The major European and American critics – Derrida, de Man, Stanley, Fish etc. – are here introduced to a reader looking for some guidance to this most complex of theories. Lucid, but by no means a spoon-feeding exercise, it offers a critique of the theorists as well as a guide to them.

David DAICHES (1912–)

A Critical History of English Literature (4 vols) 1968
Ideal for a serious student's first immersion. The author calls his method 'description, explanation and critical interpretation'. The easy range of a thoughtful mind takes the reader from Anglo-Saxon poetry to the Victorian era, with a twentieth century epilogue.

ed. Boris FORD

The Pelican Guide to English Literature 1954–1983
A series of eight period volumes from *The Age of Chaucer* to *The Present*. Each book contains a number of individual articles on literary movements and major writers, which together constitute a continuous survey of literature.

eds Anne JEFFERSON and David ROBEY

Modern Literary Theory: A Comparative Introduction 1982
An introduction to the increasingly complex world of literary theory in the twentieth century, examining the most important developments in Europe and North America. Each chapter is followed by a useful and comprehensive bibliography.

ed. David LODGE

20th Century Literary Criticism: A Reader
A large book of short extracts arranged chronologically so that the reader can follow the historical development of modern literary criticism.

Christopher NORRIS

Deconstruction: Theory and Practice 1982
A clear guide to Derrida's thought, showing that, if he is correct, Derrida has challenged the basic assumptions of literary criticism and therefore of philosophy and all other related disciplines. Useful too for showing the American connection and the critics most closely involved.

ed. David ROBEY

Structuralism. An Introduction 1973
Five essays by leading exponents of structuralist theory which encompass not just literary theory but the linguistic foundations and applications in philosophy and sociology.

George SAINTSBURY

A History of Literary Criticism (3 vols) 1900–1904
A wide-ranging, sometime rambling, but always enthusiastic survey of criticism, an earlier, and less academic (more idiosyncratic) version of Wimsatt and Brooks's work.

George WATSON

The Literary Critics 1962 (enlarged edition 1986)
A concise survey of the major figures in 'English descriptive criticism' from Dryden through to Leavis and the New Critics. The changing theories are summarized with regard to the kinds of questions asked, and the method and success of the answers offered. Second edition updated the survey.

Basil WILLEY (1897–)

The Seventeenth Century Background 1937
The book describes how the varying philosophies of Hobbes and Locke and the poetry of Milton all emerged from this age of scientific advance. Not pure literary criticism, it is a useful companion for students of seventeenth century literature.

The Eighteenth Century Background 1940
This volume continues the story, looking at the predominant theme of 'Nature' through the writings of Johnson, Butler, Swift, and Hume.

W K WIMSATT and Cleanth BROOKS

Literary Criticism: A Short History 1957
As fair as a critic can be on his fellow critics, this account is a valuable and very informed guide to critical theories from the Greeks to the present. A major achievement and a most useful reference book.

HISTORY

The study of history is an enquiry into the recorded human past and its purpose is to discover the truth about those happenings and experiences for which evidence has survived. For some people this enquiry never gets beyond the stage of historical dates, collecting names or narrating deeds and achievements.

Napoleon thought that history was 'a fable agreed upon'; for Henry Ford, history was 'bunk', philosophers and intellectuals look down on history as vague, general and without basic standards. A more popular view is that it is just boring.

These dismissive or superficial views have their supporters still and it is easy to see why. For the human past cannot be relived; it can only be reconstructed by means of the historian's intellectual and imaginative commitment to it. Such commitment is not easy and just how it occurs has given rise to a strenuous debate during this century. Works such as Trevelyan's *Clio, a Muse*, Butterfield's *Whig Interpretation of History* and Collingwood's *Idea of History* have opened new views on the historian's explanation of change. For the essence of history is change and it is the historian's function to detect and to explain change in particular, as well as in general, terms.

For the historian, every event is unique but it is unique within a framework of social generalization. Thus the study of history enriches our knowledge by imaginative participation in many modes of being: it provides a breadth of vicarious experience. This, more than anything, attracts so many people to read history, to read details of the fall of Constantinople with Gibbon or the last days of Hitler with Trevor-Roper. The mind is exhilarated by historical curiosity, imaginative sensibility, critical judgements and the freedom to move about in time.

History can be tiresome: it does not teach by direct precept nor does it provide either solutions to present problems or programmes for future action. True, something of these can be found in Toynbee's *A Study of History*, but the only way history can help us to cope with the future is by assisting in an understanding of the present by inquiring into the past.

Some historians like to make us feel that the past was perfect, especially in our own country. British nineteenth century historians have described Britain's role in building up an empire or parliamentary system in terms which tend to encourage a romantic backward look. It is necessary to be reminded that history is about change; the empire began to dissolve as soon as it was at its peak and the parliamentary system was never perfect.

267

As well as giving us a sense of change and continuity, the past affords a sense of contrast with the present. Because of the time gap and knowledge of subsequent events, the historian does more than recapture a contemporary's view of a past age. Sir Herbert Butterfield has said that the historian 'seeks to understand the people of the past better than they understood themselves'. Genuine respect for the past gives us a fuller understanding of it.

Men's thoughts and actions are moved by all kinds of ideas and conceptions: protestantism, capitalism, marxism, revolution, class, religious intolerance. Removed from their historical contexts these can be dangerous notions. History has been used nobly and dangerously by prophets and reformers, unscrupulously by power seekers to promote myths – especially the myth that history is on one's own side. It is here that the tone of Carlyle or Macaulay, unfashionable though they be nowadays, add the cautionary note to historical mythology.

Every historical work must be read critically. The works that appear in this list present evidence in many different ways. Those who are drawn to history should consider what the bias of each author is likely to be, and upon what evidence the writer's statements are based. Note how difficult it is to supply satisfactory evidence to endorse general statements which inpute common motives or purport to describe general conditions of large groups.

History then requires a critical and analytical approach. The list of books is necessarily limited: many of the books offer points of departure and the reader will soon learn the value of following up a subject by exploring books listed in the bibliographies and the footnotes of the volumes. The material dealing with the past is infinitely vast, often very accessible. Against this must be measured the severity of technique (in assembling evidence) and criticism.

Perhaps this sounds rather forbidding. The study of history may be an intellectual discipline, an extender of mental horizons and a corrective to human arrogance and pretensions, but it is also an enduring pleasure. Sales and borrowings of popular works of history have never been higher. In this section, most of the books listed are by 'professional' historians, but there are many good popular historians and the borderline between the two classifications is blurred. Excellent authors like Christopher Hibbert and C V Wedgewood can be termed 'popular' to distinguish them from their academic colleagues, while the academic A J P Taylor is one of the most popular writers of history this century.

'The justification of all historical study' says Keith Thomas 'must ultimately be that it enhances our self-consciousness, enables us to see ourselves in perspective, and helps us towards that greater freedom which comes from self-knowledge'.

Sir John ACTON (Baron Acton) (1834–1902)

Lectures on Modern History 1906
Seminal lectures delivered from 1899–1901, and the Inaugural Lecture on the study of history delivered 11 June 1895. Lord Acton planned the Cambridge Modern History, a standard work of collective scholarship.

Essays on Freedom and Power (ed. G Himmelfarb) 1956
A selection containing the famous Inaugural Lecture, eight other chapters on freedom, the political causes of the American and French Revolutions, and one chapter of selections from the Acton-Creighton correspondence.

ANON

The Anglo-Saxon Chronicle
The most important source for the pre-Conquest history of England. The period covered by the old chronicles is A D 450 to 1154.

Francis BACON (1561–1626)

The History of the Reign of Henry VII 1622
The only complete historical work of Bacon, this represented a new departure in historical method by its careful examination of evidence and its enquiry into causes.

Walter BAGEHOT (1826–77)

The English Constitution 1867
A standard introduction for lay readers.

Bernard BAILYN (1922–)

Ideological Origins of the American Revolution 1967
This discusses the role of ideas in both England and America (before the revolution) and traces those ideas through to the revolution itself.

Geoffrey BARRACLOUGH (1908–80)

History in a Changing World 1956
A distinguished mediaeval historian discusses the problems of historical study.

(The Venerable) BEDE (673–735)

The Ecclesiastical History of the English Nation
Bede, living a scholar's life in a monastery in Jarrow, wrote his famous work in Latin. It is much more than its title indicates, and is the chief source of information on the early history of Britain, the coming of Augustine and of Christianity, the invasions

and other early events, to about A D 730. There is a modern version under the title of *A History of the English Church and People*, translated by L. Sherley Price, 1955.

Robert BLAKE (1916–)

Decline of Power 1915–1964 1985
Begins with the disintegration of the Liberal Party in 1915 and moves through to the establishment of the Labour government in 1964. Britain's decline as a colonial power with the consequent economic and social upheavals are examined as is the rise of the USA and the USSR, powers which took over much of Britain's former role.

The Conserative Party from Peel to Thatcher 1985
Originally entitled *The Conservative Party from Peel to Churchill* (1970), this book does precisely what the title suggests: it traces the fortunes of the party from the point of view of one sympathetic to the cause but not overawed by it.

Asa BRIGGS (1921–)

The Age of Improvement, 1783–1867 1959
A lively study of Britain in an era of social and technological change.

John BROOKE (1920–)

King George III 1972
Although George III lost America, he also founded the Royal Academy. This study examines the nature of royalty at the time and is a lively account of the ambiguous attitude towards royalty in the eighteenth century.

James BRYCE (1838–1922)

The Holy Roman Empire 1864
A scholar and ambassador, Lord Bryce here wrote a book that time has not been superseded. It is generally accepted as a well-balanced survey in a single volume of the central European states whose rulers from the eighth century A D successively claimed the authority of Rome as spiritual and temporal supports.

H T BUCKLE (1821–62)

The History of Civilisation in England 1857, 1861
This first history of its kind immediately brought Buckle European fame as an initiator in historiography, through his conception of a quasi-scientific examination of historical changes in thought and the development of epochs in history.

Alan BULLOCK (1914–)

Hitler: A Study in Tyranny 1952 (revised 1964)
See under Biography section.

Gilbert BURNET (1643–1715)

History of His Own Time 1724, 1734 (ed. O Airy, 2 vols, 1897–1900; ed. H C Foxcroft, supplement, 1902)
A personal account of the events of the period 1659 to 1713, published posthumously. 'It seems', said Horace Walpole, 'as if Burnet had just come from the King's closet or from the apartments of the men whom he describes, and was telling his readers, in plain honest terms, what he had seen and heard.'

J B BURY (1861–1927)

A History of the Later Roman Empire, A.D. 395–565 1889, (revised ed. 1923)
This is still a standard work. Bury takes the narrative of events from the death of Theodosius I (A D 395) to the death of Justinian (A D 565).

A History of Greece to the Death of Alexander the Great 323 BC 1900 (revised 1913; ed. Russell Meiggs, 1 vol, 1951)
Bury was Professor of Greek and of Modern History at Dublin, and later at Cambridge. His edition of Gibbon's *Decline and Fall* is the standard set, for which see under **Gibbon.**

Herbert BUTTERFIELD (1900–1979)

The Whig Interpretation of History 1931
The author demonstrates that 'the understanding of the past is not so easy as it is sometimes made to appear'. This is a starting point for anyone pondering on the meaning of history.

William CAMDEN (1551–1623)

Britannia 1586
Annals 1615
Two classics by an Elizabethan writer based on massive research into the records which were available at the time.

Norman CANTOR (1929–)

Mediaeval History 1963
A gentle introduction to Europe up to the fifteenth century from an historian with no particular axe to grind; a good introduction to a broad subject.

Thomas CARLYLE (1795–1881)

The French Revolution 1837
Twentieth-century scholarship has superseded Carlyle's once widely read masterpiece, but it can be read today for its poetic, almost intuitive interpretation of events, characters and motives, and for its gallery of portraits presented in the glowing vitality of Carlyle's style at its best.

Letters and Speeches of Oliver Cromwell 1846
An important contribution to the interpretation of the Civil War and Commonwealth.

E H CARR (1892–1982)

A History of Soviet Russia 1950–71
This grand narrative appeared in four parts; *The Bolshevik Revolution 1917–23, The Interregnum 1923–4, Socialism in one Country 1924–6,* and *Foundations of a Planned Economy 1926–9* (with R W Davies).

What is History? 1961
One of the best introductions to the question by an historian who rejects the possibility of historical objectivity.

Sir John CLAPHAM (1873–1946)

The Economic History of Modern Britain 1926–38, (vol 1: *The Early Railway Age, 1820–50;* vol 2: *Free Trade and Steel,* 1850–86; vol 3: *Machines and National Rivalries,* 1887–1914; with an Epilogue, 1914–29)
This massive work was the foundation of a new approach to economic history based on statistics. Clapham wrote, '... an attempt has been made to offer dimensions, in place of blurred masses of unspecified size'.

Earl of CLARENDON (1608–74)

The History of The Great Rebellion 1702–4
A personal narrative of great events, without parallel in English historical writing until Sir Winston Churchill's *The Second World War.* Like Sir Winston, Clarendon related in glowing style, events in which he himself had played a leading part.

G S K Kitson CLARK (1900–1975)

The Making of Victorian England 1962
The opening chapter of this book, entitled 'The task of revision', counsels caution in accepting revision. Kitson Clark's own version is a masterpiece.

G D H COLE (1889–1958)

A Short History of the British Working Class Movement, 1789–1947 1925–7
A major work by a prolific writer on cooperation, trade unionism, the Labour Party, and other topics in sociology.

G D H COLE (1889–1955) and Raymond POSTGATE (1896–1971)

The Common People 1746–1946 1946
This book has become a classic of its kind: a study of the 'ordinary' people of England and how changing political, economic and social conditions altered their way of life.

Terry COLEMAN (1931–)

Passage to America 1972
A history of emigration from Britain and Ireland to America during the nineteenth century, told by thorough reference to contemporary papers and documents.

R G COLLINGWOOD (1889–1943)

Roman Britain 1932
Collingwood was also part author with J N L Myres of volume 1 of the *Oxford History of England: Roman Britain and the English Settlements* (1937)

The Idea of History 1944
An unusual book, lucidly written, in which the philosopher–historian tries to answer the question 'What is history?'

George Gordon COULTON (1858–1947)

Chaucer and His England 1908
An unrivalled monograph for literary students and for students of the history of the Middle Ages, especially of the reign of Edward III.

Social Life in Britain from Conquest to Reformation 1918
This text presents extracts from books and documents of the period to supplement formal histories.

The Mediaeval Scene 1930
Can scarcely be bettered as 'an informative introduction to the Middle Ages' for both students and the general readers for whom these broadcast talks were first delivered.

The Mediaeval Panorama 1938
Reveals the English scene from Conquest to Reformation.

George DANGERFIELD (1904–1986)

The Strange Death of Liberal England 1935
Brilliantly written and imaginatively argued this account of the collapse of a seemingly secure and morally superior ruling class between 1910 and 1914 is a masterpiece of 'amatuer' social and political history.

A V DICEY (1835–1922)

Introduction to the Study of the, Law of the Constitution 1885
Law and Public Opinion in England 1905
These are standard works that can be read without specialized knowledge of the subject, and 'indispensable reading' for the political history of the nineteenth century.

G R ELTON (1921–)

The Tudor Revolution in Government 1953
This contains the most complete statement of the 'Elton Thesis' of the Tudor 'revolution' in government, which he claims gave England a stable bureaucracy.

The Practice of History 1967
A vigorous review of the study, writing and teaching of history by one of the most intellectually combative of modern (conservative) historians.

Friedrich ENGELS (1820–95)

The Condition of the Working Class in England 1845
This early socialist study paints a black picture of working class conditions, drawing on newspaper accounts and government papers.

J A FROUDE (1818–94)

A History of England 1856–70
A glowing narrative of events from the fall of Cardinal Wolsey to the defeat of the Spanish Armada. Read in its sections, it may be enjoyed by the general reader as four separate works: vols 1–3: Henry VIII, vol 4: Edward VI; vol 5: Mary Tudor; vols 6–10: Queen Elizabeth I.

Sir Charles Harding FIRTH (1857–1936)

Cromwell's Army 1902
This monograph on the formation of Cromwell's 'New Model' of 1645, and of contrasting military systems of the Stuarts preceding Cromwell's era, provides in effect 'a history of the English soldier during the Civil Wars, the Commonwealth, and the Protectorate'.

H A L FISHER (1865–1940)

A History of Europe 1935
One of the great historical surveys of the twentieth century. It has become a standard work for students and a popular one with general readers. This distinguished humanist and liberal historian wrote: 'I begin this book with neolithic man and conclude with Stalin and Mustapha Kemal, Mussolini and Hitler ... Men wiser and more learned than I have discerned in history a plot, a rhythm, a predetermined pattern. These harmonies are concealed from me.'

Jean FROISSART (c. 1337–1410)

Chronicles of England
A fairly reliable account of his own time. The translation by Lord Berners (John Bourdrier) of 1523, is generally considered to be the best.

Samuel Rawson GARDINER (1829–1902)

History of the Commonwealth and the Protectorate, 1949–1656 1894–1901
This standard history was completed by Sir Charles Firth.

Norman GASH (1912–)

Politics in the Age of Peel 1953
A book concerned with the ordinary working world of the politician in a crucial phase of British history – the passage from an aristocratic to a democratic society.

GEOFFREY of MONMOUTH (c. 1100–1154)

Histories of the Kings of Britain 1508
The Welsh chronicler's *Historia Regnum Britanniae* is an important part of the Arthurian literature.

Edward GIBBON (1737–94)

The History of the Decline and Fall of the Roman Empire 1776–88
There are many editions of this 'greatest historical book of the century, if not of all time' (Saintsbury), but J B Bury's seven-volume edition (1909–10) is considered as standard. *The Decline and Fall* is both great history – in its scope and scholarship – and great literature in the organization, irony and elegance of Gibbon's narrative style. This English humanist's view of 'the triumph of barbarism and religion', still correctly and incorrectly influences our view of the Classical and Middle Ages.

John Lawrence HAMMOND (1872–1949) and Barbara HAMMOND

The Age of the Chartists, 1832–1854 1930
'A study in discontent' complementary to the trilogy noted below.

The Rise of Modern Industry, 1925
This standard trilogy *The Village Labourer, 1760–1832*, *The Town Labourer, 1760–1832*, *The Skilled Labourer, 1760–1832*, is the principal study of working-class life, labour, wages and conditions in the industrial and economic history of Britain before the Reform Bill.

Christopher HIBBERT (1924–)

The Great Mutiny: India 1857 1980
The French Revolution 1980
Two good examples of work by one of the best contemporary writers of modern history. *The French Revolution* is a model of concision and clarity.

Christopher HILL (1912–)

The Economic Problems of the Church from Archbishop Whitgift To the Long Parliament 1956 (corrected 1963)
Intellectual Origins of the English Revolution 1965
The World Turned Upside Down 1975
Hill, as a Marxist, is concerned with the social function of history. He explains, 'The connections of religion, science, politics and economics are infinite and infinitely subtle'. The last named title concerns the reaction of the general population to the Civil War. Hill has also written books on Cromwell, Milton and Lenin and the Russian Revolution.

R H HILTON (1916–)

A Medieval Society. The West Midlands at the end of the thirteenth century 1966
Covering the period when England was emerging from a period of civil war and the barons held enormous wealth and power. The author examines the problems of regional society, the structure of peasant holdings and the effect of fluctuating crop prices on the lives of ordinary people. A detailed but lucid study.

Bond Men Made Free 1973
The English Peasants' Revolt of 1381 is examined in the broader context of class conflict throughout Europe.

E J HOBSBAWM (1917–)

Industry and Empire: An Economic History of Britain since 1750 1968
A masterly survey of the major economic developments of the last 200 years, sharply and ironically observed.

The Age of Revolution, 1789–1848 1962
The Age of Capital, 1848–1875 1975
The Age of Imperialism, 1875–1914 1987
A three-volume study by a Marxist historian with a distinctive and clear prose style.

Sir William HOLDSWORTH (1871–1944)

Some Makers of English Law 1938
The distinguished legal historian's masterpiece was the great thirteen-volume *History of English Law*.

Raphael HOLINSHED (d. c. 1580)

Chronicles
A collective work named after the Elizabethan translator who was responsible for its planning and publishing. From its pages many dramatists drew characters and plots for their plays – most eminently Shakespeare in the writing of his History plays.

Michael HOWARD (1922–)

The Franco–Prussian War 1961
A highly detailed account of the German invasion of France in 1870–71. The conflict established Germany as a major military power, introducing an era in which showdowns led to the disaster of 1914. In many ways the book is a model of how military history should be written.

The Causes of War 1983
A collection of essays which range from the general causes of conflict to the implications behind holding a nuclear deterrent and the use and abuse of military history. Howard is a provocative writer whose essays are full of controversial points.

James JOLL (1918–)

Europe Since 1870 1973 (revised 1983)
A history of the major upheavals in Europe, the major new intellectual movements (liberalism, the growth of communism and fascism) and the artistic achievements of the period.

Peter LASLETT (1915–)

The World We Have Lost 1965
A social history, dealing with ordinary English people of the sixteenth and seventeenth centuries.

Henry Charles LEA (1825–1909)

The Inquisition of the Middle Ages 1887–8 (ed. with an historical introduction by Walter Ullman, 1963)
A modern edition, unabridged, of those chapters in volume 1 'dealing with the organisation and operation of the Inquisition throughout Europe'. This controversial American classic, praised by Lord Acton, 'still forms to-day', writes Dr Ullman, 'the basis of research into the subject'.

William Edward LECKY (1838–1903)

A History of England in the Eighteenth Century 1878–90
Much admired for its scientific approach to historical events, its firmly drawn and balanced estimates of the principal figures, its depiction of social details, and for the detachment shown by the author (who was Irish) in the last volumes dealing with Ireland.

B H LIDDELL HART (1895–1970)

The Other Side of the Hill 1948
'Germany's Generals, their rise and fall, with their own accounts of military events 1939–1945'. As a former soldier, military adviser and military correspondent Liddell Hart wrote to gain immediate influence. He was able to interview the defeated generals immediately after the war.

F S L LYONS (1923–83)

Ireland Since the Famine 1971 (revised 1973)
The authoritative account of Ireland's history from 1850–1973.

Thomas Babington MACAULAY (1800–1859)

Critical and Historical Essays 1843
The *Historical Essays* have opened the door of the historical library to generations of students, and introduced general readers to the persons and events of history in the same fluent, readable style.

The History of England from the Accession of James II 1848–61
Macaulay's *History of England* was unfinished. It does not go beyond 1700 and the end of the reign of William III. It was criticized for its Whig bias, but never before, and seldom since, has an historical work of this popular nature displayed such superb gifts of narrative and such a masterly comprehension of the English historical scene. The best edition of this brilliant, fluent and enjoyable work was edited by Sir Charles Firth, in six volumes, with 900 illustrations, (1913–15).

Sir Henry James Sumner MAINE (1822–88)

Ancient Law 1861
A classic study of primitive law, 'its connection with the early history of society, and its relation to modern ideas'.

Frederick William MAITLAND (1850–1906)

Domesday Book and Beyond: Three Essays in the Early History of England 1897
Maitland was 'England's greatest historian since Gibbon and Macaulay' according to Thomas Seccombe. This is a classic study of English society at one of its turning points.

Selections from the Writings of England's Great Historian 1960 (ed. Robert Livingston Schuyler)
The above two volumes offer a representative choice of shorter works by Maitland, whose legal training enabled him to prepare authoritative essays on legal aspects of history, including the growth of townships and boroughs, the history of law, the renaissance, the reformation and allied topics.

Frederick William MAITLAND (1850–1906) and Frederick POLLOCK (1845–1937)

A History of English Law to 1272 1895
This is still a standard work for this period.

Gervase MATHEW (1905–)

The Court of Richard II 1968
Not a history of Richard's reign, but a depiction of the 'court culture' of the time and of the changes in thought that led to the 'Renaissance'.

general editor W N MEDLICOTT (1900–)

A History of England 1953–76
Ten volumes, each by a different expert historian, trace the political, social, military and foreign development of England from the 'Anglo-Saxon Age' to 'Contemporary England'.

S E MORRISON (1887–1976)

The Oxford History of the American People 1965
The books is not as dry as its title might suggest: it is an enjoyable account of the settlement of America, enlivened by the author's often controversial comments.

John Lothrop MOTLEY (1814–77)

The Rise of the Dutch Republic 1856
This standard work by an American historian deals with the thirty year's period of the Netherlands from 1555. It has not been superseded.

J H MUNDY (1917–)

Europe in the High Middle Ages 1150–1309 1973
A scholarly work from an authority on mediaeval history. The political developments and relations between countries are thoroughly discussed.

Lewis NAMIER (1888–1960)

The Structure of Politics at the Accession of George III 1928
A major historical study of the highest importance. The author's method of approach – massive and concentrated research into the detail of political relationships – profoundly influenced other historians and students.

England in the Age of the American Revolution 1930
The revision for the second (posthumous) edition of this modern classic was carried out by Lady Namier and John Brooke.

The PASTON Family (1378–)

Paston Letters 1422–1509 (6 vols ed. James Gardiner, 1903–4)
The first editor of these celebrated letters, a source for historians and of the greatest interest for the general reader, was Sir John Fenn, who published a selection in 1787. Gardiner's edition is still the standard one; but there is a very full selection in Everyman collated with Gardiner's text, with the spelling, where necessary, modernized. The Pastons lived in the Norfolk village from which they took their name, from the fourteenth to sixteenth century. Their letters offer an incomparable account of social life in semi-feudal times.

Harold J PERKIN (1920–)

The Origins of Modern English Society 1780–1880 1969
A provocative analysis of the birth of the new class society.

J H PLUMB (1911–)

The Growth of Political Stability in England, 1675–1725 1967
After civil war, revolution and constant turbulence, England achieved stability: the process of this transformation is the theme of this important book. Plumb is an expert on eighteenth-century political history; his biography, *Sir Robert Walpole. The King's Minister* examines Walpole's rise from an ordinary middle-class background into the ranks of the Whig administration and finally to the position of prime minister.

Eileen POWER (1889–1940)

Mediaeval English Nunneries, 1275–1535 1922
This was the masterpiece of a distinguished historian, and is the most detailed specialized monograph on the subject.

Mediaeval People 1924
Written for a popular audience, but displaying the same scholarly attention to detail as the specialized work on nunneries. It is a picture of life in the Middle Ages, emphasizing the daily round of typical people by the specific example of a characteristic household.

William Hickling PRESCOTT (1796–1859)

The History of the Reign of Ferdinand and Isabella the Catholic 1837
The historian's first work, recognized immediately as an historical narrative of the greatest period of Spanish civilization (1452–1516) not likely ever to be superseded.

The History of the Conquest of Mexico 1843
The History of the Conquest of Peru 1847
These carefully documented historical narratives of two sixteenth-century conquests by the Spanish invaders under Hernando Cortes and the Pizarro brothers, have not been superseded by later researchers, although they were written under the almost insuperable difficulties of blindness.

Charles William PREVITE-ORTON (1877–1947)

A History of Europe, 1198–1378 1937
The Shorter Cambridge Mediaeval History 1952
A two-volume abridgement of the collective work in eight volumes. Previte-Orton was one of the original editors. With its 300 illustrations it has been described as 'almost an encyclopaedia of the European Middle Ages'.

The Study of Mediaeval History 1937
An Inaugural Lecture addressed to students.

Sir Walter RALEIGH (c. 1552–1618)

Selections from his Historie of the World 1614 (ed. G E Hadow, 1917)
A notable example of Elizabethan prose, with some letters and other pieces, selected to present Raleigh's genius as a writer. There is a long introduction and notes.

A L ROWSE (1903–)

The England of Elizabeth 1950
Rowse's books on the Elizabethan age reflect his detailed knowledge of social conditions. Some of his opinions — notably on Shakespeare — are fanciful.

George RUDE (1910–)

Hanoverian London, 1714–1808 1971
Rude is a social historian who is fascinated by the inner workings of the city of London. He describes the people, the places they inhabited and shows the theory – political and artistic – which underpinned the layout of London.

Simon SCHAMA (1945–)

The Embarrassment of Riches 1987
An interpretation of Dutch culture in the Netherlands 'Golden Age' of the seventeenth century. It examines not 'Culture' but 'culture': there is nothing on theatre or music or art but a great deal about society and Dutch ways of thinking and acting, interpreted through contemporary prints and paintings.

R W SOUTHERN (1912–)

The Making of the Middle Ages 1953
The formation of Western Europe from the late tenth to the early thirteenth centuries. From an examination of the relatively disparate nature of Europe at the beginning of the period, the author demonstrates that by the end of it 'Europe' had become a leader in political experiment and intellectual curiosity.

Lawrence STONE (1919–)

The Crisis of the Aristocracy, 1558–1641 1965
Stone explains: 'Statistical measurement is the only means of extracting a coherent pattern from the chaos of personal behaviour and of discovering what is a typical specimen and what a sport'.

William STUBBS (1825–1901)

The Constitutional History of England 1874–8, 3 vols 1980
A students' classic, and its complementary book of sources, illustrating English constitutional history from Edward I. See also *Select Charters* William Stubbs (9th edition revised H W C Davis, 1913)

(Sir) Ronald SYME (1903–)

The Roman Revolution 1939
The subject is the transformation of state and society in Rome between 60 BC and AD 14. Dealing largely with the rule of Augustus, Syme emphasizes the internal conflicts which took place, and examines the way in which political leaders emerged. A long, detailed study written in a clear style.

I A SYMONDS (1840–93)

Renaissance in Italy 1875–86
(vol 1: *The Age of the Despots*; vol 2: *The Revival of Learning*; vol 3: *The Fine Arts*; vols 4 and 5: *Italian Literature*, vols 6 and 7: *The Catholic Reaction*)
These studies are written with the typical absorbing thoroughness of this Victorian historian. He covers all aspects of renaissance Italy, from political upheavals to art and literature. Although not an easy read, it is a rewarding one.

Richard Henry TAWNEY (1880–1962)

The Acquisitive Society 1921
Religion and the Rise of Capitalism 1923
Equality 1931
The above three books are the most widely studied and influential writings of one of the greatest socialist teachers of the century. His work and thought on economic history and socialism gave him an international reputation.

A J P TAYLOR (1906–)

The Struggle for Mastery in Europe, 1848–1918 1954
A corrective to the textbook versions. Vigorously written study of the political and economic rivalries of the nation states.

The Origins of the Second World War 1961
Perhaps Taylor's best known book because its view – that Hitler was an opportunistic child of his time rather than the possessor of an uniquely evil master plan – and his fair assessment of appeasement still makes uncomfortable reading for those who lived through the war and its immediate consequences.

English History 1914–45 1965
In this masterly summary written by a fine exponent of modern prose style, Taylor questions many accepted views of this period.

H W V TEMPERLEY (1879–1939)

The Foreign Policy of Canning, 1822–1827 1925
Expanded from the author's contribution to the second volume of the *Cambridge History of British Foreign Policy*. The period covered is from Canning's acceptance of the post of minister for foreign affairs after Castlereagh's suicide.

Keith THOMAS (1933–)

Religion and the Decline of Magic 1971
Man and the Natural World: Changing Attitudes in England, 1500–1800 1986
The brillant study of the supernatural in everyday life (religion, magic, witchcraft) has been recently followed by a study of Man's relation with the natural.

E P THOMPSON (1924–)

The Making of the English Working Class 1965
'Neither poverty nor disease, but work itself … casts the blackest shadow over the years of the Industrial Revolution'. Thus Thompson brings before us the aspirations and efforts of working people in a book which has achieved world fame.

David THOMSON (1912–)

Europe Since Napolean 1957
A standard work, as the title implies; Thomson does not deal with each European nation individually but shows that there was a pattern of European development which he considers phase-by-phase with the aim of revealing the 'continuous whole'.

E M TILLYARD (1889–1962)

The Elizabethan World Picture 1943
A short, brilliant account of traditional thinking in late mediaeval England; of particular value to students of literature.

Arnold TOYNBEE (1889–1975)

A Study of History 1934–1954 1972
Professionals take the view that this massive theorizing study of the cyclical growth and decline of civilizations is not history but too much myth and mysticism. Nevertheless Toynbee has made an outstanding contribution to the understanding of the past. A two-volume abridged version by D C Somervell of the twelve-volume original is available.

George Macaulay TREVELYAN (1876–1962)

Clio, a Muse 1913
This is a celebrated essay, responding to Bury's 'scientific view of history'. 'History is not a scientific deduction, but an imaginative guess at the most likely generalisations'.

England Under Queen Anne 1930–34
Praised as a masterpiece for its scholarship, widely enjoyed by the general public, it is one of those twentieth-century classics that have made English historical writing world-famous both with academic students and with the ordinary reader. The three volumes are divided thus: *Blenheim; Ramillies and the Union with Scotland; The Peace and the Protestant Succession.*

English Social History 1944
'A survey of six centuries: Chaucer to Queen Victoria' and the most widely-read historical narrative of the century. It is 'polite chat about the past' and not what would be accepted as social history nowadays.

Hugh TREVOR-ROPER (Baron Dacre) (1914–)

The Last Days of Hitler 1947
A brilliant detective work that turned into standard history.

Religion, the Reformation and Social Change 1967
A collection of essays on the 'general crisis' in the middle part of the seventeenth century.

Arthur Stanley TURBERVILLE (1888–1945)

English Men and Manners in the Eighteenth Century 1926
A survey of eighteenth-century life dealing with aspects of social change.

Johnson's England 1933
A standard work of social history, contributed to by specialists on various aspects, with 180 illustrations.

Sir Charles Kingsley WEBSTER (1886–1961)

The Congress of Vienna 1919
A masterly study of the organization, methods and techniques of the epoch-making Congress held in 1815 to settle some of the problems resulting from the final defeat of Napoleon. It was originally written for the Foreign Office to provide historical background for officials and statesmen confronted with the settlement of international problems in the aftermath of World War I.

The Foreign Policy of Castlereagh, 1812–1815 1931
The Foreign Policy of Palmerston, 1830–41 1951
These texts are classic studies of nineteenth-century foreign policy.

C V WEDGEWOOD (1910–)

The King's Peace 1955
The King's War 1958
The Trial of Charles I 1964
The story of the English Revolution told by one of the best popular historians.

H G WELLS (1866–1946)

The Outline of History 1920 (revised R. Postgate, 1972)
The most widely-read survey of its kind, and the begetter of many similar outlines of great subjects for the general reader. Wells starts with 'primordial life'; in the latest revision the record is taken up to 1960.

PHILOSOPHY AND OTHER WRITINGS ON MORALS AND RELIGION

What follows is a selection of British philosophy's contribution to the best of English literature. The criteria for good literature may be different from the criteria for good philosophy, but after consideration this notion has been rejected: not because in a conflict between 'literary' quality, it is philosophical importance, that is preferred, but because it would be pertinent to see literary quality as having to do with the presentation of thought as distinct from the the nature of the thought itself. There is a sense of 'literary quality' which even novels, or plays, or poetry may lack – because they are 'badly written' – and yet they stand as significant literature.

Some of the features which often make writing attractive – imaginative, and perhaps innovatory use of language, wit, charm and even formal beauty of rhythm and structure – are positively dangerous in philosophy, for they can distract the reader from the austere questions of validity and truth which are the real business in hand. It is all too possible, for example, to be persuaded as a reader (and to imagine as a writer), that a clear point has been made, when all that has been put forward is a suggestive metaphor, or a comfortable invocation of prejudice. But happily these are dangers which have, in British philosophy, again and again been overcome with seminal philosophical thought combining with mordant wit as in Hobbes, or with relaxed civilized urbanity as in Locke, or with limpid clarity as in Russell. Our fine tradition of philosophical thought has for the most part warmed to the discipline of expressing itself, and given us more rewards than strictly it need have.

British philosophical excellence starts in the Middle Ages, with its important contribution to the logical enquiries pursued in the great centres of learning in Christian Europe. But since the language was Latin, their mention is restricted here to a few representative names gathered at the end. From that time, the seminal writers have been preoccupied, one way or another, with the emergence, associated with the break up of medieval hierarchies, of the *individual*.

The spectre of a society from which the traditional structure had been swept away was most vivid perhaps to early modern writers like Hobbes, in whose 'state of nature' the individual, a political atom, skitters about in an entirely fruitless way, driven by total and totally justifiable fear. Where Hobbes prescribes an absolute power, Locke launches the rationale of 'liberal democracy' by suggesting that the power of the state cannot properly be *all that* absolute, since its purpose is to preserve an individual's rights: but the diagnosis is essentially the same. So it is with Mill, urging that individuality must be maximized by constraining one person's freedom only at the point at which it begins to interfere with someone else's.

Beyond the problem of fashioning a political framework for the newly emerged individual is that of working out what should govern how individuals are to behave quite generally towards each other. As Alastair Mackintyre has convincingly argued (in *After Virtue*) the modern era inherited agreed notions about how men should behave to each other, but not the framework of practices, the social order, which had in the past given sense to rational defences of them. Their project therefore was to find a new rationale, one which made sense in the new world. Hume, for example, sought a justification in the individual's 'passions'. The reason for doing one's duty was that one would thus be meeting one's own needs, needs springing from one's nature as a creature with inclinations, desires, aversions and sympathies.

Post-enlightenment writers were unconvinced by this or any other attempt to offer a rational justification for accepted morality and began to query what was enjoyed by duty as well as the nature of its hold over us. Jeremy Bentham, for example, applying to human behaviour an adaptation of the mechanical approach that had been so successful elsewhere, took the view that the sole motivators of human behaviour were the pursuit of pleasure and the avoidance of pain. Morality must follow this general rubric, or be disregarded as superstition. But as Mill brought out, 'pleasure', far from being a simple sensation of quantifiable intensity, is of different incommensurable kinds and cannot be used as a simple criterion for deciding between alternative courses of action.

At this point, the struggle to find a rational justification for morality was abandoned by some philosophers. In Sidgwick, and more famously in Moore, we find the idea that moral truths are not to be deduced from anything else, but can only be grasped by a kind of 'moral intuition'. Although more recent philosophers, notably Hare and Foot, have refined both Kantian and Utilitarian appeals to objective foundations, the main interests of moral philosophers in the latter half of the twentieth century has been with the practical consequences of moral theorizing.

Somehow associated with the collapse of medieval hierarchies which yielded the individual 'citizen' and the individual 'moral agent' was the demise of an approach to human experience which had no place for the clear distinction made in the modern period between the perceiving and knowing subject and the world that is perceived and known about. For Aquinas, to perceive a thing was to assimilate its 'form', and this actually entailed *becoming* that thing, albeit in an abstract way. Because this notion of form obstructed the application of new types of explanation which the ambitious new science was developing, it became after Bacon one of the major targets of science's early protagonists – in Britain Boyle, Hobbes and Locke. In place of a parcel of matter organized under a 'form' there arose a new conception of what it was to be a thing, and with that conception a new motion of how things entered into human experience. A person was now envisaged as having dealings with the world only via 'representations' and as the stage upon which these representations performed (before an inner eye!) the modern concept of the *mind* became articulated. To see a horse, for Locke, was to have an image of the horse before the mind.

As Richard Rorty has observed, the early empiricists (no less in fact than the rationalists, which happen to be poorly represented among British philosophers) were engaged in developing these revolutionary conceptions, in their attempt to 'make the intellectual world safe for Copernicus and Galileo' (*Philosophy and the Mirror of Nature*) not in addressing the problems created by them. But this *has* been the major concern of their successors, Hume, Berkeley, Moore, Russell, the early Wittgenstein, Ayer. In what way are we really seeing a thing if all we are actually 'aware of' is a representation of it? How can there be representations of the problem of generality, properties and categories? If perceiving is having an image before the mind, what exactly is 'having' and image? Who or what is it that 'has' it? Above all, how can we ever find out whether the representations we have are accurate, or even check that they are not the merest fantasies?

The hold of these problems, and of the conceptions of experience and reality they arise from, have already been loosened by the work, beginning in the mid-twentieth century, of Wittgenstein, Austin, Ryle and the many who now write under their influence. But it will again, no doubt, be developments in science that bring about their final displacement – perhaps by conceptualizations based on the idea of 'information processing' as these emerge from advances in artificial intelligence. In deference to the fact that philosophy stands at some distance from what we have agreed to regard as the centre of English Literature, the list is restricted rather firmly to a few dozen works of long-established standing, introducing representatives of post-war work very sparingly: Wittgenstein, of course, Ryle, Austin, Strawson, Popper, Kuhn and one or two others, rather more arbitrarily chosen. This is not to suggest that in recent decades philosophizing has declined, or declined even in relation to novel or poetry writing. The reverse is probably the case. Until very recently at any rate academic philosophy has been riding high.

Under the inspiration of Austin, and later of Ryle, the graduates who flocked to Oxford in the fifties and sixties conducted their philosophizing with great enthusiasm, brilliance, and confidence, and their productions emanating from philosophy departments up and down the country (and indeed across the English speaking world) have been earnest, highly intelligent and voluminous: and perhaps important.

Under these influences new generations of philosophers have gone on to develop the techniques of analysis and respect for clarity. But clarity in itself was never enough and many have sought to apply the methods of Austin, Wittgenstein and Ryle to other disciplines. There are now Wittgenstein approaches to the natural and social sciences, religion, and art. Conceptual analysis has given way to practical reasoning in ethics and politics. In combination with these developments there has been a revival of interest in the great figures from the past. Kant continues to influence all aspects of philosophy and is treated respectfully by exponents of the new disciplines of Artificial Intelligence and Cognitive Studies. Since the late 1960s, there has been a dramatic revival of interest in Hegel amounting to an explosion of talented and imaginative interpretations of his work which has nurtured a revival of interest in the British Idealist school of the late nineteenth century. Such has been the vigour of this revival that the history of Oxford-influenced philosophy will have to be re-written to draw attention to the fact that the Hegelian tradition was never totally eclipsed by Russell, Moore, Wittgenstein and Ayer.

In this list, then, contemporary contributors are rather neglected, some of whom seem notable indeed; on the other hand, appendices have been included containing a handful of translations of works which have entered into the warp and woof of British philosophizing: Plato, Aristotle, Aquinas, Descartes, Leibniz, Spinoza, Hegel and Marx.

This section also includes books which not only discuss religion as philosophy but are notable expressions of personal religious belief and experience. It is difficult today, in a largely secular and increasingly multi-cultural society, to find major works which are both relevant to continuing religious issues and are of literary merit. In former times such works bulked very large in the literature to which people had ready access. Alongside the Bible on many a small bookshelf has stood Foxe's *Books of Martyres*, Butler's *Fifteen Sermons*, and perhaps Law's *Serious Call*, or a translation of Thomas à Kempis's *The Imitation of Christ*. To what extent works such as these remained on the shelf, or were actually read when removed is open to some doubt. In *The Mill on the Floss* we are told that in moments of solemnity it was to Baxter's *The Saints Everlasting Rest* that Mrs Glegg has resort – but more as a suitably sombre article of clothing than for its content: for all that George Eliot reports is that on 'special occasions' – 'wet Sunday mornings, or when she heard of the death in the family' – this was the work that Mrs Glegg 'was accustomed to lay before her'.

For the modern reader some of the best writing on religious experience is not to be found in sermons or individual aids, but in autobiography, as in Browne's *Religio Medici* or Newman's *Apologia Pro Vita Sua* or in the poetry of Traherne, Blake, Hopkins and Eliot. Two of the finest novelists of the twentieth century – Waugh and Greene – have made religious faith central themes of their work. In a recently secularized society, the adherence to religious principles and practices sets up fruitful conflicts and resolutions: it is an ideal attribution for an outsider-hero.

Samuel ALEXANDER (1859–1938)

Space, Time and Deity 1920
Although he was influenced by the idealism of Bradley and Bosanquet, *Space, Time and Deity* is representative of the New Realism of the early decades of the twentieth century. Alexander maintained that philosophy proceeds by description, rather than by argument, and consequently his writings appear to be closer to literature than philosophy. Insisting that we look at the world with the naive eyes of innocence, he then presents a world that is complex in the extreme.

John AUSTIN (1790–1859)

The Province of Jurisprudence Determined 1832
This work had a profound effect upon English legal theory. Austin developed the view that a law is essentially a command of the sovereign, backed up by sanctions and maintained by a habit of obedience. For Austin, unlike several other legal theorists of his time, the authority of the sovereign was absolute.

J L AUSTIN (1911–60)

How to do Things with Words 1962
Sense and Sensibilia 1962
One of the central figures in Oxford after the Second World War, Austin held that a close study of the way in which ordinary words are ordinarily used can throw invaluable light on philosophical problems. He most deserves the title 'ordinary language' philosopher, his theory of speech acts having had a decisive influence on twentieth-century Anglo-American philosophy.

A J AYER (1910–)

Language, Truth and Logic 1936
Logical positivism attempted to show, using 'logical analysis', that all knowledge is constructed from the data of experience, and that all would-be statements that could not be verified by experience were lacking significance. This is the work that presented logical positivism to British philosophy: concise, combative, exciting even today. Ayer's formulation of the verification principle consigned religion, metaphysics, and ethics to the realms of nonsense since he claimed that propositions within these disciplines were lacking in both sense and content and therefore ultimately devoid of meaning. The verification principle and logical positivism came under attack in post-war Britain and is unlikely to reappear this century.

The Concept of a Person & Other Essays 1967
A collection of papers on various topics which reveals Ayer's development beyond the logical positivism of youth. Ayer is one of the few British philosophers of the twentieth century who is known outside professional philosophy, largely because of the clear and concise presentation of his arguments.

Francis BACON (1561–1626)

The Advancement of Learning 1605
Created Lord Verulam, becoming Viscount St Albans, and before his downfall Lord Chancellor of England, Bacon wrote with wit and eloquence to urge the practical importance of gaining new knowledge of nature, and to suggest then neglected ways (based on gathering facts) of how it might be done. The precise nature, and validity of Baconian inductivism is still of continuing interest to philosophers of the natural and social sciences.

Alexander BAIN (1818–1903)

Mental and Moral Science 1868
Bain argues for the investigation of the material conditions under which mental states of particular kinds occur. Dissatisfied with the accounts of prevailing theories of belief, he defined a belief as 'that upon which a man is prepared to act', and thus became a forerunner of the pragmatist movement.

Jeremy BENTHAM (1748–1832)

Introduction to the Principles of Morals and Legislation 1789
An early, very influential statement of traditional Utilitarianism. Bentham propounded the 'greatest-happiness principle', that the best thing to do is the thing that generates the most happiness for all concerned. Although this was never recognized as a satisfactory definition of moral conduct it nevertheless had it uses as a practical guide for legislators and governments. The influence of Bentham is still felt in Anglo-American philosophy as one of the founders of practical ethics.

George BERKELEY (1685–1753)

A Treatise Concerning the Principles of Human Knowledge, 1710 (ed. G J Warnock)
Berkeley developed the empiricist and naive realist approach of Locke to arrive at the proposition that *esse est percipi* – to be is to be perceived, thus demonstrating the conceptual affinity between phenomenalism and subjective idealism. There is a paperback edition of this work and *Three Dialogues Between Hughes and Phitorus* by G J Warnock.

Isaiah BERLIN (1909–)

Four Essays on Liberty 1969
An exposition of one aspect of a liberal social philosophy which has its antecedents in Locke's possessive individualism. Determinism must be rejected and the role of human responsibility for the course of events retained. Berlin is famous for his articulation of the distinction between 'freedom from' and 'freedom to'. For Berlin the liberal ideal consists in the piecemeal removing of the barriers from free actions rather than schemes of social reconstruction to provide 'freedom to' pursue certain objectives which is what he finds objectionable in the theories of Rousseau, Hegel and Marx.

George BOOLE (1815–64)

Laws of Thought 1854
Boole was a mathematician who approached logic as a species of non-quantitative algebra. In *The Laws of Thought* he shows how logical revelations can be expressed in a thoroughgoing symbolic way and thus lays the foundations of modern symbolic logic. Boole's logic had a profound effect in England on the logicians W S Jevons and J Venn.

Bernard BOSANQUET (1848–1923)

History of Aesthetics 1892
An important and much neglected expression of late nineteenth century idealism, partly influenced by Hegel. Bosanquet also contributed to the development of nineteenth century logic, expressed a conservative political philosophy, and developed a philosophy of religion which anticipates recent scholarship in this area.

Robert BOYLE (1627–92)

The Sceptical Chemist 1661
Boyle argues for the importance of experimental evidence; an archetypal expression of seventeenth century mechanist philosophy. Like Hobbes and Descartes, Boyle's concept of scientific methodology relied heavily on mechanical models and analogies.

F H BRADLEY (1846–1924)

Principles of Logic 1883
Appearance & Reality 1893
Essays on Truth and Reality 1914
A central figure in nineteenth century philosophy, Bradley's standpoint was attacked by Russell and Moore as idealism. Bradley exhibited a conservative moral and political outlook which can be seen in his famous essay 'My Station and Its Duties'. Nevertheless his influence on metaphysics and logic was profound and his contribution to aesthetics and philosophy of literature has withstood the test of time.

C D BROAD (1887–1971)

Lectures on Psychical Research 1962
Although he survived him, Broad belonged to the Cambridge prior to Wittgenstein. Here he writes lucidly on a lifelong interest. His views on scientific method, metaphysics and ethics are found in *Scientific Thought* (1923), *The Mind and its Place in Nature* (1925) and *Five Types of Ethical Theory* (1930).

Sir Thomas BROWNE (1605–82)

Religio Medici 1643
Written as a private spiritual exercise (see Autobiography) this work became a bestseller in an age when scientific rationality began to erode religious belief.

John BUNYAN (1628–88)

Grace Abounding 1666 (1955)
A personal narrative of spiritual revelation: *Grace Abounding to the Chief of Sinners, or the Brief Relation of the Exceeding Mercy of God in Christ to his Poor Servant*. The simple, Biblical power of Bunyan's style, and the autobiographical element, make this a complementary work to his masterpiece.

The Pilgrim's Progress 1678
On his journey to the Celestial City, Christian passes through many physical and moral trials, such as those represented by the Slough of Despond, Vanity Fair and Doubting Castle. The directness and beauty of Bunyan's language, both in description and dialogue, and the humanity of his symbolic characterizations has attracted an immense readership down the centuries.

Edmund BURKE (1729–97)

Reflections on the Recent Revolution in France 1790
Classic discussion by a founder of modern (wet) Conservatism. Essential reading for any student of modern political philosophy. Burke's general philosophical outlook has been frequently compared with Wittgenstein's injunction that philosophy must 'leave everything as it is'.

Joseph BUTLER (1692–1752)

Fifteen Sermons 1726
This emphasizes the role of self-interest and benevolence in moral philosophy, and attributes an overriding authority to a rational based conscience.

Lewis CARROLL (Charles Lutwidge DODGSON) (1832–98)

Alice in Wonderland 1865
A children's tale (for modern editions see Children's Literature section) but at the same time 'a logical-philosophical *causerie*, garnished with innumerable examples of elegant and unforgettable absurdity' (Flew's *Dictionary of Philosophy*).

Samuel Taylor COLERIDGE (1772–1834)

Confessions of an Enquiring Spirit 1840
Coleridge's view that Christianity embodies symbolic truths that are unaffected by the textual uncertainties of the Bible or traditional errors gave the impetus to a broad theology which has become increasingly influential.

ed. Eric COLLEDGE

The Mediaeval Mystics of England 1962
A valuable anthology of characteristic writings of the English mystics, translated
where necessary from the Latin, and given in standard versions. Among the mystics
are Margery Kempe (see also in the Autobiography section), Julian of Norwich,
Walter Hilton, and Richard Rolle.

R G COLLINGWOOD (1889–1943)

The Idea of Nature 1945
The Idea of History 1946
Interested in ancient history and archaeology as much as philosophy, Collingwood
saw all philosophical discussion as profoundly influenced by its historical context.
His writings on the philosophy of history, philosophy of nature, and aesthetics are
some of the finest contributions of this century. His *An Autobiography* (1939) is,
perhaps, one of the most exciting and stimulating introductions to philosophical
inquiry, which not only outlines Collingwood's intellectual development, but also
captures the essential ingredient of the practice of philosophical knowledge.

Thomas CRANMER (1489–1556) and others

The Book of Common Prayer 1549; 1552
Throughout the sixteenth and seventeenth centuries the *Book of Common Prayer* was
a battleground of religious belief and national policies, leading to a series of
revisions. The 1549 edition, *The First Prayer Book of Edward VI*, was the first
authorized liturgy in English for use at Anglican services. Largely written by Thomas
Cranmer, it is a masterpiece of English prose and doctrinal ambiguity. The prose has
comforted worshippers for generations; the ambiguity has had more painful
consequences.

Ralph CUDWORTH (1617–88)

The True Intellectual System of the Universe 1678
Representative of the school of 'Cambridge Platonists', which looked to Plato and
neo-platonism for help in maintaining Christian theology on a rational basis.

Charles DARWIN (1809–82)

The Origin of Species 1859
The most forceful and influential statement of the theory of evolution which has had
its impact on almost every branch of thought. Capable, because of its date and
character, of being included under the 'English literature' rubric, the philosophical
and methodological status of Darwin's work is still controversial.

J G DAVIES

Christian Politics and Violent Revolution 1976
A contribution to contemporary Christian concern with practical morality and politics. Davies questions the possibility of violence and civil disobedience for the practicing Christian bound by the ethics of non-violence in a repressive society.

Augustus DE MORGAN (1806–71)

Formal Logic 1849
Although much neglected by contemporary logicians, De Morgan's *Formal Logic* was an important stage in the revolution in logic of the nineteenth century, and can be seen as a stepping stone towards his theory of relations according to which the word 'is' performs its functions, logically because it represents a transitive relation.

John DONNE (c. 1573–1631)

Essays in Divinity 1651 (ed. Evelyn M Simpson, 1952)
Written before Donne entered Holy Orders, and therefore of particular interest to students of the poet's temperament.

Sermons (ed. Logan Pearsall Smith, 1919)
Selected passages, with an essay by the editor. These sermons are read as examples of majestic prose, with many often-quoted sentences of poetic beauty and imagery.

James D G DUNN

Christology in the Making 1980
A detailed clarification of the full Christian belief in Christ the Son of God and the Incarnate Word. The work should be seen as an important illustration of the first century context of the meaning of key passages in the *New Testament*.

John FOXE (1516–87)

Book of Martyres 1563
A vast and often gruesome history of the Church and its martyrs. Properly titled *Acts and monuments of these latter and perilous days*, it is largely concerned with and slanted towards the causes of the Protestant martyrs of Mary's reign. For generations it was a hugely popular textbook of English Protestant and anti-Papist sentiment, although Foxe himself was to plead for the Jesuit martyrs of Elizabeth's reign.

Anthony FLEW (1923–)

God and Philosophy 1952
Written by an analytic philosopher of the post-Wittgensteinian period this closely argued book develops a sceptical thesis regarding the existence of God and the immortality of the soul.

eds Anthony FLEW (1923–) and Alasdair MacINTYRE (1929–)

New Essays in Philosophical Theology 1956
A collection of short pieces that achieved a wide readership in academic philosophy, and now conveys something of the style of conceptual analysis in the 1950s and 1960s. See also *Logic and Language*, vols I and II, edited by Flew in 1968 which contain some of the most important papers produced by the linguistic movement.

Sir James George FRAZER (1854–1941)

The Golden Bough 1890–1915
This vast twelve-volume 'study in magic and religion' by a founder of modern anthropology offers a theory of the development of human thought from the magical, through the religious to the scientific. The symbols and practices described entered a whole generation of literary writing. There is a one-volume abridgement.

Peter T GEACH (1916–)

God and the Soul 1969
A professor of logic who examines the nature of God's authority with considerable clarity, arguing that there is something so fundamentally mistaken in attempts by theologians to question the commands of an Almighty God: 'it is as if a stick tried to beat, or an axe to cut, the very hand that was wielding it'. Not many contemporary theists regard the authority of God in such an austere fashion.

Joseph GLANVILL (1636–80)

The Vanity of Dogmatizing 1661
A rejection of Scholastic Aristotelianism, which is a fair representation of seventeenth century intellectual currents.

William GODWIN (1756–1836)

An Enquiry Concerning Political Justice 1793
A work of great popularity in its time prompting Wordsworth to advise students to 'Burn your books on chemistry and read Godwin on necessity'. Government, argued Godwin, was an evil of which we should have as little as possible. The book was seen as subversive and anarchistic, and yet its strength to this day rests on its moral earnestness and sense of justice.

Robert GRANT

A Historical Introduction to the New Testament
An original and controversial introduction to New Testament studies.

T H GREEN (1836–82)

Prologemena to Ethics 1883
Green was one of the foremost thinkers of the Idealist school in Britain during the 1870s and 1880s, and *The Prologemena to Ethics* was one of the central treatises of idealism until the 1920s. It represents Green's understanding of the nature of moral conduct in the context of a philosophical history of virtue. Green's philosophy exercised considerable influence over twentieth century philosophers, particularly R G Collingwood.

Stuart HAMPSHIRE (1914–)

Thought and Action 1959
Freedom of the Individual 1965
Writing with urbanity and broad sensibility, Hampshire contributes a distinctive strand to post-war Oxford philosophy. Like Strawson, Hampshire outlines a position of commonsense metaphysics which does not completely break away from the analytic tradition. His principal concern in *Thought and Action* is with human freedom in relation to knowledge.

R M HARE (1919–)

The Language of Morals 1952
Freedom and Reason 1963
Writing from the centre of Oxford, Hare develops the Kant-inspired thesis that statements about what one morally ought to do derive much of their character from their 'universalizability' – from the fact that what is right for one person must be right for anyone else in the same position.

H L A HART (1907–)

The Concept of Law 1961
A very influential exploration, affected by the linguistic philosophy of J L Austin, of the nature of law. Here the hallmark of the linguistic movement – the patient, descriptive and sometimes laborious attempt to answer the question of how different kinds of concepts are used – is applied to the philosophy of law.

ed. Paul HELM

Divine Commands and Morality 1981
A collection of papers dealing with some of the more important of recent writings on the connections between religion and morality, e.g. whether the existence of God can be proved by reference to the requirement of morality or whether some kind of religion is necessary for appropriate moral conduct.

eds John HICK and Hasan ASKARI

The Experience of Religious Diversity 1985
An expression of the emergence of a twentieth-century ecumenical religious awareness which is described by recent representatives of Christian, Buddhist, Hindu, Jewish, Moslem and Sikh writers who explore the resources of their own religions in support of a pluralistic version.

Thomas HOBBES (1588–1679)

Leviathan 1651
Beginning with the idea that 'all men are equal, if not in strength in cunning', Hobbes reaches the conclusion that without a 'state' the human condition would be one of 'a war of every man, against every man', and thus develops, with ferocious power, a case for absolutism out of the liberal doctrines of possessive individualism. Hobbes remains one of the great figures of British philosophy, not merely for his political writings but for his application of geometrical models to philosophical discourse.

Richard HOOKER (c. 1554–1600)

Of the Laws of Ecclesiastical Polity 1594–1648
A classic statement of Anglican theology, and a famous example of Tudor prose.

Gerald Manley HOPKINS (1844–89)

Sermons and Devotional Writings (ed. Christopher Devlin, 1959)
This contains all the sermons written by Hopkins, the poet and Jesuit, during the early years of his priesthood – his commentary on the Spiritual Exercises of Saint Ignatius – together with concluding notes and discourses up to his death.

J L HOULDEN

Ethics in the New Testament 1973
Discusses the guidance for moral conduct, found in the *New Testament*, noting internal inconsistences and problems with comtemporary relevance and application. Houlden also attempts to get behind the writings to the moral teaching of Jesus.

Francis HUCHESON (1694–1746)

Inquiry into the Original of Our Ideas of Beauty and Virtue 1725
Develops the concept of 'moral sense', a faculty by which virtue is apprehended, which becomes intellectually fashionable in the eighteenth century.

W D HUDSON

Modern Moral Philosophy 1970
Hudson is both a philosopher and theologian and in this book he examines several modern ethical theories, such as intuitionism, emotivism, prescriptivism, and descriptivism, which are of immediate concern to comtemporary moral theology.

David HUME (1711–76)

A Treatise of Human Nature 1739–1740
An Inquiry concerning Human Understanding 1748
Dialogues concerning Natural Religion 1777
An Inquiry concerning the Principles of Morals 1792
The genial and much respected leader of the Scottish Enlightenment, Hume contributed generously to history, politics, aesthetics and economics as well as to philosophy. He developed the empiricist approach of Locke, holding that all we can be directly aware of are not objects in the world but the 'appearance' of them in our own minds, and it is on these that such knowledge as we may have is built. Morality, too, he bases on 'mental' *feelings* of approbation and blame, and thus offers the first thoroughly secular systematic account of ethics in the modern period. *Hume on Human Nature and the Understanding* (ed. A G N Flew, 1962) is a useful selection.

William Ralph INGE (1860–1954)

Christian Mysticism 1899
These eight lectures delivered by 'the gloomy Dean', seem likely to maintain their position as a standard exposition of the development of, and changes in, Christian mysticism from St John and St Paul to the nineteenth century.

William JAMES (1842–1910)

The Varieties of Religious Experience 1902
James, the brother of the novelist Henry, was a notable American exponent of pragmatism. Subtitled 'A study in human nature', his work is included here because of its general influence.

John Maynard KEYNES (1883–1946)

A Treatise on Probability 1921
Most famous for his work in economics, Keynes also published some significant philosophy, which was influenced by Moore and Russell. Here he argues that propositions and not events are the bearers of probability. Just as Moore had argued that goodness was indefinable, Keynes argued that the probability of a proposition was to relate to it a body of existing knowledge. Accordingly, like Moore's account of goodness, probability was irreducible and apprehended intuitively.

eds P LASLETT (1915–) & RUNCIMAN (1934–)

Philosophy, Politics and Society (Series I-V) 1963–78
Collections of papers reflecting well the direction and style of work which echoed the influence of the linguistic movement on British political philosophy in mid-century.

Hugh LATIMER (c. 1490–1555)

Sermons 1758
Sermons preached by the Protestant martyr from about 1529 to 1552. Radical in thought and direct in language, his preaching attracted large crowds and the patronage of Edward VI before his death at the stake with Nicholas Ridley.

William LAW (1686–1761)

A Serious Call to a Devout and Holy Life 1728
A much-loved classic of the Christian way of life 'adapted to the state and conditions of all Orders of Christians'.

Trevor LING

A History of Religion: East and West 1968
One of the most comprehensive introductions to world religions available, covering the period from 1500 BC to the present. Ling examines the development of the major religions as they occurred, often simultaneously, in an historical overlap where parallel developments and divergencies – generally unnoticed in studies taken in isolation – are fully covered. Ling also draws attention to the contemporary significance of various religious trends and their future potential.

John LOCKE (1632–1704)

Essay Concerning Human Understanding 1670
Two Treatises of Government 1690
Laying foundations for both empiricism in the theory of knowledge and liberal democracy in political philosophy, Locke has been one of the most influential of English philosophers. Moderation and commonsense mark his writings, as well as a relaxed elegance of style.

Alasdair MACINTYRE (1929–)

A Short History of Ethics 1967
A history which contrives to be an important contribution to ethical philosophy and a reasonably accessible introduction to the field.

After Virtue 1981
This combines the techniques of analytical philosophy and sensitivity to history to produce a prophetic analysis of the modern condition.

John Ellis McTAGGART (1866–1925)

The Nature of Existence 1921–7
An important contributor to the British idealist movement, nevertheless McTaggart's Hegelian credentials have frequently been questioned. It was probably the Hegelianism of McTaggart – selective in the extreme – which influenced the flight from Hegel by Russell and Moore. In the *Nature of Existence* McTaggart attempted to rigorously work out a deductive metaphysics from first principles, an approach which fitted his general idea that we are not entitled to our instinctive beliefs unless they can be supported by metaphysical reasoning.

T R MALTHUS (1766–1834)

Essays on Population 1798–1803
These advertise the potential of a population to increase at a geometrical rate and argue the need for control. Darwin once claimed that the inspiration for his theory of evolution by natural selection come from Malthus's *Essays*, but several sources nowadays reject this account.

John Stuart MILL (1806–73)

System of Logic 1843
The work which established Mill's reputation as a major philosopher. This is now seen as a forerunner to research in the methodology of the social sciences. On Mill's terms, the logic of science should not merely describe the methods of science; it should justify them.

On Liberty 1859
Individuality is to be valued very highly, but society must step in to prevent one person's freedom resulting in another's harm. Eloquent and finely argued.

Utilitarianism 1863
In this attempt to develop what he saw to be correct in Bentham's utilitarianism, Mill objected to the exclusive role of self-interest in the latter, and distinguishes between higher and lower pleasures.

G E MOORE (1873–1958)

Principia Ethica 1903
A work which had an impact beyond philosophy via the Bloomsbury set. It argues that goodness is an unanalysable quality of things and situations, and that we 'sense' it by a kind of moral 'sight'. According to Moore, attempts to define goodness amounted to a breach of the naturalistic fallacy, the precise meaning of which is still a subject of controversy amongst meta-ethicists. Moore's writing testifies to his tremendous thirst for clarity, which is sometimes excessive and tedious.

Thomas MORE (1478–1535)

Utopia 1516
Uses the device of a fictional society to develop a political and social philosophy
which provided for the election of officers, and shared property, work and
enjoyment. Although it is now read mainly for historical interest in Britain, interest in
More's *Utopia* as a form of social criticism has been rekindled in America and
Germany by followers of the 'Frankfurt school' of critical philosophy.

Cardinal John Henry NEWMAN (1801–90)

Apologia Pro Vita Sua 1864
An account of Cardinal Newman's religious opinions and of his spiritual
development, presented in prose of singular grace and persuasion.

Sir Issac NEWTON (1642–1727)

Philosophiae Naturalis, Principia Mathematica 1687
Although Newton's research interests included alchemy, church history, politics,
history, theology, metrology and prophecy his most famous work was primarily in
mathematics and physics, and it had profound repercussions in philosophy. One of
the greatest books ever written, is not easy to read: some real knowledge of
mathematics is required in order to appreciate its breathtaking elegance.

Michael OAKESHOTT (1901–   )

Rationalism in Politics and Other Essays 1972
A sophisticated appeal to conservatism which reflects the view that the more we
understand our own political tradition the more likely we will be to defend it and
protect ourselves from the imposition of an alien regime.

William PALEY (1743–1845)

Natural Theology 1803
Paley was an English churchman whose influence in his day was considerable but is
scarcely mentioned today except in an antiquarian sense. In *Natural Theology* he
argues with great detail that all living beings are machines which, like a watch, must
have a creator. Similar versions of the argument were advanced by Voltaire, Boyle,
and many others – all of which failed to survive Hume's attack on their analogical
character.

Michael POLANYI (1891–1976)

Personal Knowledge 1958
A scientist of considerable repute who turned to philosophy in his later years. Polanyi
sought a radical alternative to logical positivism and Popperian falsificationism.

According to Polanyi previous accounts of scientific methodology have concentrated too heavily on the objective status of scientific claims. As a counter, Polanyi proposed that essential to scientific progress was a dimension of personal knowledge according to which the subjective attitudes of scientists play a part in the discovery process. Polanyi then developed his theory of 'tacit knowledge' in opposition to the 'all facts and no nonsense' view of science.

K R POPPER (1902–)

The Open Society and its Enemies 1945
An eloquent defence of the type of society in which free criticism of the state flourishes, built partly on a savage denunciation of Plato and Marx and a complete misunderstanding of Hegel.

The Logic of Scientific Discovery 1959
Conjectures and Refutations 1963
Scientific method is identified as proposing hypotheses, attempting to falsify them, and retaining only those that remain unfalsified. The unwillingness to abandon a hypothesis after experimental falsification is seen by Popper as unscientific dogmatism of which he selects astrology, Marxism, and Freudian psycho-analysis as representatives.

Richard PRICE (1723–91)

A Review of the Principal Questions and Difficulties in Morals 1758
A deontological approach to morality, which includes a rebuttal of theological definitions of ethics. According to Price 'right and wrong when applied to actions do not signify merely that such actions are commanded or forbidden by God'. If they did, argues Price, it would always be absurd to ask whether it is right to obey or disobey a command of God.

A N PRIOR (1914–69)

Formal Logic 1955 (2nd edition, 1962)
A textbook treatment by a logician and philosopher who had made significant contributions particularly in developing tense logic before his untimely death.

ed. A M QUINTON (1925–)

Political Philosophy 1967
A collection of papers which are representative of Anglo-American political philosophy in the 1960s.

Frank RAMSEY (1903–30)

The Foundations of Mathematics 1931
Ramsey died before he was thirty but not before he had begun what would undoubtedly have been a significant contribution to British philosophy. In *The Foundations of Mathematics* the influence of Russell and Wittgenstein is noticable on Ramsey's attempt to derive mathematics from a logic which contains no empirical propositions without collapsing into paradox. Although he derived his logical apparatus from Wittgenstein, especially the latter's truth – the functional analysis of propositions – there is a pragmatic direction to Ramsey's thought which is reminiscent of C S Peirce.

Thomas REID (1710–96)

Enquiry into the Human Mind on the Principles of Common Sense 1764
Defends the 'commonsense' view that our senses put us in touch with the external world and thus helped to inspire what came to be called the Scottish 'commonsense' school of philosophy.

Bertrand RUSSELL (1872–1970)

The Problems of Philosophy 1912
Here Russell discusses in a brief and entirely readable manner a handful of what he sees as the most profound problems in philosophy. This is still one of the better introductions to philosophy, although Russell's version of philosophical scepticism has been rejected by followers of Wittgenstein and Austin.

Principia Mathemetica 1913 (with A N Whitehead 1861–1947)
Like Moore, Russell turned away from the idealist school towards commonsense realism, but during his career he grew away from Moore's style of philosophizing, seeing philosophy as 'the science of science'. His philosophical writings are vast but his most lasting contribution to philosophy is his attempt with A N Whitehead to show that mathematics could be derived from a few basic axioms of logic.

Lectures on Logical Atomism 1918, 1919
Continuing the empiricist tradition of Locke, Hume and Berkeley, Russell here attempts to show how more complex statements could be analysed into 'atomic' statements, reporting 'atomic' facts of experience.

History of Western Philosophy 1948
A sweeping survey of Western philosophy from sixth century BC to the logical atomist movement in the first half of the twentieth century. Like many of Russell's ventures into the history of philosophy, this book is probably more revealing about the author's preferences and prejudices, but it is nevertheless an enjoyable, elegant book.

Logic and Knowledge 1956
This collects together some of Russell's most important short pieces on logic and epistemology.

Gilbert RYLE (1900–1976)

Concept of Mind 1949
A philosopher's book, in spite of the charm of its style, which is a major example of 'ordinary language' philosophy and an important contribution to our understanding of 'mind'. Ryle's effort is to undermine the idea that the mind is a kind of hidden substance distinct from the body – a view he depicts as the 'ghost in the machine' analogy which was representative of Cartesian dualism.

Henry SIDGWICK (1838–1900)

The Methods of Ethics 1874
An attempt to combine utilitarianism and intuitionism by a philosopher who retains a place in nineteenth-century British philosophy.

Adam SMITH (1723–90)

An Enquiry into the Nature and Causes of the Wealth of Nations 1776
A philosopher of the Scottish Enlightenment much influenced by Hume, Smith is seen as one of the founders of classical economics. Here he lays bare the principles of *laissez-faire* economics theory which had a profound and lasting effect upon nineteenth-century values.

Herbert SPENCER (1820–1903)

The Principles of Sociology 1877–96
One of the earliest exponents of sociology and of evolution, Spencer was also an uncompromising apostle of *laissez-faire* liberalism. He opposed both absolute monarchy and absolute parliament, viewing the liberals of his day as traitors to their cause and the socialists as harbingers of slavery.

P F STRAWSON (1919–)

Individuals 1959
Formerly a representative of the 'ordinary language' school of philosophy pioneered by Austin and Ryle, Strawson develops a philosophy of commonsense or descriptive metaphysics in *Individuals*. Here he retains the belief that 'the reliance upon a close examination of words is the best, and indeed the only sure way in philosophy'. But he also saw that the philosopher must pass beyond that to 'lay bare the most general features of our conceptual structure'. Thus returning to the methods of Aristotle and Kant, Strawson attempts to map out the very structure of our thought about the world.

Pierre TEILHARD de CHARDIN (1881–1955)

The Phenomenon of Man 1959
A highly speculative, theologically inspired work that draws on ideas of evolutionary theory to develop an account of human destiny, which combines Darwin's theories with a profound belief in the truth of Christianity.

Friedrich WAISMANN (1896–1959)

The Principles of Linguistic Philosophy 1965
A follower of Wittgenstein and important figure in linguistic tradition. Waismann's attempt to systematize the methods of linguistic analysis differs from many other 'ordinary language' philosophers in that he emphasizes the need for a loose and liberal attitude towards language; against the tendency to emphasize rules and correctness. 'Correctness is the last refuge of those who have nothing to say'.

A N WHITEHEAD (1861–1947)

Process and Reality 1929
Whitehead attempts in this and other works a theory of reality as a whole, by applying generally the notion of the organic life-cycle; and achieves a 'vast, rhapsodic' system: 'the most imposing metaphysical product of modern British philosophy' (A M Quinton). He collaborated with Russell, in preparing the monumental *Principia Mathematica*.

A J T D WISDOM (1904–)

Philosophy and Psychoanalysis 1953
Paradox and Discovery 1965
One of the best known of Wittgenstein's pupils at Cambridge. Wisdom retains a level of sympathy for metaphysics which is absent in the work of many linguistic philosophers. These works attempt to say something about the nature of philosophical disputes which, as Wisdom points out, reflect views when, considered from the point of view of strict logic, are clearly false.

Ludwig WITTGENSTEIN (1889–1951)

Tractatus Logico-Philosophicus 1921 (English translation, 1922)
Tractatus is one of the most influential books in the history of philosophy. Written as a critique of language it attempts a fundamental distinction between what can be said and what must be shown. This distinction is central to Wittgenstein's proposed solutions to the problems of mathematics, logic and metaphysics outlined here. When first published, the *Tractatus* was mistakenly seen as a contribution to logical positivism, a view which was later repudiated by Wittgenstein.

The Blue and Brown Books 1958
This is one of the standard introductions to Wittgenstein's post-*Tractatus* philosophy which was originally dictated by Wittgenstein to his students at Cambridge in the early 1930s. The arguments are reproduced in *Philosophical Investigations*.

Philosophical Investigations 1958
Whereas the *Tractatus* attempted a critique of language in a once-and-for-all attempt to map out the limit of language, and is written in a rather cryptic and formal manner, the *Investigations* represents a complete change of style to something much looser, colloquial and unsystematic. Philosophy is no longer seen as the pursuit of the underlying logical structure of language. Here it is stressed that language is akin to a set of tools used in particular social contexts, or language games where the meaning of words is not determined by their correllation to objects but by the rules appertaining to the game. Wittgenstein also attacks in this work Cartesian and introspectionist accounts of the mind, as well as proposing the idea that many philosophical problems in the past have resulted from using language outside of a proper context, and that such confusion is to be cured by the patient study of the way in which our language is *normally* used. Other titles are: *Remarks on the Foundations of Mathematics* 1956, *Zettel* 1967, *On Certainty* 1969, *Lectures and Conversations on Aesthetics, Psychology and Religious Belief* 1970

Mary WOLLSTONECRAFT (1759–97)

A Vindication of the Rights of Women 1790
A classic defence of libertarian and egalitarian ideals.

MEDIEVAL BRITISH WORKS IN LATIN

St ANSELM (1033–1109)

Proslogion (trans. M J Charlesworth, 1965)
St Anselm was born in Italy, but became Archbishop of Canterbury in 1093. He is most famous for his ontological 'proof' of the existence of God.

St Thomas AQUINAS (c. 1225–74)

Summa Theologica
A sustained attempt to appropriate Aristotle on behalf of Christianity.

Roger BACON (c. 1214–92)

Opus Maius
This work feels towards the forthcoming emergence of science.

John DUNS SCOTUS (c. 1264–1308)

Opera Omnia 1639
Duns Scotus was a Scottish-born opponent of the teachings of St Thomas Aquinas, and belonged to a great tradition of logicians who flourished in Britain during the early middle ages.

William of OCKHAM (c. 1285–1349)

Summa Logices 1488 (ed. P Boehner, selections, 1951–4)
Ockham is most famous for his nominalist approach to the understanding of general terms.

WORKS IN TRANSLATIONS

Some works that have been of seminal influence on British philosophy by way of translation are briefly listed below.

ARISTOTLE (384–22 B.C.)

Three editions (among others) to choose from:

Aristotle's Works (eds J A Smith and W D Ross, 1980–52)
The Loeb Classical Library, printing Greek and English text on facing pages. The quality of the translations, and the helpfulness of the introductions that go with them differ from volume to volume.
    The Clarendon Aristotle is partial, but incorporates the most recent scholarship and volumes already published are excellent.

Rene DESCARTES (1591–1650)

Descartes' Philosophical Writings (eds G E M Anscombe and P T Geach, 1954)
A selection from Descartes's writings designed to present the major substance of his contribution to philosophy.

G W F HEGEL (1770–1831)

The Phenomenology of Spirit 1806
The Philosophy of Right 1821
Hegel's writings are rebarbatively difficult, but historically influential. Perhaps Hegel is most famous for his influence on Marx and Engels, but there was also a considerable Hegelian influence on the rather conservative British Idealists of the late nineteenth century. Many twentieth-century philosophers have turned yet again to Hegel as an alternative to the sterility of the analytic and linguistic tradition.

E Emmanuel KANT (1724–1804)

Critique of Pure Reason 1781 (trans. N Kemp Smith, 1929)
A major turning point in the history of philosophy. The influence of Kant has been felt
by all schools of philosophy which includes such diverse representatives as Mill,
Wittgenstein, Popper and Strawson.

Ground Work of the Metaphysic of Morals 1785 (trans. as *The Moral Law*, H J Paton,
1948)
Perhaps the best introduction to Kant's ethical theory.

G W LEIBNIZ (1646–1716)

New Essays on the Human Understanding c. 1705
Leibniz: Philosophical Writings (trans. Mary Morris, 1934)
These are translations of a selection of Leibniz's various philosophical works.
Leibniz was the last polymathic genius: brilliant mathematician, scientist, logician,
historian, jurist – as well as philosopher. In the latter role he is a leading contributor to
the Rationalist tradition.

Karl MARX (1818–83)

Das Kapital 1867
An attempt to understand historical change in terms of how human beings organize
the production of their necessities. A useful selection of the writings of Marx (often
with his collaborator Engels) is: *Marx and Engels: Basic Writings on Politics and
Philosophy.*

PLATO (c. 428–348 B.C.)

The Republic (trans. F M Cornford, 1941)
Possibly the greatest work by the greatest philosopher of all time, *The Republic* is one
of the most relevant texts with which to begin a reading of philosophy. Ostensibly
written as a dialogue concerning the nature of justice it deals profoundly with moral
and political issues, the status of the arts, religion, theory of knowledge,
metaphysics, and the nature of philosophy itself. It has frequently been pointed out
that the history of Western philosophy is merely a series of footnotes to Plato.

Jean-Jacques ROUSSEAU (1712–78)

The Social Contract 1762
By invoking the notion of a 'general will' which cannot but serve the common good,
Rousseau explains, ominously, how it might be necessary for people to be 'forced to
be free'. Nowadays criticized as an example of democratic totalitarianism, *The Social
Contract* had a profound influence upon nineteenth-century Romanticism.

Benedictus de SPINOZA (1632–77)

Ethics 1677
Spinoza Selections (ed. J Wild, 1930)
Spinoza was a leading Rationalist, who proposed mathematical models for the solution of philosophical problems.

WORKS OF REFERENCE

G E M ANSCOMBE (1919–)

Intention 1957
Anscombe is a former student and translator of Wittgenstein. In this text he employs Wittgensteinian techniques to resolve problems in philosophical psychology. Here it is agreed that actions we mark off as intentional are not necessarily preceded by a special kind of internal act. Intentional acts are not defined by reference to psychological process but in terms of the questions which can be applied to them.

F COPLESTON (1907–)

History of Philosophy 1959 (9 vols)
A comprehensive history from one (Thomist) pen. Clearly written, painstaking, and invaluable.

ed. P EDWARDS

The Encyclopaedia of Philosophy
Though edited and published in America, this is too useful a work to go unmentioned. Available in eight volumes, or, with smaller print in just four.

P K FEYERABEND (1924–)

Against Method 1975
Science in a Free Society 1978
A student of history, physics and astronomy with a background in German theatre, Feyerabend was introduced to Wittgenstein's later philosophy by Anscombe and came to England in the 1950s where he lectured on the philosophy of science. These two books have enlivened recent philosophy of science and outraged his critics, since they propose a Dadaist approach to scientific methodology. His style is witty, elegant and provocative. Combining these features with a passion for argument and historical case studies he has advanced, epistemological anarchism according to which the only terrible position in the philosophy of science is 'anything goes'.

Anthony FLEW (1923–)

An Introduction to Western Philosophy 1971
This introduces major philosophers and their traditions by engaging in argument with them. A vigorous and unpompous presentation by one who learnt his philosophy in the Oxford of the 1960s.

A Dictionary of Philosophy 1979
A handy and authoritative text.

ed. O HANFLING

Fundamental Problems in Philosophy 1972
A wide ranging collection of pieces designed to introduce the major dimensions of philosophy via its seminal writers.

W M KNEALE

The Development of Logic 1962
From the pre-Socratics to Church logicians: philosophically acute, lucidly written, a work of considerable scholarship.

T KUHN (1922–)

The Structure of Scientific Revolutions 1970
Kuhn is primarily a historian of science but this text has had a profound effect upon recent philosophy of science and theory of knowledge. Here it is maintained that normal scientific inquiry is conducted by scientists who share a common paradigm of background beliefs and theories which are held without question. Only in times of crisis is the paradigm questioned after which a new paradigm may replace the old in a similar fashion to the overthrow of authorities in political revolutions. Kuhn's critics have charged him with the advocacy of 'mob psychology' and Kuhn has lately reformulated his original views.

Norman MALCOLM (1911–)

Ludwig Wittgenstein: A Memoir 1958
Problems of Mind 1971
A former student of Wittgenstein and Moore, Malcolm develops their approach with contributions to the philosophy of mind and epistemology where he attacks Cortesian theory and philosophical scepticism. His short, yet sometimes moving, biography of Wittgenstein is an excellent introduction to the latter's work which demonstrates that complex philosophical topics can be communicated with clarity and simplicity of style.

ed. W MAYS

The British Journal for the Study of Phenomenology
A former student of Wittgenstein with a broad knowledge of continental philosophy. Mays has made significant contributions to both analytic philosophy and phenomenology as well as philosophy of education and the philosophy of the sciences.

ed. D J O'CONNOR

A Critical History of Western Philosophy 1964
An encyclopaedic approach, with introductory and authoritative short articles on the leading figures and ideas.

D OLDROYD

The Arch of Knowledge 1986
An introduction to the history of philosophy with specific reference to the methodology of science which spans the early Greeks and the philosophy of the sciences in post-Einsteinian times.

Derek PARFIT (1942–)

Reasons and Persons 1984
Challenges our deepest beliefs about rationality, morality, and personal identities. The author proposes a controversial account of rationality according to which it may be rational to act against our interests and that most of us hold moral beliefs that are ultimately self-defeating.

J PASSMORE (1914–)

A Hundred Years of Philosophy 1975
A history of modern ideas showing achievement in logic and metaphysics which is stimulating to the specialist and intelligible to the lay reader.

D Z PHILLIPS (1934–)

The Concept of Prayer 1965
Faith and Philosophical Enquiry 1970
An exposition of Wittgenstein's philosophy with particular bearing on problems in the philosophy of religion. Here Phillips develops Wittgenstein's technique to closely examine the contexts in which statements are made to throw light on the meanings associated with prayer and acts of faith.

Richard RORTY

Philosophy and the Mirror of Nature 1980
An examination of the current state and status of philosophy.

W H WALSH (1913–86)

Metaphysics 1963
As a historian and metaphysician, Walsh's major contribution to British philosophy lies in his exposition of Kantian and Hegelian idealism on which he continued to work until his death in 1986. His *Metaphysics* is a useful introductory survey of the standpoints of the world's greatest philosophers which include Plato, Aristotle, Descartes, Hume, Hegel, Bradley, Moore and Wittgenstein.

G J WARNOCK (1923–)

English Philosophy Since 1900
A concise and readable account of developments in the twentieth century, written from the standpoint of Oxford philosophy in the 1960s.

P WINCH (1926–)

The Idea of a Social Science 1959
An exposition of Wittgenstein's philosophical approach with specific application to the social sciences. Winch has often been characterized as a relativist with regard to the understanding of social values and standards of objectivity.

THE BIBLE

The Bible in English is an English library in itself. As a collective work of literature, it has no equal. It is fiction, history, biography and autobiography and it contains poetry, philosophic discourse and ethical instruction.

The 17 biblical books that are listed and annotated here illustrate these different attributes. It is a selection from 66 books in total and has been made with the intention of attracting the interest of those who are not already familiar with the Bible or committed to its religious message. However, the Bible only make sense if it is also recognized as a sacred text for those of Christian or Jewish faiths: the medium through which God reveals his purpose to man.

Which English version of the Bible should one read? For most general readers the choice will be between the *Authorised Version* of 1611 and the *New English Bible*, which was published in two stages: 1961 and 1970. The *New English Bible* is the first full new translation since the *Authorised Version* and is often criticized for the 'flatness' of its style. It is, however, the best version to read in order to obtain the meaning of the text. The beautiful familiar sound of the *Authorised Version* sometimes gives the impression but not the substance of a comprehensible message.

On the other hand, the *Authorised Version* is one of the great glories of the English language. Its literary excellence derives from a Hebrew original whose word order and rhetorical style closely matches that of English, the individual genius of successive translators, particularly William Tyndale, and the state of the English language in the sixteenth and early seventeenth centuries – the *Authorised Version* was published in the same year that the last of Shakespeare's plays was performed. This culmination of Renaissance English translations achieves a fusion of narrative, ideas and language which has conditioned the English response to literature for over five centuries.

The best course is to alternate one's reading between both versions, obtaining the meaning from one and the poetic effect from the other.

THE OLD TESTAMENT

The Myths of the Creation and the Fall of Man: *Genesis (Chapters 1–11.9)*
The Genesis myths of the creation of the world and the fall of man is at the psychological centre of Western civilization. The scientific facts do not devalue the symbols: Adam and Eve; the serpent and the apple; Cain, the first born and first murderer; the flood and Noah's ark; the Tower of Babel and the dispersion of man throughout the world.

The Origins of God's People: *Genesis (Chapters 12–50)*
God's promise to Abraham – 'I will make of thee a great nation' – is the origin of the Jewish people. The struggle to preserve the bond between God and his chosen people is illustrated in the vivid human dramas of Abraham's family: the destruction of Sodom and Gomorrah and the rescue of his nephew Lot, the 'miraculous' pregnancy of his wife Sarah, the near sacrifice of his son Isaac, the rivalry between his grandsons Esau and Jacob, and the trials in Egypt of his great grandsons Joseph and Benjamin. The narrative is rich in strong, visual images such as the pillar of salt, Jacob's ladder and Joseph's coat of many colours.

The Birth of a Nation: *Exodus*
Nearly 400 years after Jacob's settlement in Egypt, the Israelites were working as slaves in the brickfields: this is an epic story of liberation. The narrative of the first 15 chapters of *Exodus* covers the forced labour and attempted genocide of the Israelites, the discovery of the infant Moses in the bulrushes, his later confrontation with Pharaoh, the visitation of plagues on the Egyptian people, the mass exodus on Passover night and the miraculous crossing of the Red Sea. This is followed by a period of wandering in the wilderness during which a national identity is forged through the covenant between God and his people, and the establishment of codes of ethical conduct and religious practice.

The Rise and Fall of a Monarchy: *the First and Second Books of Samuel and the First Book of Kings (Chapters 1–11)*
The account of the rise and fall of Israel's monarchy is a magnificent human and political drama and in the so-called Succession Narrative, (2 Samuel 6–7, 9–20 and 1 Kings 1–2) it contains the world's oldest written history, dating from the 10th century BC. The story runs from Samuel's anointment of Saul as the first king, through the clashes between the two as Saul departs from the God-given rules and Samuel switches his support to the young David, and on to David's military successes and family tragedies. The struggle to succeed David ends in Solomon's favour but after the building of the first Temple at Jerusalem the regime degenerates and the Israelite kingdom splits into two. The story is dominated by the personality of David and the classic heroic–tragic curve of his career: the young poet-warrior who defeats Goliath grows into the politician-king who commits adultery and murder to gain Bathsheba and then suffers the rebellion and death of his son Absalom.

The authors' treatment of this material illustrates themes which have exercised the writers of historical literature ever since: the nature of political leadership, the relevance of a leader's personal morality and the legitimacy of a revolution against a tyrannical regime.

The Poetic Voice: *Job, Psalms, Ecclesiastes, The Song of Songs*

The poetic books of the Old Testament add to its artistic and psychological complexity. In many respects they contradict the prophetic message: they are often at their most poetically intense when their sentiment is least religious.

Job is the story of extreme and undeserved suffering and teaches the difficult conclusion that man can never sufficiently comprehend the immensity of God's creation to be able to distinguish his purpose. However the book faces, if it does not resolve, the problem of suffering and it communicates the philosophical issues with great poetic force.

Human suffering and the need for divine comfort is a frequent subject of the *Psalms*. Their popular reputation is for fine phrases isolated in catalogues of threats and complaints. Indeed, in nine verses psalm 137 does turn the beautifully plaintive opening of 'By the rivers of Babylon, there we sat down ...' into the ferocious ending of 'Happy shall he be, that taketh and dasheth the little ones against the stones'. But there are many psalms which combine both the sentiment and sustained expression of great poems, such as

> 'The heavens declare the glory of God' (19)
> 'The Lord is my shepherd' (23)
> 'The earth is the Lord's and the fullness thereof' (24)
> 'As the hart panteth after the water brooks' (42)
> 'O God of my salvation, I have cried day and night before thee' (88)
> 'O Lord, thou hast searched me and known me' (139)

Attempts to gloss acceptable religious messages out of *Ecclesiastes* and the *Song of Songs* are undermined by the poetry, which is clearly an expression of their authors' personal experience of the physical world rather than extended religious metaphors. The preacher-author of *Ecclesiastes* meditates on the transitory and insignificant nature of life and the finality of death and ends with a superb but chilling last chapter: 'Remember now thy Creator in the days of thy youth, while the evil days come not, nor the years draw nigh, when thou shalt say, I have no pleasure in them.' Among the few consolations of human experience allowed by the preacher is to 'live joyfully with the wife whom thou lovest'. In the *Song of Songs* a set of poems cast in the voice of a bride and bridegroom celebrate the feeling of physical union and separateness that is created by sexual love.

The Prophetic Voice: *The Book of the Prophet Isaiah*

The prophets provided national moral leadership against the background of colonial rule and deportations which followed on the disintegration of the two Jewish kingdoms. In their denunciations of the evils of their days and their insistence on adherence to God's laws they forged a link between religion and ethical behaviour which has conditioned Western culture ever since.

Isaiah is one name but three separate voices which span the whole of the prophetic period. The Isaiah of chapters 1–39 lived in a Jerusalem threatened by Assyria and castigates the Jews for their materialism and lack of faith. He forecasts their conquest by foreign powers but also prophesies (chapters 9 and 11) the birth of a national leader – a wonderful counseller and prince of peace – who will unite the Jewish people in a rule of religious observance and social justice. The second voice (chapters 40–49) dates from the captivity in Nebuchadnezzar's Babylon and expresses God's love for his people and his choice of them as the servant nation which will achieve God's purpose in the world. The language of the second Isaiah such as in the opening 'Comfort ye, comfort ye my people', is among the most uplifting in the Bible. The third Isaiah (chapters 55–60) was among the first to return from Babylonian exile and his concern is with the moral as well as the physical restoration of the nation.

Isaiah is the most quoted prophet in the New Testament as his prophecies about the nature of God's servant nation are personified in Jesus as the Messiah. Many of the finest passages are familiar from their use in the text of Handel's *Messiah*.

THE NEW TESTAMENT

The Life and Teaching of Jesus: *Gospels according to Matthew, Mark, Luke and John*

The New Testament provides four versions of Jesus's life and teaching. *Matthew*, *Mark* and *Luke* share a large amount of the same material presented in approximately the same order. *John* is a very different work.

Mark was the first written of the gospels and was the point at which oral tradition of stories about Jesus became 'fixed'. It is a short, forceful book which bristles with a sense of urgency: there is no nativity story and Jesus is teaching by verse 12 of chapter 1. It is a roughly written record of his life, death and resurrection made for a community which contained many who could have been eye-witnesses of these events and who expected the end of the world and the second coming of Jesus in their own lifetime. One of the fascinating puzzles in *Mark* is the apparent ambivalence that Jesus himself has towards publicizing his Messianic role and the difficulty his disciples had in determining the true nature of this mission.

Matthew uses virtually all *Mark*'s material but it is a longer, more reflective gospel. The evangelist is a Jew who wants to legitimize Jesus as the Jewish Messiah, albeit a different one from that of general expectation. He provides a miraculous nativity story, illustrates Jesus's descent from David and shows his teaching as fulfilment of the true spirit of the Mosaic Law. *Matthew*'s Messianic Jesus is concerned to achieve the kingdom of heaven rather than a worldy kingdom and this leads to rigorous statements of Christian ethics, as in the Sermon on the Mount (chapters 5–7). This lays down absolute standards which require adherence to the spirit as well as the acts of a moral code.

Luke is the most human of the gospels in the sense that it provides the most information about Jesus's personal life, shows particular interest in his healing ministry, and contains some of the most memorable human stories. In literary terms, it is the best written of the four gospels both in the dramatic presentation of incidents such as the supper at Emmaus or the short-story telling of the parables of the Good Samaritan and the Prodigal Son.

John is the last of the gospels to be written and stands on its own both in content and purpose. It relates little of Jesus's life and contains no parables and few miracles. It is dedicated to the presentation of Jesus's claims that he is the Son of God and that his life, death and resurrection is the fulfilment of God's purpose since the beginning of the world. These claims are made largely in the direct speech of Jesus himself: 'Before Abraham was, I am ...', 'I am the resurrection and the life ...', 'I am the way, the truth and the life: no man cometh unto the Father, but by me'. If *Matthew* makes the most absolute claims on Christian behaviour, *John* makes the most absolute claims on Christian belief.

The Life and Teachings of Paul: *Acts of the Apostles, Letter to the Romans and the First Letter to the Corinthians*
Shortly after the crucifixion of Jesus a young man called Saul witnesses the stoning of the first Christian martyr. Determined to root out the new belief, he sets out for Damascus on a search-and-arrest mission. On the road he sees and hears Jesus, and undergoes an immediate and total conversion. Now as Paul he begins a series of missionary journeys which spreads Christianity outside its Jewish birthland to Asia Minor and ultimately to the then world capital of Rome.

Paul is the most important person in the history of Christianity after Jesus. He wrote the first account of Jesus – his letters pre-date the earliest gospel by several years – and provided the only firsthand record of a meeting with the risen Christ. His commitment to the conversion of non-Jews is the foundation of a worldwide religion, while his acceptance of the central authority of Jerusalem helped the church to survive the sectarian divisions of the first and second century.

Paul (as Saul) appears in chapter 8 of *Acts* and from chapter 13 onwards his works are the main subject of the book. It is a story of dramatic incidents – the martyrdom of Stephen, the earthquake at Philippi, the riot at Ephesus, the shipwreck on the way to Rome – and inspirational preaching, such as Paul's address to the Ephesian elders and his defence before Agrippa. Some of the events and speeches have probably been heightened by Luke, who is the author of both *Acts* and the *Luke* gospel and a master of suspenseful narrative.

Paul's missionary message is best expressed in *Romans* and *I Corinthians*. In essence it is a threefold message: that salvation is through faith in Jesus as the Son of God; that the inspiration of faith comes from the fact of the life, death and resurrection of Jesus; and that this path to salvation is open to all people. *Romans* grounds this argument in an analysis of sin and consciousness of sin: 'For the good that I would I do not: but the evil that I would not, that I do.' The escape from this misery is through the 'grace of God', the act of divine favour which grants salvation to man. Jesus's life is the overwhelming expression of God's grace and acceptance of Jesus provides a new start in life.

I Corinthians like the later chapters of *Romans* is concerned with the way in which 'born again' Christians should conduct their lives, but its emotional high point is the personal affirmation in chapter 15 of the resurrection of Jesus and the essential nature of this fact : 'And if Christ be not risen, then is our preaching in vain and your faith is also in vain'.

Both letters illustrate Paul's rhetorical style, especially in the rhythmical prose of the *Authorised Version*. In such passages the sense of his argument is repeated and carried forward in a continuous surge of phrases such as *I Corinthians'* famous chapter 13: 'Though I speak with tongues of men and of angels, and have not charity I am become as sounding brass, or a tinkling cymbal' or the encouragement to the persecuted in chapter 8 of *Romans* 'Who shall separate us from the love of Christ? shall tribulation, or distress, or persecution, or famine, or nakedness or peril or sword? As it is written, for thy sake we are killed all the day long: we are accounted as sheep for the slaughter. Nay in all these things we are more than conquerers through him that loved us.'

FINE ARTS

It is tempting to attribute the paucity of English contributions to the literature of the visual arts in the sixteenth and seventeenth century to a similar dearth of achievements (relative to those of Italy or Germany) in the arts themselves. Is it really surprising that we have no Alberti or Vasari and nothing remotely equivalent to the letters of Poussin, given that we have no Raphael, Leonardo or Dürer? The most prominent Jacobean and Carolingian painters are themselves foreigners.

It is with the eighteenth century that a wealth of aesthetic debate and art criticism begins to appear. Much of this is concerned with the debate between rationalist and idealist aestheticians on concepts that may now seem largely outmoded: the social value of connoisseurship, definitions of the sublime and picturesque. By and large English contributions to these matters are less influential than those of Kant or Diderot and much of what is worth preserving is to be found in Burke. Perhaps only the aesthetic antiquarian still reads Payne Knight, Kames, Allison, Bailie and Hutchinson. The discourses of Reynolds belong to the rather more urgent reflections of the practising painter, albeit one perhaps excessively concerned with the then modish concept of 'taste' as a socially distinctive 'faculty'.

It is however, in the realm of the applied arts that the eighteenth century introduces the pragmatic concern for integrating art and daily life. This is manifested in innumerable major contributions to the literature of craftsmanship and design. In fields as diverse as architecture, pottery, and landscape gardening; Campbell, Repton and others demonstrate that happy talent for compiling readable inventories that leads to Pevsner's sweeping achievement. Wedgwood and Walpole go further and demonstrate a gift for common-sense reflection on the psychological and social function of the fine and decorative arts alike. Perhaps it is in them and their intellectual inheritors – Ruskin, Morris, Fry and Bell – that the major English writing on the arts is to be found.

C R ASHBEE

Should We Stop Teaching Art? 1911
An important pamphlet by the prolific publisher and leading proponent of the Arts and Crafts movement.

Clive BELL (1881–1962)

Art 1914
Stresses the importance of 'significant form' in art using Cezanne as an example. Bell was a leading member of the Bloomsbury Group and promoter of the Post-Impressionists.

John BERGER (1926–)

Ways of Seeing 1973
A lively Marxist approach to art criticism.

John BETJEMAN (1906–84)

Ghastly Good Taste 1933
His first book of prose, a witty polemic on architecture and related subjects.

William BLAKE (1757–1827)

A Descriptive Catalogue 1809
The accompaniment to an (unsuccessful) exhibition of Blake's 'Poetical and Historical Inventors'. An account of his views on the prehistoric origins of art, and a justification of his preference for linear clarity.

Edmund BURKE (1729–97)

A Philosophical Enquiry into the Origins of our Ideas on the Sublime and the Beautiful 1757
The most widely-read English contribution to the subject and a key contribution to the emergence of an aesthetic of Romanticism. His emphasis on the terror in the sublime fired the gothic imaginings of artists such as Fuseli and novelists such as Mrs Radcliffe.

William CHAMBERS (1726–96)

Treatise of Civil Architecture 1759
A statement of the academic principles upheld by Chambers, drawn from his study of Italian renaissance architecture.

Kenneth CLARK (1903–83)

The Nude: A Study of Ideal Art 1956
Nearly 300 illustrations accompany this study of how the nude has dominated classical sculpture and painting, showing the different attitudes and theories that accompanied the representations.

R G COLLINGWOOD (1889–1943)

Principles of Art 1938
A theory of Expressionism by the philosopher-historian.

Alexander COZENS (1717–86)

A New Method of Assisting the Invention in Drawing Original Compositions of Landscape 1778
Pre-Romantic suggestions on means of stimulating the imagination, aimed largely at practitioners of the newly-fashionable hobby of sketching.

Walter CRANE (1845–1915)

Ideals in Art 1905
The views of the poet, painter, illustrator and socialist.

Charles EASTLAKE (1836–1906)

A History of the Gothic Revival 1872
The first account of the Gothic Revival, written at a time when it was only just beginning to be on the wane, and still a useful sourcebook.

James FERGUSSON (1808–86)

An Historical Inquiry into True Principles of Beauty in Art, More Especially with Reference to Architecture 1849
Fergusson was a popular writer on art and architecture in the nineteenth century.

John FLAXMAN (1755–1826)

Lectures on Sculpture 1829
The first serious consideration of sculptural values by an English artist of renown.

Roger FRY (1866–1934)

Vision and Design 1920
An infectiously enthusiastic and often republished selection of essays that constitute a down-to-earth analysis of the bonds between culture and society. Personal assessments ranging from the art of the bushman to Post-Impressionism.

Eric GILL (1882–1940)

Art Nonsense and Other Essays 1929
Essays by the sculptor, engraver, letter cutter and typographer, who also wrote prolifically on artistic, religious and social matters.

William GILPEN (1724–1804)

Three Essays: On Picturesque Beauty; On Picturesque Travel; and on Sketching Landscape 1792
One of the major propagators of the idea of the 'picturesque', especially in the appreciation and painting of landscape. Judgements based as much on moral and social as on aesthetic grounds.

E H GOMBRICH (1909–)

The Story of Art 1950
An introduction to the history of art which has become a standard textbook and is available in a generously illustrated paperback edition. Discarding connoisseurship and based on the author's wide knowledge of arts and ideas it sets out to place the works it discusses in their historical setting and thus to lead towards an understanding of the masters' artistic aims.

Art and Illusion. A Study in the Psychology of Pictorial Representation 1960
'Is everything concerned with art subjective, or are there objective standards in such matters?' Approaching such questions from a scientific viewpoint this book awakened widespread interest in the psychology of the visual arts.

William HAZLITT (1778–1830)

Criticisms on Art 1843
An easy-going appreciation of painting.

William HOGARTH (1697–1762)

The Analysis of Beauty: Written with a View of Fixing the Fluctuating Ideas of Taste 1753
Some startlingly modern views on psychological responses to form.

Sir Ebenezer HOWARD (1850–1928)

Tomorrow: A Peaceful Path to Real Reform 1898
One of the main sources of inspiration of the 'Garden City' movement.

William Holman HUNT (1827–1910)

Pre-Raphaelitism and the Pre-Raphaelite Brotherhood 1920
Autobiographical sourcebook for the movement, written by one of its leading participants.

Richard Payne KNIGHT (1750–1824)

An Analytical Inquiry into the Principles of Taste 1805
An important document in the literature of the picturesque.

William Richard LETHABY (1857–1931)

Architecture, Mysticism and Myth 1891
A remarkable book by the architect, craftsman and first Principal of the Central Schools of Arts and Crafts.

Percy Wyndham LEWIS (1882–1957)

Blast: The Review of the Great English Vortex 1914
The 'puce monster', edited and largely written by Lewis, that forcefully asserted his aesthetic views.

James Leslie MARTIN, Ben NICHOLSON, Naum GABO (eds)

Circle: An International Review of Constructive Art 1937
Essays by the editors, and by Herbert Read, Barbara Hepworth, Henry Moore etc.

William MORRIS (1834–96)

Hopes and Fears for Art 1882
A collection of the lectures by the poet, artist, craftsman, decorator and social reformer. His identification of art with self-expression and fulfilment through labour is the major influence in the Crafts Movement.

Francis Turner PALGRAVE (1824–97)

Essays on Art 1866
Essays by the poet and critic.

Walter H PATER (1839–1984)

The Renaissance: Studies in Art and Poetry 1873
The seminal English text on aestheticism that influenced Oscar Wilde and the poets of 1890s. It contains the famous, floridly expressed essays on the Schools of Giorgione, Leonardo, Botticelli, etc.

Nickolaus PEVSNER (1902–83)

The Englishness of English Art 1956
The Buildings of England 1951–74
The latter is arranged in 46 volumes by county and shows the differing architecture that can be found throughout England; a thorough guide by a leading expert.

Sir Uvedale PRICE (1747–1829)

Essays on the Picturesque 1794
One of the principal statements of the picturesque doctrine.

A W N PUGIN (1812–52)

Contrasts 1836
The full title continues 'or a Parallel between the noble Edifices of the fourteenth and fifteenth centuries and similar buildings of the present day. Showing the decay of taste'. By linking a spiritual decline to the assumed aesthetic inferiority of the classical architecture of his time, Pugin laid the basis for the Gothic Revival.

Herbert READ (1893–1968)

The Meaning of Art 1931
Art Now 1933
Surrealism 1936
The Form of Things Unknown 1960
The champion of modern art and friend of leading artists, especially the Neo-Romantics and Surrealists, Read wrote extensively on art and society, including the influential *Education through Art* (1943).

Humphrey REPTON

Sketches and Hints on Landscape Gardening 1794
Fragments on the Theory and Practice of Landscape Gardening 1816
A leading practitioner's guide to landscape gardening from the golden age of the art.

Joshua REYNOLDS (1723–92)

Discourses on Art 1794
Lectures initially delivered at the Royal Academy from 1769. The most widely-known English exposition of the Classical ideal.

Jonathan RICHARDSON (1665–1745)

Essays on the Theory of Painting 1715
In this and other writings the portrait painter established the claim of painting as an art rather than just recreation.

John RUSKIN (1819–1900)

Perhaps the greatest English writer on the fine arts and their position in a civilized society. In spite of frequent mental breakdowns and an uneven response to the painting of his own day – he promoted the Pre-Raphaelites, disliked the Impressionists – his style and sincerity communicates a taste that is still a powerful influence on the British response to art.

Modern Painters 1843–60
'Truth to nature' is the most important value in art with Turner shown (most succinctly in volume one) as the supreme example.

The Seven Lamps of Architecture 1849
The Stones of Venice 1851–3
The general principles and values of the Gothic in art are identified in the first book and expressed in the second through a detailed examination and illustration of the work of the medieval artists and craftsmen of Venice.

Unto this Last 1860
Four essays developing Ruskin's art criticism into an attack on the social and economic consequences of *laissez-faire* capitalism.

Geoffrey SCOTT (1883–1929)

The Architecture of Humanism 1914
Discusses the theory and form of classical architecture and remains relevant to the current and growing interest in classicism.

Sir George Gilbert SCOTT (1811–78)

Remarks on Secular and Domestic Architecture, Present and Future 1857
Surveys English architecture and 'predicts' its future, making it an interesting 'companion' to Ruskin's views on Venice.

Earl of SHAFTESBURY, Anthony Ashley Cooper (1671–1713)

Characteristics of Men, Manners, Opinions and Times 1711
Multi-volume set of analytic essays, many concerned with pragmatic reflections on the relationship between art, nature and society.

Richard Norman SHAW (1831–1912) and Thomas Graham JACKSON (1835–1924)

Architecture: A Profession or an Art 1892
A controversial collection of articles by various architects of the period.

Walter SICKERT (1860–1942)

Free House! 1947
A great painter and fine teacher who wrote polemical journalism, letters and incidental pieces which were edited in this collection by Osbert Sitwell. A direct and witty expression of ideas.

Sir John SOANE (1753–1837)

Lectures on Architecture, 1809–1836 1925
The collected Royal Academy lectures by one of the most original neo-classical architects (edited by A T Bolton).

Adrian STOKES (1902–72)

Critical Writings (ed. L Gowing) 1978
By the painter and writer on art.

Sir John SUMMERSON (1904–)

Heavenly Mansions 1949
A collection of brilliant essays in architectural criticism.

C F A VOYSEY (1857–1941)

Individuality 1915
A statement of principles by a quintessentially English architect and designer.

Josiah WEDGWOOD (1730–95)

Letters of Josiah Wedgwood 1982
Belatedly published correspondence between Wedgwood and his partner, highlighting the links between industry and artists, especially Stubbs and Flaxman.

Horace WALPOLE (1717–97)

Anecdotes of Painting in England 1761–71
An entertaining but rather unsystematic early attempt to collate source material for English art history in four volumes.

A Description of Strawberry Hill 1784
A guidebook for intending visitors to the famous cottage-into-castle example of the Gothic Revival.

J A McN WHISTLER (1834–1903)

Ten O'Clock Lecture 1885
A brief but biting lecture on the artist and the critic that defends the artist's right to express himself as he sees fit.

The Gentle Art of Making Enemies 1890
Various polemical writings by the celebrated pyrrhic victor in the 'paint pot' libel case which he brought against Ruskin.

Edgar WIND

Art and the Will 1960
The 1960 Reith Lectures. An eloquent humanist synthesis of the significance of the arts in history.

Art and Anarchy 1965
How and why do artists engage our attention? The author, in a whirlwind of knowledge and reference, embraces art theory, history and philosophy.

H WOTTON (1568–1639)

The Elements of Architecture 1624
An early exposition of artistic taste by a diplomat-poet.

REFERENCE

This selection of reference books has been drawn up with the requirements of those who have a special interest in English literature in mind. Most of the titles are purchasable, but inevitably a few works of reference are too bulky, or too expensive, or too esoteric to be held anywhere but in a library.

The first section includes general 'Quick Reference' books and dictionaries, encyclopaedias, atlases and yearbooks. The second, Specialist Reference section, sketches what is available for those who wish to explore the many avenues of interest that radiate from any particular piece of reading.

Tracking down book information is possible through the major bibliographical sources and these are included in the first section. Reference works such as *British Books in Print*, available to all libraries, publishers and bookshops, are the key to the full range of books published within the British copyright system.

Reference books can be expensive but many now appear in paperback editions and some of the hardbacks, such as the *Oxford Companion to English Literature* are generously priced. For pure pleasure, a personal copy of a good reference book is one of the best literary investments.

In *The Three Princes of Serendip*, as Horace Walpole noted in 1754, the heroes 'were always making discoveries, by accident and sagacity, of those things they were not in quest of'. This is one of the incidental benefits of having the wherewithal to 'look it up'.

QUICK REFERENCE

BOOK AUCTION RECORDS (*ed. W Y Health & Wm Dawson, annual*)

Lists full bibliographical and condition details of books sold at auction during the previous year, with sale price; can be seen at most public reference departments.

BRITISH BOOKS IN PRINT (*Whitaker, annual*)

The reference catalogue of current literature. In two volumes the work lists every British book in print, with author, title, editor, translator, reviser, year of publication or latest edition, number, size, number of pages, illustrations, series, binding and price. Alphabetical by author and title with subject index. Current information can be found in *British Books in Print on Microfiche*, updated monthly. The whole database, including forthcoming titles and recently out-of-print titles, can be searched on *Bookbank CD-Rom*, a CD-Rom disc which is updated monthly. A similar range of information services covering books published in the USA is available from Bowker under the *Books in Print* label.

CHAMBERS BIOGRAPHICAL DICTIONARY 1984 (*ed. J O Thorne and T C Collocott, 3rd edition*)

Very full and detailed one-volume biographical dictionary: for use on personal reference shelves and for those who find the *Dictionary of National Biography* a little unwieldy. Available in paperback.

CHAMBERS TWENTIETH CENTURY DICTIONARY 1983 (*ed. E M Kirkpatrick, 4th edition, Chambers*)

The most detailed of the single-volume dictionaries, the words and definitions are up-to-date and include many foreign language words. Numerous appendices include proper names and modern abbreviations.

CONCISE OXFORD DICTIONARY OF CURRENT ENGLISH 1982 (*ed. J B Sykes, 7th edition, OUP*)

Based on the Oxford English Dictionary and its supplements, this records 'what is found to exist in the educated use of modern English', with two extra aspects; D = disputed by a significant number of educated writers; R = racially offensive. It contains 75,000 words including derivatives, components and abbreviations. Those seeking a 'broader canvas of English words and their history' should use the 20-volume *Oxford English Dictionary* or the *Shorter Oxford English Dictionary*.

DICTIONARY OF NATIONAL BIOGRAPHY (*OUP, decennially*)

The reference tool for anyone wishing to glean information about anyone famous or notorious. The *Dictionary of National Biography* is arranged alphabetically, in 63 volumes up to 1900, and then there is a single volume for each decade of the twentieth century. Only those people who died in a particular decade are recorded.

ENCYCLOPAEDIA BRITANNICA 1980 (*ed. Warren E Preece, 15th edition*)

The lay-out of the 15th edition, with its 10 volumes of short micropaedia entries and 19 volumes of macropaedia articles on selected subjects, has infuriated many users. The propaedia (Outline of Knowledge) volume is no substitute for a comprehensive index and there is a North American bias in the coverage as viewed by British readers. It remains invaluable and can fulfil the sales claims as a family investment.

EVERYMAN'S ENCYCLOPAEDIA 1978 (*ed. D A Girling, 6th edition, Dent*)

First published in 1913 'to satisfy the reader's desire for rapid information on all subjects in the general course of reading or in the affairs of everyday life', the alphabetical sequence of entries covers in succinct style the major areas of knowledge.

PEARS CYCLOPAEDIA 1982 (*ed. Christopher Cook, 91st edition, Pelham*)

A book of background information and reference for everyday use which covers a range of information from nuclear reactors, sport, medicine, politics, leisure and literature to events, people and places. The index directs the reader to the appropriate section and page.

READER'S DIGEST GREAT WORLD ATLAS 1978 (*3rd revised edition, Reader's Digest*)

This contains maps of the world; in relief, in detail of physical geography, population, geology, flora and fauna; the solar system; pictorial information about gems, food, health, exploration and many other aspects of life. These all go to form a work of reference for many purposes.

WATERSTONE'S GUIDE TO BOOKS (*2nd edition, Waterstones*)

A large 'catalogue' listing books with some useful annotations and 'book choices' by personalities. Gives current prices.

WHITAKER'S ALMANAC (*Whitaker, annual*)

This handy reference book covers thousands of items of information on a wide range of subjects, which can only be reached via the detailed index at the beginning of the work. First published in 1868, the annual volumes take account of the political and scientific changes and provide the answers to official and unofficial questions.

WILLING'S PRESS GUIDE (*Thomas Skinner Directories, IPC Business Press, annual*)

Newspapers and periodicals are arranged alphabetically by name within each country of the world, with a list of publishers and their periodicals, reporting, news and press cutting agencies.

WORLD BOOK ENCYCLOPAEDIA 1981 (*Macmillan*)

Suitable for a wide age range of readers, the entries are brief but informative, with good cross referencing and plenty of pictures. The 24-volume size and price make it more likely to be seen in the public library than the home.

WRITERS' AND ARTISTS' YEARBOOK (*A & C Black, annual*)

A directory for writers, artists, playwrights and writers for film, radio and television. International coverage of newspapers, magazines, book publishers, theatre, television and radio agents, art music, prizes, clubs, copyright, tax and services.

SPECIALIST REFERENCE

ABC FOR BOOK COLLECTORS 1981 (*John Carter, 6th revised edition, Granada*)

This highlights the perils, pitfalls and joys of collecting first editions. Themes, authors, forms and formats are placed in alphabetical sequence of subject, to aid the collector, in this standard work revised by N Barker.

BARTLETT'S FAMILIAR QUOTATIONS 1980 (*ed. Emily Morison Beck, 14th revised edition, Macmillan*)

Originally published in 1855 from John Bartlett's collection of quotations, authors are arranged chronologically from ancient Egypt, the Bible and Greek philosophers to J D Salinger, James Baldwin and Yevtushenko, with an index of authors and full alphabetic index to the texts.

BATTY, BLOOMERS AND BOYCOTT 1982 (*Rosie Boycott, Hutchinson*)

The origins of 300 eponymous words, (e.g. Mudd, Batty and McCoy) are traced, with examples of use.

BLACK BRITISH LITERATURE: AN ANNOTATED BIBLIOGRAPHY 1986 (*Prahta Guptara, Dangaroo*)

Annotated entries on works by black British authors

BLOOMSBURY GOOD READING GUIDE 1988 (*Kenneth McLeish, Bloomsbury*)

Over 300 authors are surveyed with a 'read on' feature which indicates similar authors and works and 'menus' of suggested reading within similar genres.

BREWER'S DICTIONARY OF PHRASE AND FABLE 1981 (*Ivor H Evans, 12th revised edition, Cassell*)

The original aim of Dr Brewer in 1870, 'an alms-basket of Common Phrases, Allusion and Words which have a Tale to Tell' is maintained. Additions include Commonwealth and American phrases, folklore from Wales and Ireland and current expressions.

The CAMBRIDGE GUIDE TO LITERATURE IN ENGLISH 1988 (*ed. Ian Ousby, CUP/Hamlyn*)

Appearing three years after the rival *Oxford Campanion*, it covers the same ground in much the same way. Well worth having both.

The CAMBRIDGE HISTORY OF ENGLISH LITERATURE 1949–53 (*ed. Sir Adolphus William Ward and A R Waller, revised by Margaret Drabble, CUP*)

A chronological survey of English Literature, from Anglo-Saxon times to the twentieth century. Factual and useful as a reminder where all those writers fit in.

CENTURY CHILDREN'S WRITERS 1983 (*ed. D L Kirkpatrick, 3rd revised edition, Macmillan*)

Signed critical essays on English language authors of fiction, poetry and drama for children and young people arranged alphabetically by author. An author's biography and bibliography is followed by an analysis of their major works.

CHAMBERS BIOGRAPHICAL DICTIONARY 1975 (*J O Thorne, Chambers, paperback*)

The editor's criterion for including a subject was whether he or she 'was likely to be looked up', so Don Bradman, cricketer and de Havilland, aircraft designer appear, as do Kierkegaard and Rossini.

CHILDREN'S BOOKS IN ENGLAND 1982 (*F J Harvey Darton, revised by Brian Alderson, 3rd revised edition, CUP*)

This is a survey of children's books from the Middle Ages to the end of the nineteenth century. The standard work on children's literature, this is an authoritive description and discussion of the subject.

CONCISE CAMBRIDGE HISTORY OF ENGLISH LITERATURE 1970 (*ed. George Sampson, 3rd revised edition, CUP, paperback*)

A useful little survey of over nine centuries of literature.

The CONCISE OXFORD DICTIONARY OF PROVERBS 1982 (*ed. J A Simpson, OUP*)

Smaller than the standard *Oxford Dictionary*, it nevertheless provides readers with a tool to enable them to check English proverbs, their meanings and origins.

The CONCISE OXFORD DICTIONARY OF QUOTATIONS 1981 (*2nd revised edition, OUP, paperback*)

Based on the 1979 edition of the ODQ but omits proverbs, nursery rhymes, hymns, pop songs and catchphrases.

The DICTIONARY OF IMAGINERY PLACES 1981 (*Alberto Manguel and Gianni Guadalupi, Granada*)

The lands created by Tolkien, LeGuin, Lloyd Alexander, C S Lewis, Samual Butler, J M Barrie, Anthony Hope and many others, are described in text and maps, like a gazetteer with an index of authors and titles.

DICTIONARY OF LITERARY PSEUDONYMS 1981 (*Frank Atkinson, Bingley*)

Agatha Christie wrote as Mary Westmacott, Ellery Queen was Frederick Dannay and Manfred B Less; John Creasey had at least twenty-four pseudonyms and James Kirkup at least three. This selection of popular modern writers in English lists about 2500 real names with their pseudonyms while a second list works in the reverse order.

A DICTIONARY OF LITERARY TERMS 1982 (*J A Cudden, 2nd revised edition, Penguin, paperback*)

2000 terms in regular use are listed alphabetically in ten main categories from technical terms such as *pentameter* through forms such as *sonnet* and *clerihew*, to schools, -isms, themes and modes – with description, definition, cross references and examples of use.

DICTIONARY OF MODERN CRITICAL TERMS 1973 (*Roger Fowler, Routledge, paperback*)

Definitions are arranged alphabetically with a cross section of critical attitudes, designed to 'open up potentialities for literary enquiry (rather than) providing finished definitions.'

DICTIONARY OF MODERN ENGLISH USAGE (*Henry Watson Fowler, revised by Sir Ernest Gower, OUP, 2nd edition 1965, paperback edition 1983*)

Intended to guide clear thinking and the orderly use of words.

EVERYMAN'S CLASSICAL DICTIONARY 1961 (*John Warrington, Dent*)

Alphabetical arrangement of information from 8th century BC to the death of Constantine AD 337.

EVERYMAN'S DICTIONARY OF LITERARY BIOGRAPHY, ENGLISH AND AMERICAN 1972 (*D C Browning, Pan, paperback*)

Provides 2,300 brief biographies of literary people, for all tastes from James Joyce to Ella Wheeler Wilcox and Adrian Bell to Shakespeare.

GLOSSARY OF THE BOOK 1982 (*Geoffrey Ashall Glaister, 2nd revised edition Allen & Unwin*)

Terms used in papermaking, printing, bookbinding and publishing, with notes on illuminated manuscripts and private presses. 4,000 entries in alphabetical order make this a useful book for the book person to own or consult in the public library.

GUIDE TO MODERN WORLD LITERATURE 1986 (*Martin Seymour-Smith, 3rd revised edition, Macmillan, paperback*)

Massive one-man, one-volume survey of modern world literature. Bold opinions challenge the reader on almost every page. A necessary companion to more circumspect reference books.

GUINNESS BOOK OF RECORDS (*ed. Norris McWhirter, annual*)

The twelve sections cover anything that can be measured as the most or the least, the highest or the lowest, the longest or the shortest or any other extreme, with facts and figures and photographs.

The LIBRARIAN'S GLOSSARY 1984 (*Raymond Prytherch, 5th revised edition, Gower*)

Previously edited by L Harrod, this is a completely revised work covering technical, literary and librarianship terms, organizations and subjects internationally.

LITERARY HISTORY OF ENGLAND 1967 (*ed. Albert C Baugh, 2nd revised edition, Routledge*)

A comprehensive survey connecting one period with another, discussing the subject critically and providing extensive bibliographical information.

NAMING NAMES 1981 (*Adrian Room, Routledge*)

This contains stories of pseudonyms and name changes with a who's who. The introductory chapters discuss reasons for changing names. These are followed by lists of categories of pseudonym (e.g. female to male), anagrams, embarrassing changes and five appendices (e.g. the 173 pseudonyms of Voltaire).

The NEW CAMBRIDGE BIBLIOGRAPHY OF ENGLISH LITERATURE 1974 (*ed. George Watson, 5 vols, CUP*)

Each volume is assigned a period and can be used independently of the others. Vol. 1 AD 600–1660; Vol. 2 1600–1800; Vol. 3 1800–1900; Vol. 4 1900–1950; Vol. 5 1950–80.

The NEW PELICAN GUIDE TO ENGLISH LITERATURE 1982–4 (*ed. by Boris Ford, 10 vols, Penguin*)

An updated edition of a guide that was originally and successfully published in the 1950s as a survey of fiction and poetry for both the general reader and formal students of literature. It provides background and critical guidance on authors and works in nine volumes: *Medieval Literature*; *The Age of Shakespeare*; *From Donne to Marvell*; *From Dryden to Johnson*; *From Blake to Byron*; *From Dickens to Hardy*; *From James to Eliot*; *The Present*; *The Literature of the United States*. The useful bibliographical material which is contained in appendices to each volume is also gathered in a separate tenth volume – a *Guide to Readers*.

NOW READ ON 1990 (*complied by Mandy Hicken and Roy Prytherch, Gower*)

A guide to contemporary popular English-language fiction. Divided up into various genres such as historical novels and science fiction, this book guides the reader further into favourite areas – and encourages the development of further reading in unexplored regions.

The ORIGINALS: WHO'S REALLY WHO IN FICTION 1985 (*William Amos, Cape*)

This identifies (or discusses claimed identifications of) originals of characters in world fiction. Some photographic illustrations.

The OXFORD CLASSICAL DICTIONARY 1970 (*ed. N G L Hammong and H H Scullard, 2nd revised edition, OUP*)

Previously edited by Max Carey, the entries are the work of eminent contributors, making this the standard work on the classics.

The OXFORD COMPANION TO AMERICAN LITERATURE 1975 (*ed. James Hart, 4th revised edition, OUP*)

An alphabetical arrangement of information about writers, books, allusions and the American literary scene, including biographies, analytical summaries of works, with a chronological index of literary history.

The OXFORD COMPANION TO CLASSICAL LITERATURE 1959 (*ed. Sir Paul Harvey, OUP*)

Covers Latin and Greek authors showing their major works and tracing the history of the 'greats' and their influences.

The OXFORD COMPANION TO ENGLISH LITERATURE 1985 (*ed. Margaret Drabble, 5th edition, OUP*)

Covers authors, works, schools of literature and literary criticism and many literary allusions and characters in alphabetical sequence intended for 'ordinary everyday readers of English literature'. A reliable and up-to-date guide which contains a lot of information at a very reasonable price.

The OXFORD COMPANION TO FILM 1979 (*ed. Liz Anne Bawden, OUP*)

Information is arranged in alphabetical order from AA Certificate to Zuoboda, a French film director, aimed at the 'amateur of film in … reading and filmgoing'.

The OXFORD COMPANION TO FRENCH LITERATURE 1959 (*ed. Sir Paul Harvey and Janet E Heseltine, OUP*)

The French and Belgian literary scene is covered up to 1955 with its historical, geographical and political background, about 6000 entries in alphabetical order.

The OXFORD DICTIONARY OF ENGLISH PROVERBS 1970 (*ed. Joana Wilson, 3rd edition*)

Alphabetical arrangement by the significant word of the proverb, quoting usage.

The OXFORD DICTIONARY OF NURSERY RHYMES 1951 (*Iona and Peter Opie, OUP*)

Covers the origins and literary appearance of more than 500 rhymes and songs and over 100 illustrations. Arranged alphabetically by the most significant word of the rhyme, with an index of notable figures and of the first line, the work is an erudite guide to every child's heritage.

The OXFORD DICTIONARY OF QUOTATIONS 1979 (*3rd edition, OUP*)

The most substantial revision since 1941 includes major twentieth century writers and public figures alphabetically by author, with keyword index.

The OXFORD ILLUSTRATED LITERARY GUIDE TO GREAT BRITAIN AND IRELAND 1981 (*Dorothy Eagle and Hilary Carnell, 2nd revised edition, OUP*)

Refers readers to places relevant to literature. Arranged in two sections; alphabetical list of place names with their literary connections; index of over 900 writers (excluding the living) with their place connections.

The OXFORD SHAKESPEARE GLOSSARY 1976 (*Charles Talbot Onions, 2nd revised edition, OUP, paperback*)

Analyses Shakespeare's vocabulary in his drama and verse.

The PENGUIN COMPANION TO LITERATURE 1969–71 (*4 vols, Penguin, paperback*)

Alphabetical entries include biographical sketches, critical assessments, selective bibliographies, forms and styles, in volumes concerned with Britain and the Commonwealth, USA and Latin America, Europe, and Classical, Byzantine, Oriental and African literature.

The PENGUIN DICTIONARY OF MODERN QUOTATIONS 1980 (*ed. J M and M J Cohen, Penguin, paperback*)

Includes 4000 predominantly English quotations from poets, politicians, novelists, lawyers, comedians and others from 1900 on, e.g. Kingsley Amis, Duke of Edinburgh, Trygve Lee, Spike Milligan, Picasso, Proust, and Harold Wilson.

READER'S ADVISER: A LAYMAN'S GUIDE TO LITERATURE 1986 (*13th edition, Bowker*)

Vol. 1 Best in American and British fiction, poetry, essays, literature and biography.
Vol. 2 Best in American and British drama and world literature in English translation.
Vol. 3 Best in general reference literature, the social sciences, history and the arts.
Vol. 4 Best in the literature of philosophy and world religions.
Vol. 5 Best in the literature of science, technology and medicine.

ROGET'S THESAURUS OF ENGLISH WORDS AND PHRASES 1982 (*ed. Susan Lloyd, Longman*)

How to find another word for the same thing. This first revision since 1962 has added new terms and subjects in literary, technical, scientific, philosophic, colloquial and social fields.

A SHAKESPEARE COMPANION 1564–1964 1964 (*Frank E A Halliday, Duckworth*)

Covers the plays, life and literature of Shakespeare and the critical works about him.

The SHORTER OXFORD ENGLISH DICTIONARY 1973 (*Charles Talbot Onions and G W S Friedrichsen, OUP*)

Originally based on the OED the revisions take account of new words and definitions up to 1972. In two volumes.

THE SPHERE HISTORY OF LITERATURE 1971–88 (*general editor: Roger Lonsdale, Sphere*)

A rival to the *New Pelican Guide*; the essays are more up-to-date and tend to deal with individual authors and their works rather than filling in a great deal of background. Very good bibliographies. The 10 volumes are: *The Middle Ages*; *English Poetry and Prose 1540–1674*; *English Drama to 1710*; *Dryden to Johnson*; *Literature of the Romantic Period*; *The Victorians*; *The Twentieth Century*; *American Literature to 1900*; *American Literature since 1900*; *The English Language*.

WHERE'S THAT POEM? 1979 (*Helen Morris, 2nd revised edition, Blackwell, paperback*)

Lists poems under subject and refers to named volumes of poetry in the bibliography. Covers the kinds of poem commonly used by schools.

WHO DONE IT? 1969 (*Ordean A Hagen, Bowker*)

A guide to detective, mystery and suspense fiction which covers 1841–1967 by author and then by subject, e.g. crime involving advertising, libraries, atomic research, mystery novels on screen, anthologies, collections and awards, heroes, heroines, villains, with an index to it all.

WHO WAS REALLY WHO IN FICTION 1987 (*Alan Bold and Robert Giddings, Longman*)

Over 600 are unmasked. A rival to *The Originals*.

WHO'S WHO IN CHILDREN'S BOOKS 1975 (*Margery Fisher, Weidenfeld & Nicholson*).

Identifies and describes in text and illustration many characters in children's books through the ages, thus enabling the reader to recall the original story and provides a fascinating introduction to children's books. It is out of print but available through libraries.

WHO'S WHO IN TWENTIETH CENTURY LITERATURE 1979 (*Martin Seymour Smith, Weidenfeld & Nicholson*)

A guide to modern writers in the world; the 700 entries provide critical annotation.

WRITER'S BRITAIN: 1979 (*Margaret Drabble, Thames and Hudson*)

A guide to places where writers wrote and the landscapes they wrote about. A useful literary travelling companion.

THE WRITER'S DIRECTORY (*4th edition, Macmillan, biennial*)

15000 living writers from Australia, Canada, Ireland, New Zealand, South Africa, UK and USA, with name, pseudonym, citizenship, birth, nature of writing, major current and past appointments, detailed bibliography and address. A subject list indicates authors writing in each field.

AUTHOR INDEX

TITLE INDEX